ULSTER LIBERALISM, 1778–1876

To Jewell, Peggy, Diane, Maeve, Aileen and Iona

Ulster Liberalism, 1778–1876

The Middle Path

Gerald R. Hall

FOUR COURTS PRESS

Typeset in 10.5 pt on 13 pt Ehrhardt for
FOUR COURTS PRESS LTD
7 Malpas Street, Dublin 8, Ireland
www.fourcourtspress.ie
and in North America for
FOUR COURTS PRESS
c/o ISBS, 920 NE 58th Avenue, Suite 300, Portland, OR 97213.

A catalogue record for this title is available
from the British Library.

ISBN 978-1-84682-202-5

Printed in England
by Antony Rowe Ltd, Chippenham, Wilts.

Contents

Tables

Abbreviations

AG	*Armagh Guardian*
BMM	*Belfast Monthly Magazine*
BNL	*Belfast News-Letter*
BU	*Banner of Ulster*
EC	*Enniskillen Chronicle*
HC	House of Commons sessional papers
HMC	Historical Manuscripts Commission
IHS	*Irish Historical Studies*
LJ	*Londonderry Journal*
NW	*Northern Whig*
ODNB	*Oxford dictionary of national biography*
PRO	Public Record Office
PRONI	Public Record Office of Northern Ireland
NW	*Northern Whig*
TC	town commission
UO	*Ulster Observer*
Vin	*Vindicator*

Acknowledgments

This book would not have been possible without the kind assistance of the following people and institutions. Thanks to the British Council for timely financial support. The arduous task of research was made tolerable, sometimes even enjoyable, by the staff and fellows of the Institute of Irish Studies at Queen's University in Belfast, the staff of the Linen Hall Library, the staff of the Public Record Office of Northern Ireland, the librarian and staff of the Gamble Library at the Union Theological College in Belfast, and the keeper of the Armagh Public Library. Nourishment for the soul, mind and body were graciously provided at various times by Bill and Judy Riches, Jim and Alita Miller, David Miller, Cassie Adcock, Sean Farrell, Stéphanie Bouffort and Michelle O'Neill. Ben Jacobson provided sage counsel and caring comfort during a time of crisis. The guidance and patience of Professor Emmet Larkin have been indispensable.

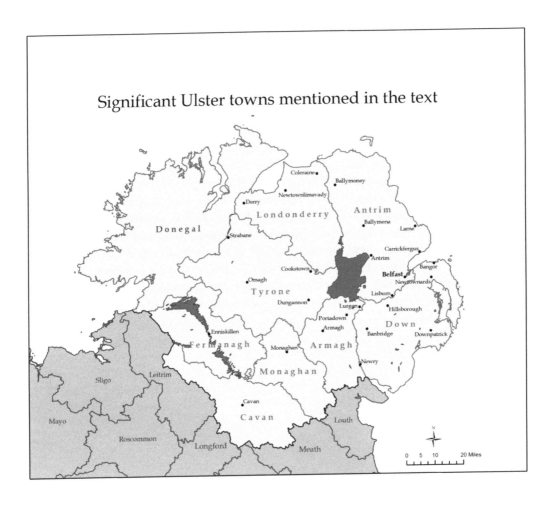

Significant Ulster towns mentioned in the text

Introduction

This book aims to rescue the history of a political tradition in Ulster in which neither nationalism nor unionism was the foremost consideration. For the people who form the focus of this study the world was not as yet immutably divided between Catholic and Protestant, nationalist and unionist. Instead, their primary concerns were social and political policies that are best described as liberal. This is not to say that the subjects of this study did not express opinions that would divide the sheep from the goats on some imagined day of political judgment. It would also be a gross oversimplification not to recognize that Ulster liberals lived in a world that was becoming practically divided between Protestant and Catholic, unionist and nationalist. Much of the tension and drama of this story derives from the struggles of men and women to maintain their principles despite changing circumstances.

It has long been recognized that the history of Ulster is complicated by the development of two narrative traditions, nationalist and unionist, whose advocates have made remarkably comprehensive divisions of people and events in their efforts to establish the continuing legitimacy of their claims. The danger is that systematic classifications often make nonsense of the complexities and ambiguities of history. During the past two decades many aspects of Irish history have been closely re-examined and past conclusions questioned or qualified. Using a variety of approaches to gather evidence for what have been rightly described as 'heroic reconstructions of the proportions and dynamics of demographic, economic and social change', historians have begun to reconsider fundamental assumptions about Irish society. Yet, despite contentious and occasionally uncivil discussions concerning new discoveries and interpretations, there continues to be a rarely challenged presupposition concerning Irish history. Most historical writing is still framed within a nationalist historiography founded upon a belief that there has been (or should have been) a natural progression within Irish history 'through protest, strife and rebellion to politicization'.[1] Whether the fulfilment of that progression is conceived as having been accomplished with the achievement of legislative independence or as an incomplete promise to be realized at some future date, the inexorable rise of the Irish nation continues to be the premise of most studies.

1 T.C. Barnard, 'Historiographical review: farewell to old Ireland' (1993), 909–10. For an apposite summary by a prominent actor in this on-going re-evaluation see S.J. Connolly, 'Eighteenth-century Ireland: colony or *ancien régime?*' (1996).

The endurance of the nationalist paradigm derives both from its suitability as a conceptual framework and its political utility. Nationalism is a primary theme of modern Irish history. Given the need to understand the development of nationalism, historical studies might be expected to focus on past events that seemed to foreshadow subsequent developments. However, a nationalist framework that becomes too teleological, that is overly concerned with the search for precursors of modern parties, states and conflicts can become an impediment to understanding. Other themes and explanations are neglected until, in the words of Nancy Curtin, 'a history that is defined as nationalist struggle excludes those who did not partake in or benefit from that struggle'.[2]

Surprisingly, unionist narratives also have accepted the idea of an autochthonous and indefatigable Irish nation. Accepting the belief that essential qualities in the Irish nation were manifested in an historical struggle with Britain became useful to unionists. Incompatibility between British Ulster and the rest of Ireland formed a rationale for the existence of Northern Ireland and, in some cases, an excuse for the exclusion of nationalists in Ulster from full participation in political life. If nationalists were determined to resist anglicization then unionists became equally determined to resist celticization. Some writers are questioning aspects of this dramatic schema of Irish history, this conceived Manichaean opposition between a native culture and colonial hegemony. It is increasingly recognized that these groups had cultural interactions and exchanges beyond confrontation or domination. Historians inspired by the works of J.G.A. Pocock and others have begun to speak of a 'Britannic' and 'archipelagic' framework for study.[3] Likewise, cultural critics such as Declan Kiberd have begun to consider whether the Irish have been a 'hybrid people' rather than 'a pure, unitary race, dedicated to defending a notion of integrity'.[4] The history of Ulster liberalism demonstrates the usefulness of questioning the polarized frame of Irish history. Ulster liberalism was comprised of a variety of cultural and social strands and its history elucidates important social and cultural changes that are sometimes overlooked in the overarching narratives of nationalism and unionism.

Any definition of Ulster liberalism is fraught with difficulty. Much of the political language of Ulster liberalism – its historical and cultural references – derived from a British political vocabulary. Given the political subordination of Ireland to Britain and the subsequently strong social and cultural connections that developed between Ulster and Britain this is not surprising. Because of these connections the British context of Ulster liberalism, particularly the

---

2 N. Curtin, '"Varieties of Irishness": historical revisionism, Irish style' (1996), 212.   3 I. McBride, 'Ulster and the British problem' (1996), pp 3–5.   4 D. Kiberd, *Inventing Ireland* (Cambridge, MA, 1996), p. 7.

development of the categories liberal, Whig, Tory and radical, is an indispensable part of the story. Unfortunately historians have described these categories in schema so complicated that practical application becomes difficult. For that reason, the definition of 'liberal' adopted here will be broadly inclusive. This means applying the term 'liberal' to people and movements who before the 1820s often continued to describe themselves and others as Whigs, reformers, independents, or patriots when it is clear that something had changed. Something had made the descriptions Whig or patriot seem somehow incomplete or even quaint.

Political language in Ulster has not been subjected to the kind of rigorous analysis practiced by J.G.A. Pocock and others with regard to British and American politics. Pocock's observation that 'it is a large part of the historian's practice to learn to read and recognize the diverse idioms of political discourse' available in a culture at a particular time has been neglected until recently, and on occasion positively dismissed.[5] At the most basic level, there has been no serious consideration of when the word 'liberal' began to be used substantively in Ulster. In the more closely studied British context, the substantive use of the words 'liberal' and 'liberalism' only gradually developed during the 1820s when they were borrowed, at first as pejorative terms, from discussions concerning political developments on the continent and in Latin America.[6] Before that time 'liberal' had been used as an adjective to describe what was considered generous, unrestrained or bountiful, often with an added social connotation of gentility.[7]

In Ulster the term 'liberal' seems to have gained some currency as an adjective with reformist connotations concerning the removal of civil disabilities of Catholics since at least 1809 when the *Belfast Monthly Magazine* called upon 'the liberal of the Protestant part of the community' to consider the 'hurtful tendency' of party processions celebrating the anniversary of the Battle of the Boyne.[8] The word 'liberal' was beginning to be used substantively by around 1826 to denote advocates of parliamentary reform and Catholic emancipation. In 1825 the *Belfast Magazine and Literary Journal* described the ideals of the various parties in Ireland, including 'the liberal reformer' who ascribed the ills of society to the effects of maladministration that might be remedied by parliamentary reform.[9] At a political meeting in Newry in August

5 J.G.A. Pocock, *Virtue, commerce and history* (Cambridge, 1985), p. 9. For a challenge to this approach see 'A note on the title', in J. Smyth, *Men of no property* (New York, 1992), pp ix–x. 6 E. Halévy, *The liberal awakening, 1815–1830*, ii: *A history of the English people in the nineteenth century*, 6 vols (New York, 1961), pp 81–2; A. Briggs, *The making of modern England, 1783–1867* (New York, 1965), p. 218. 7 J.C.D. Clark, *English society, 1688–1832* (Cambridge, 1985), p. 348. 8 'Monthly retrospect of politics', *BMM*, 2 (June 1809), 474. 9 'On the present state of Ireland', *Belfast Magazine and Literary Journal*, 1 (February

1826, the radical writer George Ensor asserted that, 'the aristocracy were all liberal' but, 'the minor gentlemen, those called the "squireens," were for most part of an opposite tendency'.[10] By 1827, the author of pamphlet on Catholic emancipation believed that 'Dr. Miller must once have been a "*liberal*"'.[11]

Because the word liberalism was not substantively used before the 1820s, some historians have been either anxious or hostile to the anachronistic use of the terms 'liberal' or 'liberalism'. For some historians, the broad consensus that defined liberalism by its political emphasis 'on the representation of individuals rather than corporate bodies, ranks, orders, or "interests"',[12] has been undermined by misguided efforts to describe too precisely when the traditional, hierarchical polity was supplanted by a modern, market society.[13] The continuing importance of Whiggish political ideals during the nineteenth century has been commented upon by a number of authors.[14] The persistence of traditional political ideals has led sceptics such as J.C.D. Clark to insist upon giving priority to the dominant political categories of the period in order to avoid teleological conclusions more concerned with today's polemics than understanding the past.[15]

Other historians have conceded that although the *ancien régime* was not supplanted during the last decades of the eighteenth century, there were significant challenges to traditional, hierarchical understandings of society that might merit the use of the term 'liberal' decades prior to the substantive use of the word or the emergence of an organized Liberal party. Even the rigorous analysis of Pocock concedes the existence of 'liberalism' in the eighteenth century.[16] Likewise, J.W. Burrow, another critic of 'the elision of the word "Whig" in favour of the prospective use of "liberal"', favourably cites studies of the period between 1780 and 1832 in which scholars have deliberately used the anachronism 'liberal' to describe significant changes in political language and practice among some Whigs.[17] In one of those cited works, J.E. Cookson observes that 'while the noun was in its long gestation, "liberal", the adjective, was given full employment' by a group of Whigs and radicals struggling with social and political questions during the period of Britain's wars with France.[18] In examining political language in Ulster the deliberately anachronistic use of the word liberal for the period between 1778 and 1828 also seems to be justified.

1825), 21.   10 *NW*, 10 August 1826.   11 Presbyterian Layman, *Historical view of the Catholic question* (Belfast, 1827), p. 60.   12 S.H. Beer, *British politics in the collectivist age* (New York, 1969), p. 34. Beer's descriptions of the distinctions between liberal, Whig, Tory and radical might be considered archetypal.   13 Pocock, *Virtue*, pp 70–1.   14 See for example J.W. Burrow, *Whigs and liberals* (Oxford, 1988), pp 2–4; P. Mandler, *Aristocratic government in the age of reform* (Oxford, 1990), p. 3.   15 Clark, *English society, 1688–1832*, p. 383.   16 Pocock, *Virtue*, p. 71.   17 Ibid., p. 8. Burrow specifically cites: J.E. Cookson, *The friends of peace* (Cambridge, 1982); B. Fontana, *Rethinking the politics of commercial society* (Cambridge, 1985).   18 Cookson, *The friends of peace*, p. 2.

Before 1778 a Whig or patriot element existed in Ireland but it was not particularly strong in Ulster. After 1778, Ulster became a centre of politics and contributed significantly to the development of the kinds of political language and activity that are described as liberal rather than Whig.

Although the British context is indispensable to the understanding of Ulster liberalism, the Irish context is inescapable. Ulster liberalism developed in the context of a heritage of conquest, plantation, and immigration that fundamentally affected its development. An essential aspect of this heritage was the often antagonistic relationship between descendants of the native, Catholic population and the descendants of Protestant settlers. As the late Frank Wright observed, this relationship has been described inadequately by studies that only outline Protestant perspectives without describing the dynamic interactions between communities. The tendency to omit references to Catholic concerns and actions, admittedly only beginning to be recovered in adequate detail, casts Catholics as passive observers of events and tends to make the story of liberalism in Ulster 'only partly intelligible'.[19] Catholics were not merely passive victims of political repression or indefatigable rebels. For this reason, I will attempt to describe a more complete context for Ulster liberalism by considering the effect of the neglected interactions between Catholics and Protestants upon liberal fortunes.

While the study of political ideas forms a considerable part of this study, those ideas were closely associated with the reality of social changes. A considerable number of people believed that economic changes fundamentally affected their society and acted upon that belief. Ulster liberals came to believe that social developments made changes in government at both the local and national levels both possible and desirable. They even hoped that social change might ameliorate the relationship between Catholics and Protestants by making many of the institutions and principles derived from historical conquest and civil strife obsolete. They discovered, however, that neither the institutions nor the legacy of distrust and antagonism were quickly or easily overcome.

19 F. Wright, *Two lands on one soil* (New York, 1996), p. 3.

CHAPTER ONE

The forging of Ulster liberalism, 1778–1814

> Thus monarchy becomes tyranny, aristocracy degenerates into oligarchy, and popular government lapses readily into licentiousness […] Such is the circle which all republics are destined to run through […] But it may well happen that a republic lacking good strength and counsel in its difficulties becomes subject for a while to some neighbouring state, that is better organized than itself; and if such is not the case, then they will be apt to revolve indefinitely in the circle of revolutions.
>
> Niccolò Machiavelli, *Discourses*, book 1, chapter 2

The Volunteers and the origins of Ulster liberalism, 1778–91

On 22 July 1781, William Bruce, the minister of the Presbyterian congregation at Lisburn, a sizeable town six miles to the south and west of Belfast, delivered his sabbath sermon dressed 'in a short blue swallow-tail coat, with brass buttons (lettered "Lisburn True Blues"), red cuffs, collar and facings, white breeches, and black leggings'.[1] Whether Bruce leaned a musket against the pulpit like a colleague in Belfast is unknown, but since 1778 the spectacle of a Presbyterian minister preaching in military uniform was not singular in towns and villages in Ulster. Many ministers were caught up in what Revd Thomas Witherow, professor of church history and pastoral theology at Magee college in Derry and editor of the *Londonderry Standard*, described in 1880 as the 'mania' of the Volunteer movement – 'when gilded visions of national independence and liberty dazzled the eyes of the populace'.[2]

Perhaps more astonishing than the abandonment of customarily sober garb by Presbyterian ministers was the developing genre of the Volunteer sermon. Ministers exhorted the men of their flocks to come together and learn the use of arms. They hoped to see, as one pastor put it, 'the manners of the soldier grafted upon the principles of the Christian'. They believed a martial education would instil the virtues necessary for citizenship, and by 1781 many were also convinced that 'her military associations' had raised Ireland from 'a state of insignificancy' to one of 'estimation, dignity and respect'.[3] There was a

1 *Belfast Literary Society, 1801–1901* (Belfast, 1902), p. 29.   2 T. Witherow, *Historical and literary memorials of Presbyterianism in Ireland, 1731–1800* (Belfast, 1880), pp 204, 222, 243–4, 266.   3 J. Crombie, *The propriety of setting apart a portion of the Sabbath for the purpose of acquiring the knowledge and use of arms* (Belfast, 1781), p. 38; see also J. Rogers, *A*

widespread conviction both at the time and subsequently that the emergence of the Volunteer movement was a critical moment in Irish history. Men with divergent political principles, principles that during the 1790s divided many of them into opposing armed camps, agreed that the Volunteer movement had been the mainspring of efforts to preserve – or perhaps to create – constitutional government in Ireland. My decision to begin this study in 1778 derives from a belief that by examining the Volunteer movement and its concern with constitutional ideals the beginnings of a liberal tradition in Ulster can be better understood.

The outlines of the history of the Volunteer movement are well known. Having begun as voluntary military associations with the ostensible aim of defending the coasts against French or American raids during the American Revolution, Volunteer units subsequently became involved in political agitation concerning fundamental issues of trade, Catholic emancipation and parliamentary reform. They contributed to the transitory achievement of increased autonomy for the Irish parliament between 1782 and the Act of Union in 1800. The Volunteers, Grattan's parliament and the so-called Constitution of 1782 became models, albeit much-debated models, for Irish nationalists and were often cited as the origin of liberal ideals in Ulster society.

The more recent judgments of posterity have not been so kind to the Volunteers. At present, the assertion that the origins of Ulster liberalism can be discerned within the Volunteer movement might arouse considerable dissent. The reputation of the Volunteers has diminished from that of enlightened Irish patriots asserting Ireland's rights in the face of unwarranted British interference to that of an armed gentry forming 'the cutting edge of the establishment at the local level'.[4] The early cultural nationalists in Young Ireland expressed a mild ambivalence about these patriots who, despite many admirable qualities, 'seemed as if they had resolved not to be English, rather than to be positively Irish'.[5] During the twentieth century ambivalence gave way to increasingly severe censures that eventually amounted to a thorough iconoclasm.

In the overlooked vanguard of the iconoclasts were writers such as C. Litton Falkiner and J.R. Fisher who, respectively, represented the conservative and liberal aspects of unionism. Both writers believed that advocates for home rule absurdly misinterpreted the Volunteers in a vain search for positive historical precedents for an autonomous legislature. Both writers described the history of the Volunteers in terms of a struggle within the British polity, 'a family quarrel

sermon preached at Lisnavein (Edinburgh, 1780), p. 32.   **4** P. Ó Snodaigh, 'Some police and military aspects of the Irish Volunteers' (1978), 229.   **5** D.O. Madden (ed.), *The speeches of the Right Hon. Henry Grattan* (Dublin, 1871), pp xvii, xxi

based on rights guaranteed under the British Constitution'.[6] Neither the Volunteers nor Grattan's parliament would or could come to terms with the continuing antagonism between Protestant settlers and Catholic natives, an antagonism described with increasing frequency in racial terms during the second half of the nineteenth century. While clamouring for free trade and parliamentary reform, the Volunteers 'were not unwilling to rivet the fetters which bound a subject race and proscribed a detested religion'.[7] Furthermore, the Volunteers' support for increased autonomy was misplaced. Only the framework of the Union could control or ameliorate such antagonisms.

Many nationalist authors were all too willing to endorse most of these conclusions. Ambivalence about fallible patriots developed into a conviction that an unbridgeable gulf existed between the Protestant gentry who made up the Volunteers and a distinct Gaelic and Catholic society living under penal repression. According to Michael Davitt, the Constitution of 1782 secured by the Volunteers was the 'utmost measure of Anglo-Norman-Irish patriotism' and 'any thought of carrying national freedom to its just and logical goal was as repugnant and treasonable to Henry Grattan as to any member of the ruling pro-British party'.[8] The Volunteers were patriots but not Irish patriots.

These early writers were animated by a degree of partisanship that would become less acceptable as history became more professionalized, but significant issues had been raised and monumental history challenged. More recent analyses have been built upon the ground-breaking scholarship of R.B. McDowell. While acknowledging that his sources were limited somewhat to 'the thinking few', McDowell was the first writer to describe the wide spectrum of Irish opinion by adding an extensive examination and thorough citation of the voluminous corpus of periodical and pamphlet literature produced during the period to the more widely known correspondence of influential leaders.[9] From this foundation, a clearer understanding of the social and cultural complexity of the Volunteer movement has emerged. Understanding the society and culture that had shaped the principles and actions of the Volunteers became more important than judging them by a party standard.

Out of this broader appreciation of the rhetoric and ideals of the Volunteers the central question became – did the Volunteers represent a significant moment of change in Irish society? Writing before the upsurge of violence during the last decades of the twentieth century, McDowell and M.R. O'Connell believed the Volunteers of the eighteenth century personified significant new developments in Irish society. These developments had resulted in an increased

6 J.R. Fisher, *The end of the Irish parliament* (London, 1911), p. 109.   7 C. Litton Falkiner, *Studies in Irish history and biography* (London, 1902), p. 28.   8 M. Davitt, *The fall of feudalism in Ireland* (London, 1904), pp 114–15.   9 R.B. McDowell, *Irish public opinion, 1750–1800* (London, 1944), p. 5.

dissatisfaction with the existing political framework and an expansion of deliberative public opinion.[10] Writing later, against the backdrop of paramilitary violence, Padraig Ó Snodaigh and David Miller perceived a more foreboding continuity in the society and culture that produced the Volunteers. For Ó Snodaigh in particular, the Volunteers did not spring fully armed with constitutional declarations from the enlightened heads of men such as the earl of Charlemont, but continued a traditional pattern of Protestant settlers independently organizing themselves into public bands for their own defence, typically against a perceived threat from Catholics. These public bands emphasized Protestant solidarity and acted primarily as instruments of social control directed against an increasingly restive population, especially Catholics.[11] The struggle between settler and native endured.

While accepting the Volunteers as part of the legacy of conflict between settler and native, Miller provided a critical insight into how the history of Ulster liberalism might begin with the Volunteers. Acknowledging the importance of the public band tradition, Miller also accepted the earlier observations of McDowell and O'Connell that important social changes were occurring that significantly affected the public band tradition as manifested by the Volunteers. Specifically, the expansion of commercial textile manufacturing had created a leadership struggle between two élite groups within the Protestant community; the traditional Church of Ireland landlord élite and a new Presbyterian élite founded upon textile manufacture and commerce.[12] Ironically, the Volunteer movement served for a time as the common ground for these very different élites.

This short-lived common ground was undermined by the different choices these élites made when confronted with social change and the prospect of Catholic emancipation. The landed élite, in sympathy with the desires of the Protestant lower orders who felt threatened by economic changes and the prospect of competition with Catholics, tried to restore and re-emphasize the sectarian exclusivity of the public band. The most obvious symbol of this development was the Orange Order. On the other hand, the Presbyterian élite advocated parliamentary reform, Catholic emancipation and agrarian reform. These principles eventually led some to become involved with the United Irishmen.[13] The Volunteer movement therefore might be said to have contained the seeds of both the Orange Order and the United Irishmen. The Volunteers originated from within the public band tradition that had developed during

10 Ibid., p. 26; M.R. O'Connell, *Irish politics and social conflict in the age of the American Revolution* (Philadelphia, 1965), p. 98. 11 Ó Snodaigh, 'Some police and military aspects of the Irish Volunteers', 229. 12 D. Miller, *Queen's rebels* (New York, 1978), pp 50–1. 13 Ibid.

Ulster's colonial past, but they were clearly affected by modernization so that from within their ranks new ideas, such as Ulster liberalism, might emerge.

Miller's analysis has been somewhat challenged by doubts about the relevance of the enlightenment principles espoused in many Volunteer pronouncements. Were these principles empty rhetoric? For Thomas Bartlett, sectarian disdain and animosity formed the bedrock of Volunteer agitation. Constitutional agitation was possible precisely because the *philosophes* confirmed existing sectarian prejudices and contempt for a supposedly moribund Catholicism.[14] Moving beyond Bartlett's belief in the irrelevance of enlightenment ideals when compared to the tradition of anti-Catholicism, Gerard O'Brien questioned whether there was any role for public opinion in eighteenth-century Ireland. The rhetoric of the Volunteers was inconsequential because the governing élites in Ireland used the limited means of expression available to those outside of government as a means of social control. Petitions, with their conventions and restrictions, became 'a covert instrument of repression' whereby 'the government could identify and head off political unrest'. The possibility of public opinion affecting government policy through parliamentary elections was undermined by the infrequency of elections, the severely restricted franchise in most constituencies and the extensive patronage network maintained by the government to influence members of parliament. Given the structure of politics, the power of the republic of letters was illusory; the idea that 'a loud press and a multiplicity of pamphlets would wring results from an apprehensive government was and is fallacious'. O'Brien therefore contended that the primary importance of the Volunteers was the threat of force that ultimately influenced the government.[15]

This recent scepticism about the ideals of the Volunteers and their likely effects upon politics and society has in some ways been salutary. First, a closer examination of the apparent contradictions within Volunteer rhetoric has led to a clearer understanding that a 'cacophony of political languages' was spoken in eighteenth-century Ireland.[16] The story is complex. Second, not only has the heterogeneity of the Volunteers become widely accepted, but the very real problem of judging the relationship between ideas and events has been acknowledged if not resolved. A careful consideration of the political languages of the Volunteers may not provide a simple explanation of events but it can help our understanding of both the ideas and actions of the people as they adapted to the circumstances in which they lived. Ulster liberalism was one of the political languages that emerged from the Volunteer movement.

14 T. Bartlett, *The fall and rise of the Irish nation* (Savage, MD, 1992), pp 67–9, 91. 15 G. O'Brien, 'The unimportance of public opinion in eighteenth-century Britain and Ireland' (1993), 116, 120, 124. 16 S. Small, *Political thought in Ireland, 1776–1798* (Oxford, 2002), p. 1.

In 2002, shortly after the completion of the dissertation which forms the foundation of this book, Stephen Small published a significant study of political thought in eighteenth-century Ireland in an attempt to 'shed new light on the origins of Irish republican nationalism and place late eighteenth-century Irish political thought in the larger context of British, Atlantic and European ideas'.[17] Small identifies and describes five distinct political languages in Ireland – Protestant superiority, ancient constitutionalism, commercial grievance, classical republicanism, and natural rights. Aspects of Small's schema are similar to the development of political languages described here, both being strongly influenced by J.G.A. Pocock's ideas. However, because this study focuses on Ulster rather than Ireland as a whole and the development of liberalism rather than Small's stated themes of patriotism, radicalism and republicanism, I have retained my original categories. Small's careful documentation of the existence of these political languages also permits this study the luxury of an abbreviated discussion of shared categories in order to concentrate on distinct elements.

While sharing many beliefs and assumptions, four distinct categories are discernible among the Volunteers in Ulster – Whigs, civic republicans, covenanters and nascent liberals. With the exception of the covenanters, a small but important element among the Volunteers who will be considered later, these traditions were concerned with an idealized Irish constitution of supposedly ancient origin. Neil York has recently described this Irish constitutional tradition as consisting of a belief that:

> from 1172 on Ireland had been a commonwealth as well as a kingdom, governed by the rule of law; that Ireland's legal tradition was linked to Magna Carta and rights enjoyed under common law, custom, royal proclamation, and parliamentary statute.[18]

The differences among Whigs, civic republicans, and nascent liberals concerning that constitutional tradition were at first matters of emphasis that often permitted cooperation. Over time, however, these differences became more pronounced and more difficult to reconcile.

The Whigs, personified by the earl of Charlemont, conceived of a constitution founded upon classical precepts, especially interpretations of Polybius, favouring a mixed government composed of monarchy, aristocracy, and democracy. By themselves or combined in the wrong proportions, these three forms of government were likely to degenerate into parlous parodies of themselves.[19] Monarchy would become tyranny, aristocracy an oligarchy and

---

17 Ibid.   18 N.L. York, *Neither kingdom nor nation* (Washington, DC, 1994), p. 26.   19 For the influence of Polybius upon political thought see J.G.A. Pocock, *The Machiavellian*

democracy an anarchy. In the case of Ireland the balance of the constitution was threatened by the ambitions of the monarchy as well as the grasping interests of a powerful neighbour, England. For the Whigs, the primary bulwark against these encroachments was an aristocracy with sufficient means to maintain a virtuous independence. In his memoirs Charlemont described his political strategy as an aspiration to keep –

> one individual at least of rank and property wholly independent, as a standard to which, upon any emergency, men might resort, whether actuated by real public principle, or, as is too often the case, by motives of an interested nature, which last species, base as it is, may however often be rendered useful to the public cause.[20]

More recently, Jacqueline Hill has suggested that the sartorial extravagance favoured by some Volunteers may have been an outward and visible symbol of a resurgence of an aristocratic ideal that was a hallmark of Whiggery.[21]

Like the Whigs, civic republicans believed that an ancient Irish constitution was threatened or already had been subverted. Unlike the Whigs, civic republicans did not emphasize the role of the Irish aristocracy in preserving that constitution. Instead, drawing inspiration from the commonwealth tradition described by Caroline Robbins and others, civic republicans believed that the constitution required each of the three estates to play an equal and independent part in government.[22] The democracy was as important as the aristocracy or the monarchy. A balanced constitution required citizens to be active, independent and virtuous. Evidence of the virtue or corruption of the commonalty could be found in two institutions – the unpaid militia and the municipal corporation. Civic republicans feared that both these institutions were being undermined. Unpaid service in the militia, an important emblem of the willingness to sacrifice self-interest for the common good, was threatened by the increasing reliance of monarchs upon professional soldiers. This trend threatened to undermine the constitution by subverting the public spirit and independence of the commonalty in the militia. The zeal for volunteering, particularly when it reached beyond the aristocracy, might be taken as a manifestation of civic republicanism.

Very often the principles of civic republicanism were presented and explained in the sermons of Presbyterian ministers delivered to Volunteer units. A typical example of this kind of discourse was delivered by Revd James

moment (Princeton, 1975), pp 77–80, 365–6. 20 HMC, *Manuscripts and correspondence of the James, first earl of Charlemont* (London, 1891–4), i, p. 7. 21 J. Hill, *From patriots to unionists* (Oxford, 1997), p. 9. 22 Ibid., p. 14.

Crombie, the Scottish-born minister of the First Presbyterian Congregation of Belfast, to the First Company of Belfast Volunteers in July 1778. For Crombie, fear of the Polybian cycle was the foundation for a British constitutional tradition. The balance of the constitution provided, 'against the turbulence of the people, the ambition of the nobles, and the usurpations of the crown'. For that constitution to function, however, 'activity must pervade every link of the political union'; the aristocracy cannot say to the commonalty 'we have no need of you' without threatening the 'health and soundness' of the social body. Crombie cites the example of the Greeks who 'with a handful of her virtuous citizens' were able 'to repel and disperse the mighty armies of the East' because 'every citizen was a patriot, and every interest gave way to that of country'. If that active virtue failed, however, even the mightiest of states might fail, as Sparta had when its people had fallen away from their 'simplicity of manners' and 'manly virtues'.[23]

Along with volunteering, active participation in municipal life was also a prominent concern of civic republicans. The municipal charters established during the plantation of the seventeenth century had provided for some representation of the interests of the mass of inhabitants by the admission of freemen. The corporation was meant to be a commonwealth in miniature, consisting of a sovereign – known variously as mayor, provost or portreeve – a limited number of burgesses, and a commonalty consisting of a greater number of freemen. For civic republicans, these charters were modelled on those of London, that rampart of resistance to Stuart tyranny, and had been intended to allow the lesser orders a limited role in both local and national politics, every corporate town being also a parliamentary borough. The corporation was a school for the 'civil arts' of local government where virtues necessary to preserve the constitution might be learned by the commonalty.[24] Recent research has demonstrated that civic republicanism persisted within the corporate structure of Dublin, but in municipal corporations in Ulster civic republicanism was handicapped by the almost complete decay of the democratic elements in the municipal charters.[25]

By the end of the eighteenth century freemen were a rare species throughout Ireland but especially so in Ulster. The combination of denominational requirements for membership in the Church of Ireland enacted in 1704, the lapsing of residential requirements in 1747, and the widespread practice of co-option to supply or more often not to supply new freemen rendered the ideal of an active and independent commonalty an illusion in Ulster. T.C. Barnard

23 J. Crombie, *A sermon on the love of country* ([Belfast], 1778), pp 16, 24–5, 30.   24 T.C. Barnard, *A new anatomy of Ireland* (New Haven, CT, 2003), p. 16.   25 Hill, *From patriots to unionists*, p. 145.

estimates that during the period before 1770 there were still some 30 to 50 towns where somewhere 'between 3000 and 5000 provincial townsmen were given a chance to participate' in civic life.[26] That number seems small enough, but the practical monopoly of aristocratic patrons or oligarchies over municipal life in Ulster was almost complete.

At the end of the eighteenth century there were twenty-nine parliamentary boroughs in Ulster that returned two members each to the Irish parliament. In general, parliamentary borough and municipal corporation were synonymous terms. There were, however, six anomalous towns in Ireland where the status of parliamentary borough was granted without a municipal charter.[27] Three of these rare exceptions were the Co. Antrim boroughs of Antrim, Randalstown, and Lisburn. All three towns were so-called potwalloping boroughs. The term referred to the right of all inhabitants who boiled a pot in the borough to vote. Theoretically, therefore, all of the Protestant householders might vote. This franchise might have been expected to preserve the democratic aspect of the civic republican ideal, but in practice all three towns were pocket boroughs completely controlled by aristocratic patrons. With the franchise simply dependent on residency, politically adroit landlords were careful in their choice of tenants and grant of leases. This confirmed the contemporary complaint that 'no potwalloping town, the soil of which is the property of an individual, can possibly be free'.[28] Without a charter, the independence of the commonalty valued by civic republicans was moribund.

Chartered liberties were no less threatened. In the remaining twenty-six boroughs the corporate charters included provisions for the creation of freemen. All of the official titles for these corporations contained a reference to the 'commonalty'. For example, the official title of the corporation in Strabane was – the Provost, Free Burgesses, and Commonalty of the Borough of Strabane. By the last two decades of the eighteenth century, however, these charters were dead letters in all but two towns in Ulster, Carrickfergus and Derry. Entire corporations typically consisted of a dozen or so burgesses, allied to a patron by family and interest, who perfunctorily approved the parliamentary candidates chosen by the patron and conducted municipal affairs, generally in secret, without regard to the interests or needs of the inhabitants. Often the only circumstance in which freemen were created was when the charter required that a new burgess be selected from among the freemen of the corporation. This deterioration of the commonalty in Ulster was a prime factor in the efflorescence of civic republican ideals among the Volunteers. In Belfast,

---

26 Barnard, *New anatomy*, p. 16.   27 *First report of the commissioners appointed to inquire into the municipal corporations in Ireland*, HC 1835 (23, 24, 25, 27, 28), xxvii–xxviii, p. 6.   28 *A letter to Henry Flood, esq., on the present state of representation in Ireland* (Belfast, 1783), p. 7.

for example, the corporation consisted of twelve burgesses (the majority of them non-resident) and the sovereign. The lack of a role for the commonalty contributed to the widespread enthusiasm for volunteering.

The remaining two political languages of the Volunteers, the covenanting tradition and the nascent liberals, were strongly influenced by their Scottish cultural heritage. I have conceived of the covenanting tradition as comprising two closely related Presbyterian groups, the Covenanters and Seceders, who both believed the Solemn League and Covenant of 1643 was a cornerstone of an Irish constitutional tradition. That pledge to support the English parliament against the crown in exchange for the establishment of Presbyterianism and the extirpation of prelacy and popery throughout the three kingdoms fostered an attitude of resistance that remained an important foundation of religious and political faith for them. As the rubric for an ideal constitution, the covenant had been subverted by the Glorious Revolution and the Hanoverian succession, but in the words of Ian McBride, 'the intellectual inheritance of the Scottish Reformation offered a rich and complex legacy of resistance and radicalism' continued to affect all Presbyterians but especially those belonging to the covenanting tradition.[29]

The divisions between the Covenanters and the Seceders might seem overly subtle to modern readers but they significantly affected the history of Ulster liberalism. The Covenanters never fully accepted the Hanoverian regime, and as a result they were at times particularly persecuted or discriminated against by the state. Known officially as the Reformed Presbytery, the Covenanters were by far the smallest of the Presbyterian sects in Ulster with only 6 ministers for 12 congregations in 1792. By comparison, the mainstream represented by the Synod of Ulster had 185 ministers. The other distinct component of the covenanting tradition, the Seceders, had 46 ministers at that time. The small number of Covenanter ministers and congregations somewhat belies their influence. Their pastors often travelled to 'preaching stations' and supervised 'meetings' other than their own congregations so that the popularity of the Covenanters with the common people became a common source of complaint by orthodox ministers in the General Synod.[30]

The Seceders were less extreme in their opposition to the Hanoverians than the Covenanters. Citing the precedent of early Christians having been commanded to obey pagans in civil matters, the Seceders conceded that pristine orthodoxy was not a precondition for obedience to existing authorities.[31] Unfortunately for them, however, the Hanoverian regime at times did

---

29 The political attitudes of the covenanting tradition are magisterially outlined in I.R. McBride, *Scripture politics* (Oxford, 1998), pp 78–83, 109. **30** Ibid., pp 65, 706. **31** Ibid., pp 81–3.

not fully acknowledge the Seceders' careful distinctions in belief and practice from the Covenanters. In 1740 the Seceders were expelled from the Church of Scotland for their refusal to accept lay patronage in the choice of ministers and formed their own Associate Synod. In Ulster the Seceders flourished despite being divided into burgher and antiburgher synods over the question of a civic oath in Scotland until 1818. From the establishment of the first congregation in 1746 the number of secession congregations increased steadily until there were 41 in Ulster in 1770.[32] The rate of increase then slowed somewhat so that there were only 46 congregations in 1792 when the Seceders were given a portion of the *regium donum* provided annually by parliament for the support of Presbyterian ministers in Ireland.[33] In 1809 there were 91 seceding congregations in Ulster, and by time of the reunion of the synods in 1818 there were 114.[34] The greater flexibility of the Seceders was to be of critical importance in their ability to adapt the covenanting tradition to social and political change during the nineteenth century.

Combining a contractarian theology resonant of Locke's social contract with a strong sense of themselves as a distinct community or even a chosen people, the covenanting tradition encouraged both a distrust of the state and a prophetic attitude of instruction and correction with regard to the civil authorities. Whereas civic republicans considered their participation in the Volunteers as a sign of their worthiness to be citizens, the covenanting tradition gathered as a community to enforce the laws of God upon the state. These attitudes led the covenanting tradition to play a role in the Volunteer movement disproportionate to its numbers. The covenanting tradition's views of the British constitution were estimably summarized by Revd John Rogers, minister of a Seceding congregation in Co. Monaghan, in a Volunteer sermon delivered in 1780. Unlike the civic republicanism evident in the previously cited Volunteer sermon of Crombie in Belfast, Rogers placed the mixed constitution firmly within the covenanting tradition. He emphasized that 'no man is born with a crown on his head, or a sword in his hand, as if nature had designed him to be a ruler', but instead the crown was a 'gift of the people' confirmed by the contract of the coronation oath that bound both a ruler and his subjects. Most importantly, this constitution conformed to divine law – 'the affections of the people, and the broad basis of the constitution, under God' was the surest foundation for rule. Every patriot was obliged –

---

32 D. Hempton and M. Hill, *Evangelical Protestantism in Ulster society, 1740–1890* (New York, 1992), pp 17, 26, 109. 33 J.S. Reid and W.D. Killen, *History of the Presbyterian church in Ireland,* 3 vols (new [3rd] ed., Belfast, 1867), iii, p. 368. Reid died in 1851 before the manuscript of the third volume was published. Killen completed the work, carrying the narrative from the middle of the eighteenth century until 1867. 34 W.T. Latimer, *A history of the Irish Presbyterians* (2nd ed., Belfast, 1902), p. 467; A.R. Holmes, *The shaping of Ulster Presbyterian belief and practice, 1770–1840* (Oxford, 2006), p. 5.

to support both the civil and religious rights of mankind, and not to separate what God has joined together. If we consider civil rights, and are indifferent about religion, we are lukewarm patriots. Or, if we consider religion and disregard civil rights, we are fiery zealots, and our zeal is without knowledge; for God informs us, that there are duties to be performed both to God and man.

This position led many Seceders to oppose the complete removal of penal disabilities against Catholics. 'Humanity enjoins' the removal of most impediments against Catholics or any persecution on account of their religion, but 'Christianity forbids' patriots from 'building up their [Catholic] altars, or permitting them to tear down ours'.[35] Rogers was one of the two delegates at the Volunteer convention in Dungannon in 1782 to dissent from a resolution supporting the removal of Catholic disabilities.[36] As Elaine McFarland points out, the ability of the covenanting tradition to cooperate with the Volunteer consensus on these grounds explains how 'political libertarianism and religious sectarianism could coexist comfortably within Ulster Presbyterianism, both ideologies drawing on the Scottish intellectual legacy'.[37]

Along with the intermingling of covenanting tradition and civic republicanism the Scottish intellectual influence upon Ulster also included ideas from the Scottish Enlightenment. Many Ulster Presbyterians travelled to Glasgow and Edinburgh for their education and several scholars have described the close personal and intellectual connections that developed between Scotland and Ulster during the eighteenth century.[38] In Scotland, the students absorbed the enlightenment ideals of Francis Hutcheson, Adam Ferguson and John Millar, as well as aspects of the commonwealth tradition. It was these ideas that contributed most to the development of nascent liberalism among the Volunteers.

Hitherto the most widely recognized influence of the Scottish enlightenment in Ulster was the spread of so-called 'new light' ideas among Presbyterians. Because the 'new light' emphasized human reason and private conscience in opposition to tradition and the authority of institutions some scholars have considered it to be an important source of the radicalism of the United Irishmen.[39] The debate concerning private judgment as opposed to community engendered within Ulster Presbyterianism would have consequences in the nineteenth century that extended beyond questions of sectarian religion or the United Irishmen. A concern for the ideals of private conscience and rationality and its relationship with community and nation would become a distinguishing feature of Ulster liberalism.

35 Rogers, *A sermon preached at Lisnavein*, pp 11–12, 24, 34. 36 Witherow, *Historical memorials*, p. 249. 37 E.W. McFarland, *Ireland and Scotland in the age of revolution* (Edinburgh, 1994), pp 89, 25. 38 A.T.Q. Stewart, *A deeper silence: the hidden origins of the United Irishmen* (London, 1993), pp 81–101. 39 McFarland, *Ireland and Scotland*, p. 11.

However, while A.T.Q. Stewart, McFarland and Small have made convincing arguments about the intermingling of covenanting, civic republican, and new light ideals within the Volunteer movement, they have curiously neglected an important aspect of the Scottish enlightenment that was critical to nascent liberalism in Ulster. It is clear that a number of Ulster writers were influenced by the debates concerning the Scottish school of sociology that developed in the writings of David Hume, Adam Ferguson and John Millar. From these writers, nascent liberals in Ulster came to emphasize the role of social developments in political history.

Rather than imagining an ancient constitution that ought to be preserved, the Scottish sociologists and their adherents in Ulster described a more evolutionary development of society and political institutions. The ancient constitution depended on a balance of interests as represented by king, lords, and commons together with a virtuous independence on the part of the individual. For both Whigs and civic republicans any imbalance between the interests or diminution of virtue would almost inevitably result in a cycle of corruption, despotism and anarchy. The only possibility of preventing degeneration was a return to original principles.[40] The covenanting tradition likewise believed in the need for a return to a more precisely defined set of theologically derived original principles.

The Scottish sociologists and nascent liberals in Ulster were increasingly sceptical about the existence of an ancient constitution and the desirability of preserving unaltered any constitution in inevitably changing circumstances. The Scottish sociologists, according to Pocock, 'employed the notion of a progress of society, from savagery to commerce, as a means of vindicating the Whig order and presenting commercial and specialized society as superior to the classical republics and their ancient virtue'.[41] The classical societies were not the utopian models of virtue that some imagined and, furthermore, the nature of political virtue itself had been transformed by social developments. The societies and circumstances of classical Rome, Athens and Sparta differed so markedly from those of Britain and Ireland in the eighteenth century as to make wholesale adoption of their political principles a procrustean absurdity.

A particular example of the ideological community that developed between Ulster and Scotland was the influence of John Millar, professor of law at Glasgow from 1761 until 1801.[42] While direct intellectual connections are notoriously difficult to establish, three developments seem to confirm the Scottish sociological heritage in general and Millar's influence in particular. First, doubts concerning both the idea of the ancient constitution and a simple

---

40 Pocock, *Virtue*, p. 97. 41 Ibid., p. 298. 42 C. Robbins, *The eighteenth-century commonwealthman* (New York, 1968), p. 214.

restoration of principles began to appear in pamphlets and public speeches. Commercial men were no longer suspected of lacking the virtue necessary for political life but were cast as ideal citizens. Second, there is evidence of the works of the Scottish sociologists among the lists of books owned by prominent Ulster liberals.[43] Thirdly, during the period between 1792 and 1813, prominent figures in the history of Ulster liberalism specifically cited their exposure to Millar's lectures and books as important intellectual influences.

The significant change in attitude toward the ancient constitution and classical virtue among some Volunteers can be understood by comparing pamphlets written by two well-known reformers, William Bruce and Joseph Pollock. In 1784, William Bruce, then minister of an influential Presbyterian congregation in Dublin, wrote a caustically satirical pamphlet criticizing the Irish parliament.[44] Using the pseudonym Gracchus, Bruce constructed a tongue-in-cheek defence of the majority in the Irish parliament who had rejected the proposals for parliamentary reform drafted by the Volunteer convention in Dublin during 1783. Bruce mockingly praised the majority for rejecting 'the arrogant usurpations of the people' and hoped his solitary apology for their conduct would not be lost to posterity 'least it should erroneously regard you as the UNANIMOUS OBJECT of public contempt, public disgust and public execration'. Bruce systematically reduced the arguments of the majority concerning trade, the Volunteers, corruption and reform to absurdities. Bruce subverted, for example, the traditional defence of places and pensions. Gracchus ironically dismissed the principle that 'wealth is highly prejudicial to a state unless there be a strict integrity in those that have the management of it', and he further reasoned that 'the whole system of places, pensions, preferments, promises &c. which is petulantly denominated a system of corruption' was entirely attributable to the patriot policies of the Volunteers because 'in plain English the Patriot is to be bribed, and as it is vulgarly said the receiver makes the thief, so it may be safely alleged that the Patriot makes the bribe'.[45]

In the dramatic volte-face that concludes the pamphlet, Bruce casts aside his satirical mask and in the direct language of civic republicanism derided the government and its supporters as 'strong in wickedness', 'corrupt' and 'venal'. Bruce even suggested that a system of government might become so corrupt that the use of force might be necessary to restore the commonwealth. By exposing the sophistry of the majority Bruce hoped that the people of Ireland would understand 'that the words in which they have expressed their enmity

---

43 Catalogue of books belonging to William Tennent c.1807, PRONI, D1748/A/3/4/4. 44 *Belfast Literary Society*, p. 29. 45 Gracchus [W. Bruce], *A vindication of government addressed to the people of Ireland* (Dublin, 1784), pp iii, 19.

and their attachment, have been equally fatal to their interests', and in the future they might adopt 'another language, besides that of words, that nations make use of to enforce redress, and to which needs only to be uttered to be obeyed'.[46]

Bruce's background and education help to explain his adherence to the civic republican tradition. His family was steeped in the traditions of the common-wealthmen described by Caroline Robbins. An uncle in Dublin had published editions of several works in this tradition, such as James Harrington's *Oceana*.[47] Unlike most Presbyterians of his day Bruce did not receive the bulk of his education at Glasgow, but rather received his BA from Trinity College, Dublin and then spent a single session at Glasgow before proceeding to the famous dissenting academy at Warrington for two years. His exposure to the ideas of the Scottish sociologists was certainly less extensive than many of his contemporaries. Yet, as will be seen, by end of his life, even Bruce would view history more sociologically.

In contrast to Bruce's straightforward indictment of the characters of members of parliament was the influential *Letters of Owen Roe O'Nial* written by Joseph Pollock, a young barrister from Co. Down who served as captain of the First Company of Newry Volunteers. Pollock's historical reputation has probably derived as much from his influence on the more widely known William Drennan and Theobald Wolfe Tone than from any close consideration of his writings. To most modern readers the striking aspect of Pollock's work was its extended apology for Irish independence. According to N.L. York, for example, Pollock had little faith in British intentions towards Ireland and 'threaded his way through the past to show that, as he put it, the Irish had been to the English what the helots had been to the Spartans'.[48] Pollock's work was much more sophisticated than a simple catalogue of English mistreatment of the Irish.

For Pollock, the difficulty was not the English as such but the natural limits of political institutions. In Pollock's estimation political institutions, 'act uniformly from the narrowest kind of selfishness, and are totally incapable of a steady or uniform principle of generosity'. Although 'morality is felt' by men as a natural faculty akin to that described by Francis Hutcheson, politics are an artificial product of human reason that diminishes the natural conscience. In addition, the faith that Whigs and civic republicans placed in a balance of interests to preserve virtue and liberty was misplaced. All political bodies, 'whether sole or aggregate, whether composed of one person or a multitude', are incapable of generosity and justice beyond circumscribed limits. Indeed,

46 Ibid., pp 34–5. 47 Stewart, *Deeper silence,* p. 113. 48 York, *Neither kingdom nor nation,* p. 119.

citing Hume, Pollock observes ironically that, 'those nations who enjoyed the most liberty themselves have been ever the greatest tyrants of others, and the provinces of a despotic King have generally been treated more kindly than those of free states'. Unlike despotic states where one will and interest governs, free states, where 'every man is in a degree one of the *government*', allow a multiplicity of interests to arise and this 'opposition of interests disunites the Lords of a free state from their subjects in the province'. In this way 'Athens the brave, the polite, the lettered and the wise', oppressed Sicily. Even Sparta, usually considered the epitome of a virtuous state where the public interest was the sole object of government and society, oppressed its helots.[49] Pollock's acerbic iconoclasm extended to the tradition of liberty among the English who, despite having 'sacrificed kings themselves at the altar of freedom', oppressed Ireland. Given the inevitable difference in interests between Ireland and England the best way to restore and maintain its liberty was independence. The foundation of Pollock's justification for Irish independence was not, however, the ancient constitution. It was rather an appeal to apply constitutional principles with a regard to circumstances. No amount of virtue, not the classical virtue of Athens or Sparta or the civic republican virtues derived from the English commonwealthmen, could overcome the limits of social institutions and circumstances.

The sociological approach of Pollock was almost certainly derived in large part from his time as a student at Glasgow where he attended lectures by John Millar.[50] Although Pollock's pamphlet represents the most detailed expression of the sociological aspect of nascent liberalism among the Volunteers, he was not alone in his use of this political language. The older language of civic republicanism was predominant but references to the manners and customs of society in history were evident in the writings of other Volunteers such as Revd William Crawford, chaplain of the First Tyrone Regiment, and Revd William Steel Dickson.[51] Pollock's work had a significant effect upon the ideas of William Drennan, Wolfe Tone and other later Irish radicals.[52] In particular, Pollock's scepticism about the existence or utility of an ancient constitution led to a willingness to question the very ideas of mixed government and

---

49 [J. Pollock], *Letters of Owen Roe O'Nial* (Dublin, 1779), pp 7, 10; see for example Adam Ferguson's descriptions of the Spartans originally published in 1767, A. Ferguson, *An essay on the history of civil society* (Edinburgh, 1966), pp 160–1. 50 Pollock explicitly acknowledged his debt to Millar in Joseph Pollock, *Letters to the inhabitants of the town and lordship of Newry* (Dublin, 1793), pp 42–3. 51 W. Crawford, *A history of Ireland* (Strabane, 1783), i, p. 21; W.S. Dickson, *Sermons on the following subjects* (Belfast, [1778]), p. 11; subsequently Dickson explicitly acknowledged the influence of John Millar upon his thought in W.S. Dickson, *A narrative of the confinement and exile of William Steel Dickson* (Dublin, 1812), p. 4. 52 For his influence on Drennan see York, *Neither kingdom nor colony*, p. 188; for Tone see M. Elliott, *Wolfe Tone* (1989), pp 103–4.

parliamentary sovereignty. William Drennan mocked both in his widely read *Letters of Orellana*.[53] The willingness to question the traditional constitutional orthodoxy likewise may have fostered an enthusiasm for the kind of constitutional innovations heralded by the French Revolution. It is interesting to note that Joseph Pollock was present at the founding of the Dublin society of United Irishmen in October 1791.

Before the French Revolution, Whigs, civic republicans, covenanters and nascent liberals could find sufficient common ground to cooperate within the Volunteer movement without significantly compromising their principles. That cooperation and those principles would be put to the test during the 1790s. The violence of 1790s would act as a crucible for the formation of Ulster liberalism. Some of the elements that had formed the alloy of the Volunteers would be diminished, while others would be mixed in new proportions.

Republics, commonwealths and war, 1791–1800

As the Volunteer movement loomed large in the historical imagination of a nineteenth-century Ireland transfixed by the idea of an autonomous Irish parliament, the United Irishmen mesmerized a twentieth-century Ireland hopeful for social reform and confronted with conspiracy and violence in Northern Ireland. Since the late 1960s the legacy of the United Irishmen has been debated with renewed vigour and occasionally new insights. Anniversaries of important events in the history of the society have resulted in a myriad of publications ranging from detailed analyses of the ideology and social composition of the movement as a whole to more popular narratives of a regional scale. A detailed examination of the development of this burgeoning historiography is beyond the scope of this book.[54] However, the events of the 1790s were of sufficient importance in the development of Ulster liberalism that a concise consideration is warranted.

In October 1791 a group of twenty-eight men gathered in Belfast to establish the Society of United Irishmen. The goals of the society as outlined in its first declaration were extraordinarily simple. Impressed by the examples of the American and French revolutions the society was established to rescue 'our Constitution' from the corrupting influence of England by means of radical parliamentary reform.[55] Neither the declaration of grievances nor the

53 [W. Drennan], *Letters of Orellana, an Irish helot to the seven northern counties* (Dublin, 1785). 54 Two important reviews of recent work on the United Irishmen and other aspects of Irish history during the 1790s are H.T. Dickinson, 'Irish radicalism in the late eighteenth century' (1997), 266–84; and I. McBride, 'Reclaiming the rebellion: 1798 in 1998' (1999), 395–410. 55 Quoted from the 'Declarations and resolutions of the Society of United Irishmen of Belfast' reproduced in Elliott, *Wolfe Tone* (New Haven, CT, 1989), pp 139–40.

proposals for their redress were extraordinary. They were easily recognizable as those of the radical elements of the Volunteers. As Marianne Elliott has observed, nearly all of the core members of the new society had been Volunteers who 'felt betrayed by the movement's aristocratic and parliamentary leaders and shocked at the dismissive treatment meted out to their conventions and reform congress' during the 1780s.[56] From its inauguration until 1794, the society was in many ways a typical eighteenth century reform society. It was a voluntary association that attempted to influence public opinion through the recruitment of prominent and successful men and the dissemination of political propaganda in its innovative and successful newspaper, the *Northern Star*.[57] Like many other such societies, the United Irishmen were not highly regimented during the first few years of their existence. Apart from agreement about the necessity of parliamentary reform as the primary goal and Catholic emancipation as a means to achieve that reform, 'there appear to have been as many opinions on detail as there were individuals'.[58]

In December 1792, the Dublin society of United Irishmen began to formulate a program of parliamentary reform that was eventually published in January 1794. Despite serious internal divisions the plan was radically ambitious, espousing universal manhood suffrage. The program was an attempt to shore up support for society in difficult circumstances. The Whig opposition in parliament threatened to steal their thunder by introducing plans for parliamentary reform, and the political potential of the Catholic question was threatened by significant relief legislation in 1792 and 1793.[59] To make matters worse, when war broke out with France in 1793 the government suppressed the remnants of the Volunteers that had provided support for the society and passed a convention act forbidding political assemblies other than municipal corporations and parliament itself. The Terror in France further contributed to an 'unusual reticence' on the part of the society during 1793.[60] When they published their program in January 1794 the United Irishmen, in the words of Nancy Curtin, 'had little membership or public credibility to lose'.[61]

This combination of circumstances resulted in significant changes in the society. During 1794 and the first half of 1795 the society fitfully evolved from an open voluntary association espousing parliamentary reform into a revolutionary conspiracy dedicated to the establishment of a republic modelled on

---

56 Elliott, *Wolfe Tone*, p. 115. 57 For the surprising social influence in the society, particularly in comparison with its British counterparts, see M. Elliott, *Partners in revolution: the United Irishmen and France* (New Haven, CT, 1982), pp 24–6; for the *Northern Star*, see John Gray, 'A tale of two newspapers: the contest between the *Belfast News-Letter* and the *Northern Star* in the 1790s' (1996), pp 175–98. 58 Elliott, *Partners in revolution*, p. 26. 59 N.J. Curtin, *The United Irishmen* (Oxford, 1994), p. 267. 60 Elliott, *Partners in revolution*, p. 31. 61 Curtin, *The United Irishmen*, p. 27.

that of France. The doubtful prospects for reform led some to consider seriously an overture in the spring of 1794 from an element within the embattled French republican government for an invasion of Ireland. After a series of further setbacks, including government prosecutions for the ostensibly treasonous communications with France, a new oath-bound, underground Society of United Irishmen emerged in May 1795.

Two important changes resulted from this transformation. First, the society no longer concentrated on enlisting the respectable but instead began recruiting the lower orders into a broader revolutionary conspiracy. This led to a second fateful decision. In order to increase their numbers, the society allied themselves with the Catholic and agrarian secret society known as the Defenders. Originating in sectarian conflicts along the border between the provinces of Ulster and Leinster, the Defenders were a violent secret society whose principles were a mixture of revolutionary ideals, agrarian grievances and sectarian Catholicism. Revolutionary ideas were, in the words of Tom Dunne – 'filtered through a number of traditional perspectives and their associated vocabularies – Jacobite hope of foreign deliverance from usurping colonists, or millenarian expectations of Divine intervention to overthrow religious enemies'.[62] The relative importance of these elements is difficult to measure in a secret society operating in a culture with significant numbers of people, 'who were not only illiterate but between languages', and has been hotly debated.[63] Whatever the balance, there can be little doubt that there were serious underlying differences between the Defenders and United Irishmen that could not always be papered over with revolutionary catechisms.

Because of the Defenders, the heterogeneity of the participants in the rising of 1798 has become the central issue in the historiography. What was the meaning of the rising in 1798? Kevin Whelan has described how various groups have attempted to foster their own interpretations in order to advance their particular political agendas. He broadly divides the approaches into three categories – the sectarian plot, the reluctant rebellion, and the republican revolution. Conservative loyalists portrayed the failed insurrection as a sanguinary Catholic plot that had seduced gullible Presbyterians as well as a few foolish members of the Church of Ireland. Liberals described the men of '98 as reluctant rebels forced into rebellion by events they could not control.[64] According to Whelan, both of these interpretations deliberately ignored or underplayed the role of republican ideology in the insurrection.

Whelan, together with a number of collaborators in what one recent

<hr />

62 T. Dunne, 'Popular ballads, revolutionary rhetoric and politicisation' (1989), p. 147.
63 Dunne, 'Popular ballads', pp 145–52; Dickinson, 'Irish radicalism', pp 274–6; Elliott, *Partners in revolution*, p. xvii. 64 K. Whelan, *The tree of liberty* (Cork, 1996), pp 157, 174.

reviewer has described as a growing 'collective enterprise',[65] have sought to prove that the United Irishmen and their Defender allies are best understood as dedicated revolutionaries whose republicanism was not a matter of desperation or expedience.[66] Citing new kinds of evidence of widespread politicization and organization, particularly concerning the Defenders, Whelan and his colleagues have cast considerable doubts upon any attempt to describe the rising as primarily a jacquerie of a normally loyal population. Whelan has been less successful in his attempts to describe the ideals of the rebels. When speaking of the French Revolution, Whelan and his collaborators at times seem to have imagined an established canon of beliefs and principles rather than a complex historical process that bitterly divided partisans of the republic in France at least as much as in Ireland. Whelan imagines the rebels were liberated from the circumstances of history and culture by the revolutionary moment in a transcendent 'window of opportunity'.[67] The world was simply divided between those who supported the revolution and those who did not.

This was, of course, far from the truth. Scales did not fall from the eyes of contemporaries exposed to a fulgent republican canon. Men and women interpreted events and circumstances in terms of their particular cultural and historical perspectives.[68] Indeed, 'much of the fascination' of the subject of revolutions, Ian McBride observes, 'lies in the interaction between revolutionary thought and older clusters of ideas'.[69] Revolutionary ideals, furthermore, were not simply translated into practice but often involved, whether due to revolutionary zeal or necessity, violence and intimidation that troubled many. Observers of the progress of events on the continent also soon realized that the promise of the French republic to aid revolutionary minorities might become problematic. Hugh Gough observes 'that very few so-called "oppressed peoples" welcomed French troops when they appeared over the horizon'.[70] This was due in part to the difficulties the French had in applying their revolutionary model to particular circumstances.[71]

Resistance to the United Irishmen and their Defender allies was not limited to a corrupt government or a frightened Ascendancy and its Orange auxiliaries. The Catholic church and moderate reformers, some of whom had been supporters of the society in its constitutional phase, opposed the revolutionary

---

65 McBride, 'Reclaiming the rebellion', 396. 66 Whelan, *The tree of liberty*, p. 167. 67 K. Whelan, 'Reinterpreting the 1798 rebellion in County Wexford' (1996), pp 9–10. 68 A cogent analysis of the adaptation of French republican ideals to Irish circumstances has been constructed by Hugh Gough and Gilles Le Biez, 'Un républicanisme ambigu: l'Irlande et la Révolution Française' (1994) pp 321–30. 69 McBride, 'Reclaiming the Rebellion', 400. 70 Hugh Gough, 'France and the 1798 Rebellion' (1998), p. 39. 71 See S. Wahnich, Les républiques-soeurs, débat théorique et réalité historique, conquêtes et reconquêtes d'identité républicaine' (1994), 165–78.

United Irishmen. The militia, comprised mostly of Catholics, refused to back the rebels at the critical moment. Like the French Revolution itself, the rebellion seems to have been not simply a struggle between a unified people and a corrupt government but also 'a civil war over the kind of government and society that Ireland should have'.[72] During the agitations surrounding the wars with revolutionary and Napoleonic France, many former allies of the Volunteer movement came to differing conclusions about the best course of action under the circumstances. During the rising, friends found themselves in opposing armed camps.

For various reasons, veterans of the campaign for radical parliamentary reform enlisted in the yeomanry to fight against members of the United Irishmen with whom they had paraded and dined together as Volunteers. In the aftermath of the rebellion, reconciliation was difficult for these reformers who shared many goals and principles. While some abandoned politics and a few became conservatives, some measure of reconciliation was eventually achieved, after great acrimony, by a portion of the Volunteer movement. Former civic republicans, Whigs, and covenanters found a new common ground for cooperation in the principles of the nascent liberals of the eighteenth century that were gaining wider acceptance in society at large. During the nineteenth century this new coalescence became the basis of Ulster liberalism.

In order to understand the extent to which the legacy of the United Irishmen threatened to shatter the new coalition for reform that had emerged from the Volunteer movement, it is useful to consider the history of a section of Ulster society representative of the Volunteer coalition. The Belfast chamber of commerce was in many respects representative of the Volunteer movement. Founded in October 1783, the chamber was a voluntary association intended to provide the mercantile community with means to pressure government for legislation and improvements needed to encourage trade and industry in Belfast. The establishment of such an association was a considerable political innovation. In theory the municipal corporation was the chartered body through which petitions for legislation ought to have passed. When the Dublin chamber of commerce, established in March 1783, presented its first petition to the Irish parliament in November 1783, several MPs wanted to reject the document on the grounds that parliament ought not to accept petitions from an unchartered body. Jacqueline Hill has suggested that the reticence of parliament was a reaction to the Volunteer movement – 'the possibility that *ad hoc* bodies such as the Volunteer convention would be regarded as the real organs of public opinion had made the Irish parliament sensitive to any unaccredited body claiming to speak for particular interests'.[73]

---

72 Curtin, *The United Irishmen*, p. 4.   73 Hill, *From patriots to unionists*, p. 172.

In both Dublin and Belfast the leading spirits behind the foundations of the respective chambers of commerce were prominent in the Volunteer movement. In Dublin, the prominent radical Napper Tandy was a founding member and chief supporter of the chamber during its first years. The first president of the chamber in Dublin was Travers Hartley, an independent member of parliament for Dublin whose election in 1782 was a Volunteer *cause célèbre* even in Belfast.[74] In Belfast, Waddell Cunningham, the leading radical Volunteer leader discussed previously with regard to Carrickfergus, was elected the first president of the chamber at its foundation in October 1783.[75]

The membership of the chamber of commerce in Belfast was composed almost entirely of supporters of the Volunteer movement. Forty-five of the founding 59 members were certainly Volunteers.[76] For a further 8 the evidence strongly suggests involvement in the Volunteer movement. For 6 of the members there is insufficient evidence to make any judgment. Beyond these numbers, the chamber of commerce also seems to have been comprised of the more zealous Volunteers. They were supporters of parliamentary reform who continued to be involved in the movement even after the failure of the Volunteer convention in Dublin in 1783.

Of the 59 founding members of the Belfast chamber of commerce, 7 certainly became members of the United Irishmen.[77] These included 4 founders of the society – William Sinclaire, William Tennent, Robert Simms and Henry Haslett. Another 4 may reasonably be suspected of involvement.[78] In contrast, 17 of the original members joined the yeomanry raised in Belfast in 1797 and 1798. A further 8 either made subscriptions to the yeomanry or were signatories of statements supporting them. It is perhaps not surprising that with such clear political divisions that the survival of the chamber of commerce became doubtful during the 1790s. In February 1794 the chamber ceased to exist and was not revived until February 1802.[79]

At its foundation in 1783 the chamber had been operating within a political consensus in which the Volunteer movement's support for parliamentary reform was the core principle. There was also broad support for gradual

---

74 Ibid.; [Henry Joy], *Historical collections relative to the town of Belfast from the earliest period to the Union with Great Britain* (Belfast, 1817), pp 190–2.   75 G. Chambers, *Faces of change: the Belfast and Northern Ireland chambers of commerce and industry* (Belfast, 1984), p. 43.   76 The names along with brief biographies for most of these members have been supplied in Chambers, *Faces of change*. To augment these biographies, accounts of signatories to petitions and public notices taken from *Historical collections relative to the town of Belfast* attributed to Henry Joy, former owner and editor of the *Belfast News-Letter,* together with some from the *Belfast News-Letter* itself have been tabulated.   77 These were: John Boyle, Hugh Crawford, Robert Getty, Henry Haslett, Robert Simms, William Sinclaire, and William Tennent.   78 These were: Thomas Andrews, Cunningham Greg, James Hyndman and John Luke.   79 Chambers, *Faces of change*, p. 121.

Catholic emancipation. In 1784, 14 of the original 59 members of the chamber of commerce signed a requisition for a town meeting to consider the question of Catholic suffrage as a means to advance the cause of parliamentary reform. At the meeting, it was resolved that,

> the gradual extension of suffrage to our too long oppressed brethren, the Roman Catholics, preserving unimpaired the Protestant government of this country, would be a measure fraught with the happiest consequences, and would be highly conducive to the security of civil liberty.[80]

A cautious compromise had been reached over the divisive tactical issue of Catholic emancipation.

When immediate Catholic emancipation was adopted by the United Irishmen as a tactic to bring about parliamentary reform, however, the majority of former Volunteers as represented by the chamber of commerce seem to have baulked at the prospect. Only 10 of the original 59 members of the chamber of commerce signed the requisition for a town meeting in January 1792. That requisition had as its premise a desire 'to see all distinctions on account of religion abolished and all narrow, partial maxims of policy done away'.[81]

The majority of that town meeting accepted the premise of immediate Catholic emancipation. As with all such public meetings, however, it is difficult to ascertain whether the meeting was truly representative of public opinion or packed with enthusiasts. A consideration of the reaction of the members of the chamber of commerce suggests the latter. A sizeable number of the original members of the chamber of commerce dissented from the majority of the meeting. Twenty-two of them signed a public notice explaining their opposition to immediate emancipation in the aftermath of the meeting. They asserted that the 'only point of difference' between themselves and the majority at the town meeting was whether emancipation should be immediate or progressive, 'from time to time, and as speedily as the circumstances of the country, and the general welfare of the whole Kingdom will permit'.[82]

A consideration of the behaviour of members of the chamber of commerce during the period surrounding the rising in 1797 and 1798 suggests, as might be expected, some correlation between support for immediate emancipation and involvement in revolutionary conspiracy. Of the 10 supporters of immediate emancipation in the chamber of commerce in 1792, 7 were at that time or subsequently United Irishmen. This correlation should not be exaggerated. Of the 10 supporters for immediate emancipation, 6, including 5 of the 7 United Irishmen who were original members of the chamber, joined,

80 [Joy], *Historical collections*, p. 298.   81 Ibid., p. 363.   82 *BNL*, 21 Jan. to 3 Feb. 1793.

subscribed to, or signed a declaration in support of, the yeomanry. This suggests that between 1792 and 1797 the political circumstances had altered so much that even supporters of immediate emancipation who had joined the United Irishmen were willing to support the civil authorities against both their former Irish and French allies.

Of the 22 who supported a more gradual emancipation, 17 either joined, subscribed to, or signed a declaration in support of the yeomanry. Many historians have commented upon the changes in political opinion among former radical Volunteers or even a number of United Irishmen. These changes have been ascribed variously to a deep-seated fear and prejudice against Catholicism, irrational fear of the French Revolution, simple venality or government repression. Upon consideration, however, the changes in political opinion and behaviour may be more apparent than real. For example, although in subsequent years the yeomanry in Ireland became a by-word for sectarianism, recent research by Allan Blackstock and J.E. Cookson has demonstrated that this reputation should not be exaggerated.[83]

The administration of Lord Camden in Ireland was interested in harnessing the tradition of volunteering among the reformers after 1796. They soon discovered, however, that it was difficult to bind what one contemporary referred to as, 'old royalists and the republican reformists now disposed to loyalty', in the same yeomanry corps. Therefore, they connived at the creation of separate yeomanry corps – those comprised of loyalists that sometimes became infused with Orangeism, as opposed to others comprised of critics of the government and advocates of reform. Blackstock demonstrates the existence of two politically opposed yeomanry units in Armagh city.[84] In Belfast, the veterans of the Volunteer movement who joined the unpaid, therefore more like the virtuous Volunteers, supplementary yeomanry signed a declaration stating that their political opinions had not changed, that they remained 'firmly attached to the rights and liberties of ALL the people of Ireland', and had joined the yeomanry in order to protect persons and property from the scourge of foreign invasion and civil war. The captain of the yeomen cavalry in Belfast, Charles Ranken, had presided over a town meeting in January 1795 to petition the Irish parliament on Catholic emancipation. In March 1795 he presided over another meeting which prepared an address to the recalled Earl Fitzwilliam that stated their anticipation of 'the complete liberation of our Roman Catholic brethren'.[85]

In order to understand the processes by which many of the reformers of the 1780s and 1790s came to reject the United Irishmen without rejecting reform

83 J.E. Cookson, *The British armed nation, 1793–1815* (Oxford, 1997), pp 161–4. 84 A. Blackstock, 'The social and political implications of the raising of the yeomanry in Ulster: 1796–1798' (1993), pp 238–9. 85 [Joy], *Historical collections*, pp 431–2, 469.

or betraying their principles it is useful to examine probably the two most important apologies for moderate reform of the period – Joseph Pollock's *Letters to the inhabitants of the town and lordship of Newry* and the collaborative work of Henry Joy and William Bruce titled *Belfast politics*. As will be recalled, Pollock first gained fame with his pseudonymous *Letters of Owen Roe O'Nial* published in 1779 that outlined the philosophical case for Irish independence and even made a case for French intervention in pursuit of that end. Pollock continued to be active in Volunteer politics. Having been an early advocate for the admission of the Catholics into the ranks of the Volunteers, Pollock knew Theobald Wolfe Tone from the Historical Society at Trinity College in Dublin and was a founding member of the first Dublin Society of United Irishmen in 1791.[86] However, Pollock quickly became estranged from the United Irishmen and by early 1793 he had become a member of the Friends of the Constitution, Liberty and Peace, a reform club that attempted, with limited success, to establish branches throughout Ireland.[87]

The society advocated, 'radical and effectual Reform in the Representation of the People in Parliament' as well as the complete 'abolition of all civil and political distinctions arising from difference in religious opinions'. Although acknowledging serious defects in its practice in Ireland, the society were attached to a constitution comprised of king, lords, and commons and critical of any attempt 'tear down our constitution and efface its ancient landmarks and foundations', as had been done in France. Membership in the society required a declaration of principles that included the phrase,

> And seriously apprehending the dangerous consequences of certain levelling tenets, and seditious principles, which have been lately disseminated, I do further declare, that I will resist all attempts to introduce any new form of Government into this country, or in any manner to subvert or impair our Constitution, consisting of King, Lords, and Commons.[88]

Given Pollock's earlier espousal of separatism and his scruples concerning the existence of an ancient constitution, his decision to join the Friends of the Constitution was a sign of his growing concern about revolutionary France.

In February 1793, Pollock was a delegate for County Down to the reform convention at Dungannon. At Dungannon, Pollock was a strident opponent of any of radical resolutions favoured by the United Irishmen. In the aftermath of the convention, Pollock wrote a defence of his conduct in the form of *Letters to*

86 Elliott, *Wolfe Tone*, pp 103, 113. 87 Pollock, *Letters to the inhabitants.* 88 *The proceedings of the association of the Friends of the Constitution, Liberty and Peace, held at the King's Arms Tavern, in Fownes-street, Dublin, Dec. 21, 1792* (London, 1793), pp 8, 10–12.

the inhabitants of the town and lordship of Newry. Surprisingly, Pollock's explanation of his recent conduct reiterated many of the principles outlined in his *O'Nial* letters of 1779. In 1779 Pollock had suggested that French intervention in Ireland would be benign because France, as had been the case in America, would be unequal to the task of conquest and therefore offer instead an alliance. Furthermore, even if a conquest were attempted, Pollock believed there was little reason to fear great social upheaval. The French were unlikely to 'involve themselves in the perplexed disputes and antiquated claims of families, that have suffered by forfeiture'.[89] The France of 1793 was, however, a different creature from the France of the *ancien régime.*

Pollock feared that republican France, if tempted by the loud complaints of the disaffected, might not simply establish Ireland's parliamentary sovereignty but fundamentally change its constitution without respect for its particular history and social institutions. He defended his concern by referring to French conduct in Belgium where after liberating that nation from Austria the French did not permit the re-establishment of the constitution or institutions of the short-lived United States of Belgium founded in 1790 but instead sought to alter fundamentally Belgian institutions and society.[90] In 1793, the French 'might think of offering us *their protection*, and their assistance in *reforming* our Constitution, as they had done in *Belgium*'.[91]

Pollock also believed a sudden, coercive change in political and social institutions was bound to result in civil war, and anyone who would advise people to attempt 'an improvement of their Constitution, *by a civil war*, can be little better than a desperate quack, an incorrigible fool, or a ready-handed ruffian'. Pollock instead advocated a '*middle line*, or anything before them but the *alternative*, which I call a desperate one, of immediate and complete concession on the part of government, or war, on the part of the people'. The instrument of Pollock's middle line was to be a 'civil association' rather than a martial one. The instruments of coercion were to be voluntary non-importation and non-consumption agreements rather than weapons. Indeed, in keeping with the nascent liberal devaluation of martial virtue, Pollock prayed 'that we may have no *heroes*, nor any *miserable occasion for heroes*, but live the life, and walk in the ways of *men*'.[92]

As for government itself, Pollock stressed two points. First, government must not abandon its authority, even if force were required to maintain it. Second, 'THE ONLY MEASURE which can finally and for-ever soften, subdue and disarm this half-reasoning, half-methodical madness' would be a 'reasonable,

---

89 Pollock, *Letters of Owen Roe O'Nial*, pp 21, 26.   **90** J.L. Polasky, *Revolution in Brussels, 1787–1793* (Brussels, 1985), pp 233–9.   **91** Pollock, *Letters to the inhabitants*, p. 39.
92 Ibid., pp 55, 58, 203.

moderate and *unquestionably safe reform*.[93] In Pollock's opinion, true friends of reform recognized that peace and order were necessary conditions to their success. In July 1793, Pollock was so concerned by his perception of a real threat of civil war that he sent a copy of his *Letters to the inhabitants of the town and lordship of Newry* to the government. Confessing that his political connections had 'been with persons in opposition to the administration of Mr Pitt', Pollock believed the circumstances required men 'to give to those in Administration any information or assistance in their power, forgetting all distinctions of prejudice or party, & only thinking how they can add to public happiness or security'.[94] Pollock's thinly-veiled offer of service to the administration was not overlooked and he was eventually appointed assistant-barrister for County Down, much to the disappointment of his former radical friends.

As assistant-barrister Pollock gained first-hand experience of the difficulties involved in balancing the needs of peace and security with civil liberty. His greatest fear continued to be civil war. In November 1796 Pollock proposed writing a pamphlet to explain to the populace the two principle dangers 'they must incur if they join any party but England' in the event of a French invasion. First, because the English believed that 'to give it [Ireland] up to France is to give up herself', England would choose to 'fight France here rather than at home, and must desolate this country rather than give it up'. Second, the population needed to understand the suffering to be expected not only from opposing armies but also from 'internal sects and factions and plunderers, murderers and marauders'.[95] In July 1797 Pollock came into conflict with the notorious General Gerard Lake, commander of forces in Ulster at the time, over the imprisonment of some of the suspected leaders of the United Irishmen. When Pollock concluded that some of the committals were insufficient and that prisoners ought to be released Lake complained but ultimately submitted to Pollock's recommendation. Pollock's experiences of the excesses of ill-disciplined and over-zealous troops in and around Newry led him to compose a memorandum to the chief secretary Thomas Pelham in December 1797 that accepted the need for extraordinary powers in a time of civil disorder but recommended restraint. The troops' behaviour should demonstrate the gravity of the situation that required a curtailment of normal civil liberties. While it was at times necessary that soldiers be 'on proper occasions feared [...] it may be ruinous that they should be hated'.[96] For Pollock, the 1790s were spent trying to rein in the abuses of both the reformers and the authorities.

An emphasis upon moderation and gradual change aligned with an

93 Ibid., p. 208.   94 Chatham papers, Joseph Pollock to William Pitt, 11 July 1793, PRO, 30/8/329/ff 370–1.   95 Downshire papers, Joseph Pollock to Lord Downshire, 10 November 1796, PRONI, D607/D/D302.   96 R.B. McDowell, *Ireland in the age of imperialism and revolution* (Oxford, 1979), pp 573, 589.

increasing awareness of the contributions of commercial society is to be found in the work of Henry Joy, Jr, editor of the *Belfast News-Letter*, and William Bruce, the Presbyterian minister and principal of the Belfast Academy. In their *Belfast politics* published in 1794, Joy and Bruce described how the broad Volunteer consensus had given way to an acrimonious division between radicals who supported the United Irishmen and moderate reformers like themselves.[97] In the case of Bruce, this moderation was a significant change from his writings ten years before when under the pseudonym Gracchus he had suggested the Volunteers force reform upon the Irish parliament. Like so many others, Joy and Bruce had been optimistic about the French Revolution until the execution of the French king and the outbreak of war.

Among the collected documents in *Belfast politics* was a series of essays entitled 'Thoughts on the British Constitution' that attempted to show the superiority of a mixed constitution to republican forms of government. Despite including an epigraph from Millar's *An historical view of the English government* at the head of the first essay, Joy and Bruce were still primarily concerned with a balanced constitution, speaking more like civic republicans than nascent liberals. On several occasions, however, the authors seem to consider the development of society rather than the machinery of the constitution or the increasing or decreasing virtue of citizens. Parliament had gained its proper influence in the constitutions 'from the introduction of commerce'. Commerce is 'that great spring of political independence'. Whereas commerce had been considered a threat to republican governments, in England 'commerce was the parent and nurse of liberty'.[98]

The history of another newspaper and its editor also demonstrates how many nascent liberals continued to support reforms while distancing themselves from certain radical principles. In 1772, George Douglas, a Scotsman who had been a printer in Dublin, established the *Londonderry Journal and Donegal and Tyrone Advertiser*. Douglas published the newspaper until 1796 when he sold the business and emigrated to the United States where he continued to publish, including several works relating to Ireland. While not as earnestly polemical as the radical *Belfast Mercury* during the early 1780s or the *Northern Star* of the 1790s, the *Londonderry Journal* was an independent paper that provided favourable coverage of the Volunteer movement and parliamentary reform. Douglas had played an important role in the growth of civic republicanism in Derry through his organization of the centennial celebrations of the siege.

Douglas, however, might better be characterized as a nascent liberal rather

---

97 [H. Joy and W. Bruce], *Belfast politics* (Belfast, 1794), pp iv–vii.   98 Ibid., pp 182, 201, 260.

than a civic republican. His positive attitude towards commerce was evident in 1786 in his comments concerning the participation of the radical earl of Bristol in political meetings in Derry. Douglas asserted that with the participation of the gentry and aristocracy, 'we may expect that such a spirit of commerce and enterprise may become more universal among us', and that the gentry, 'will no longer be remarked for pride, and a contempt for trade'.[99] Douglas lacked both the overwhelming concern about the corrupting influence of commerce and opulence upon civic virtue that was typical among civic republicans and a faith in the bulwark of a virtuous aristocracy that was a hallmark of Whig thought.

In his preface to *Derriana*, a collection of contemporary historical accounts of the siege published in 1794, Douglas also exhibits considerable distaste for aristocratic and martial ideals. Commenting upon historical writing, Douglas criticized 'the practice of passing over the most useful and most numerous class of mankind, and of only noticing the sons of Rank and Fortune'. He praised instead the renunciation of the 'false glory of battles and sieges and human slaughter' that was 'leading the public mind to the contemplation of the arts of peace, and the improvement of civil and domestic life'.[1] Douglas seems to echo the works of the Scottish enlightenment that emphasized a progression of societies through stages from those that prized martial skills to the more 'polished' stage of commercial societies where martial skills were of less importance.

Douglas' belief in progress was further evidence of his nascent liberalism. Unlike civic republicans who often spoke of an ancient constitution threatened by moral degeneration, Douglas believed that society had improved over time. 'Who', Douglas asked, 'would prefer the dark and barren ages of the 10th, 11th, and 12th centuries, to the enlightened and enlightening periods of the 16th, 17th and 18th centuries?' Although an advocate of constitutional reforms, Douglas described the current constitution as 'mild and liberal'.[2] Douglas was both witness and participant in the development of an independent challenge to the group of families that had controlled politics in Derry.[3] Douglas endorsed independent candidates for parliament and in 1791 supported the establishment of a chamber of commerce that became involved in a series of disputes with the municipal corporation concerning the civic constitution and the parliamentary franchise.[4]

As might be expected, Douglas and the other reformers in Derry were quick to compare the early events in France with the history of the Glorious Revolution. At the celebration of the siege in August 1790, 'the French

99 *LJ*, 18 Apr. 1786. 1 G. Douglas, *Derriana* (Derry, 1794), p. vi. 2 Ibid., pp vii–ix. 3 Murphy, *Derry, Donegal and modern Ulster, 1790–1921* (Derry, 1981), p. 5. 4 *LJ*, 13 July 1790, 19 Oct. 1790, 25 Oct. 1791, 10 Jan. 1792, 15 Apr. 1794.

Revolutionists', was among the many Whig and radical toasts offered by the Londonderry Independent Volunteers. By 1791 the drama of the French Revolution even began to overshadow the memory of 1688. In 1791, in addition to the celebration of the anniversary of the lifting of the siege in August, the anniversary of the fall of the Bastille was an occasion for public celebration in July. The resolutions were now infused with more revolutionary language praising the 'natural Rights of Man' and denouncing 'feudal Tyranny'.[5] An edition of Thomas Paine's *The rights of man* secretly published in the city in 1791 'at the desire of a society of gentlemen' may have been the source of some of the new revolutionary rhetoric. It is possible, furthermore, that the pamphlet was published by Douglas himself as only two printers were working in the city during this time and Douglas was by far the more prolific of the two.[6]

By 1792, however, there was growing concern among reformers about events in both Ireland and France. Opinion in the city was increasingly anxious about proposals for Catholic relief. On 30 January 1792 the common council of the corporation of Derry comprised of the mayor, aldermen, sheriffs and burgesses, met and approved a series of resolutions expressing support for very limited Catholic relief. The council criticized the, 'Resolutions of different Roman Catholics of this Kingdom, expressive of their Discontent of the present Constitution', and urging alterations that would destroy that constitution established at the 'glorious revolution'. The council vowed to oppose any measure, 'that may tend to subvert the Protestant Ascendancy'. The contrasting deliberations and resolutions of the common hall comprised of the freemen of the corporation were of more interest. On 4 February 1792, a meeting of the common hall was called to consider a Catholic relief bill brought before the Irish parliament. The freemen supported moderate measures of relief but like their counterparts in the common council opposed any immediate admission of Catholics to the franchise or parliament. During the debates, it was clear that the resolutions were supported by a group of reformers led by William Armstrong, a draper and leading member of the chamber of commerce.[7]

It would be an exaggeration, however, to assert that the independent interest in the city temporarily 'realigned themselves with the old oligarchy of the city to denounce Catholic rights'.[8] The tone of the resolutions from the freemen differed markedly from those of the common council. Whereas the common council's resolutions began with criticism of Catholics for attacks upon the constitution, the freemen instead commended Catholics, 'peaceable and loyal

---

5 Ibid., 17 Aug. 1790, 19 July 1791. 6 Derived from the English Short Title Catalogue database. 7 *LJ*, 7 Feb. 1792, 21 Feb. 1792. 8 Murphy, *Derry, Donegal and modern Ulster*, p. 8.

conduct'. On the one hand, the common council spoke of a 'Protestant Ascendancy' founded by forbears who 'gallantly fought and conquered' in order to establish their privileges. In contrast, the freemen's resolutions defended the continued maintenance of the 'Protestant Interest' by ascribing to Protestantism a mildness and tolerance 'that is friendly to Freedom of Enquiry, and to civil and religious Liberty' so that 'there is nothing to be dreaded by any party'. While the smug tone and the invidious comparison of Catholicism by the freemen may have been more galling in some ways than the forthright triumphalism of the common council, they at least had liberal pretensions. It is clear that the common council conceived of its ascendancy as permanent and enduring. Limited relief 'ought not to be exceeded'.[9] For the freemen, however the admission of the Catholics to the polity was both desirable and inevitable, if not yet feasible. Caution in momentous times should be distinguished from conservatism and reaction.

In 1792 Douglas felt compelled to publish a defence of the proposal to celebrate the fall of Bastille. For Douglas, only the 'Bigotted' and the 'Corrupt' would misinterpret the celebration of French liberty as a sign of disaffection with the 'British Constitution'. When the Friends of Civil and Religious Liberty met in Derry to celebrate the fall of the Bastille, they also voiced concern about the turn of events in France but ascribed them to the nature of revolutions, citing the sanguinary experience of Ireland during the Glorious Revolution. They regretted 'the menaces of Despotism, and the violence of Party', but were hopeful that the 'genuine Friends of Freedom, who look with abhorrence on the outrages of the Despot or of a Mob' were gaining an ascendancy in France. They also believed themselves in a similar predicament. Although 'blest with a Constitution whose spirit is congenial with the purest Liberty', Ireland also had to defend that constitution both against 'those who boldly and professedly project its overthrow' as well as others who would more slowly undermine it 'by sanctioning abuses' and 'resisting every effort toward a constitutional Reform'.[10] Frightened by the disorder in France, the reformers in Derry were beginning to construct an image of a middle path between revolution and reaction.

The construction of this middle path in Derry was also made more evident in December 1792 when a parochial meeting was held to choose delegates for a provincial meeting on parliamentary reform to be held in Dungannon during February 1793. At the meeting, the 'anarchy' in France was cited as evidence of 'the danger of overthrowing any settled form of Government' as opposed to peaceful constitutional reform. The marking out of a middle path was reiterated at the meeting by Revd Robert Black, a veteran Volunteer and

9 *LJ*, 7 Feb. 1792, 21 Feb. 1792.   10 Ibid., 3 July 1792, 17 July 1792.

Presbyterian minister who during the early 1780s had preached before his first congregation in Co. Down in uniform. Black spoke of the –

> *middle men*, who saw the abuses of the Constitution and wished to remove them, but who saw also, and would steadily oppose, the workings of a few seditious spirits, who wished to commit the Country in hostilities, to overturn the Constitution, and to try 'unproved theories'.

Black cautioned those who were impatient against any ill-conceived insurrection. Not only would government act decisively to quell the 'madness', but the insurrection would also be 'suppressed by the voluntary exertions of the Nation'. Although the abuses of the constitution were great, none of them would 'justify the risk of a civil war, or the shedding of blood to remove'.[11]

The opposition to the use of force by the former Volunteer contrasted sharply with more radical voices. When the parochial delegates from Londonderry, Donegal and Tyrone had met in Derry in January 1793, the delegates unanimously approved resolutions for radical parliamentary reform and 'rapid emancipation from oppressive Laws', for Catholics. They also denounced proposals for a militia act as having, 'Ministerial influence for its object'. Three United Irishmen led by Dr John Caldwell of Magherafelt were not, however, satisfied and sought to have a list of grievances accompany the resolutions. Caldwell believed 'the people needed to be rouzed to a sense of their wrongs' and 'disapproved and suspected such soft, silky Reformers as the Gentlemen of Derry', a group led by Robert Black. Caldwell further believed, 'one Volunteer was better than thirty Grattans'.[12] The contrast between Caldwell's exaltation of armed force and the nascent liberal devaluation of martial skill as a basis for virtuous citizenship is striking. At the meeting, Caldwell's proposal was rejected. That rejection was a sign of the growing strength of moderate opinion, whether in the form of the 'middle line' of Pollock or the 'middle men' of Black.

With the onset of war between Britain and France in 1793, overt support for the French Revolution was no longer possible, and expressions of public opinion were severely curtailed. Even the commemorations of the siege that had in the past been opportunities for expressions of political opinion were effectively suppressed. The next significant expression of the continued support for reform occurred in 1795 at the close of the ill-fated viceroyalty of Lord Fitzwilliam. When Fitzwilliam's recall became known, a group of Derry freemen requested that the mayor convene a common hall to discuss the matter. Recognizing that under the provisions of the convention act, no meeting of the

11 Ibid., 15 Jan. 1793. 12 Ibid., 22 Jan. 1793.

inhabitants other than the freemen called to a common hall in order to form a petition could gather, the mayor attempted to suppress the meeting by refusing his permission. The freemen, however, persuaded two aldermen, John Ferguson and William Lecky, to preside over the common hall. Among the one hundred and ten freemen who requested the meeting were almost all of the leading members of the chamber of commerce as well as Robert Black and George Douglas. The resolutions of the common hall praising Fitzwilliam and condemning his recall were as thoroughly radical as any passed before the war.[13]

Although the spirit of reform seemed to maintain itself during the war, the economic crisis it created severely affected journalists throughout Ulster and in April 1796 Douglas was forced to sell the *Journal*.[14] Before his departure for the United States in August of 1796, Douglas offered a summary of his views on, 'the two greatest events that have occurred in history of the world since the Reformation, namely, the Revolutions of America and France'. Douglas admitted that he had 'rejoiced at the emancipation of 25 millions of people from Despotism and Superstition' at the outset of the French Revolution only to lament, 'the massacres, the murders and the atrocities which tarnished and disgraced their efforts'. He hoped, however, that the end of the war would 'give to France a rational and settled government'. As for Ireland, Douglas once again expressed a belief in progress. Although Ireland had not arrived at political perfection, 'the exertions of the People and Parliament of Ireland, during the last sixteen years, have exalted the Kingdom to an higher degree of consequence and reputation than at any former period'. While more work was to be done, the disorders in France convinced Douglas,

> that it is wiser to obtain political perfection (if such a thing can be obtained) by the slow but peaceful means of gradual Reform, than by rash and violent measures to precipitate the nation into all the horrors of a bloody and destructive Revolution.[15]

Douglas remained an advocate of reform rather than revolution.

Upon arriving in the United States, Douglas resumed his trade as printer, publisher and bookseller. Like other emigrants during the 1790s, Douglas settled into a burgeoning Irish-American community and remained concerned with Irish affairs. In Philadelphia, Petersburg, Baltimore and New York, Douglas published a variety of works concerning American and Irish subjects. In Baltimore, differences began to emerge between Douglas and more radical

13 Ibid., 31 Mar. 1795, 14 Apr. 1795.   14 For the hardships faced by journalists see Gray, 'A tale of two newspapers'; *LJ*, 26 Apr. 1796; A. Aspinall, *Politics and the press, c.1780–1850* (London, 1949), pp 116–17.   15 *LJ*, 26 Apr. 1796.

Irish emigrants. In 1802 and 1803 Douglas published speeches of Thomas Paine that were clearly intended to damage Paine's reputation.[16]

The following year, Douglas demonstrated his continuing sympathy for reform if not for the radical republicanism of Paine. In the preface to *Forensic eloquence: sketches of trials in Ireland for high treason,* Douglas included an historical sketch of Ireland that described, 'the disastrous consequences of a bad system of government'. Douglas' work was not, however, characterized by the Anglophobia of other emigrant writers. In echoes of his time in Derry, Douglas praised the Glorious Revolution as 'famous for its beneficial consequences to the liberties of mankind'. Even Americans, though they had serious grievances against the present English ministry, had to admit 'that when liberty was extinct in every other nation in the world, England was the parent and nurse of civil and religious liberty'.[17]

In his description of the United Irishmen and the insurrection of 1798, Douglas' tone differed markedly from the more ardent accounts of exiled United Irishmen. Perhaps most interesting was his candid description of the rising as 'a Civil War, wherein many brave and good men on both sides lost their lives'. In the aftermath of the insurrection, Douglas described the extraordinary abuses involved in passing the Union but frankly admitted that the fear of French intervention was a legitimate and defensible rationale for the course of events. Douglas furthermore believed it was in 'the interest of Ireland to be connected with England, if such connexion can be obtained on fair and honourable terms'. This might be accomplished by abandoning the coercive policy of the present for the kind of conciliation shown to the 'Scotch Highlanders for the past fifty-years'.[18] The nascent liberal ideals of the Scottish enlightenment led some to consider the Union as a possibly beneficial social and political institution.

A new frame? Ulster liberalism and the Union, 1800–14

During the nineteenth century the Act of Union became a defining political issue in Irish society. For practically all Ulster Protestants, the Union would become a cornerstone of their social and political ideals. This is in sharp contrast to the outcome elsewhere in Ireland where the Catholic majority progressively questioned the legitimacy of the Union, the British constitutional tradition and even British culture. This dramatic contrast between Protestant and Catholic responses to the Union has sometimes overshadowed the signif-

16 T. Paine, *Letter from Thomas Paine to George Washington* (Baltimore, 1802); George Douglas (ed.), *Paine versus religion; or, Christianity triumphant* (Baltimore, 1803). 17 George Douglas (ed.), *Forensic eloquence* (Baltimore, 1804), pp ii, 12, 26. 18 Ibid., pp 23, 27–8.

icant diversity of opinion among Protestants about the meaning of the Union. The distinctive conceptions of the Union affected political opinion and policy and are an important aspect of the story of Ulster liberalism.

For conservatives, the Union became, despite their initial opposition, a reaffirmation of the contract between the Protestants of Ireland and the British nation as established during the Glorious Revolution. David Miller has demonstrated that conservatives in Ulster viewed the constitution as a covenant with established obligations for both themselves and the British state.[19] Indeed, their role in the establishment and preservation of what they described as constitutional liberty entitled the Protestants of Ireland not merely to equality but to ascendancy. For the conservatives, there was little discussion of the adoption, tacit or otherwise, of the British constitution by the Irish nation. Conquest had established liberty and force would be used to preserve it.

Almost instinctively, those Volunteers who had belonged to the covenanting tradition also came to judge the Union in contractarian terms. The contract in question, however, was not between Irish Protestants and the British nation but rather between themselves and their ideal of a godly commonwealth. Initially, the Union itself was of little importance. The events of the 1790s were shattering for the most radical adherents of the covenanting tradition, whether former Volunteers who had hoped for parliamentary reform and greater legislative independence from Britain or those few who joined the United Irishmen, perhaps believing seventeenth century prophecies that the French would be God's instrument of establishing Christ's crown and covenant.[20] After 1798, both the Covenanters and the Seceders seemed to have withdrawn from active involvement in politics. Ian McBride suggests that as early as the 1790s the Seceders began to eschew politics. While radical laymen at the time ascribed this to their obtaining a portion of the *regium donum,* McBride believes that the Seceders were the first among Ulster Presbyterians to be affected by an evangelical concern for inward salvation rather than transformation of the state into a godly commonwealth.[21]

As for the Covenanters, the extent of their withdrawal might best be extrapolated from the exiles of 1798 who went to the United States. Unlike many Irish émigrés, the exiled Covenanters did not for the most part become heavily involved in republican politics. Because the federal constitution was 'radically and wilfully defective in that it does not recognise the existence of God, the supremacy of Christ the King of Nations, and the word of God as the supreme law', the Covenanters denied its legitimacy and refused to vote or pursue public office. Samuel Wylie, a leading Covenanter minister in exile in America,

19 Miller, *Queen's rebels,* pp 62–3. 20 R.F.G. Holmes, *Our Irish Presbyterian heritage* (Belfast, 1985), p. 89. 21 McBride, '"When Ulster joined Ireland"', 83–5.

asserted in 1803 that the federal constitution allowed 'gross heresy, blasphemy, [and] idolatry under the notion of liberty of conscience'.[22]

In Ulster, there were a few in the covenanting tradition who remained active in politics. The seceding layman John Barnett was prominent in radical causes in Belfast during the period between 1815 and 1832, and in 1820 he complained 'that the Union had so debased the Irish mind' that it lacked the gallantry to support the cause of the injured Queen Caroline.[23] Among the Covenanters, Revd John Paul, 'who came closest to the spirit of the United Irishmen', according to Peter Brooke, was an advocate of voluntaryism and led his supporters to support reform policies in 1835. Both men were, however, struggling against the tide within their denominations. Among the Covenanters, Paul's position was challenged from within his own synod and in 1839 he separated from the Covenanters.[24] While David Miller has outlined social changes that contributed to the transformation of Ulster Presbyterians forms of piety, the traumatic disappointments of the late 1790s also seem to have contributed to a withdrawal from active political participation.

For civic republicans, the Union was a more complicated question. For some, the Union was anathema. The newly-won independence of the Irish parliament, indeed the Irish constitution itself, was effectively destroyed by incorporation with Britain. For William Drennan, who despite his membership in the United Irishmen continued to be as determined a defender of the concept of the ancient constitution as might be imagined, Pitt, as the architect of the Union, had 'put an extinguisher on a constitution with as little ceremony as he would upon a candle'. Furthermore, in Drennan's estimation, the independence of the Irish parliament was an essential part of the enduring constitution and the Irish parliament itself could no more 'surrender the constitution to Mr Pitt, than King John could, by himself, or even *with* the other estates, to surrender his crown to the Pope'. Drennan believed that the passage of the Union would have been impossible had the virtue of the nation as represented by the Volunteers not been undermined by Pitt's policies. He also, recognized, however, that his fellow civic republicans who had marched together as Volunteers were now divided. He lamented that '*some* of my volunteer comrades, have been forced, *purely,* by their hysteric horror of the French Revolution, to accept offices under the State', in complete violation of the civic republican ideal of virtuous independence. Others, namely those civic republicans who had become prominent United Irishmen, 'are at this moment, silent sufferers in the living grave of the prison'. Drennan attempted to

22 M. Durey, *Transatlantic radicals and the early American republic* (Lawrence, KS, 1997), p. 194.   23 P. Brooke, *Ulster Presbyterianism* (New York, 1987), p. 145; *Irishman*, 25 Aug. 1820. 24 Brooke, *Ulster Presbyterians*, pp 159–60, 162.

persuade his former allies that the best bulwark against French invasion would be an independent and reformed Ireland that would reclaim those who had been forced 'to become Frenchmen, because they were not suffered to be Irishmen', by allowing 'the genius of the British constitution, *to* encounter the genius of Jacobinism in the covert recesses of the human heart'.[25] For Drennan the Union meant destruction of the ancient constitution.

Drennan did not, however, convince all of the civic republicans nor the nascent liberals that the Union meant destruction of the constitution. For many the Union did away with the most glaring abuses of the constitution. The Union, as many of the plans for parliamentary reform that emanated from the entire spectrum of reform sentiment had proposed since 1783, removed the great majority of the rotten and close borough constituencies. By increasing the percentage of the reputedly more representative county constituencies from just over twenty per cent of the Irish parliament to 64 of the 100 representatives sent from Ireland to the Imperial parliament, the Union might be seen as a measure of parliamentary reform. It was this fact that led Archibald Hamilton Rowan, the celebrated Volunteer and founding member of the United Irishmen, to welcome the Union as putting an end 'to one of the most corrupt assemblies, I believe ever existed', and replacing it instead with 'a source of industrious enterprize for the people, and the wreck of the feudal aristocracy'.[26] Rowan was not alone. According to Mary McNeill, biographer of a sister of a leading United Irishman in Belfast, the 'opinion of the old liberal groups was divided'. Even the ardent United Irishman Samuel Neilson came to believe that because the Irish aristocracy who controlled the rotten and close boroughs were the most dangerous foes, 'representation at Westminster might be preferable to the concentrated corruption of College Green'.[27]

In the aftermath of 1798 and the Union, former Volunteers from the civic republican and covenanting traditions had much to reconsider. Not surprisingly, there were recriminations that seemed unlikely to be overcome. Men held one another responsible for the deaths, imprisonments and betrayals of loved ones. As they examined the wreck of many of their ambitions and the bitter divisions that now separated them, some of them began to adopt some aspects of the practical constitutionalism of the nascent liberals. This struggle to come to terms with new circumstances is evident in the developing ideas of one of the most consistent civic republicans, William Drennan, in the pages of the *Belfast Monthly Magazine*.

Until 1812, Presbyterians in Ulster were surprisingly quiet with regard to

25 W. Drennan, *A second letter to the right honorable William Pitt* (Dublin, 1799), pp 5, 10, 16, 22, 44. 26 A.H. Rowan, *Autobiography of Archibald Hamilton Rowan, esq.* (Dublin, 1840), p. 340. 27 M. McNeill, *The life and times of Mary Ann McCracken, 1770–1866* (Dublin, 1960), pp 204–5.

the rising of 1798. For Presbyterians, the violence of the rebellion and its repression 'made a deep impression upon minds accustomed to interpret disaster as divine judgment'.[28] The government also had made efforts to influence Presbyterians by increasing the annual grant or *regium donum* as well as regulating its disbursement through sympathetic clergy. Beginning in 1812, however, the legacy of the rebellion was a central theme in a number of controversies in which former friends and associates from the various strands that had comprised the Volunteer movements accused one another of betraying their principles.

In 1812, William Steel Dickson, a Presbyterian minister and confessed United Irishman who was imprisoned in Scotland on suspicion of involvement in the rebellion but never put to trial, published an account of his ordeal. In that account Dickson accused the Synod of Ulster of unjustly punishing him for his past political associations by denying him, though never tried or convicted of treason, his fair portion of the *regium donum*, the annual grant from government towards the support of the Presbyterian clergy in Ireland. Dickson suggested that his continued support for Catholic emancipation contributed to his plight. Indeed, Dickson had been beaten by a mob in Armagh in 1812 while returning from a meeting in support of emancipation. Dickson ascribed these circumstances to the synod's betrayal of its independent, liberal principles for a mess of pottage in the form of an augmented *regium donum*.[29] The synod was now a mere instrument of the state. According to Dickson, the worst example of the synod's servility was its unjust and ignoble denial of the widow of James Porter, the minister of Greyabbey, Co. Down executed in 1798, her portion of the synod's widow's fund.

The particular target of Dickson's accusations was Robert Black, the minister from the city of Derry responsible for the disbursement of the *regium donum*. Black, the former Volunteer, had been elected agent for the *regium donum* by the synod in 1788. Black successfully obtained, with the help of Charlemont and Grattan, a significant increase in the *regium donum* from the Irish parliament in 1792.[30] Black was a friend and adviser to Viscount Castlereagh and in the aftermath of 1798 he cooperated with Castlereagh's plan to foster government influence among Presbyterians by significantly increasing the *regium donum*. In 1804, the grant was augmented again and the agent for its disbursement was appointed by the government rather than elected by the synod. The government retained Black in the position.

Black vehemently denied Dickson's allegations, and the bitter conflict that

28 R.F.G. Holmes, 'United Irishmen and Unionists: Irish Presbyterians, 1791 and 1886', p. 182. 29 Dickson, *A narrative*, pp 246–7. 30 *ODNB*, www.oxforddnb.com, accessed 17 Jan. 2008.

ensued between the two men reflected the very personal divisions that existed among reformers as a legacy of the violence of the 1790s. Many of Dickson's claims were undoubtedly exaggerated. Black correctly pointed out, for example, that Dickson's congregation in Keady came into existence after negotiations for the increase in the *regium donum* had commenced. The list of congregations already had been submitted to the government for classification. Furthermore, the widow of James Porter had not been excluded from the widow's fund. There had been a debate about her right to be included among the beneficiaries for the simple reason that people who died 'by the hands of public justice, duelling, or suicide', were as a rule excluded. There had been, however, no effort to punish Porter's family. Rather the debate centred upon whether Mrs Porter, given the circumstances, ought to be provided with an extraordinary pension rather than included among the usual list of benefici-aries. Black averred that there was no systematic exclusion of ministers implicated at the time of the rebellion. Some of those implicated in 1798 were respected ministers of congregations receiving the *regium donum* in 1812.[31] Recent scholarship on Ulster Presbyterianism concurs with this judgment. The disbursement of the grant, according to Peter Brooke, did not 'provide any evidence of discrimination against ministers who were associated with the United Irishmen'.[32] Neither was support for Catholic emancipation an imped-iment. Black reaffirmed his support for Catholic emancipation in his riposte to Dickson and in 1813 supported a resolution passed by the synod calling for such a measure.[33]

The gravamen of Black's case against Dickson was more visceral. In his narrative, Dickson was defiant about his involvement in political affairs during the 1790s. Black felt strongly that Dickson ought to be penitent. By either design or foolhardiness Dickson had unnecessarily led other men to their destruction. At the annual meeting of the synod in 1812 Black publicly challenged Dickson to 'declare solemnly, that he was not concerned in origi-nating, fomenting or fostering the rebellion of 1798'. Black was enraged by Dickson's references to James Porter. Porter had been a close friend of Black – 'I married him, and to my countenance and friendship afterwards, it was chiefly owing that he became a member of this synod'. Porter's zeal for reform, perhaps imbibed from Black himself, had been taken advantage of by men such as Dickson who had not cautioned enthusiastic younger men against rash or desperate measures. Black boasted to the synod that at the time of the rebellion he had poured oil upon troubled waters –

---

31 R. Black, *Substance of two speeches, delivered of the General Synod of Ulster at its annual meeting in 1812* (Dublin, n.d.), pp 24, 31, 467.   32 P. Brooke, *Ulster Presbyterianism*, p. 135.
33 Black, *Substance*, p. 56; Brooke, *Ulster Presbyterianism*, p. 142.

> Wherever, in those awful times, I possessed influence, tranquillity prevailed. No congregation charges *me* with having drawn them to *the brink of a precipice;* whoever was guided by my opinions, stood safe. No widow imputes to *my* councils [sic] and society the loss of her *husband,* no child ascribes to my advice the regrets associated with the name of *Father.*

In 1812 the synod agreed with Black that Dickson's account contained 'a number of gross mistatements and misrepresentations' and ordered Dickson to retract these errors.[34]

The unseemly interchanges about perceived past wrongs continued. Flushed with his triumph at the synod's annual meeting in 1812, Black unwisely published a more complete refutation of Dickson's narrative, ostentatiously promising any profits from the work to be donated to the very widow's fund that had been at the emotional centre of the controversy. Black's unrelenting attack on Dickson together with the continuing controversy surrounding Black's position as an appointed agent for the newly augmented and reorganized *regium donum* and his opposition to a government grant for the Belfast Academical Institution aroused fresh controversy at the synod's annual meeting in 1813. A group of younger ministers attempted to have the condemnation of Dickson's narrative rescinded. After a series of protracted and bitter debates, during which an elder actually had his name 'expunged from the roll of the synod', the synod remained convinced that Dickson's narrative was inaccurate but at the same time was displeased with Black's pertinacity in the controversy.

In the first of the several resolutions concerning the two ministers, Dickson's supporters offered a motion stating that the synod had acted 'inconsiderately, in declaring without inquiry and without evidence, that two members of their body, then in confinement, were implicated in treasonable or seditious practices'. The majority of the synod refused to accept such an interpretation but offered a face-saving compromise to Dickson and his supporters. After a long debate, a resolution was approved stating that the central phrase, 'implicated in treasonable or seditious practices', was 'inaccurately used, inasmuch as it appears to be liable to an unfavourable construction respecting' the imprisoned ministers.[35] In other words, the phrase ought not to have been understood as a judgment concerning the guilt or innocence of Dickson but only as a factual statement that he had been arrested and held for suspicion of treason. The resolution might be construed as a small victory for Dickson, who denied involvement in the rebellion despite compelling evidence to the contrary

---

34 Black, *Substance,* pp 39, 49.   35 *BMM,* 11 (Aug. 1813), 130.

from friends and foes as well as the subsequent judgment of historians, but it was far from a vindication.

Subsequent resolutions proposed by Dickson's supporters also achieved little towards his rehabilitation. The synod, while admitting that it regretted not having dealt with the question of Dickson's past in 1805 when Dickson had first sought to raise the issue, refused to support any suggestion that Black had persecuted Dickson for his past political associations. Dickson's supporters attempted to salvage something from the debacle by proposing a resolution that the synod disavow responsibility for Black's book on the affair published since the last meeting.[36] The synod was not usually considered responsible for the publications of its ministers as individuals and Black obviated the need for such a resolution by immediately declaring that the responsibility was entirely his own.

A further defeat for Dickson was the synod's reaction to his retraction ordered at the synod's meeting the year before. More of a vindication than a retraction, the statement offered by Dickson resulted in a call by some for his expulsion from the synod. Sensibly, the synod attempted to put the issue behind it with a resolution stating – 'That this Synod disapprove of what Dr Dickson has offered as an apology; but that under all the circumstances, they dismiss this subject, and order said paper returned to Dr Dickson'.[37] Ironically, the final insult to Dickson may have been the synod's approval of a public declaration supporting Catholic emancipation. Dickson played no part in the affair while Black warmly supported the measure and thereby seemed to undermine Dickson's claim to martyrdom for his political principles. In 1793, when Dickson had been elected moderator, the synod had advocated both parliamentary reform and Catholic emancipation in its annual address to the lord lieutenant. In 1813 the synod was still willing to endorse considerable political reforms. The synod was not, however, willing to countenance a rehabilitation of the revolutionary principles of the United Irishmen.

Outside the Synod of Ulster, many of the themes and controversies of the 1790s were also the subtext of a new and important journal in Ulster. In 1808, after having spent thirty years as a struggling physician in Belfast, Newry and Dublin, William Drennan was able, with capital from an inheritance, to fulfil a long held ambition of establishing a magazine.[38] Drennan, together with assistance from John Templeton, John Hancock and, later, Francis Dalzell Finlay, edited the *Belfast Monthly Magazine* from 1808 until 1814. Established ostensibly as a literary journal with the declared intention of excluding 'theological controversies and intemperate politics', the magazine promised to report only briefly 'the facts which give rise to those political differences that

36 Ibid.   37 Ibid., p. 132.   38 McBride, *Scripture politics*, p. 159.

agitate the public mind'.[39] In practice, every issue contained not only a 'retrospect of politics', in which local, national and international affairs were analysed but also detailed reports of important public meetings. If Drennan truly intended his magazine to be less concerned with politics than art and science, an improbable ambition given his past penchant for public debate, the times were not propitious.

In the year 1808 the Catholic question began to dominate public affairs to an extent perhaps unmatched since the Catholic convention of 1792. After having subordinated their efforts to attain political emancipation to the needs and circumstance of British political parties, the so-called veto controversy of 1808 contributed to a new sense of self-consciousness and self-reliance among Irish Catholics. The debate and eventual rejection of the proposal that Irish Catholics were amenable to some governmental voice in the appointment of their bishops in exchange for emancipation was, in the estimation of Thomas Bartlett, 'the first major expression of Catholic nationalism in the nineteenth century'.[40] In the atmosphere of re-animated public discussion that developed during the years between 1808 and 1814 many of the issues and events of the 1790s were reconsidered. As these issues and debates were presented in the *Belfast Monthly Magazine* the conflict between the principles of civic republicanism and nascent liberalism in the mind of William Drennan gives us an insight into the debates that occurred among Ulster reformers. While Drennan continued to speak the language of civic republicanism when discussing aspects of the Act of Union or Catholic emancipation, the growing influence of nascent liberalism can be gauged not only by Drennan's cooption or adaptation of some elements of nascent liberal discourse but also, perhaps more importantly, by his failure to revive the civic republican tradition. Rather than attempt to restore the spirit of the Volunteers that seemed to haunt the mind of the older Drennan, Ulster reformers began to adopt new tactics and policies.

Drennan's continuing adherence to many of the civic republican ideals was evident in the first issues of the magazine. Drennan reiterated his opposition to the Union as sapping Ireland's civic virtue. He hoped, however, that the independent public spirit represented in the Catholic community's struggle for emancipation might be harnessed to the larger struggle for political reform.[41] During the years that followed, however, Drennan's beliefs changed. Drennan increasingly feared the atomization of Irish society and devoted considerable effort to condemning any movement or institution that contributed to further divisions between Protestants and Catholics. Instead, Drennan wished to foster the development of what he described as 'civil society', by developing shared needs and interests into shared institutions.[42]

---

39 *BMM*, 1 (Sept. 1808), 3. 40 Bartlett, *The fall and rise of the Irish Nation*, p. 295.
41 *BMM*, 1 (Sept. 1808), 1. 42 Ibid., 11 (Oct. 1813), 335.

In July 1809, Drennan reaffirmed his civic republican conception of the British constitutional tradition in Ireland and explained how that tradition was threatened by reaction to, 'the ill success which has attended the French Revolution'. Exaggerated perceptions of the Napoleonic threat had so frightened Irishmen that they suffered a loss of memory similar to that caused by a grave illness. Irishmen had forgotten 'to what glorious height the Irish people were exalted in the year 1782', when the Volunteers had met in Dungannon to reassert the principles of the constitution. Furthermore, the exigencies of the wars with France threatened to undermine the '*manners, customs and habits* of the people, which preserve the vitality of the constitution and resist its decay and putrefaction'. Specifically, Drennan believed that there was a growing trend towards expressing loyalty to the monarchy as a symbol of resistance to the French that threatened to undermine the balance of the constitution so that 'loyalty, which ought to embrace with equal warmth the whole constitution is converged upon the monarch'.[43]

Fear rather than corruption threatened to undermine the balance of the constitution. This new loyalism was part of the effort 'to reconcile the people, a common-sensical, commercial people, to war', by presenting them with 'a model of one master mind, which guides and inspirits the whole mass, as it were *Napoleonizes* a whole nation'.[44] The past praise of martial training by citizens as a necessary means of fostering civic virtue and public spirit that characterized his nostalgic descriptions of the Volunteer movement was now mingled with a new ambivalence about the effects of prolonged warfare upon society. Drennan remained sympathetic to the ideal of a national unity of purpose which might be derived from war. The unity of legislation and policy of, 'the French writers, called *economists*', might be more efficient as a result of being 'unrestrained by the prejudices and local interests of popular assemblies', but Drennan denounced this ideal as too much akin to the warlike Spartan constitution and its despotic tendencies. Drennan still longed for the strong sense of common purpose and community that he had felt within the Volunteer movement but was beginning to recognize that martial solidarity might not always produce the public virtue he yearned for. Although the ideals of civic republicanism had not been abandoned, seeds of doubt had been sown.

By September 1810, these seeds were beginning to bear new fruit. In response to a campaign that originated within the Dublin corporation for repeal of the Union, Drennan discovered potential merits in the Union not unlike those earlier hoped for by Neilson and Rowan.[45] Drennan maintained his conviction that the manner in which the Union had been passed was

---

43 Ibid., 3 (July 1809), 68–9. 44 Ibid., 69–70. 45 For a history of repeal sentiment in Dublin see Hill, *From patriots to unionists*, pp 257–75.

'disgraceful' and 'justly deserving of execration', but conceded that 'considered abstractly', the Union, 'had a tendency to allay party feuds, and to relieve us from the rough riding of some of our Irish unprincipled jockies'. There was little reason to grieve the dissolution of the Irish parliament as it had been. Could, Drennan asked, any parliament have been 'more obsequious to ministerial leading strings' or have mismanaged Irish affairs worse. Furthermore, the Union might, under other circumstances, provide a blueprint for beneficial parliamentary reform not only in Ireland but in the United Kingdom as a whole. Speaking of the terms of the Act of Union, Drennan observed –

> To a certain degree parliamentary reform has been introduced into Ireland, and through the operation of counteracting causes, this abolition of rotten boroughs produces no effect in the general scale at present, yet a precedent is set, which might under a change of circumstances, be useful, and serve as a model for effectual and radical reform.[46]

Drennan believed that any agitation for repeal was misguided. Rather than risk division among reformers in the two islands, they should join forces with their British allies to seek parliamentary reform as they had done during the time of the Volunteers.

In subsequent years, Drennan continued to criticize the manner of the Union's passage, its administration and its deadening effect upon political life. At the same time, rather than advocate repeal and the restoration of an Irish parliament, Drennan consistently stated that his goal was to make the Union a reality. In February 1811, he hoped 'to accomplish an honourable and faithful union between the yet dissevered portions of the empire'. In September of the same year Drennan expressed the belief that both internal union, the conciliation of conflicting parties within Ireland, and external union, the conciliation of Britain and Ireland, were mutually dependent and desirable aspirations. Drennan concluded 'that without *both*, being accomplished really and substantially, *neither* of them will ever be realized'. In March 1813, Drennan denied accusations that he and his supporters comprised a '*Republican party*', but instead averred that their 'actuating principle at the present hour, is, IRISH CONCILIATION, and BRITISH CONSTITUTION'. A year later, March 1814, Drennan hoped that the defeat of Napoleon would allow the government to dispense with a policy of partiality in Ireland that may have seemed a necessity in time of war and endeavour instead, 'to unite and permanently consolidate the British Islands, into one continent of free constitution'.[47] While the Union was,

---

46 *BMM*, 5 (Sept. 1810), 224.   47 Ibid., 6 (Feb. 1811), 157; 7 (Sept. 1811), 227; 10 (Mar. 1813), 264; 12 (Mar. 1814), 249.

in Drennan's estimation, clearly flawed in both its conception and its operation, it was now part of the British constitutional tradition in Ireland that must be made to work for the good of Irish society.

Drennan's tentative acceptance of the Union was the result in part of his fear that Irish society might be irretrievably divided if some sense of what he described as 'concord' were not created. As mentioned previously, Drennan believed that one of the considerable drawbacks to the Union was its undermining of public spirit. Though a constant concern from the first issue, perhaps the best explanation of this phenomenon was put forth by Drennan in October 1813. Using language clearly derived from the work of Francis Hutcheson, Drennan asserted that the end of the Irish parliament deprived Ireland of a focus for the 'generous affections of the heart, reflecting as *they* were designed to do, a pure and permanent happiness to the individual, from the pursuit of the public good'. As a result of this lack of focus for public spirit, apathy and selfishness increased until, 'the whole society resolves as it were into its primitive particles, into a heap of uncemented sand'. The genuine patriotism of the Volunteers that 'spontaneously poured forth its armed thousands in defence of country' was replaced by a 'putrefaction of patriotism; a sort of inferior life, a maggotty animation which swarms upon the carcase of our country'.[48] Without the benefit of public spirit, the effect of war is simply to create a more passionate self-interest, a hope for personal advancement rather than defence of the community.

One particular distortion of genuine public spirit referred to by Drennan was Orangeism. The growth of Orangeism became a frequent subject of the magazine in the aftermath of a number of public conflicts involving yeomanry units who refused to serve under officers who had signed a petition in favour of Catholic emancipation. In April 1812, a segment of the Lurgan yeomanry threatened to lay down their arms unless a lieutenant who had recently signed the Protestant petition in favour of Catholic emancipation was removed from command. Similarly, in June of 1812 some members of the local yeomanry corps in Armagh city refused to serve under an officer who had signed the Protestant petition favouring emancipation. In this case, the government was compelled to dissolve the unit.[49]

Drennan described further pathological expressions of public spirit in the Synod of Ulster. A minister near Tandragee in Co. Armagh outraged a section of his congregation by signing the Protestant petition in favour of Catholic emancipation. When attempts by the presbytery of Armagh to reconcile the congregation with its minister failed, a segment of the members claiming to represent the majority barred the doors of the meeting house against their

48 Ibid., 11 (Oct. 1813), 334–5.   49 Ibid., 8 (Apr. 1812), 315; 9 (Aug. 1812), 157.

pastor and refused to surrender the keys to representatives of the synod sent to adjudicate.[50] Pathological loyalism was not merely a threat to Protestant unity. Such loyalism had a clear potential to unleash a continuing cycle of sectarian violence. In his October 1813 description of the atomization of Irish society created by the combination of the Union's deadening effect upon public spirit and the passions aroused in a nation at war, Drennan cited a lengthy passage from Germaine de Staël describing the nightmare of a society where violence made any concord impossible:

> Voyez des persécuteurs toujours agités, des persécutés toujours implacables; aucune opinion qui paraisse innocente, aucun raisonnement qui puisse être écouté; [...] aucun parti fidèle aux mêmes principes; quelques homme réunis par le lien d'une terreur commune, lien que rompt aisément l'espérance de pouvoir se sauver seul; [...] L'action inhumaine sème la discorde, perpétue les combats, sépare en bandes ennemies la nation entière.[51]

Recent evidence of this potential for violence had been demonstrated by a riot between Orangemen and Catholics in Belfast in July 1813 that left two men dead. In addition to the violence of the riot itself, the attempt to hold a public meeting to discuss the event and possible measures to prevent its recurrence had resulted in further civil discord. The mayor of the corporation, Edward May, refused to preside over the meeting and declared it in violation of the convention act. During the commotion that followed May's pronouncement, a prominent liberal, Dr Robert Tennent, attempted to remonstrate with May and laid his hand upon May's shoulder to gain his attention. As a result, Tennent was charged, convicted, and imprisoned for assault.[52] The case against Tennent was closely watched by the *Belfast Monthly Magazine* as an example of the pernicious effects of Orangeism upon social harmony and justice.

While a pathological patriotism in the guise of Orangeism was probably foremost in Drennan's conception of the threats to civil society in Ireland, he recognized and commented upon dangers within the Catholic community as well. In general, Drennan believed that the campaign for Catholic emancipation

---

50 Ibid., 8 (Mar. 1812), 227; 9 (Sept. 1812), 232. **51** Ibid., 11 (Oct. 1813), 335–6. A search of the Project for American and French Research on the Treasury of the French Language (ARTFL) database reveals that the quote is from de Staël's *De la Littérature* published in 1800. www.lib.uchicago.edu/efts/ARTFL/databases/TLF07/ accessed January 2008. Translation: See the persecutors always agitated, the persecuted always implacable; no opinion can appear innocent, no argument can be heard; [...] no party faithful to the same principles; some men are reunited by the tie of a common fear, a tie easily broken in the hope of saving oneself. Inhumanity sows discord, perpetuates the conflicts, separates a whole nation into warring bands. **52** *BMM*, 11 (Oct. 1813), 314–17.

was the best hope to restore a sense of pubic spirit to Irish society. In March 1811, however, Drennan criticized the prospectus for a new Dublin newspaper that promised to cater specifically to Catholic interests. Drennan cautioned Catholics against cooperating with 'the errors, the follies, and the crimes of past and present administrations, in perpetuating a distinctness; a separating instead of an associating spirit'. Drennan instead proposed the establishment of Emancipation Clubs 'where the Protestant and Catholic should sit alternately, and a Catholic and Protestant chairman elected in their turn'. Drennan also insisted that Catholics should not attempt to gain emancipation entirely through their own efforts and prophesied that if such an exclusive effort were made, 'it will fail'.[53]

Furthermore, Drennan made it clear that while Catholic emancipation was essential, his ultimate goal remained, as it had in the 1790s, parliamentary reform. In October 1811, Drennan spoke to a meeting of Catholics in Co. Antrim in Belfast. After emphasizing the need for sectarian cooperation, Drennan described emancipation as 'a great step in the attainment of that grand political measure without which, all in my mind is as nothing – I mean, *a Reform of the representation of the people in the Commons House of Parliament'*. Drennan emphasized his point by proclaiming that if Catholics were –

> adopted into the constitution, as into a corpulent and corrupt corpo-ration, without adding any spirit, any purity, any renovation, but merely fixing more firmly the crying abuses, and shameful pollution of the constitution, I for one, would be a sincere and single negative against unanimity of the present day, and present hour.[54]

In October 1812, Drennan spoke again before the Co. Antrim Catholic meeting in Belfast. Drennan once again made it clear that to be worthy of emancipation Catholics must unite with, 'the true lovers of peace, and union, and reform', in order to attain, 'a real and efficient representation, a more fair distribution and an annual election'.[55] Despite his firm and constant commitment to emancipation, it is clear that Drennan was concerned about the possibility that Catholics might decide to pursue their own community interests while ignoring the greater goal of creating a common civil society.

When it became clear in 1814 that the current campaign for emancipation would fail, in part because of serious divisions among its advocates, Drennan became increasingly despondent about the state of public virtue in Ulster. Much affected by the conviction and imprisonment of his friend Dr Robert

---

53 Ibid., 6 (Mar. 1811), 233–4. **54** Ibid., 7 (Oct. 1811), 329–30. **55** Ibid., 9 (Oct. 1812), 332.

Tennent, in August 1814 Drennan ascribed the widespread 'indifference to the public weal', that had contributed to Tennent's conviction to corruption created by widespread government influence. The independence of the gentry had been undermined by the wholesale distribution of place so that 'the interests of almost every family in the upper classes hang upon, or are inter-woven with the will of the government'. There were no more Charlemonts to sustain the Whig cause. Even the 'middling classes', previously famed for their 'bold independence', were 'encumbered with the lower links of the same debasing chain' in the form of the licensing system for merchants arising out of the economic blockade of the continent during the war against Napoleon.[56]

In September 1814, Drennan bitterly complained of the lack of any public dinner or demonstration when Tennent was released from Carrickfergus gaol. Resonant of the rhetorical flash of his writings from the Volunteer era, Drennan condemned the inactivity of his fellow citizens, their 'pomposity in planning' and 'poverty in executing'. There was 'a cant of moderation, veiling timidity or corruption, which affects to object to all decisive measures, and would level all public spirit to the grovelling views of conveniency and a trimming expediency'. Even the gracious allusion to Tennent's confinement during a lecture before the Belfast Historic Society, an organization that seems to have been comprised mostly of allies and associates of Drennan, was offset by rejection of a motion of thanks to Tennent, an honorary member of the society. Drennan complained bitterly that some were competing 'in spreading the contagion of timidity to destroy public spirit'.[57]

Whether from the very same lack of public spirit which Drennan had raged against or some other cause, the *Belfast Monthly Magazine* ceased publication in December 1814. Its demise in many ways marked the end of the founding period of Ulster liberalism. Drennan witnessed the dissolution of the Volunteer movement as its various elements reacted differently to the whirlwind of events in the 1790s. As an ardent proponent of the civic republicanism that had been the predominant component of the Volunteer consensus, Drennan was disen-chanted by its particular fate. Not only had civic republicanism failed to sustain the united, virtuous patriotism of the Volunteers, but a portion of its followers had been grossly corrupted. Drennan might be loath to admit it, but the dislike and distrust of Catholicism that was intertwined with the contempt for tyranny in the founding texts of civic republicanism that he so admired was, in some men, transformed by the fear or the zeal aroused by the war into the 'putre-faction of patriotism', that was Orangeism.

Drennan's strong attachment to the civic republican tradition greatly influ-enced his judgment of the course of politics in the aftermath of the Union.

---

56 Ibid., 13 (Aug. 1814), 174–5.　**57** Ibid., 13 (Sept. 1814), 263.

While understanding that the era of civic republicanism had passed, that the French Revolution had discredited the idea of being able to restore the ancient constitution, Drennan failed to recognize that faith in the constitutional tradition had not been destroyed. The evolutionary principles of nascent liberalism derived from the Scottish enlightenment allowed many Irish reformers to reconcile themselves to the Act of Union. These men and women hoped that by accepting changes in society and reforming their institutions to accord with those changes they might escape the nightmarish cycles of revolution and discord described by writers from Polybius to Machiavelli to Germaine de Staël. These reformers were descendants of the Volunteer movement who had been forged and tempered in an era of revolution and war into Ulster liberals. During subsequent decades these Ulster liberals would be confronted with the reality that not all Irishmen accepted the Union as part of a liberal, evolutionary constitutional tradition.

CHAPTER TWO

Ulster liberalism and the birth of public opinion, 1814–42

The apparent lack of political vigour among Ulster liberals described by William Drennan in the first decades after the Union has been explained in a variety of ways. Some writers have eagerly accepted Drennan's analysis and concluded that the political virtue of Belfast's reformers had been sapped by government corruption like that purportedly used to secure the Union.[1] Other writers have pointed to a transformation of Ulster Presbyterianism into a more orthodox and evangelical sect that made the formation of a pan-Protestant conservative coalition possible.[2] It has also been suggested that the significant cultural and economic development of Belfast during the early nineteenth century provided alternative outlets for the public spirit that previously had animated the Volunteers and the United Irishmen. A sort of sublimation of political energy occurred. The number and variety of cultural associations, clubs and societies increased in inverse proportion to the declining number of political meetings and conventions.[3]

The appearance of political quiescence after the Union belied the reality. Rather than abandoning politics, many Ulster reformers simply began to doubt the wisdom or practicality of violent constitutional change. As a result of both developing principles and altered circumstances Ulster liberals adopted new tactics during the period between 1814 and 1842. As they experimented with these new tactics, liberals soon realized that neither the Union nor the end of the war had substantially affected the structure of politics. The local levers of power and administration that had allowed landlords to control politics remained largely intact. In addition, during the 1820s Ulster liberalism confronted a new political problem that affected its fortunes well into the future. Under the dynamic leadership of Daniel O'Connell, Irish Catholics became a political force to be reckoned with. The existence of an independent Catholic political movement strained cooperation between Catholic and Protestant reformers. The strength and immediacy of any movement for Irish autonomy, whether in the form of agitation for repeal of the Union or estab-lishment of a Home Rule parliament, substantially affected the fortunes of Ulster liberalism. Even with these difficulties, however, Ulster liberalism

---

1 F. Campbell, *The dissenting voice* (Belfast, 1991), pp 107–36. 2 A.T.Q. Stewart, *The narrow ground* (London, 1989), pp 98–101. 3 R.B. McDowell, *Public opinion and government policy* (London, 1952), pp 52–9.

survived because of changes in the structure of local politics achieved in part because of their efforts. In a number of places the authority of urban patrons was challenged in an unprecedented fashion.

Testing the frame: the structure of politics

Perhaps only time could have assuaged the rancour that had arisen during the years of war with France. That rancour had hindered the efforts of William Drennan and his allies to rally enthusiasm for their reform agenda. Drennan's nostalgia for the era of the Volunteers also caused him to undervalue some modes of political activity. He could not completely put aside the Volunteer uniform for plainer dress. The quotidian procedures of a voluntary association, improvement commission, or municipal council must have seemed anticlimactic when compared to the drama of a national convention or revolutionary conspiracy.

Drennan and his allies clung to an increasingly outmoded form of civic republicanism. In June 1813, Revd William B. Neilson, a radical Presbyterian minister and accomplished classical scholar, reminded the Belfast Historic Society that the habits produced by commerce in a town such as Belfast 'threatened to smother all that is noble, generous and candid in the breast of man'. In both classical and modern states, the pursuit of commerce might begin well, but such societies 'soon proceeded to luxury', went down 'the stream of vice and dissipation' and were then 'swallowed up for ever in the whirlpool of destruction'. Concern with the classical model of political corruption continued to haunt the minds of these reformers. Even for Neilson, however, fear of the insidious effects of commerce upon virtue did not elicit a call for excluding commercial men from public life. That tide was simply too strong to resist. Rather, Neilson hoped that associations like the Belfast Historic Society, by emphasizing 'virtue and knowledge', might act as a 'salutary check' upon the pernicious effects of commerce and allow Ireland to escape the classical cycle of corruption.[4]

Some of Drennan's allies, however, also began to doubt whether commerce posed such a dire threat to public virtue as had been imagined. In an address to the Belfast Historic Society in August 1814, H.W. Tennent, member of an influential Belfast radical family, argued that far from contributing to social atomization, commerce strengthened and preserved the virtue of citizens. Those who derided commerce forgot 'the true character of a merchant'. They forgot that to be a merchant required as much of an 'ease of manners,

---

4 'Speech delivered by William B. Neilson, as president of the Belfast Historic Society', *BMM*, 13 (Aug. 1814), 114.

independence of mind, ardour, perseverance, industry [and] research' as any of the learned professions claiming gentility. The commercial ethos outstripped the professional ethos 'in the universality of its speculations', and counteracted the vices of the aristocracy by tending 'to dissipate prejudices and to remove the petty distinctions arising from pride and vanity'.[5] Far from being a threat to the virtue of a nation, a commercial ethos might provide the foundation for a peaceful civil society.

Much of the energy of liberalism in Ulster during the nineteenth century resulted from changes in social relationships at the local level that were more widespread and enduring than has been generally recognized. As the population and commerce of towns in Ulster increased during the period between 1780 and 1830, the merchants, manufacturers, shopkeepers and professionals who comprised the middle classes became increasingly influential in society. That increasing influence did not result in a significant increase in political power. This disparity between social influence and political power became a matter of contention in the aftermath of the defeat of Napoleon in 1815. During the period between 1815 and 1828, liberals in towns and cities in Ulster attempted to rein in the power of the traditional, aristocratic élites by the creation of voluntary associations or the manipulation of the existing legal and political framework with only limited success. By the late 1820s, however, neither the voluntary associations nor the traditional institutions could assimilate the changes in society. There occurred in Ulster what has been described in Britain as the 'rise of the notion of "public opinion"' whereby it was increasingly accepted that '"middle class" values were so widespread, and middle-class politicisation so developed' that they could not be safely ignored.[6] From the 1820s Ulster liberals made concerted efforts to establish new political channels. They sought to move from voluntary associations by reforming existing political institutions and creating new institutions more representative of public opinion. Until these new channels were better established, however, the political situation in Ulster continued to be fluid.

Because of this fluidity an examination of local politics is necessary. In Ireland, the structure of parliamentary politics magnified the role of the landed élite rather than the growing commercial interests of towns and cities. Unlike England, the parliamentary representation of Ireland after the Union was composed primarily of county rather than borough constituencies. The size and structure of these constituencies made the Irish MPs of the period between 1800 and 1820 'more representative of the established and wealthier sections of landed society' while reducing 'the opportunities open to the professional and mercantile classes of Protestant society'.[7]

5 Ibid., 13 (Oct. 1814), 305–6.   6 J.P. Parry, *The rise and fall of liberal government in Victorian Britain* (New Haven, CT, 1993), p. 23.   7 R.G. Thorne (ed.), *The history of*

In England, even with its greater proportion of borough constituencies, the social changes caused by urbanization and industrialization created a disjuncture between local and national politics. The influence of the middle classes upon local politics in England was considerable, but even after parliamentary reform in 1832 parliamentary politics continued to be dominated by the aristocracy.[8] In Ulster this disjuncture was even greater. The structure of politics in Ireland was less able to reflect the social changes occurring in an industrializing region such as Ulster.[9] Because the parliamentary representation of Ireland after the Union comprised primarily county constituencies rather than boroughs, there were fewer opportunities for new men to enter politics.

Until recently Irish urban history was a neglected topic. Scholars are beginning to recover the histories of lesser cities and towns with which to analyse the broader trends in Irish urban history.[10] In 1988, R.F. Foster examined the limited research on urban politics and concluded that by the 1830s the Protestant bourgeoisie throughout Ireland was increasingly involved in conservative and sectarian politics, but Ulster was the worst of a bad lot. Foster cited the work of Ian D'Alton on the city of Cork that described how the aristocratic, oligarchic politics of Ireland during the eighteenth century were supplanted by popular, sectarian politics during the 1820s.[11] In Ulster, Foster believed the Protestant middle classes, including the Presbyterians, had abandoned the liberalism of their forefathers as early as the 1820s.[12] Foster interpreted the frequently cited theological divisions among Ulster Presbyterians as evidence of the development of sectarian politics.

The exception to this tale of liberal perversion has been Peter Jupp's analysis of urban politics in Ireland during the period between 1801 and 1831. Jupp considered 28 of the 33 parliamentary boroughs in Ireland and concluded that the various types of oligarchy in those boroughs came 'under increasing pressure' as a result of larger populations and commercial prosperity. The oligarchs had to contend with efforts to establish alternative institutions of local government more broadly based than the corporations and increasing resistance to the actions of the municipal corporations, particularly the

parliament, 5 vols (London, 1986), i, pp 105–6. This conclusion is reinforced by I.R. Christie, *British 'non-elite' MPs, 1715–1820* (Oxford, 1995), p. 110. 8 R.J. Morris and R. Rodger, 'An Introduction to British Urban History, 1820–1914' (1993), p. 35. 9 For the industrialization of Ulster see L.M. Cullen, *An economic history of Ireland since 1660* (1981), pp 120–2; L.A. Clarkson, 'Population change and urbanisation, 1821–1911' (1985), pp 137–57; S.A. Royle, 'Industrialization, urbanization and urban society in post-famine Ireland *c.*1850–1921' (1993), pp 267–9. 10 P. Borsay and L. Proudfoot, 'The English and Irish Urban Experience, 1500–1800' (2002), pp 5–13. 11 I. D'Alton, *Protestant society and politics in Cork* (Cork, 1980), p. 112. 12 R.F. Foster, *Modern Ireland, 1600–1972* (London, 1988), pp 302–3. Similar conclusions are found in M.E. Daly, 'Irish urban history: a survey' (1986).

collection of local taxes upon commerce. At the parliamentary level, Jupp concluded that this challenge to the prevailing interests was also evident in 'a popular enthusiasm on the part of Catholics and Protestants for a range of political and economic reforms'.[13]

Not directly concerned with the political history of Irish towns, the geographer L.J. Proudfoot has studied the social authority of landlords in Irish towns and come to conclusions consonant with many of Jupp's observations. For Proudfoot, the influence of the landed élites in Irish towns diminished during nineteenth century in the face of a broad 'process of modernization that increasingly eroded the colonial polarities of seventeenth-century society'. Examining the history of towns on the estates of the dukes of Devonshire in Ireland, Proudfoot describes how the institutional framework created to support landlords was undone 'by the creation of various municipal institutions whose authority was sanctioned by the state' and economic changes that were accelerated by the Famine.[14]

After the end of the wars with France, Ulster liberals attempted to capitalize on grievances with two broad strategies. Some were actively involved with the debates of a wider British political culture such as opposition to proposed changes in the corn laws. In February and March of 1815 mass meetings and petitions against the enactment of the corn laws were organized throughout the United Kingdom.[15] The depth of feeling that the issue aroused was evident in March 1815 at Antrim town when inhabitants rioted against a meeting of local landlords who supported strengthening the corn laws.[16] A more peaceful and organized expression of discontent occurred at Carrickfergus where the freemen of the corporation instructed their MP to oppose any change in the corn laws. Similar efforts to organize meetings in concert with reformers in Britain were undertaken concerning proposed alterations of the window tax in 1816, parliamentary reform in 1817, and the treatment of Queen Caroline in 1818 and 1820.[17] While these meetings were evidence of the continuing existence of a small group engaged with the significant issues of British politics, little of substance was accomplished. These mostly *ad hoc* reactions to the political events of the day neither created enduring voluntary associations nor significantly affected institutions of government.

Of more lasting importance was a second tactic that over time developed into a broader strategy of challenging the social and political authority of the landed élite in many towns. After the end of the wars with France, Ulster

---

13 P. Jupp, 'Urban politics in Ireland, 1801–1831' (1981), pp 109, 111–12, 115. 14 L.J. Proudfoot, *Urban patronage and social authority* (Washington, DC, 1995), pp 7, 324. 15 E. Halévy, *England in 1815*, i: *A history of the English people in the nineteenth century*, 6 vols (New York, 1961), p. 158. 16 *BNL*, 3 Mar. 1815, 28 Mar. 1815. 17 Ibid., 17 Mar. 1815, 15 Nov. 1816, 14 Feb. 1817, 16 Jan. 1818; *The Irishman*, 25 Aug. 1820.

liberals attempted to capitalize on the discontent with local taxes on commerce that had developed throughout Ireland. The right to collect various imposts was granted to landlords or municipal corporations by royal authority, mostly during the seventeenth century. For example, cattle brought to a fair were driven through a turnstile for payment of a 'toll'. At markets the imposts included among others – stallage for the right to erect a stall in the market, market toll for goods sold on market day, and cranage for the use of public cranes to transfer goods. Together these charges were loosely referred to as the 'tolls and customs' of a town or city.[18] In late 1814, legal challenges to these imposts began to occur throughout Ireland.[19] By 1817 successful challenges were reported in Cork, Waterford, Belfast, Tuam, Wexford and Naas.[20]

Little has been written about these challenges to local taxes on commerce or their significance. They appear to have originated in Dublin under the leadership of Whig and radical lawyers such as Robert Holmes, Louis Perrin and John Finlay. Recently described as the 'most prolific of Irish legal authors', Finlay wrote several practical manuals dealing with the seemingly quotidian issues of game laws, parish officers and local taxes.[21] These were in fact contentious issues related to the cause of Catholic emancipation and directly impinged upon the authority of the Protestant Ascendancy in Ireland. Associated with the Catholic Board and a friend and ally of Daniel O'Connell, Finlay was the son of brewer from Co. Londonderry, and received his early education at the Free Grammar School in Derry.[22] Described by O'Connell as 'having no very considerable portion of this world's means', Finlay attended Trinity College, Dublin as a sizar student, was admitted to the bar in 1809 and first practiced law on the north-west circuit. According to the journalist George Douglas, Finlay was of Catholic lineage but conformed to the Church of Ireland for the sake of his education.[23] Finlay challenged the legality of tolls and customs throughout Ireland and helped to force the abandonment of some tolls in Dublin and other places.[24] It is interesting to note that in 1794 the young Finlay could have witnessed a legal challenge by the chamber of commerce in Derry to the right of the municipal corporation to collect quayage.[25]

In Belfast, the first popular challenge to local taxes seems to have occurred in October 1814 when the collection of tolls on the Long Bridge connecting the

---

18 *Report of the commissioners to inquire into the state of the fairs and markets in Ireland*, HC 1852–3 (1674), xli, p. 3. 19 *BMM*, 13 (Oct. 1814), 333. John Finlay, *Letters addressed to the Irish government, on local taxes* (Dublin, 1822), p. 10. 20 J. Cantwell, *A treatise on tolls and customs* (2nd ed., Dublin, 1829), p. 1. 21 W.N. Osborough, *Studies in Irish legal history* (Dublin, 1999), p. 262. 22 John O'Connell, *The select speeches of Daniel O'Connell* (Dublin, 1867) ii, p. 410; *Alumni Dublinenses* (London, 1924), p. 280. 23 *Western Star and Harp of Erin*, 31 Oct. 1812. 24 Finlay, *Letters addressed to the Irish government*, p. 10; for example in Castleblayney in 1819, *Connaught Journal*, 11 Dec. 1823. 25 *LJ*, 4 Apr. 1794.

town to Co. Down was questioned. In July 1815 an important legal case concerning the control of markets and their associated tolls and customs in Belfast was decided at the assizes in Carrickfergus. Claiming that a royal patent for a market granted to his forebears bestowed an exclusive right, the marquess of Donegall sought damages from the proprietor of a new market established in Belfast. Both at the assizes and on appeal in the court of common pleas, the case was decided against the Donegall interest.[26] This successful challenge of the control of local taxation became part of a broader struggle for power in the town that soon became focused on the local improvement commission established in Belfast in 1800 by the penultimate act of the Irish parliament.

The failure of the Donegall-controlled municipal corporation to cope with the rapid expansion of the town was the impetus for the creation of the original improvement commission in Belfast in 1800. Between 1782 and 1791 the population of the town had increased from 13,105 to 18,320. Concomitantly, the housing stock had increased from 2,026 in 1782 to 3,099 in 1791. By 1809 the population reached 27,000 and the number of houses amounted to 5000.[27] In order to deal with the inevitable problems arising from such rapid growth, a town meeting in Belfast had petitioned parliament in 1786 for a police commission. Some reformers expressed concerns about such a plan. Charlemont, for example, feared that the government might use a police commission to control local affairs, citing the precedent of a Dublin police bill that many believed had been intended to muzzle the Dublin corporation and its sometimes obstreperous freemen. Charlemont's trusted source for information regarding Belfast politics, Alexander Haliday, assured the earl that the proposed measure was not a government intrigue. Belfast had been, 'plagued and tormented' by 'porters and carmen, higglers, forestallers and butchers, dunghills, coal measurers and pigs'. Haliday prophesied that the only groups likely to petition against the proposed bill would be the, 'porters, pigs, dunghills, etc.' and even they were divided as 'the butchers have come to blows lately with the pigs'.[28] Furthermore, unlike Dublin, the corporation in Belfast lacked any body of freemen for the government to muzzle. Therefore the practical benefits of a police commission seemed to outweigh any political risks. Reformers nevertheless continued to be concerned. Although the 1786 police proposals for Belfast came to naught, dissatisfaction with the Donegall interest's management of municipal affairs did not abate, and in December 1794 the *Northern Star* complained that 'the lighting, paving and watering of

26 *BNL*, 25 July 1815, 28 Nov. 1815.   27 R. Gillespie et al., *Belfast: part I to 1840*, Irish Historic Towns Atlas 12 (Dublin, 2003), p. 10.   28 HMC, *Manuscripts and correspondence of the James, first earl of Charlemont* (London, 1891–1894), ii, pp 43–4. Charlemont's fears about Dublin were somewhat exaggerated as the struggle against the legislation in Dublin continued for years, Hill, *From patriots to unionists*, pp 183–90

the town' were still 'worth some notice'. Yet, the newspaper also cautioned its readers against accepting any offers of 'pecuniary aid' by the Donegall interest 'to accomplish either, or all of these objects'. The improvements would be 'best done under their own inspection' rather than controlled by the marquess of Donegall.[29]

Improvement commissions, variously referred to as street, sewer, water, paving or police commissions were approved by parliaments in Britain, Ireland, and, subsequently, the United Kingdom in order to provide services and facilities for growing urban centres. In Britain the establishment of improvement commissions were often an occasion for challenges to municipal oligarchies. Some scholars believe the improvement commissions 'extended and diversified the governing élites' by including the middling ranks and religious dissenters.[30] Other writers have cautioned against reading too much into the greater diversity represented in improvement commissions. Local oligarchs 'exploited the legislative supremacy of Parliament' to create forms of local government they might easily control.[31] It was not until the early decades of the nineteenth century that elections by ratepayers were regularly added to the long-standing oligarchical method of co-option.[32] Research on improvement commissions in Ireland has been very limited but Peter Jupp theorized that during the period between 1800 and 1831 improvement commissions in Ireland seemed to be the product of practical 'alliances between wealthy inhabitants and MPs conscious of the inability of the corporations to cope with expansion' rather than politically motivated attacks upon exclusive corporations.[33] Closer examination bears out Jupp's conclusions concerning the considerable wealth and influence necessary to obtain an improvement act. Other evidence, however, demonstrates that improvement commissions were frequently a source of political contention. The alliances that Jupp perceived may in fact have been the result of a legislative process for improvement bills that practically compelled would-be reformers to compromise with urban patrons. The history of the 1816 amendment of the Belfast Police Act of 1800 demonstrates this process.

The eventual passage of the Belfast Police Act by the Irish parliament in 1800 was intended to cope both with the practical problems of the town and the growing discontent with the Donegall interest's monopoly of municipal affairs. Improvement commissions at the time used a combination of four criteria to select members – *ex-officio* membership, property qualification, co-option, and

29 *Northern Star,* 26 to 29 Dec. 1794.   **30** R. Sweet, *The English town, 1680–1840* (New York, 1999), pp 49–56; D. Eastwood, 'Local government and local society' in *A companion to eighteenth-century Britain* (Oxford, 2002), pp 49–50.   **31** N. McCord, *British history, 1815–1914* (2nd ed., New York, 2007), p. 79.   **32** S. Webb and B. Webb, *English local government: statutory authorities for special purposes* (London, 1922), pp 374–5.   **33** Jupp, 'Urban politics in Ireland, 1801–1831', p. 112.

election.[34] The Belfast police act of 1800 combined all of these methods to establish a bicameral improvement commission comprised of a police commission and police committee.[35] The police commission was comprised of 25 members, appointed for life, who represented the town élite. Of those 25 police commissioners, 13 were *ex officio* members from the corporation, namely the 12 burgesses and the mayor. Because the corporation was completely controlled by the Donegall interest, these 13 *ex officio* commissioners guaranteed Donegall control of the police commission. The remaining complement of 12 members was named in the act. Vacancies among those 12 members were filled by co-option from among inhabitants meeting substantial property requirements. Of the 12 police commissioners named in the act, 7 were members of the chamber of commerce with a record of involvement in reform movements. During the late 1790s, however, these reformers had demonstrated their loyalty when 5 of the 7 either joined the Belfast supplemental yeomanry or signed a declaration supporting that body. In this way, the composition of the police commission recognized the longstanding social authority of the Donegall interest while also including new men active in public affairs.

The police committee was comprised of 21 members meeting a more modest property qualification who were elected annually by householders assessed twenty shillings in parish rates. There was a division of responsibilities between the two police boards and all by-laws required joint approval. Although the presence of the *ex-officio* members from the corporation guaranteed that the Donegall interest would have a majority within the police commission, the inclusion of new men from the chamber of commerce in the police commission together with the creation of a representative police committee brought to an end the monopoly of municipal authority by the Donegall interest.

By the time of the markets decision in 1815 the Donegall interest had reason to fear that its influence in civic affairs was further threatened. When the second marquess of Donegall succeeded his father in 1799, he had accumulated prodigious debts and squandered the resources and influence husbanded by earlier generations. In early 1815 he was reported by a contemporary to have been 'obliged to raise money upon the tenantry in the speediest manner possible'.[36] The Donegall interest hoped to preserve their vanishing ascendancy by increasing their influence within the improvement commission established in

34 Sweet, *The English town*, pp 44–56. Practically nothing has been written concerning Irish improvement commissions before or after the Union. Little can be said with regard to such matters as the parliamentary procedures for their passage in the Irish parliament.   35 An Act for paving, cleansing, lighting, and improving the several Streets, Squares, Lanes, and Passages within the Town of Belfast, 40 Geo. III, c. 37.   36 The pathetic history of the second marquess is described in W.A. Maguire, *Living like a lord* (Belfast, 1984), p. 59.

1800. In September 1815, while the final appeal concerning the control of markets in Belfast was still before the court of common pleas, they announced their intention to bring forward a private bill to amend the Belfast police act of 1800.[37] The story of this bill is important not merely for its provisions and the contention they aroused but also for the changing conception of the relationship between local government and public opinion reflected in its passage.

During the first three decades of the nineteenth century improvement commissions in Ireland were created and amended primarily by means of private bills, but private bill procedures were increasingly a source of complaint. Between 1801 and 1832, 49 bills came before parliament for establishing or amending improvement commissions in Ireland. Of those 49 bills, only 12 were public bills. The other 37 bills originated as petitions to parliament and were designated private bills. Successful private bills were classified variously as 'local and personal acts declared public and to be judicially noted' or 'private and personal acts'.[38] Theoretically public legislation concerned the welfare of the entire kingdom while private legislation affected the interests of a segment of the population.[39] Private acts delegated limited powers to collect taxes or fees to individuals, local authorities and private corporations.

In order to protect the public good, private bills were subject to special procedures. They were examined in both houses of parliament by select committees that, in theory, included members of parliament not directly interested in the legislation. In practice by the end of the eighteenth century the committees considering private legislation were often controlled by peers with a personal interest in the measures being considered so that 'there was no pretence of impartiality'.[40] Parliamentary committees in 1824 and 1825 investigated the question of private bill select committees and concluded that the public good was being damaged 'by an almost exclusive attendance' on private bill committees by members 'directly or indirectly personally interested in the issue of the proceedings'.[41]

The efforts to amend the Belfast police act illustrated many of the

---

37 *BNL*, 12 Sept. 1815.   **38** F. Clifford, *A history of private bill legislation*, 2 vols (London, 1885), i, pp 267–9. This tripartite classification of the acts of parliament dated from 1798 in Britain and was applied to Ireland at the Union. In 1814 a further division of private legislation was added so that the four classes were – 1) public general acts, 2) local and personal acts declared public and to be judicially noticed, 3) private acts printed by the queen's printer, copies of which may be given in evidence, and 4) private acts not so printed. In 1868 this number was reduced to the three official categories: 1) public general acts, 2) local acts, and 3) private acts. The last category now almost exclusively concerned with such personal matters as naturalization.   **39** M.F. Bond, *Guide to the records of parliament* (London, 1971), p. 70.   **40** A. Adonis, *Making aristocracy work* (Oxford, 1993), p. 97.   **41** *Report from select committee on the constitution of committees on private bills*, HC 1825 (457), v, p. 2

complaints against private bill procedures. The first grievance of the bill's opponents concerned the issue of publicity. Although the Donegall interest ostensibly complied with the standing orders requiring notification of their intention to seek an amending act in November 1815, that notice lacked any meaningful details. To the bill's opponents, the 'vague and indefinite' notice afforded 'just grounds for apprehending that other objects may be in view which are perhaps unfit for public scrutiny'.[42] This was a common criticism. John Finlay asserted that the promoters of such private bills believed that, despite the requisite notifications in the newspapers, the parliamentary proce- dures for such bills might paradoxically shield unpopular proposals from the kind of scrutiny and debate that accompanied public bills. Of a particular private bill for Dublin, Finlay asserted that its proponents 'published that intention in a manner the least public'. Indeed, they 'published it, to keep it private'.[43]

When details of the improvement bill finally became known in February 1816, the apprehensions of its critics proved well-founded. The plan clearly intended to shore up Donegall influence in the town. For example, the bill added the lord of the manor to the list of *ex-officio* members of the police commission so that the Donegall interest would control 14 of the 26 commis- sioners. The bill also would have permitted the police commission alone to make by-laws rather than requiring the approval of both boards. The Donegall interest hoped to forestall any opposition from within the existing police boards by proposing significant increases in the boards' authority for badly needed town planning.

In order to maintain some semblance of representation, the bill proposed that the portion of the police commission that was not *ex-officio* should in the future, like the police committee, be elected by qualified ratepayers rather than selected by co-option. Because the *ex officio* portion of the police commission represented the Donegall interest, the bill could meet the increasing demand in parliament for representation in improvement bills without actually putting Donegall power and influence at risk.[44] Indeed, the Donegall interest might conceivably win further representation within the police commission. To add insult to injury the qualification for voting in the annual elections for the police committee were to be increased from 20s. to £2.

The Donegall interest tried unsuccessfully to quell opposition to the bill through its control of corporate institutions. In April 1816 the mayor refused permission for an official town meeting to discuss the bill, daring the opponents to risk prosecution under the Convention Act of 1793 if they proceeded. The

42 *BNL*, 17 Nov. 1815.   43 Finlay, *Letters addressed to the Irish government*, p. 69.   44 Sweet, *The English town*, pp 48–9.

leading opponents of the bill consisted of advanced reformers aligned to William Drennan, such as W.B. Neilson and Robert Grimshaw, who not only wanted to defeat the Donegall interest but to establish longstanding radical principles. They hoped to limit police commissioners to a specific term, require *ex officio* members to be residents (a number of the burgesses at the time were non-residents), increase the term of the more representative police committee members to three years, continue a proportional rate of taxation, and preserve the existing requirement for joint approval by the boards for by-laws.[45]

In April 1816, the reformers hoped to join with the existing police commissioners not connected with the Donegall interest to alter or obstruct the bill. With the important exception of maintaining the requirement for joint approval of by-laws, all of the reformers' proposals were rejected. Cooperation between the radicals and the members of the commission not connected with the Donegall interest was hindered by two factors. First, the events of 1790s continued to be a source of antagonism. Several of the commissioners named in 1800 were reformers who had sided with the government during the war. On the other hand, the opposition to the improvement bill was led by men who had been vocal critics of the government during the war. While the bill was being debated during March and April 1816, these old wounds were disturbed once again by a much publicized St Patrick's Day dinner at which local radicals, including leading opponents of the bill, offered controversial toasts, particularly two praising prominent supporters of Napoleon.[46]

The second factor affecting cooperation between the elected police commissioners and the more radical opponents of the bill was simple practicality. If the elected commissioners had acceded to the demands of the reformers, there would have been no new police bill and the very real need for urban improvements left wanting. The procedures for improvement bills in parliament were not intended to represent the will of the citizens, however defined, but to consider various interests. A bill opposed by the Donegall interest would mean that both the lord of the manor and the municipal corporation were against the measure. An improvement bill opposed by both the lord of the manor and the municipal corporation would be difficult to pass so long as the existing procedures 'put a premium on promoters of bills gathering a broad band of local support for a bill in advance of the presentation of a petition'.[47] Even an unopposed bill required an experienced parliamentary agent to ensure compliance with standing orders as well as to arrange payment of the various fees for private bills that were due to sundry parliamentary officers. According to one expert 'every official in both Houses from the chancellor down to the

45 *BNL*, 4 April 1816, 19 Apr. 1816.   46 McBride, *Scripture politics*, pp 212–13; *Shamrock*, 11 May 1816.   47 P. Jupp, *British politics on the eve of reform* (New York, 1998), pp 182–3.

doorkeeper' was due a fee for a private bill.[48] A rough idea of the considerable expenses of such a process can be gauged from English towns where an unopposed improvement bill during the 1830s cost on average of about £1600.[49]

When a bill was opposed the expenses increased considerably as partisans were compelled to marshal an increased number of counsel and witnesses to appear before select committees in both houses of parliament.[50] Costs were further inflated by tactical delays. The select committee investigating private bills concluded that resolute proponents of a measure with sizeable war chests sought 'to drive opponents from the field by expense', while determined adversaries with sufficient cash hoped 'to render it impossible, for want of time, to pass the Bill into law'.[51] In one case proponents of a failed improvement bill for Manchester spent £6000.[52] With expenses of this magnitude it is not surprising that proponents would make every effort to avoid antagonizing either local MPs or wealthy inhabitants who might make trouble for them in committee. In Belfast in 1816, the commissioners had to weigh the need for effective town planning against the transparent efforts of the Donegall interest to preserve their threatened influence. After having removed the most obvious effort of the Donegall interest to control the police board through by-laws approved by the police commission alone, the commissioners considered the likely gains to outweigh the defects of the proposed legislation.

The passage of the 1816 police act for Belfast illustrated the difficulties confronting Ulster liberalism. Not only were the divisions of the 1790s an impediment, but the very structure of politics and administration was an obstacle to liberal success. While there was no longer an Irish parliament comprised of the Irish gentry and solicitous of the interests of fellow aristocratic families such as the Donegalls, the customs and procedures of the imperial parliament tended to preserve the status quo. The imperial parliament governed through the same institutions that had existed prior to the Union. Improvement bills might modify the existing system of administration but they were subject to parliament's preference for consensus and the preservation of existing interests. Ulster liberals were confronted with the reality that improvement bills were, under the existing conditions, likely to be sought by aristocratic interests eager to secure or expand their power.

---

48 Bond, *Guide to the records of parliament*, p. 70; S. Lambert, *Bills and acts* (Cambridge, 1971), p. 29. **49** J. Prest, *Liberty and locality* (Oxford, 1990), p. 5. **50** Ibid. **51** *Journals of the House of Commons*, v. 80, 1825–6, 968. **52** Prest, *Liberty and locality*, p. 5

Battle of the synods: Presbyterians and Ulster liberalism

If the enduring structure of politics were not a sufficient obstacle for Ulster liberalism during the period between 1815 and 1830, the Presbyterian Synod of Ulster, one of the primary foundations of liberalism in Ulster, became involved in a bitter and painful struggle that has been a focus of historical analysis for those attempting to understand Ulster society and politics. Elsewhere in Ireland the campaign for Catholic emancipation became a triumph for reform and the foundation of a democratic and nationalist tradition in Ireland, but the fate of Ulster liberalism seemed to hang in the balance. Many have considered this a critical moment of divergence between Ulster and the rest of Irish society, the occasion when the liberal and radical traditions that had previously existed in Ulster during the eighteenth century were all but destroyed.

The general narrative is well known and deceptively simple. In 1821, building upon battles to control the education of candidates for the ministry at the Belfast Academical Institution, a party of self-described orthodox clergy and laymen led by the Revd Henry Cooke began a campaign to remove what they described as a growing heterodox element threatening the vitality of the Synod of Ulster. They believed that a number of ministers had embraced and were attempting to propagate what they described as Arianism, a heresy denying the triune nature of God. Two groups opposed Cooke and his allies. One group consisted of a small number of ministers and laymen led by the Revd Henry Montgomery who were either truly heterodox or outspoken advocates of a right to private judgment on issues where they perceived the scriptures were silent or unclear. The second, larger group comprised orthodox clergy and laymen unwilling to press the issue of subscription to the Westminster Confession lest it result in schism and a diminution of the synod's strength and prestige. Due to similarities with a conflict that had occurred a century before within Presbyterianism throughout the British Isles, labels from the past were adopted to identify the opposing groups. Cooke and his allies were identified as the Old Light while Montgomery and his supporters were described as the New Light. Rather than adopting the terms Unitarian or Remonstrant or the pejorative Arian to describe a group that included many confirmed Trinitarians, I will refer to Montgomery and his allies as Non-subscribers.

The conflict was further complicated by the fact that the most active partisans were at odds politically as well as theologically. Cooke and his close allies have been considered for the most part conservative while Montgomery and his foremost supporters were characterized as liberals. Until 1828 the orthodox campaign had been remarkably unsuccessful. Unable to persuade the synod to expel the heterodox party, in 1828 Cooke and his allies finally made the position of Montgomery and his supporters untenable by convincing the synod to appoint a special committee to examine licentiates for the ministry before their ordination. It was understood that the committee would only approve those who subscribed to the orthodox beliefs. In 1829 a small group of ministers and elders who were unwilling to accept this imposition stayed away from the annual meeting of the synod but sent a remonstrance. When this remonstrance was rejected 17 of the 219 ministers who composed the synod in 1829 formally withdrew and organized themselves into the so-called Remonstrant synod.[53]

From an early date Cooke's victory was viewed as a watershed in Ulster's history. The Presbyterian minister W.D. Killen, author of a magisterial account of Ulster Presbyterianism during the eighteenth and nineteenth century and a witness to the confrontation, described the secession of the Non-subscribers as the key event in the onset of a period of unparalleled growth and revival for Presbyterianism in Ulster. According to Killen, Cooke garnered great influence in Ulster society from his role and his popularity 'was such as perhaps has never been attained by any other minister of any denomination in this country'.[54] The critical question became whether the victory for theological orthodoxy wrought by Cooke could be translated into victories for political conservatism. Not explicitly addressing this question in his history, Killen, though an admirer of Cooke in political as well as theological matters, later admitted that, 'many members of his church objected to his strong Conservatism, his scorching sarcasms, or his occasional ebullitions of temper'.[55]

Over time, Cooke's political influence was called into question. Among the first to challenge Cooke's legacy were two Presbyterian ministers who taught at Magee college, the Presbyterian seminary established in Derry in 1865. In 1872 Richard Smyth published a critique of Cooke's career that dealt more forthrightly with political issues. Smyth, an active liberal politician, evangelical and future MP, asserted that Cooke, while a paladin of Presbyterianism in the struggle for orthodox and evangelical religion, was unable to capitalize on his theological influence to promote his conservative political agenda. Smyth bluntly concluded that 'Dr. Cooke's real life-work began and ended with the purgation of the Synod of Ulster from the leaven of Arianism'. Examining the issues that Cooke advocated after 1830, Smyth determined that 'almost every wall which was buttressed by his eloquence has been thrown down, and the principal movements to which he gave the impulse have fallen upon check and disaster' until there was hardly 'any more striking instance of the total collapse of public policies'.[56] In 1902, W.T. Latimer reiterated many of Smyth's

53 This narrative is a heavily influenced by R.F. Holmes, *Henry Cooke* (Belfast, 1981). 54 J.S. Reid and W.D. Killen, *History of the Presbyterian*, iii, p. 463. 55 W.D. Killen, *Reminiscences* (London, 1901), pp 175–6. 56 R. Smyth, 'The life and times of Dr Henry

observations but with the added conclusion that Cooke's crusade had been unnecessary. Orthodoxy was winning the day and 'Arianism would soon have died a natural death in the Synod'. Furthermore, Cooke's immediate victory was less resounding than it appeared as 'many of the ministers who remained were favourable to Non-Subscribing or even to Arian opinions, but the pronounced orthodoxy of their congregations prevented their withdrawal from the Synod'.[57]

The controversy clearly created a volatile environment in which even the most orthodox minister might feel threatened with the loss of his pulpit or the disruption of his congregation. In 1829, W.D. Killen, an exemplar of theological orthodoxy and evangelical fervour, encountered difficulty when another minister suggested that Killen was somehow heterodox. Despite his public refutations, Killen recalled that 'a young mechanic, who was a notorious mischief-maker and a mob orator of no little ability, sought to mortify one of my chief supporters, who had in some way given him umbrage, by taking the field against me, harangued the people, and got up an opposition' that eventually forced Killen to leave.[58] Given this threatening environment, only the most strong-willed and principled minister or layperson would be willing to participate actively in the debate.

Less than fraternal tactics were employed as both parties enlisted worldly influence. The New Light party was supported by a number of substantial merchants and factory owners who during the battles over the Belfast Academical Institution had brought financial pressure to bear. Cooke's party enlisted the landed aristocracy who, though not immediately concerned in the affairs of a church to which they did not belong, wanted to assist men they considered their political allies. The influence of the landed aristocracy was sometimes critical in deciding whether a particular congregation or minister remained within the synod. At Greyabbey, Co. Down, the minister and the majority of the congregation favoured joining the remonstrant synod but the minority of the congregation, in a policy explicitly advocated by Cooke's supporters, challenged the majority's rights both to the meeting house and the portion of the *regium donum* that accompanied it. The local landlord who had provided the ground for the meeting house sided with the orthodox minority and the Non-subscribers were forcibly excluded from their church. These tactics were widely publicized by the *Northern Whig*, a liberal newspaper founded in 1824 by F.D. Finlay, a printer and contributor to Drennan's *Belfast Monthly Magazine* with close connections to the Non-subscribers. The *Whig* asserted that in this case and many others 'the *great* engine' of the orthodox

Cooke', *British and Foreign Evangelical Review*, 21 (1872), 210–13.   **57** Latimer, *A history of the Irish Presbyterians*, p. 443.   **58** Killen, *Reminiscences*, pp 28–9.

party 'was the terror of the landlord's displeasure – no puny engine, when it is considered that he is proprietor of perhaps *three-fourths* of the Parish'.[59] In this way, landlords, almost all of whom were members of the Church of Ireland, were able to affect dramatically matters in the Synod of Ulster.

Perhaps the most terrifying tactic was the simple imputation of heterodoxy. The *Northern Whig* described how Cooke used this stratagem to intimidate an orthodox minister who dared to question his methods. When the minister ably argued for 'a more tolerant course', Cooke effectively silenced the perceived challenge with a menacing reply – 'I see how it is with you: I understand you have been lately in company with Dr Bruce [an admitted Arian and New Light advocate]'. According to the *Northern Whig,* the imputation 'might have essentially injured' the young minister 'had not his character and respectability counteracted its efforts'.[60] It would hardly be surprising if few ministers were willing to risk the complete disruption of their congregations on behalf of a truly Arian or Non-subscribing minority. They had prevented Cooke from actually expelling these brethren with whom they fundamentally disagreed, but there were limits to fraternal charity. The assertion that Cooke's support within the synod was more broad than deep is certainly credible.

Despite the early analyses of Smyth and Latimer, the correlation between Cooke's triumph over Arianism in 1830 and a precipitous decline in the fortunes of Ulster liberalism became widely accepted for a time. Cooke was credited with, or blamed for, having secured confessional solidarity among Protestants and extinguishing the liberal and radical aspect of Presbyterianism prominent during the eighteenth century. As recently as 1989 Oliver MacDonagh described the Arian controversy as the death knell of Ulster liberalism in the *New history of Ireland,* a volume intended to summarize current scholarship.[61] However, in that same volume, S.J. Connolly cited new research discounting a correlation between the increasing influence of conservative, evangelical theology and conservative politics.[62]

The dramatic confrontation between Cooke and Montgomery is a convenient and striking metaphor for those seeking to explain the development of the historic confrontation between unionism and nationalism in Ulster.[63] That drama does not, however, reflect the trend of scholarship. Aided in particular by publication of a modern, critical biography of Cooke by R.F.G. Holmes it is increasingly clear that Cooke's victory was not the resounding triumph some subsequently portrayed it.[64] His efforts to expel the Arians met

59 *NW,* 15 Feb. 1830. **60** Ibid., 28 Dec. 1829. **61** O. MacDonagh, 'The economy and society, 1830–1845', in *New history of Ireland,* v: *Ireland under the Union* (Oxford, 1989), pp 236–7. **62** S.J. Connolly 'Mass politics and sectarian conflict, 1823–30', in *New history of Ireland,* v: *Ireland under the Union* (Oxford, 1989), p. 77. **63** F. O'Ferrall, *Catholic emancipation* (Atlantic Highlands, NJ, 1985), pp 167–9. **64** Holmes, *Henry Cooke,* pp 31–4, 207;

with strong resistance from the beginning and he was repeatedly forced to back down on his demands. Even when the remonstrance was presented to the Synod of Ulster in 1829 and Cooke appeared to be at the height of his influence, he could not convince the synod 'to bow to conservative and ultra-Protestant pressure to join in a last ditch resistance to the imminent concession of Catholic emancipation'. The synod, while distrustful of Daniel O'Connell and many of his goals, continued to support Catholic emancipation as it had done in 1793 and in 1813.[65] Cooke and Montgomery attempted to use existing divisions to further not only their theological causes but also their political interests. The question is whether they were successful.

If liberalism among Ulster Presbyterians were only represented by Montgomery and the Non-subscribers, then Cooke and conservatism had gained the victory. This was not the case. In many ways Cooke's theological victory was pyrrhic in political terms. The conqueror of the Arians was unable to persuade the synod to follow his lead on such subjects as Catholic emancipation. Interestingly, Peter Brooke has suggested that the secession of the Non-subscribers allowed the synod to regain its confidence and enter into a period of growth and renewal in Ulster Presbyterianism because Cooke was weakened rather than strengthened by the event. It was neither the ideas of the Non-subscribers nor the disputes, as unpleasant and disputatious as they often were, which had undermined the confidence of the synod. The Non-subscribers were unimportant except in the fact that they provided Cooke with a stick with which to threaten the rest of the synod. Any disagreement with Cooke could bring insinuations of heterodoxy. After the departure of the Non-subscribers, Cooke's stick was gone. Political liberals within the synod could, and did, successfully oppose Cooke on many issues. It would be their turn to question Cooke, to ask why Cooke kept company with Tory leaders who often opposed the interests of Presbyterians.

Both contemporaries and historians have grossly underestimated the religious influences within Ulster liberalism. Aside from a small, albeit dispro-portionately influential, number of Non-subscribers, the bulk of Ulster liberalism became increasingly evangelical in its outlook during the course of the nineteenth century. Some writers, having either a more secular vision of society or a desire to create and sustain a common ground of agreement between Ulster liberalism and southern nationalism, have sought to minimize the religious element in Ulster liberalism. While all too willing to acknowledge the role of sectarian religion in the divisions that arose between Catholic and Presbyterian liberals, these writers have wittingly or unwittingly ignored the role of religion as inspiration for liberal political organization and action.

see also Brooke, *Ulster Presbyterianism*, pp 145–6.   **65** Holmes, *Our Irish Presbyterian heritage* (Belfast, 1985), p. 105.

The willingness, sometimes enthusiastic willingness, of evangelical Ulster Presbyterianism to challenge both the conservative ascendancy as well as government policy was due in part to a series of conflicts that had aroused a strong sense of grievance. Judicial decisions in Scotland and Ireland together with the policies of the Peel administration contributed to the survival of Ulster liberalism. These events helped Ulster liberals counter Cooke's efforts to garner support for conservative politics among Presbyterians. In particular, the controversy concerning lay patronage in the Church of Scotland aroused much interest in Ulster. Opinion in Ulster was solidly behind the opponents of lay patronage led by Thomas Chalmers, and when the administration of Sir Robert Peel proved unwilling and unable to resolve the affair Ulster Presbyterianism became hostile towards the Peel government. This weakened the position of Cooke and the conservatives.

In July 1841, Cooke appeared to be gaining the position and influence that he had hoped to achieve during the previous decade. Cooke had been a significant actor in the union of the Synod of Ulster with the Secession Synod to form the General Assembly of the Presbyterian Church in Ireland in 1840. As a result of this union, the 292 congregations of the Synod of Ulster joined with the 141 congregations of the Secession Synod.[66] In recognition of his role in this union, Cooke was chosen moderator of the general assembly. By the autumn of 1841, however, Cooke was, in the words of his biographer R.F. Holmes, 'on the rack' in his efforts to resist intense pressure to call an extraordinary meeting of the general assembly to demonstrate support for the opponents of lay patronage in Scotland. Cooke was deeply anxious about the possible effects of affairs in Scotland upon the political scene in Ulster. In a letter to J.E. Tennent, the conservative MP for Belfast, Cooke expressed his concern that Peel had much to lose from failing to succour the grievances of Presbyterians in Ireland and Scotland –

> Let him refuse – and I fear he will refuse – and he not only loses Scotland and Ulster, but he converts them into opponents to his measures and partisans to his enemies. This last result I dread [...] I see in it the elements of a revolution in public sentiment and in public institutions, which a little concession – no, a little justice – would avert now, but which if not granted now, cannot be averted hereafter. In Belfast this process will begin, and no living man could retard it.

Cooke also found himself placed at political peril. His opponents attempted to undermine his position by informing leaders of the opponents of lay patronage

---

66 Latimer, *A history of the Irish Presbyterians*, p. 466.

in Scotland that Cooke's political sympathies would interfere with his support for the claims of Presbyterians in Scotland.[67] By the spring of 1842, Cooke could no longer control the situation.

Ironically, Cooke's predicament was in part a result of the union of the synods which he and others had believed would increase his influence. During the 1830s, after the withdrawal of the Non-subscribers, there seemed little separating the bodies in theological terms and discussions about a union began.[68] There were, however, significant underlying differences that would trouble the newly created general assembly for more than a decade. The growth of the Seceders has been described previously. The Seceders, it will be recalled, had 46 congregations when they first received the *regium donum*. The financial support seems to have played a major role in their development so that by 1809 there were 91 congregations. In 1818, when a breach among the Seceders concerning the burgess oath in Scotland, an oath with absolutely no relevance to Ulster, was healed there were 97 Seceding congregations.[69] In 1829 there were 114 Seceding ministers in Ulster as opposed to 209 congregations in the Synod of Ulster in 1830.[70] It is clear that before 1830 the Seceders were outpacing the Synod of Ulster in the establishment of congregations. Whereas between 1746 and 1829 the Seceders had established 114 congregations between 1729 and 1829 the Synod of Ulster had only created 73 new congregations.[71] The Seceders might in some ways be considered a much older and perhaps more effective opponent of non-subscription or Arianism in Ulster than Henry Cooke. After the issue of non-subscription was settled in the Synod of Ulster, the Seceders were relatively less successful in establishing new congregations. While the Synod of Ulster erected 83 congregations between 1830 and 1840 the Seceders only managed 27. The orthodoxy and evangelical emphasis that had been the hallmark of the Seceders became less distinguishing in light of the changes that were occurring within the Synod of Ulster.

If the theological differences between the Seceders and the Synod of Ulster had been mostly resolved, considerable social and cultural differences remained. First, the Secession Synod appealed more to 'those in humbler circumstances' than did the Synod of Ulster and was comprised primarily of 'respectable middle-class farmers' rather than the merchants and manufacturers who wielded considerable influence in the Synod of Ulster.[72] This social difference was reflected both in the devotional practice and church

67 Porter, *Life and times of Henry Cooke*, p. 373.   68 Hempton and Hill, *Evangelical Protestantism in Ulster society*, p. 75.   69 Latimer, *A history of the Irish Presbyterians*, p. 467.   70 Hempton and Hill, *Evangelical Protestantism in Ulster society*, p. 70; Latimer, *A history of the Irish Presbyterians*, p. 449.   71 Killen in Reid, *History of the Presbyterian church in Ireland*, p. 465.   72 Hempton and Hill, *Evangelical Protestantism in Ulster society*, p. 109; Latimer, *A history of the Irish Presbyterians*, p. 467.

government. The Seceders had a reputation for popular piety more often attributed to sects other than Presbyterians.[73] This was almost certainly due in part to their particular form of church government. Before the creation of the general assembly, the Synod of Ulster made the choice of ministers dependent upon securing the votes of members who contributed two-thirds of the stipend that together with the portion of the *regium donum* allotted to each congregation provided the financial support for the minister. In the Synod of Ulster, communicants who did not contribute to the stipend were excluded from voting. Among the Seceders, however, all communicants were eligible to vote and the question of the stipend was irrelevant, the votes of two-thirds of the communicants in a congregation being the sole criterion for confirming the call of a minister.[74] When the general assembly was formed a compromise was agreed upon whereby ministers were chosen by two-thirds of the communicants who contributed to the stipend of a congregation. The influence of both the humblest and the wealthiest segments of Presbyterian opinion were sacrificed in the quest for unity. In religion as well as politics there was an increasing *embourgeoisement* of Ulster society during the nineteenth century. For some time after the union of the synods, however, the vast majority of the general assembly's ministers had been called to their profession under the previous rubrics. It would have been extraordinary if there had not been some tension over social questions within the general assembly given the social disparities represented there.

Second, the Seceders were for historical reasons even more closely influenced by the crisis in the Church of Scotland than their counterparts in the Synod of Ulster. The issue of lay patronage in Scotland had been the Seceders' *raison d'être* and they had maintained close relationships with their brethren in Scotland. It was unfortunate for Henry Cooke that the crisis of the Church of Scotland occurred so shortly after the union of the synods. His perceived lack of support for the independence of the Church of Scotland aroused the particular ire of many former Seceders.

This ire was compounded by a contemporaneous controversy affecting Ulster directly. In 1840, the Armagh consistorial court of the Church of Ireland had determined that marriages performed by Presbyterian ministers, when one of the parties was a member of the established Church of Ireland, were invalid. Though alarmed, Presbyterians hoped that the civil courts would not uphold this decision. When the House of Lords itself ultimately failed to overturn the decision in 1842, thereby threatening the property interests and legitimacy of the children of such unions, Presbyterian opinion became outraged. Assailed

---

73 Hempton and Hill, *Evangelical Protestantism in Ulster society*, p. 26.   74 Latimer, *A history of the Irish Presbyterians*, p. 466.

by emotional appeals, including personal communications from Cooke, the government agreed to address the matter with remedial legislation. However, during the process the government only managed to add insult to injury. The proposed legislation approached the problem pragmatically by legitimating existing marriages and securing inheritances. For Ulster Presbyterians this was not the point. Not only did the bill not address future marriages but, more importantly, it did not contradict what they perceived as a challenge to the legitimacy of their church. Rather than assuaging opinion, the bill antagonized Presbyterians. Cooke himself stated that the proposal 'said virtually that many of their people had been living in a state of concubinage for many years' and was 'a gross insult upon them'.[75]

In March 1842, outrage at the perceived insult finally compelled Cooke to convene an extraordinary meeting of the general assembly during which the announcement that a select committee of the House of Lords would consider the issue provided a timely respite from the hue and cry against the Peel administration.[76] It was a brief respite. At the annual meeting of the general assembly in July 1842 Cooke was severely tested. After being informed that the proceedings in the Lords would be delayed a further six to nine months, a group of ministers and elders led by John Brown, a minister from Aghadowey, Co. Londonderry, directly assailed Cooke's efforts to ally Presbyterians with conservatives. Brown complained that Presbyterians had mistakenly supported 'striplings of nobility' whose pledges to defend Presbyterian interests had been of little use. Cooke countered with demagogic levity and yet another assurance that his influence with leading conservatives would eventually bear fruit, that the assembly ought to make a distinction 'between support which seeks to aid us with loud words, and that unseen, though not less useful, support which can exert an influence in high quarters for the good of our common cause'.[77]

Cooke's opponents sensed that his continual references to allies in high places was wearing thin and pressed him to reveal the contents of his correspondence with the government while he was moderator. When Cooke reluctantly outlined the details of a bill that he had helped draft for the government the meeting turned hard against him. Cooke dug in his heels, and when further importuned to disclose the contents of the remaining private correspondence with the government he threatened, if such demands were not abandoned, to deny the assembly the boon of his presence. In response, Samuel McCurdy Greer, a barrister from Coleraine educated in Scotland, proposed the establishment of congregational 'Church Defence Associations' to disseminate information about the Church of Scotland and marriage controversies, arrange petitions to parliament, bring pressure upon their representatives and 'if

75 *BU*, 8 July 1842.   76 Holmes, *Henry Cooke*, p. 153.   77 *BU*, 8 July 1842, 13 July 1842.

necessary, lead them to choose members who might more fairly represent their feelings'. Cooke and his allies were in disarray. They argued that such associations were unnecessary, that 'associations of defence against Protestant brethren' would 'create open war between brethren to the exceeding delight of O'Connell and the whole Church of Rome'.[78] In the end, it was procedure rather than Cooke's persuasion that delayed Greer's victory. It was ruled that Greer's proposal, under the normal procedures of the general assembly, would have to be submitted in the form of an overture during this session and acted upon during the next general assembly.

If Cooke believed his tribulations for that year were finished, the closing address of John Edgar as the newly elected moderator, the first moderator from the former secession synod, soon disabused him of that miscomprehension. During the course of a review and commentary upon the proceedings, Edgar launched a bitter attack upon the 'prelatic' established church. This attack upon the church of many of his political allies led Cooke to the extraordinary action of protesting against the newly installed moderator's closing address – 'No moderator should in future be permitted in his closing address to the House, to review and comment upon the proceedings'. Cooke could not leave unchallenged the assertion that the general assembly was hostile towards their fellow Protestants in the established church. They should have no quarrel with the evangelical majority within that body. Cooke declared he was 'a Presbyterian, but not less a Presbyterian than a Protestant'. When one of Cooke's allies unsuccessfully moved a resolution that would have forbidden future moderators from such commentaries, he provoked impassioned denunciations of Cooke's efforts on behalf of 'the preservation of Protestant peace' at the expense of Presbyterian interests.

Whatever Cooke's hopes for Protestant union might have been, at this juncture a growing and vocal element within Ulster Presbyterianism wanted nothing to do with such rough suitors as the established church and conservatives. When the general assembly met in 1843, the seal was placed upon Cooke's embarrassing defeat. The assembly approved the overture of the year before by John Brown that called upon Presbyterians to defend their 'rights and privileges' from the 'powerful influences' arrayed against them by 'a united and faithful discharge of their duty as Christian electors' to elect Presbyterians to parliament.[79] Cooke fulfilled his threat of the year before and withdrew from the general assembly's proceedings until 1847 when another political crisis compelled him to return. The evangelical nature of Presbyterianism in Ulster was secure, but the political sympathies of the church were still a matter of vital contention.

78 Ibid.   79 Holmes, *Henry Cooke*, pp 156–8; *BU*, 16 July 1847.

Fire brands thrown among us: Ulster liberalism and O'Connell

The withdrawal of the Non-subscribers from the Synod of Ulster removed a scourge that Cooke had used against his opponents, but another weapon soon came to hand. When Daniel O'Connell began to agitate for repeal of the Union, Cooke and his allies quickly seized upon the opportunity to attack liberal Presbyterians for their cooperation with Catholics. In particular, the issue of repeal of the Union threatened to undermine opportunities that first parliamentary and then municipal reform presented to Ulster liberals. The history of their efforts to win the two-member constituency of Belfast during the period between 1832 and 1842 demonstrated that even under the most favourable circumstances the issue of repeal might diminish if not destroy liberal chances at the parliamentary level.

Ulster reformers imagined the year 1832 to be a watershed. They believed parliamentary reform and the rapid growth of industry and commerce were transforming politics and society. R.J. Tennent, a leading Belfast radical, declared that they were 'in the middle – disguise it as we may – of a *great social Revolution*'. Tennent's enthusiasm was fed by the prospect of storming a citadel of aristocratic and Ascendancy privilege and, 'for the *first time*', exercising 'the inalienable rights of freemen'.[80] Members of parliament for Belfast would no longer be chosen by the thirteen members of the close corporation, the derided 'boroughmongers' of the Donegall interest. There was cause for optimism. The 1832 general election was in many ways more of a contest among factions of reformers than a battle between Whigs and Tories or liberals and conservatives. Eagerly anticipating an end to their wanderings in the political wilderness, in August 1832 a committee of the Belfast Reform Society selected two candidates – W.S. Crawford, a Co. Down landlord and R.J. Tennent, a young lawyer – to represent the reform cause. These official reform candidates were eventually opposed by Lord Arthur Chichester, son of the second marquess of Donegall, and James Emerson Tennent, a cousin by marriage of R.J. Tennent. Emerson Tennent had been born James Emerson but adopted the name Tennent in 1832 as a result of marrying the heiress of R.J. Tennent's wealthy uncle, William Tennent.

This contest has sometimes carelessly been represented as a contest between Whigs and Tories but political alignments and ideologies were still very much in flux.[81] All of the candidates cast themselves as reformers. Even Chichester, despite being maligned as the 'stripling nominee' of the Donegall interest, seems to have understood the temper of the new electorate and campaigned not

---

80 *NW*, 27 Aug. 1832.   81 The best account of the 1832 election is in G.J. Slater, 'Belfast politics, 1798–1868' (PhD, New University of Ulster, 1982), pp 32–40.

as a Tory but as a Whiggish moderate who even his opponents at the *Northern Whig* reluctantly admitted was a 'Reformer, although one of very moderate description'.[82] Chichester wisely enlisted supporters from a variety of political viewpoints and kept his head down, concentrating on using what remained of Donegall proprietorial interest in the town.

The other three candidates possessed impeccable reform credentials. Since the end of 1830 all three had frequently spoken at public meetings organized by the Belfast Reform Society in support of parliamentary reform. Crawford and R.J. Tennent also had strong familial connections with past reform movements, the former's father having been a well-known Volunteer and the latter's family leaders of Belfast radicalism since the 1790s. For his part J.E. Tennent had first reported on and then participated in the Greek War of Independence in the company of R.J. Tennent.[83] The choice of two candidates from among these three men by a committee of the Belfast Reform Society was a disaster. Although there was a clear consensus for Crawford, the eldest of the three at 51, the choice between the two Tennents, both in their late 20s and just beginning legal careers, became an unseemly drama.

Upon R.J. Tennent's selection, J.E. Tennent protested that the committee had undermined an agreement between the Tennents to submit to a test of public opinion in deciding who should stand with Crawford. When efforts to heal the rift failed, J.E. Tennent decided to contest the seat without the support of the committee. At a personal level, the quarrel was clearly hurtful to the former comrades-in-arms. Both men seemed to waver at a critical juncture, offering to retire from the campaign, only to be held to the sticking point by embarrassed supporters. The dispute not only divided reformers, but also opened the Belfast Reform Society up to the accusation that they were not much better than the boroughmongers of the Donegall interest they so often derided. They were 'Barnett's burgesses', a reference to a prominent Belfast radical, John Barnett.[84] This gibe was given greater force by the fact that R.J. Tennent could have been described as a 'stripling' of Belfast's radical aristocracy, his father and uncle having been probably the most visible radicals in Belfast since the 1790s.

The primary strategy of the committee working for R.J Tennent and Crawford was simple. Their likely supporters were divided between two groups – Catholic reformers who supported O'Connell, and Protestant reformers, mostly Presbyterians of one sort or another, who were suspicious of O'Connell and positively hostile to repeal. Having recognized this division as far back as January 1831, the committee co-opted a number of prominent Catholics and

---

82 *NW*, 3 Sept. 1832.   83 *BNL*, 8 Mar. 1869; James Emerson, *Letters from the Aegean* (New York, 1829), p. iv.   84 *BNL*, 7 Sept. 1832, 14 Sept. 1832.

emphasized issues that they believed united the two groups, such as the abolition of tithes and the introduction of the ballot, while avoiding any official position on repeal.[85] When their opponents, particularly the *Belfast News-Letter*, tried to sow division between the groups by forcing a discussion of repeal, R.J. Tennent refused to give either 'a public pledge or expression of opinion on the question of Repeal'.[86] If the issue were to come before parliament, Tennent promised to consult his constituents and either act according to their wishes or resign. At the same time, the supporters of Crawford and R.J. Tennent did not scruple to use the issue of repeal against J.E. Tennent. Citing past statements critical of the operation of the Union by J.E. Tennent, they tried to undermine their opponent by suggesting that he had been an advocate of repeal in the past.[87]

The ability of Belfast reformers to sidestep the issue of repeal depended not only on the willingness of Belfast reformers to disregard the issue, but also on the forbearance of Daniel O'Connell. Elsewhere in Ireland during the general election of 1832, O'Connell, estranged from the Whig administration of Lord Grey, had required a pledge of support for repeal from all the reform candidates in the constituencies that he could control. He also tried to use his influence to press candidates for pledges to support repeal in almost every constituency outside of Ulster.[88] In Ulster, however, O'Connell did not force the issue. This forbearance by O'Connell made the cooperation between Catholic and Protestant reformers possible, but the question was would such a coalition succeed?

In Belfast in 1832 it did not. Chichester and Emerson Tennent were returned at the head of the poll. Although the candidates of the Belfast Reform Society received almost all the votes of the Catholic reformers, a large number of Presbyterians voted for Chichester and J.E. Tennent. Was this defection among the Presbyterians, however, a victory for conservatives? The nature of the support for J.E. Tennent is difficult to gauge. The most conservative element in Belfast, represented by the *Guardian and Constitutional Advocate*, was unwilling to support J.E. Tennent, asking 'Why seat one radical for the sake of unseating another?'[89] On the other hand, J.E. Tennent was supported by the then moderate *Belfast News-Letter*. Indeed, the young editor of the paper, James McKnight, played a critical role in convincing J.E. Tennent to persevere in his candidacy. The *News-Letter*'s primary motivation was not, apparently, a desire either to injure the cause of reform or to advance conservative principles. McKnight characterized his opposition to the official reform candidates as being motivated by a refusal to submit to the 'dictation' of the 'Natural

85 Ibid., 21 Jan. 1831. 86 *NW*, 27 Aug. 1832. 87 Ibid., 4 Oct. 1832. 88 O. MacDonagh, *The emancipist* (London, 1989), pp 72–4. 89 *NW*, 27 Sept. 1832.

Leaders', as he described the committee that had chosen Crawford and R.J. Tennent. McKnight further confessed to somewhat regretting this decision because the 'Natural Leaders' had 'done good service to Belfast, and to the community at large'.[90]

McKnight's distaste for the 'Natural Leaders' was likely in part theological as well as political. Born the son of a small farmer near Rathfriland, Co. Down, McKnight had studied at the Belfast Academical Institution with the intention of becoming a Presbyterian minister. Of modest means, McKnight had worked while pursuing his education, first for a short term as librarian of the Belfast Society for Promoting Knowledge (better known as the Linen Hall Library) during 1826 and then as editor of the *Belfast News-Letter* from the spring of 1827. Although some of his fellow students had abandoned their clerical vocations because of the efforts to establish orthodoxy among students for the ministry, McKnight, an orthodox Trinitarian, had passed his examination by the theological committee of the Synod of Ulster in 1828. In the meantime, McKnight had developed, in his words, 'a rooted dislike of Theology as a profession' because of having witnessed and reported on the dramatic contest between Henry Cooke and Henry Montgomery at Cookstown in 1828.

Despite his orthodoxy and confession to being 'a fiery Zealot for Protestantism', McKnight opposed Cooke and 'his detestable overtures' that had forced 'honest, independent, and event talented young men', such as his future rival at the *Northern Whig*, James Simms, from the Synod of Ulster. On the other hand, he had no love for Henry Montgomery either, blaming him for having done more 'to raise Cooke, and to create sympathy in his favour' than Cooke himself 'could have done in a century'.[91] McKnight's role in 1832 led contemporaries and later scholars to conclude that conservatives were the real force behind J.E. Tennent's candidacy. This conclusion is seemingly supported by J.E. Tennent's own subsequent description of events in a letter to his son, written nearly twenty-five years after the fact, in which Tennent laments the effects of the feud that developed between him and the 'natural leaders' in Belfast upon his career. Even Tennent's own confession that his conduct was 'a virtual desertion my own party' and 'positive junction with their enemies' should be considered as a retrospective simplification of events. Some of the opponents of the 'natural leaders' that Tennent cooperated with subsequently formed the nucleus of a much stronger conservative party in Belfast. Such a party, however, did not exist yet.[92]

90 The orthography of McKnight's surname was variable. At this time M'Neight or McNeight seem to have been the accepted forms with M'Knight being adopted later. McKnight is the form followed here in accordance with modern practice. Letter from James M'Neight to Miss Barber dated 1 Jan. 1833, from Presbyterian Historical Society of Ireland, *Extracts from original letters of James McKnight, LL.D.* (Belfast, 1915–16), p. 8.   **91** Ibid., pp 5–6.   **92** Slater, 'Belfast politics', p. 37.

Emerson Tennent's strategy was to appeal to moderate opinion. He praised the accomplishment of parliamentary reform but declared that, 'the question now should be with every patriot *how best* to render that reform of *practical utility'*. Emerson Tennent also attacked the radical associations of Crawford and R.J. Tennent by denouncing the 'headstrong *revolutionist'*, the 'phrenzied *leveller'*, and most importantly 'the fiery *republican*, ready to bring ruin upon himself and his country, in the wild attempt to give practical effect to the fanciful abstractions of boyhood, or to sanguine speculations on the possibility of reviving the departed glories of ancient Greece and Rome'.[93] The recurrent theme of the violence of the 1790s was still resonant in 1832. In 1832, a member of the committee for Crawford and R.J. Tennent, C.H. Teeling, had published a sequel to his personal account of the 1798 rebellion that resulted in a public controversy when the widow of one of the supposed insurgents, the Presbyterian minister Samuel Barber, publicly refuted Teeling's sympathetic account of the rebels along with the assertion of Barber's involvement with insurrection.[94] Emerson Tennent also emphasized his independence. He was 'unfettered and unpledged' except for one issue – repeal.[95] Emerson Tennent's pledge to oppose repeal almost certainly helped him with the sizeable number of Presbyterian liberals whose aversion to repeal was sufficiently intense to prevent them from cooperating in any broad coalition where the question of the Union was ambiguous.

In the general elections of 1835 and 1837 cooperation between the Presbyterian and Catholic reformers was made possible again because O'Connell temporarily abandoned the repeal agitation. When Sir Robert Peel formed a conservative government in November 1834, O'Connell decided upon a policy of cooperation with Whigs and reformers of all shades. Eventually, this cooperation resulted in the so-called Lichfield House compact whereby O'Connell agreed to give up the agitation for repeal for the promise of Liberal support for reform in Ireland. In Ulster, this cooperation took the form of active support for reform candidates who were not repealers. For example, O'Connell provided a seat at Dundalk for W.S. Crawford. In addition, O'Connell acted with great sensitivity to the conditions in Ulster. O'Connell's determination not to alienate Protestant reformers, for example, was made evident by his declining invitations to visit Belfast and Derry at this time. On receiving invitations to public dinners from Catholic and Protestant reformers, O'Connell expressed his gratitude for their consideration but declined 'lest the dinner should be considered in a party light, and increase, instead of, as I should wish, diminish party spirit'.[96]

---

93 *BNL*, 2 Oct. 1832.   94 C.H. Teeling, *Sequel to personal narrative of the 'Irish rebellion' of 1798* (Belfast, 1832); *BNL*, 14 Dec. 1832.   95 *NW*, 27 Sept. 1832.   96 *NW*, 28 Sept. 1837.

As a result of these changed circumstances, at the general election in January 1835 the liberals in Belfast were somewhat more successful. Although Emerson Tennent was returned at the head of the poll, the reformers were able elect John McCance, a wealthy linen merchant, and chairman of the Northern Banking Company, in place of Lord Arthur Chichester.[97] Unfortunately McCance died before the year was out, and at the by-election in August 1835, the liberal candidate R.J. Tennent was defeated by the conservative George Dunbar. The limited success of liberals during this period was attributable to one fact – repeal was no longer a serious issue. O'Connell's decision to abandon repeal and test the union permitted the reform candidates to speak unequivocally on that issue. McCance had been unequivocal in his opposition to repeal, and at the by-election in 1835 R.J. Tennent explained that in 1832 he, reluctantly, had acted on the injudicious advice of friends with regard to repeal. He had been opposed to repeal then and was still convinced that such a policy would be impracticable and injurious.[98] In this way, R.J. Tennent hoped to gain the support of those Presbyterian reformers whose scruples concerning repeal led them to support Emerson Tennent. O'Connell's foregoing of repeal likewise insured that, despite this unequivocal rejection of that policy by their Presbyterian allies, the Catholic reformers of Belfast would remain constant in their support.

Along with the victory of McCance in January of 1835, Ulster reformers were gratified that W.S. Crawford was compensated for his efforts in Belfast in 1832 by being returned for Dundalk, a virtual pocket borough of O'Connell. Before Crawford entered parliament for Dundalk in early 1835, O'Connell and Crawford thought very highly of one another. Soon after Crawford entered parliament, however, the relationship between the two became strained. Crawford, despite the fact that he had been provided with a seat by O'Connell, was openly critical of O'Connell's willingness to compromise with the Melbourne government on the question of tithes by accepting commutation instead of abolition. By 1837 O'Connell finally became exasperated by Crawford's continued public criticism of both the ministry and his own policies that he decided to break with Crawford. In a letter to Crawford, on January 17, 1837, O'Connell bluntly explained that, 'hostility to the Mulgrave government of Ireland is in my humble opinion tantamount to hostility to the People of Ireland' and would certainly 'find few responses amongst the hitherto misgoverned Irish nation'.[99] The break between the two was complete, and the O'Connellite electors of Dundalk sought Crawford's resignation. Crawford accused the group of acting as the 'executioners' of O'Connell's 'anathema'.[1]

---

97 H. Montgomery, *A funeral sermon of the death of John McCance* (Belfast, 1835).   98 *NW,* 27 Aug. 1835.   99 D. O'Connell, Kilkenny to W.S. Crawford, Crawfordsburn, 17 Jan. 1837, Crawford papers, PRONI, D856/D/53.   1 *NW,* 28 Jan. 1837.

The dispute between O'Connell and Crawford has often been ascribed to Crawford being, as were so many radicals, overly 'independent and crotchety'. In his biography of O'Connell, Oliver MacDonagh asserts 'O'Connell dismissed Crawford as the sort of visionary who would invariably sacrifice an achievable good for an impossible ideal'.[2] Crawford's correspondence, however, makes it clear that there was more than an abstract idealism involved in his opposition. When a difference arose between O'Connell and Crawford over the coercion bill introduced in the summer of 1835 to provide extraordinary powers for the repression of disturbances in Meath, Crawford wrote to his son – 'It will be great sport to our Northern Friends if we should be on opposite sides: I have no objection at all that they should perceive I am not one of the Tail'.[3] Crawford believed it no great political disadvantage to distance himself occasionally from O'Connell. By the end of 1835 relations between the two reformers were rapidly approaching the point of no return. In late December, Crawford described to his son the reaction in Ulster to a public letter by him critical of O'Connell's position on the tithe question published during December 1835.[4] 'The letter', he explained, 'has attracted public attention more than anything I ever published – and I think it will be highly important in increasing my influence in Ulster – because it will be clearly manifest that I am not a joint of the Tail of the Great man'.[5] Crawford's differences with O'Connell had as much to do with how they would affect public opinion in his favour in Ulster as with principles.

In the general election of 1837, the Belfast reformers once again concentrated their efforts upon conciliating the more moderate reformers. They fielded a candidate, James Gibson, whose opposition to repeal had always been vocal. They paired Gibson with a moderate Whig, Lord Belfast, representing the Donegall interest. In the end the reformers plan succeeded. Gibson and Belfast were returned, though they were later unseated on petition.[6] The reformers' policy of conciliating cautious Protestant reformers, however, resulted in an increasing resentment among Catholic reformers who provided a significant portion of the liberal voting strength but did not feel they were commensurately rewarded.[7]

This resentment was not expressed overtly until the spring of 1839 when Charles Gavan Duffy launched the Catholic newspaper the *Vindicator*. The liberal coalition was severely tested by Duffy and his successor's caustic attacks upon their Presbyterian allies but survived until O'Connell again declared for

2 MacDonagh, *The emancipist,* p. 154. 3 W.S. Crawford, London to J.S. Crawford, date unknown [between 31 July 1835 and 5 Aug. 1835], Crawford papers, PRONI, D856/D/37. 4 *NW,* 2 Dec. 1835. 5 W.S. Crawford, Crawfordsburn, Co. Down to J.S. Crawford, care of New York, 31 Dec. 1835, Crawford papers, PRONI, D856/D/44. 6 I. Budge and C. O'Leary, *Belfast* (1973), pp 46–7. 7 Brooke, *Ulster Presbyterianism,* pp 182–3.

repeal in April 1840. The results of the break-up of the liberal coalition of Presbyterians and Catholics were soon made evident in 1841 and 1842. First, whereas in 1835 O'Connell had declined invitations to visit Ulster, in January 1841 he made a celebrated visit to Belfast to launch the campaign for repeal in Ulster. The visit was denounced by virtually all Presbyterian reformers. Then, in the general election of 1841, the liberal candidates Lord Belfast and David Robert Ross were easily defeated by the conservatives James Emerson Tennent and William G. Johnston. When the two conservatives were unseated on petition, Belfast reformers arranged to share the constituency with their former conservative enemies, each party taking a seat.[8] This arrangement endured for a decade, and marked the end of any Catholic political influence in the constituency for more than twenty-five years.

The disastrous effects of repeal upon the parliamentary hopes of the liberal cause in Ulster were made even more evident when local rather than parliamentary politics are considered. Belfast in the 1830s had the reputation of being a liberal town. The political strength of the liberals was evident in their dominance of those local bodies that provided the essential services for the town. The care of the poor, the development of the port and harbour, and the general maintenance of services over the course of time had been all assigned respectively to the Belfast Charitable Society, the Ballast Board and the bicameral improvement commission comprised of the Police Commission and Police Committee.[9] Reformers dominated all of these bodies. The Belfast Charitable Society was a voluntary association whose leadership was primarily made up of reformers. The society was a civic outlet for those growing mercantile and industrial interests that were excluded from the closed municipal corporation. The Ballast Board and improvement commission were incorporated institutions that included an elective element chosen by ratepayers of varying qualifications. The liberals dominated these bodies as well. For example, in 1837 the newly reformed Ballast Board, or 'Corporation for preserving and improving the Port and Harbour of Belfast', as it was officially known, comprised eighteen members – the Lord of the Castle of Belfast, the Sovereign of Belfast, and sixteen elected members.[10] Among the elected portion of the board in 1837, the Liberals outnumbered the conservatives by nearly two to one.[11] Numbered among them were most of the leading reformers, including the dominant personality in the selection of the parliamentary candidates for Belfast in 1832 and 1835, Robert Grimshaw.

The bicameral constitution of the improvement commission in Belfast has

8 Budge and O'Leary, *Belfast*, pp 48–9. 9 R.M.W. Strain, *Belfast and its Charitable Society* (London, 1961), pp 15–16. 10 D.J. Owen, *A short history of the port of Belfast* (Belfast, 1917), p. 32. 11 *Ulster Times*, 7 Nov. 1837.

been described previously. In November 1837 five seats on the Police Commission were bitterly contested by liberals and conservatives. Though the margin was narrow, liberals won all five seats, and among their number was the twice-defeated parliamentary candidate Robert J. Tennent.[12] On the Police Committee, the liberals had maintained a majority of about three to one between the years 1827 and 1832. During the election for the Police Commission, John Bates, a conservative activist, complained that this was precisely the kind of exclusion denounced by liberals with regard to the municipal corporation.

In Belfast, the resurrection of the issue of repeal proved almost as politically ruinous to the reformers on the local level as it had been on the parliamentary level. When the election for the first reformed municipal corporation in Belfast was held in the autumn of 1842, the reformers of Belfast were sanguine about the outcome. The *Northern Whig* looked forward to a liberal majority being elected and the equally optimistic *Vindicator* stated that Catholics would settle for nothing less than eight of the forty seats on the council as a their fair portion. The *Whig* denounced the demand as both sectarian and divisive. The inability of the Presbyterian and Catholic reformers to accommodate each other proved to be politically disastrous for both. The technicalities of the registration were neglected by the divided reformers and the conservatives won all forty seats on the new council. After this first victory the conservatives established a political machine powerful enough to prevent the election of a single liberal of any creed for another thirteen years.

The fortunes of Belfast liberalism in the decade 1832–42 were a portent of the future. Ulster liberals, though they represented a sizeable and influential portion of the community, depended upon a delicate coalition of Presbyterians and Catholics for any hope of translating their substantial economic and social influence into political power. This delicate coalition could be wrecked at any time by the issue of repeal. From the beginning in 1832, it was clear repeal would not only divide Presbyterian and Catholic reformers, but also divide Presbyterians themselves. When repeal was not a serious threat, Presbyterians followed a middle path between repeal and conservatism. If, however, repeal were a threat, the Presbyterian reformers were divided between those who chose to pursue to the middle path and those, perhaps the majority, who were willing to cooperate with the conservatives in order to preserve the Union.

12 Ibid.

Challenges to traditional authority: local government

Fortunately for Ulster liberals, when the issue of repeal complicated their chances to win parliamentary seats important changes in local government afforded them new opportunities. These changes were in part the result of the unpopularity and inefficiency of the existing institutions. The corruption and incompetence of municipal corporations in Ireland has been thoroughly studied and described. The shortcomings of the system of private bills for improvement commissions that might have served as an alternative to municipal corporations was illustrated in the history of the police commission in Belfast. Dissatisfaction with private bills led to increased opposition. Of the five improvement bills proposed in Ulster between 1820 and 1832, four were opposed in parliament by some segment of the communities concerned. Over time even the established improvement commissions were no longer compliant tools of a local patron or oligarchy. In Derry during the 1830s a coalition of Protestant and Catholic liberals 'made some initial progress in capturing control from the Tories of the police committee'.[13] Elections for improvement commissions in both Belfast and Derry had become party contests by the 1830s.[14]

In addition to the evidence that proposed improvement bills were increasingly contested and established improvement commissions politicized, recent research outside Ulster demonstrates that improvement commissions also became regarded as a means to oppose close corporations. In Limerick a coalition of Protestants and Catholics successfully by-passed the close corporation by means of a series of local acts that included an improvement commission.[15] They established an area outside the authority of the corporation, the so-called Newtown Pery. The wealth and trade of this enclave subsequently surpassed the area of the city controlled by the corporation and efforts were made to bring the entire city under an improvement commission.[16] In July 1823 the liberals in Limerick succeeded, at an estimated cost of £30,000, in passing the Limerick Regulation Act that reformed the old corporation and 'amounted to a virtual appropriation by the Newtown of the medieval core'.[17]

Protracted and costly struggles like that of Limerick encouraged reformers elsewhere to search for alternative means of dealing with the both the practical and the political problems of municipal government. It was in Newry that an

---

13 Murphy, *Derry, Donegal and modern Ulster*, p. 50. 14 *Ulster Times*, 2 Nov. 1837; *Londonderry Sentinel*, 16 Sept. 1837. 15 É. O'Flaherty, 'Urban politics and municipal reform in Limerick, 1723–62', *Eighteenth-Century Ireland: Iris an dá chultúr*, 6 (1991), 106. 16 Ibid.; M. Potter, *The government and people of Limerick, 1197–2006* (2006), p. 270. 17 M. Lenihan, *Limerick; its history and antiquities* (Dublin, 1884), p. 461; O'Flaherty, 'Urban politics and municipal reform in Limerick', 106.

important change in local government was accomplished. During the first half of the eighteenth century Newry had prospered. That prosperity was aided by the comparatively benevolent proprietorship of the Needham family who supported important commercial improvements, such as the channelling of the Newry river.[18] By the nineteenth century, however, the Needham family's domination of local affairs was increasingly at odds with social and political developments. The history of the efforts of the Needham interest to maintain its influence in Newry demonstrated significant changes in the role of public opinion in society.

The Needham interest was handicapped by the lack of a municipal corporation in Newry that might be controlled in the manner of the Belfast corporation. This want of a municipal instrument was especially felt after 1806 when William Needham died without obvious heirs and bequeathed his estate to a distant English cousin, Robert Needham, the then Viscount Kilmorey.[19] In 1811 the politically ambitious Viscount Kilmorey proposed an improvement commission in the hope of strengthening his political influence, particularly in Newry itself where elections for the open and unruly borough seat had proven costly, with the patronage such an institution might afford.[20] The proposal became ensnared in the rivalry between the Stewart and Downshire families for control of the parliamentary representation in Co. Down.[21] The Downshire interest, fearing that the proposed improvement commission could be used to aid their rivals, orchestrated the opposition to the bill. Indeed, a leading opponent of the bill in Newry confessed that 'but for your Lordship, we should have been without any knowledge of the proceedings on the bill'.[22] The meeting that resulted in the abandonment of the proposal had the appearance of a contest between aristocratic interests mobilizing their retainers rather than a forum for deliberation and the expression of public opinion.[23]

Kilmorey also had to contend with Newry's increasingly prosperous and assertive commercial and professional classes. Their growing restiveness was demonstrated in November 1816 when the Needham interest arranged a town meeting to express support for Lord Castlereagh, then foreign secretary in the Liverpool administration, during his visit to Ireland. The proposed meeting was arranged in the customary fashion. The seneschal of the manor, chief

---

18 Canavan, *Frontier town*, pp 75–6, 90. 19 Ibid., p. 116. 20 V. Crossman, *Local government in nineteenth-century Ireland* (Belfast, 1994), p. 65. 21 For the competing interests in Newry in particular see the history of the constituency in Thorne (ed.), *The history of parliament*, 5 vols (London, 1986), ii, p. 647; for an account of the enmity between the Downshire and Stewart interests that affected politics throughout Co. Down see W.A. Maguire, *The Downshire estates in Ireland, 1801–1845* (Oxford, 1972), pp 7–10. 22 Patrick O'Hanlon to Arthur Hill, 3rd marquess of Downshire, PRONI, D671/C/12/83. 23 Crossman, *Local government*, p. 65.

magistrate of the town and representative of the Needham interest, solicited a requisition for a meeting from a few trustworthy inhabitants. The requisition was then posted at a strategic municipal locus, in this case a wall in the private news-room maintained by subscribers from the commercial and professional classes. Few inhabitants had access to that location as entrance without a subscription was punishable by a fine.[24] The notice was not published in the local newspaper.

The Needham interest did not intend the meeting to be a public, deliberative expression of the opinions of the inhabitants. After the defeat of its improvement proposals in 1811, they intended to convene an essentially private meeting. By publishing the address of the select gathering as the outcome of a public meeting, the Needham interest hoped to safely demonstrate their influence and authority. Some of Newry's inhabitants had differing conceptions of the procedures and significance of public meetings. After the seneschal peremptorily arranged the approval of the address before a score of men gathered in the news-room, a few dissidents criticized the gathering for being both insufficiently advertised and conducted in a private place, a 'coffee room', despite claiming to represent the 'inhabitants of Newry'. When the seneschal attempted to adjourn the meeting ten minutes after it began, he was chided by a Mr O'Hanlon for forgetting that he was a 'servant of the public' who should remain in the chair until he was voted from it by a majority of the meeting. It was further asserted that in order for the 'wisdom of public councils' to remedy 'public evils' it was necessary for the inhabitants to express themselves freely and truthfully 'as rational men should speak' rather than simply approving or disapproving resolutions.[25] The meeting and the address were abandoned in the face of this opposition.

The differences between the two meetings resemble developments described in a number of European societies by Jürgen Habermas. Previously public gatherings were occasions where rulers 'represented their lordship not for but "before" the people'. They were characterized by ritual and pageantry intended to emphasize the status and authority of the ruler. By the late eighteenth and early nineteenth century public meetings became occasions when 'private people, come together to form a public, readied themselves to compel public authority to legitimate itself before public opinion'.[26] Such meetings were intended to be deliberative rather than ritual.

The Needham interest did not abandon its hope of increasing its influence. In September 1823, they formulated another private bill for an improvement

24 *The Exile,* 11 Jan. 1817. 25 Ibid. The O'Hanlon in question was almost certainly Patrick O'Hanlon. 26 J. Habermas, *The structural transformation of the public sphere* (Cambridge, MA, 1989), pp 8, 25.

commission.[27] This proposed body was, its opponents complained, 'designed to procure for its author, and his successors, an inordinate accession of patronage and influence'. The body was to be bicameral, composed of 21 police commissioners and a police committee with 13 members. The first members of both bodies were to be appointed; 'absolutely nominated' by the Needham interest according to the bill's critics. Furthermore, 8 of the 21 members of the police commission were to be *ex officio*, consisting of 6 officials directly connected with the Needham interest – the lord of the manor, the member for parliament, the seneschal, the land agent for the estate, and the 2 churchwardens. Mindful that the Downshire interest had wrecked earlier improvement plans, Needham also now included the marquess of Downshire and his land agent as the other two *ex officio* members of the proposed improvement commission. The *ex officio* provisions coupled with significant financial requirements for both the municipal office and municipal franchise convinced critics that the bill would ensure 'complete and absolute dominion' by the Needham interest.[28]

The Needham interest attempted to quash any public debate on the proposals of 1823 by having the seneschal deny a requisition for an official meeting to consider the bill.[29] In response, opponents organized a committee and quickly presented a petition to parliament in March 1824 with the help of the prominent British liberal Henry Brougham.[30] The bill was eventually abandoned in the face of this organized opposition, but the inhabitants of Newry hoped to secure their victory by obtaining legislation 'generally applicable to the Police of Towns' like Newry. This legislation was to be based on already existing statutes of the former Irish parliament and founded on the principle 'that in the people at large, who supply the funds, should reside the substantial controul over the expenditure'.[31]

The primary architect of this strategy was Patrick O'Hanlon.[32] O'Hanlon's career illustrates the neglect by historians of those practical men, who after their experience of radical politics in the 1790s, adopted new strategies for reform. Born in 1771, O'Hanlon was descended from an influential Catholic family involved in the linen trade.[33] O'Hanlon took up the law and in 1796 was the first Catholic in Ulster called to the bar after the legal profession was opened to Catholics in 1793.[34] O'Hanlon's family was associated with radical politics during the 1790s. In August 1792, they cooperated with a mission by Wolfe Tone to soothe sectarian tensions in Co. Down, and two brothers of

27 *Journals of the House of Commons*, vol. 79, 5 Mar. 1824, pp 126–7. **28** *Documents relative to Lord Killmorey's intended police bill for the town of Newry* (Newry, 1824), pp 7–8, appendix II. **29** *NCT*, 19 Aug. 1828. **30** *Journals of the House of Commons*, vol. 79, 5 Mar. 1824, pp 126–7; *NCT*, 19 Aug. 1828. **31** *NCT*, 19 Aug. 1828. **32** *Documents relative to Lord Killmorey's intended police bill*, p. 11. **33** E. Keane et al., *King's Inns admission papers, 1607–1867* (Dublin, 1982), p. 380; *BNL*, 18–21 June 1793. **34** *BNL*, 13–16 May 1796.

Patrick, Hugh and Felix, later fled Ireland as suspected United Irishmen, at least one and possibly both serving with the French.[35]

In September 1792, Patrick O'Hanlon was secretary at a meeting in Newry to found a Union Society dedicated to lessening sectarian tensions.[36] Unlike many other places, in Newry the society does not seem to have become a compliant adjunct to the United Irishmen. Instead, in December 1792 the Newry Union Society aligned itself with the more moderate Friends of the Constitution, Liberty and Peace that included Joseph Pollock among its members.[37] Patrick O'Hanlon escaped the 1790s with his reputation relatively undamaged. This was perhaps because he was away from Ulster at times during the 1790s. He was admitted to Lincoln's Inn in London in 1794 and seems to have remained in England at least until March 1798 when he married the daughter of an Irish banking family from Liverpool that became connected to the Holland House Whigs.[38] After returning to Ireland, O'Hanlon abandoned the law for commerce and was appointed to the magistracy where he achieved some notoriety by being twice removed and then restored to the bench. O'Hanlon's difficulties were related to his support for Catholic emancipation and the reputations of his brothers. O'Hanlon's restoration to the bench was a *cause célèbre* among Whigs and radicals in parliament. Noted politicians such as Henry Brougham, Henry Parnell, Sir John Newport, Leonard Horner and George Ponsonby spoke on his behalf.[39]

O'Hanlon called upon his political allies to help defeat the Needham bill and to assist in framing alternative legislation. With the help of his son Hugh Marmaduke O'Hanlon, a barrister in London, O'Hanlon's plan for a public bill for municipal improvements was eventually supported by government. After a four-and-a-half-year struggle, the first town commission in the United Kingdom was established in Newry in 1828. The town commissions were expected to provide the services and regulations necessary for increasingly complex urban life in an unprecedented manner. Under the act any twenty-one inhabitants of a town who occupied houses valued by the parish vestry at more than £20 per annum could petition the lord lieutenant for permission to hold a meeting to consider adopting all or part of the act. All the inhabitants occupying houses valued at £5 or more per annum would deliberate, and a simple majority could establish a town commission.[40] Rejection of the act at the

35 T. Wolfe Tone, *Life of Theobald Wolfe Tone*, ed. T. Bartlett (Dublin, 1998), p. 143; J. Trail to Major General Sir Arthur Wellesley, University of Southampton, WP1/173/14; Elliott, *Partners in Revolution* p. 249. 36 *BNL*, 11–14 Sept. 1792. 37 *Northern Star*, 2–5 Jan. 1793. 38 *The Records of the Honorable Society of Lincoln's Inn*, 2 vols (London, 1896), i, p. 550; C.W. Heckethorn, *Lincoln's Inn Fields and the localities adjacent: their historical and topographical associations* (London, 1896), p. 224; *ODNB*, William Smyth, www.oxforddnb. com, accessed 17 Jan. 2008. 39 *Freeman's Journal*, 18 June 1816. 40 An Act to make

meeting precluded any re-application for three years. Once approved, the qualified inhabitants defined the boundaries of the municipality and decided upon the number of commissioners appropriate for the town, at least 9 but not more than 21. The property qualification for election to a three-year term as commissioner was the occupation of a house valued at £20 or more per annum. The franchise for the triennial elections was extended to all inhabitants occupying a house valued at £5 or more per annum.

The potential powers of the town commissions were considerable. Even before undertaking the basic functions of cleansing, lighting and watching outlined in the title of the act, the town commissioners were 'immediately on their entering into office' required to appoint professionals to survey, 'with an estimate and a valuation of the fully improved yearly value', all of the property in the town. Town commissions might purchase lamps and lamp posts; employ watchmen and construct bridewells; pave and clean streets; supply water by well, pipe or pump; construct and inspect sewers and drains; name streets and number houses. With the approval of the lord lieutenant towns might even construct and operate their own gas or water works. To pay for these services the commissions were permitted to strike a limited rate with established proportions for ratepayers of differing valuations. All residences, shops, warehouses, cellars, mills, yards and gardens valued at £5 or more were subject to taxation, but land used for agriculture was exempt. To enforce payment the commissions could bring recalcitrant ratepayers before the local magistrates in order to seize and sell the offender's property. To carry out these functions the town commissioners held monthly meetings and appointed a treasurer, a clerk, a collector, and other lesser servants such as scavengers, lamplighters and watchmen.[41] The right to participate in local government was verified by oath and subject to appeal.

The town commission was a radical political departure in local government both for the United Kingdom as a whole and for Ireland in particular. It was an attempt to ensure that the broad interests of towns were served rather than the narrow desires of aristocratic patrons or local oligarchies. This was accomplished in three ways. First, the town commission was one of the earliest examples of permissive legislation intended to provide simple, inexpensive paradigms for the creation of local institutions. This was in contrast to the complicated, expensive and increasingly ineffective private bill system for improvement commissions. Any town in Ireland, even those with municipal corporations, could establish a town commission without significant expense. This model would later be adopted for towns in Britain as well. Second, and

Provision for the lighting, cleansing, and watching of Cities, Towns Corporate and Market Towns in Ireland, in certain cases, 9 Geo. IV, c. 82. **41** 9 Geo. IV, c. 82.

even more radically, the town commission established the principle of broader representation in local government. As demonstrated by the Donegall proposals for Belfast and the Needham plans for Newry, the representative nature of an improvement commission, while in theory protected by the standing orders for private bills, was in practice largely dependent upon the will and influence of the sponsor. The franchise established for town commissions, although not democratic by modern standards, afforded a significant portion of the middle classes of Ulster their first opportunity to participate in local government.

The third radical departure of the town commission was the abandonment of a significant symbol of the Protestant Ascendancy in Ireland – the parish vestry.[42] As late as 1826, Robert Peel had described these assemblies 'as so many little parliaments in their several parishes'.[43] Certainly vestries were not limited to collecting money to support the established Church of Ireland. During the course of the eighteenth century the Irish parliament increasingly tried to provide for some of the temporal needs of growing towns and cities by means of the vestry.[44] One of the earliest examples of the creeping involvement of the vestry in urban improvements was the lighting of Irish cities. When the 1719 act for the lighting of Dublin, Cork and Limerick first made lighting a public issue rather than a private enterprise, the vestry was not at all involved. Inhabitants paid a fee, varying according to their proximity to the lamps, directly to contractors named in the legislation. However, because in Dublin this arrangement was perceived as 'unequal and buthensome to the poorer sort', an amending act of 1737 required the parishes in Dublin where lamps were erected to assemble the vestry and divide the expenses in proportion to the amount of minister's money, the urban equivalent to the tithe, paid by the inhabitants. The vestry could not determine the extent of the lighting or choose the contractors, but simply organized the payments. In 1741, the vestries in Cork and Limerick also became bill collectors for lighting, but the money was now paid to the respective municipal corporations.[45]

---

42 I have deliberately avoided the term 'civil parish' later adopted to delineate the historic parishes from the parochial systems of the Catholic church and the Church of Ireland that diverged for reasons of ecclesiastical administration. The term 'civil parish' is absent from the statutes of the period and contemporary legal treatises concerning the parish, such as that of John Finlay first published in 1824 or the earlier work by Edward Bullingbroke, *The duty and authority of justices of the peace and parish officers for Ireland* (Dublin, 1788). **43** *Hansard 2*, 21 Apr. 1826, xv, cc 553. **44** T. Barnard, 'The eighteenth-century parish', in FitzPatrick and Gillespie (eds), *The parish in medieval and early modern Ireland* (2006), pp 298, 307. **45** An act for erecting and continuing lights in the city of Dublin, and the several Liberties adjoining; and also in the cities of Cork and Limerick, and liberties thereof, 6 Geo. I, c. 18; An act for further explaining and amending the several acts of parliament now in force for erecting lamps in the city of Dublin and liberties thereof, 11 Geo. II, c. 19; An act to

With an act of 1759 the responsibilities of the vestry expanded beyond applotment to include at least the possibility of deliberation. The chief magistrates in cities and corporate towns, or the justices of the peace in market towns, were empowered to call a vestry to consider the question of lighting. This expansion of responsibility was part of an attempt to extend lighting to cities and towns beyond Dublin, Cork and Limerick. When the 1759 act did not meet expectations, a law introduced in 1765 required the ministers or curates of all towns without lighting to call a vestry to consider installing lamps. Although this requirement was backed by the threat of fines, the vestry continued to be such a poor instrument for local improvements that in 1774 another amending act allowed the mayor and common council of corporate towns where vestries neglect their obligations to assume the responsibilities of lighting for a year.[46]

The difficulty in using vestries in Ireland for the kinds of improvements often undertaken by vestries in England was that Catholics came to detest the vestry. Not only was the vestry a central part of the administrative machinery that compelled Catholics to support the established Church of Ireland, but the just over 2,400 parishes in Ireland were the most ubiquitous symbols of the Church of Ireland Ascendancy.[47] In some ways the vestry was more offensive than other exclusively Protestant institutions, such as the municipal corporations, because it maintained a pretence of representing all parishioners.[48] Before 1725, by common law, Catholics who paid church-rates might attend and vote at vestries. After that date, Catholics were forbidden by statute to vote on issues concerning Church of Ireland property or the election and payment of parish officers. According to John Finlay, the business of the parish ought to have been divided between two vestry meetings. At the first, the only issue was how much money was needed for the continued functioning of the Church of Ireland in the parish. Finlay suggested that Catholics might attend and even comment upon this process, at 'the discretion of the Church-wardens, or their Protestant brethren', but they could not vote. At the second meeting, all of the parishioners who paid church-rates might raise objections to the applotment, but only Protestants could vote on those objections. At the same time, all of the inhabitants who paid church-rates could, according to Finlay, deliberate and vote upon any issues dealing with temporal matters, such as lighting, watching or assistance for the poor.[49]

revive and amend an Act made in the sixth year of his late majesty King George the First, 15 Geo. II, c. 11. **46** An act for the more effectual enlightening of the city of Dublin and the liberties thereof; and for the erecting of public lights in the other cities; towns-corporate, and market-towns in the kingdom, 33 Geo. II, c. 18; An act for continuing, reviving, and amending several temporary statutes, 5 Geo. III, c. 15; An act for amending the laws relative to the lighting and cleansing of several cities, and for establishing market juries therein; and for other purposes, 13 & 14 Geo. III, c. 20. **47** Barnard, 'The eighteenth-century parish', p. 324. **48** Hill, *From patriots to unionists*, p. 174. **49** J. Finlay, *The office and duty of church-*

During the nineteenth century, supporters of Catholic emancipation frequently complained about the vestries. In his influential *Statement of the penal laws* published in 1812, Denys Scully contended that Catholics were often excluded from all vestry business, even those proceedings concerning temporal matters. 'This parochial tyranny' involved 'the middling and lower orders of Catholics in continual vexations and contests' that aggrieved them 'fully as much as the severest exactions, for even tithes or county cesses'.[50] These grievances along with the criticisms directed against them, whether in the hammering rhetoric of Scully or the subtle legalism of Finlay, made many vestries practically inoperable. Later, after the disestablishment of the Church of Ireland, the journalist James Godkin recalled the sordid conflicts of vestries assessing the church-rate:

> a sort of civil war raged in every parish in Ireland on Easter Monday, when the Roman Catholics assembled to denounce it, and to tell the chairman that he was not their pastor, but a tyrant, a persecutor and a robber.[51]

The legislation for the town commission was intended to distance the town commission from the disorder and discontent surrounding the vestry. When the first bill for town commissions was drafted in 1824, Hugh Marmaduke O'Hanlon had adopted some of the forms of the eighteenth-century legislation for improvements that relied upon the vestry. In particular, in the 1824 bill the inhabitants were to direct their request for a meeting to consider the act to the churchwardens. The churchwardens would then preside at the meeting. In addition, the valuations for the right to vote at the meeting were to be based on the rating of the parish vestry. When the final version of the bill became law in 1828, the requisition by the inhabitants was directed to the lord lieutenant who then ordered the chief magistrate to preside. The only reference to the vestry was the initial valuation needed to vote at the meeting. However, the first duty of a town commission upon entering office was to arrange its own valuation. Subsequently, the parish valuation was replaced by that of the poor law union for towns wishing to consider the act. The town commission was an important step in undoing the confessional aspect of local government in Ireland.

Over the course of the nineteenth century town commissions were established in a steadily increasing number of towns throughout Ireland, but during the first few decades of the legislation's existence towns in Ulster were

warden and parish officer in Ireland (Dublin, 1824), pp 298, 307.   **50** D. Scully, *A statement of the penal laws which aggrieve the Catholics of Ireland* (Dublin, 1824), p. 161.   **51** J. Godkin, *The religious history of Ireland: primitive, papal and protestant* (London, 1873), p. 250.

particularly quick to adopt this new form of local government. By the end of 1829, 18 town commissions were established in Ireland, 10 in Ulster.[52] (For the specific towns as well as increases over time, see Table 2.1 and Table 2.2.) Most of the town commissions established between 1828 and 1840 were in market towns rather than corporate towns. Two factors made market towns more likely than corporate towns to establish town commissions. First, without even the dubious blessing of a municipal corporation, many market towns lacked effective institutions to organize and to pay for the facilities and services needed to cope with increasing population, commercialization and industrialization. Second, market towns were not confronted with the well-established corporate interests tenaciously defending their privileges and authority. After 1840, municipal reform in Ireland would dramatically increase the number of corporate towns adopting town commissions. The municipal reform act stipulated that the property and functions of the thirty-eight corporations abolished throughout Ireland should be transferred to town commissions.[53] This transfer of municipal properties and duties resulted in a further series of disputes which provide interesting insights into the changing nature of Ulster society which will be described later.

The first town commissions created before municipal reform were established at a time when the issues of public opinion and its representation were being debated. Disagreements arose not only over matters of local policy, the specifics of providing services, but were also concerned with broader social and political issues. Citing a traditional radical criticism of the existing institutions as having operated for private rather than public benefit, Ulster liberals used the town commission to mount a surprisingly widespread, prolonged and effective challenge to the traditional, conservative order in Ulster towns.

Along with Newry, the politicization of the town commissions in market towns was evident in Lurgan. When the inhabitants of Lurgan considered establishment of a town commission in October 1828 political tensions in Ulster were particularly heightened. Lurgan was located in an area of Co. Armagh where Orangeism had 'found its most enthusiastic response' and the fear that it created was such that in July 1827 a local liberal magistrate, John Hancock, had been unable to find anyone willing to sign an affidavit that would have permitted action against an anticipated Orange procession.[54] In

52 *Return of the names of all cities and towns in Ireland, which have made application to the lord lieutenant for permission to adopt the provisions of the 9th Geo. IV c. 82*, HC 1829 (140), xxii, p. 1. 53 *Report from the select committee on local government and taxation of towns (Ireland); with the proceedings of the committee*, HC 1878 (262), xvi, p. v. 54 S. Gribbon, 'The social origins of Ulster Unionism' (1977), 69; John Hancock, Lurgan to Daniel O'Connell dated 6 July 1827, No. 1401 in M. O'Connell (ed.), *The correspondence of Daniel O'Connell*, 8 vols (Dublin, 1974), iii, pp 333–4.

Table 2.1: Town Commissions in Ireland, 1829–42

1829	1836	1842	
Banbridge	*Armagh*	*Armagh*	Bandon
Castleblayney	*Banbridge*	*Ballymena*	Callan
Coleraine	*Coleraine*	*Ballyshannon*	Carrick-on-Suir
Downpatrick	*Downpatrick*	*Banbridge*	Cashel
Limavady	*Dungannon*	*Belturbet*	Charleville
Lurgan	*Lurgan*	*Cavan*	Clonakilty
Newry	*Newry*	*Coleraine*	Clonmel
Omagh	*Portadown*	*Downpatrick*	Dundalk
Portadown	*Strabane*	*Dromore*	Ennis
Strabane	*Tandragee*	*Dungannon*	Fethard
Ballina	Bandon	*Lisburn*	Kinsale
Carrick-on-Suir	Carrick-on-Suir	*Lurgan*	Longford
Castlebar	Clonmel	*Monaghan*	Loughrea
Clonmel	Dundalk	*Newry*	Mallow
Kingstown	Longford	*Newtownards*	Maryborough
Longford	Tipperary	*Portadown*	Mitchelstown
Tullamore	Westport	*Strabane*	Nenagh
Westport	Youghal	*Tandragee*	Roscommon
		Athlone	Tipperary
		Athy	Tralee
		Ballinasloe	Wicklow
18 total	18 total	42 total	

Towns in **bold italics** in Ulster.
Sources: *Return of the names of all cities and towns in Ireland, which have made application to the lord lieutenant for permission to adopt the provisions of the 9th Geo. IV c. 82 […]*, HC 1829 (140), xxii; *Cities and towns improvement, Ireland*, HC 1836 (306), xlvii; *Return of the names of those towns in Ireland in which the act of 9 Geo. 4 c. 82 has been brought into operation wholly or in part*, HC 1843(632), L.

September 1828, the local Orangemen were particularly animated by a proposed mass meeting in favour of Catholic emancipation at nearby Ballybay, Co. Monaghan. The Orangemen threatened to use force to prevent this 'invasion' of Ulster. Under these tense circumstances the qualified inhabitants of Lurgan, with Hancock in the chair, met in October 1828 and agreed to establish a town commission. An alternative institution was proposed at the meeting. A group of local Orangemen called upon the local magnate, Lord Lurgan, to assist in establishing an institution the residents of Lurgan truly required – a Brunswick club – a conservative association opposed to Catholic emancipation. Lord Lurgan refused that honour, and instead he delivered a speech endorsing Catholic emancipation that, according to press reports, was cheered by the meeting.[55] In the context of Lurgan, the establishment of a town

55 *NCT*, 14 Oct. 1828.

Table 2.2: Town commissions in Ireland, 1852–76

1852

Armagh	*Monaghan*	Dundalk	
Aughnacloy	*Moy*	Ennis	
Ballymena	*Newry*	Enniscorthy	
Ballymoney	*Newtownards*	Fethard	
Ballyshannon	*Omagh*	Kells	
Banbridge	*Portadown*	Kinsale	
Belturbet	*Strabane*	Loughrea	
Castleblayney	*Tandragee*	Mallow	
Cavan	Ardee	Nenagh	
Coleraine	Athlone	New Ross	
Downpatrick	Athy	Parsonstown	
Dungannon	Ballinasloe	Roscommon	
Enniskillen	Bandon	Tipperary	
Holywood	Caher	Tralee	
Larne	Callan	Trim	
Limavady	Carrick-on-Suir	Tuam	
Lisburn	Cashel	Westport	
Lurgan	Clonakilty	Wicklow	
		Youghal	

55 total

1876

Antrim	*Dromore*	Athlone	Enniscorthy	Nenagh
Armagh*	*Dungannon**	Athy	Fermoy	New Ross
Aughnacloy	*Gilford*	Bagenalstown	*Fethard**	Newbridge
Ballybay	*Holywood*	Balbriggan	Gorey	Parsonstown
Ballymena	*Keady*	Ballina	Kells	Queenstown
Ballymoney	*Larne*	Ballinasloe	Killarney	Rathkeale
Ballyshannon	*Letterkenny*	*Bandon**	Killiney	Roscommon
Banbridge	*Limavady*	Boyle	Kinsale	Skibbereen
Bangor	*Lisburn*	Callan	Lismore	Templemore
Belturbet	*Lurgan*	Carlow	Longford	Thurles
Castleblayney	*Monaghan**	Carrickmacross	Loughrea	Tipperary
Cavan	*Newtownards*	Cashel	*Mallow**	*Tralee**
Clones	*Omagh**	Castlebar	Maryborough	Trim
Coleraine	*Portadown*	Clonakilty	Middleton	Tuam
Cookstown	*Strabane*	Dundalk	Mountmellick	Tullamore
Cootehill	*Tandragee*	Dungarvan	Mullingar	Westport
Downpatrick*	Ardee	Ennis	Naas	*Wicklow**
			Navan	Youghal

88 total

*In 1876 all towns with * still operating under 1828 act, remaining towns under 1854 act.
Towns in **bold italics** in Ulster.
Sources: *Return of the names of the several towns in Ireland for which town commissioners are now appointed under the act 9 Geo. 4. c. 82,* HC 1852–3 (678, 971), xciv; *Report from the select committee on local government and taxation of towns (Ireland)* HC 1876 (352), x.

commission was not merely a practical effort at improving sanitation and safety but also a pointedly political act.[56]

In other market towns the politicization of the town commission was more subtle. There was no explicit reference to party, public opinion or Catholic emancipation. Instead, conflicts over policy pitted town commissioners against the traditional social order within towns. For example, in Portadown a seemingly mundane matter of commerce resulted in a violent conflict between the town commissioners and the local gentry. Portadown was advantageously located on a navigable portion of the river Bann that connected it with the Newry canal. The combination of improvements in transportation and increased trade in grain during the late eighteenth and early nineteenth century transformed Portadown from a village of 'little importance' to a thriving town whose grain market was 'equal to any town in Ireland'.[57] Between 1821 and 1831 the population increased some sevenfold from a mere 231 to 1591. By 1841 the population had reached 2502 and continued to increase until by 1881 there were 7,850 inhabitants.[58] Like Lurgan, Portadown was located within the cockpit of Orangeism and while there is no record of controversy at the establishment of the town commission in October 1829 there was considerable controversy during its first term of office.

The genesis of the controversy was less than heroic. In September 1830 the town commission ordered the shambles removed from the open street, where it was a public nuisance, to an enclosure. Local opposition to the change resulted in a series of 'riots and disturbances'. After a riot in early 1831, a local magistrate and notorious Orange leader, William Blacker, threatened to prosecute a town commissioner who had tried to enforce the removal of the shambles from its customary location. The town commissioners construed Blacker's action as a challenge to their authority. In order to defend that authority, they decided to supervise the removal of the shambles from the street in person, defray the legal expenses of their fellow commissioner charged in the disturbances, and support the prosecution of those 'rioters' who had resisted their orders.[59] A seemingly inconsequential matter had resulted in a protracted and violent confrontation about the exercise of municipal authority.

The disputes in Portadown occurred in the context of the often violent resistance to the collection of tolls and customs at fairs and markets throughout Ireland. However, in Portadown these particular affrays were not a matter of

---

56 The issue of establishing town commissions was politicized elsewhere in Ireland as well. See the failure of the inhabitants of Cork to establish a town commission in *NCT*, 26 Sept. 1828.   57 Thomas Bradshaw (ed.), *The general directory of Newry* (Newry, 1819), p. 92; Lewis, *Topographical dictionary*, ii, p. 463.   58 W.E. Vaughan and A.J. Fitzpatrick, *Irish historical statistics: population, 1821–1971* (1978).   59 Portadown TC, 4 Mar. 1831, 4 Apr. 1831, LA/64/2B/1.

resistance to tolls and customs. These rioters were not striving to overthrow the town's status quo but rather to defend it. One of the leading opponents of the removal of the shambles from the main street was a local conservative who testified that the whole incident resulted from a neglect of the patent by the proprietor of the town, Lord Mandeville. That neglect allowed the town commissioners, some of whom were shareholders in a private market built in 1829, to compel 'parties to occupy the new market and pay a revenue'.[60] The affair was cast as an aristocrat's ill-considered abandonment of his rights and duties that benefited a usurping merchant oligarchy. As it turned out the private company constructed a 'large and commodious market-place, with shambles and every requisite' that was the only enclosed market facility in the town.[61] In Portadown it was the 'new men' who were exerting their increasing power over local affairs.

The town commission established in Downpatrick in February 1829 was usually distinguished by an indolent tranquillity. The stakes were small. The town had only adopted the provisions regarding lighting, and there were few 'new men' to disturb matters. Downpatrick's economy was stagnant, and unlike other towns in Ulster its population decreased during the nineteenth century.[62] Even in Downpatrick, however, there was evidence of social and political conflict surrounding the town commission. When the royal commissioners investigating municipal corporations visited Downpatrick in October 1833 to gather information regarding the defunct corporation, the chairman of the town commission, Aynsworth Pilson, testified that he believed that the chairman of the town commission ought to be made a magistrate. This reform was needed because the local 'Magistrates are not very well disposed to support the [town] Commissioners in carrying the provisions of the Act into operation'.[63] Indeed in 1832, the town commission hired a lawyer to prove 'their right to remove nuisances or levy fines for the non-removal of such'.[64] Pilson ascribed this lack of cooperation to the fact that the act establishing town commissions 'has been considered too popular' by some magistrates.[65]

It is not possible to determine simply and precisely how many of the nine town commissions in market towns in Ulster were politicized. The town commissions at Newry and Lurgan were clearly politicized. Likewise Portadown was the scene of considerable controversy. Even in Downpatrick there was evidence of the growing importance of the middle classes in Ulster politics. Unfortunately, in the cases of Banbridge, Limavady, Omagh and

---

60 *Report of the commissioners appointed to inquire into the state of the fairs and markets in Ireland, part II, minutes of evidence*, HC 1854–5 (1910), xix, pp 345–52. 61 Lewis, *Topographical dictionary*, ii, p. 63. 62 Royle, 'Industrialization, urbanization and urban society', pp 286–9. 63 *BNL*, 29 Oct. 1833. 64 Downpatrick TC, 11 Jan. 1832, PRONI, LA/31/2B/1. 65 *BNL*, 29 Oct. 1833.

Tandragee the extant records date from later periods. In Castleblayney it is unclear whether any records have survived. Yet, it is significant that in every case where records have survived there was evidence of the increasing influence of public opinion in Ulster local politics.

Town commissions were also perceived as an instrument of reform in corporate towns. In 1833 the royal commissioners investigating municipal corporations in Ireland described 17 corporations in Ulster. Of those 17, 13 were described as functioning – Armagh, Bangor, Belfast, Belturbet, Carrickfergus, Coleraine, Dungannon, Enniskillen, Hillsborough, Killyleagh, Derry, Monaghan and Strabane. The remaining 4 corporations, Cavan, Charlemont, Lifford and Newtownards were vestigial; their activities limited to some minor exercise of municipal functions such as controlling remnants of corporate property. Of the 13 functioning corporations in Ulster only 2, Carrickfergus and Monaghan, were 'open' corporations where the freemen had some role in the election of corporate officers and the management of corporate affairs. The remaining corporations were controlled by landed magnates or oligarchies and subject to the kinds of abuses and inefficiencies that the royal commissioners ascribed to the withdrawal of 'the management and direction of municipal affairs from the control and vigilance of the community'.[66] Critics of the Irish corporations, including the royal commissioners, went so far as to suggest that town commissions might replace corporations entirely.[67] In the abortive municipal reform bill brought before parliament in 1836, town commissions were proposed as a replacement for all of the existing corporations.[68] When municipal reform became reality this plan was essentially adopted for all but ten of the corporations in Ireland.

Of the 17 corporate towns in Ulster, the largest 2, Belfast and Derry, established and subsequently modified improvement commissions before 1828. The history of the relationships between the improvement commissions and the corporations in those towns is as yet untold. Of the remaining 15 towns, 6 did not establish a town commission until after municipal reform – Bangor, Belturbet, Cavan, Enniskillen, Monaghan and Newtownards. In an anomalous neglect of statutory responsibilities, Carrickfergus did not establish regular municipal government until 1898.[69] Of the remaining 8 corporate towns, 4 were not only waning in economic importance, but also decreasing in population. As a result,

66 *First report of the commissioners appointed to inquire into the municipal corporations in Ireland*, p. 9. 67 Peter Gale, *An inquiry into the ancient corporate system of Ireland* (London, 1834), p. 129; *First report of the commissioners appointed to inquire into the municipal corporations*, pp 22, 39. 68 A. Macintyre, *The liberator* (New York, 1965), p. 242. 69 The corporate property was, by law, vested in a municipal commission that was charged with caring for that property until either a new corporation or a town commission (TC) was established.

the negligible corporate property and responsibilities of Charlemont, Hillsborough, Killyleagh and Lifford were never devolved to town commissions but under the terms of municipal reform were instead transferred to their respective boards of poor law guardians. It is the remaining four corporate towns that were the most interesting. In Armagh, Coleraine, Dungannon and Strabane town commissions were set up alongside existing corporations before municipal reform and eventually became rivals to those corporations and their patrons.

The town commission in Armagh was established in the midst of a political conflict involving the close corporation and its patron, the archbishop of Armagh. This conflict was focused on the corporation grand jury, an anomalous organ of the corporation established during the first half of the eighteenth century and apparently modelled on the leet court of the manor. It was composed of approximately twenty jurors (the number varied) appointed annually by the sovereign of the corporation to levy a 'corporation cess' to fund city services such as lighting, watching and the regulation of markets.[70] This system collapsed amidst the political conflict that brought about the end of the archbishop of Armagh's control of the borough's parliamentary seat.

In December 1832 the first parliamentary contest in the borough under the new parliamentary reform act was fought between Leonard Dobbin, a prominent local merchant, and A.I. Kelly, the land agent for the archbishop of Armagh. Standing as a liberal proponent of parliamentary reform Dobbin defeated Kelly in a bitter campaign that the *Belfast News-Letter* described as 'the first *public* election for the Archepiscopal City'.[71] The rancour of that campaign spilled over into local government. In January 1833, the sovereign of the corporation, who was also the seneschal of the archbishop of Armagh's manor, selected a new corporation grand jury. Previously the membership of the corporation grand jury had been drawn from a small group of prominent families that varied little from year to year. In 1833 the membership was markedly different. Of the 21 families who comprised the corporation grand jury in 1833 only 5 had been represented on that body in 1832.[72] The corporation grand jury was now a clearly partisan body composed 'almost entirely' of conservatives.[73] Although at least one liberal, a venerable veteran of the Volunteer movement, survived the purge, most of the perennial grand jurors were now excluded, including the new MP for the borough, Leonard Dobbin.[74]

Such high-handed tactics were no longer tolerated in Armagh. The liberals resolved to resist any cess approved by the partisan corporation grand jury. In

---

70 *First report of the commissioners appointed to inquire into the municipal corporations*, pp 673–4; Armagh corporation grand jury minute book, Dec. 1827, Armagh Public Library [Primate Robinson's Library]. **71** *BNL*, 18 Dec. 1832. **72** Armagh corporation grand jury minute book. **73** *First report of the commissioners appointed to inquire into the municipal corporations in Ireland*, pp 676–7. **74** Armagh corporation grand jury minute book.

the face of this opposition and its own dubious legal foundation, the corporation grand jury decided not to levy a new cess and essentially abdicated responsibility for improving the town.[75] Under these circumstances a town commission was established in Armagh in November 1833. A new era in local government was inaugurated as the corporation grand jury, entirely appointed and controlled by a patron, was supplanted by a town commission elected by ratepayers.

In Strabane the conflict concerning the town commission was more complicated. By the time a town commission was proposed in 1829 the corporation was no longer a vital force. Instead, the town commission was opposed by a group of inhabitants who wanted to leave local improvements to the traditional patron of the corporation, the marquess of Abercorn. From its creation in October 1829 one of the primary goals of the town commission was to pipe clean water to the town. As work began it became clear that the costs would be significant, eventually amounting to more than £1,200. Citing a depressed local economy incapable of supporting increased taxation, a group of inhabitants opposed the town commission's efforts.[76] The disagreement became more than a matter of the cost. The fundamental question became whether or not the town should continue to be dependent upon the patronage of the Abercorn interest.

The opponents of the new water scheme did not approach the town commission in their initial efforts to stop the plan. Instead, they directed their petition against the policy to the provost of the corporation, the traditional representative of authority in the town. That appeal failed when the provost informed them that while he sympathized with their concerns and believed the town commission's policy unsound, he could do little as the law made the town commission's decision 'final'. Having failed to subvert authority of the town commission by appealing to the moribund corporation, opponents of the water policy then tried to persuade the town commissioners that the traditional authority in the town, the Abercorn interest, was better able to undertake improvements. Unfortunately for them, the ability of the Abercorn interest to oppose or influence the town commission was handicapped by the circumstance that the current marquess was a minor. They nevertheless asked the town commission to defer its plans 'with the hope that when the Marquis of Abercorn comes of age he will contribute handsomely towards supplying the town with Pipe water'. The town commission was not impressed and persisted with its plan.[77] The town commission had successfully challenged the role of

75 *First report of the commissioners appointed to inquire into the municipal corporations in Ireland*, p. 677.   **76** Strabane TC, 29 Oct. 1829, 15 Mar. 1830, 4 Jan. 1831, PRONI, MIC159/reel 2.   **77** Ibid., 15 Mar. 1830, 15 Dec. 1840, PRONI, MIC159/reel 2.

Abercorn interest as the primary agent of improvement in the town. The issue of local authority and influence was not, however, conclusively decided at this time. The conflict between the Abercorn interest and the town commission resumed in the aftermath of corporate reform in 1840.

Unfortunately the early records of the town commission in Dungannon are unavailable (the earliest surviving records date from 1844). Other evidence, however, suggests that the town commission was the focus of growing opposition to the local patron. When the Ranfurly domination of the borough was seriously challenged for the first time in 1841, the protagonist was a prominent figure in the town commission. In the first contested parliamentary election since the Union, the liberal candidate was John Falls, owner of a local distillery, who had been a long-time member and occasional chairman of the town commission.[78] Falls asserted that he entered the parliamentary campaign because of the 'very great *unpopularity* of the Ranfurly Family here, caused, in a great measure, no doubt, by the gross mismanagement and oppression used by those in power'.[79] The Ranfurly interest won that parliamentary election but with 71 votes to 50 votes for Falls, but the seriousness of the threat to their control of the borough led the Ranfurly interest to strengthen its position by purchasing a number of houses in which to place politically reliable tenants.[80] These purchases seem to have had the desired effect. Whereas John Falls had been the chairman of the town commissions elected in 1834 and 1840, the chairman of the town commission elected in 1843 was the land agent of the earl of Ranfurly.[81] In Dungannon, as in Armagh and Strabane, Ulster liberals found the town commission a useful tool in their political struggles against established patrons or oligarchies. This did not mean, however, that Ulster liberalism could easily overcome the accumulated power and influence of their opponents.

The history of Coleraine will serve as a useful case study of the role of the town commission in the growth and survival of Ulster liberalism.[82] Coleraine

---

78 Hutchison, *Tyrone*, pp 178–9; *Return of the names of those towns in Ireland in which the act of 9 Geo. 4 c. 82 has been brought into operation wholly or in part*, HC 1843 (632), l, pp 14–15.
79 Broadsheet of election address by John Falls, dated 22 June 1841, PRONI, T2181.
80 Hutchison, *Tyrone*, p. 179.   81 Despite the lack of minute books Falls' position as chairman can derived from – *First report from the select committee on fictitious votes, Ireland; with the minutes of evidence and appendix*, HC 1837 (308), xi, appendix g, p. 206; *Return of the names of those towns in Ireland in which the act of 9 Geo. 4 c. 82 has been brought into operation* pp 14–15; Dungannon TC, 6 July 1844, PRONI, LA/34/2B/1.   82 The history of Coleraine is particularly well documented with a number of useful local histories and abundant primary sources. The numerous local histories of Revd T.H. Mullin, rector of Killowen, and Julia Mullin have been of particular value. Julia E. Mullin, *New Row: the history of the New Row Presbyterian church, Coleraine, 1727–1977* (Antrim, 1976); J.E. Mullin, *The presbytery of Coleraine* (Belfast, 1979); T.H. Mullin, *Coleraine in Georgian times* (1977); T.H. Mullin, *Coleraine in modern times* (Belfast, 1979).

has been characterized as an archetypal rotten borough, a prime contender in the 'corruption stakes' of nineteenth century Ireland, where patronage and profit mattered more than political abstractions.[83] In Coleraine, a group of merchants and professionals established a town commission as an alternative to the close corporation that had developed in the town. There was a continuous partisan political struggle with ideological dimensions reflected in the town commission. Even in the supposedly trim little borough of Coleraine there was clear evidence of social conflict that provided Ulster liberals with opportunities. The travails of the town commission in Coleraine also demonstrated some of the very considerable difficulties confronting liberalism in Ulster.

Beginning in 1815, the shortcomings of the corporation were publicized by a series of deputations from the Irish Society. The corporation in Coleraine had been established in the seventeenth century under the aegis of the Irish Society, a chartered company of the City of London founded to assist in the plantation of Ulster by Scots and English settlers. During the eighteenth century, the Irish Society had neglected its authority in Coleraine and was supplanted in the corporation by the marquess of Waterford's interest. During the nineteenth century, however, the Irish Society came under the influence of reform-minded politicians of the City of London who renewed its involvement in Irish affairs.[84] The most important representative of this new influence was John Thomas Thorp who served as Governor of the Irish Society from 1817 until his death in 1835. As a member of a livery company of London, Thorp was active in the politics of the city and became one of the twenty-six aldermen elected for life in 1817. Thorp was elected to parliament for London in 1818 as an advocate of parliamentary reform. Closely associated with fellow city politicians and reformers Robert Waithman and Matthew Wood, Thorp was, according to Ian Christie, one of the less than a dozen opposition members of the parliament elected in 1818 who could be described as radicals. As governor of the Irish Society, Thorp tried to put some of his reformist ideals into practice.

In 1815 Thorp served on a committee that submitted a series of questions concerning the Irish Society's charter to legal counsel. In these questions, the Irish Society considered whether its charter intended it to operate as a private business venture dividing its profits among the other London livery companies involved in the plantation, or as a public interest that ought to use its assets for the good of those people living on its estates in Ulster.[85] By 1822, the answer

83 K.T. Hoppen, *Elections, politics and society in Ireland, 1832–1885* (Oxford, 1984), p. 77.
84 A.B. Beaven, *The aldermen of the City of London*, 2 vols (London, 1908–1913), ii, p. 142; V. Hope, *My Lord Mayor* (1989), p. 136; J.A. Hone, *For the cause of truth* (Oxford, 1982), p. 279; Christie, *British 'non–elite' MPs* (Oxford, 1995), p. 199.   85 *A report of the committee of the Irish Society respecting their charter* (London, 1815), p. 11.

was clear. In the preface of a brief history published by the society that year it was forthrightly asserted that the purpose of the Irish Society, 'independently of the pecuniary benefit to arise to the original planters and their successors, was to ameliorate the condition of the inhabitants on their plantation'.[86]

As part of this new mission the Irish Society was determined to free Coleraine from the Waterford interest. The reports of its deputations from 1815 until 1832 chronicled their efforts to ascertain the extent of property and authority usurped by the Waterford interest and to provide the kinds of improvements for the town usually considered the responsibility of a municipal corporation or urban patron.[87] The developing competition between the Irish Society and the Waterford interest fundamentally affected the town commission in Coleraine. The society's activism raised hopes among local inhabitants wishing to open up the corporation.[88] Dissatisfaction with the corporation increased until in November 1828 that usually secretive body took the extraordinary step of organizing a public meeting to refute charges of municipal abuses.[89]

It was under these circumstances that a town commission was founded in December 1828. There is little evidence of overt opposition to the establishment of the town commission by the municipal corporation. The publicity surrounding the rivalry between the corporation and the Irish Society as well as the willingness of the Irish Society to go to court may have dissuaded the Waterford interest from the kinds of obstruction and chicanery employed in other places. In addition, in comparison with the considerable resources and authority possessed by the corporation, the town commission may not have been perceived as a serious threat. Shortly after its establishment, however, the town commission became involved in a series of bitter and expensive contested parliamentary elections between 1830 and 1837.

It is both interesting and instructive to consider the political composition of the town commissions during the course of these political battles.[90] The initial

86 [H. Schultes], *A concise view of the origin, constitution and proceedings of the Honorable Society of the Governor and Assistants of London of the New Plantation of Ulster, within the Realm of Ireland* ([1st ed.], London, 1822), p. 188. It was a position that the Irish Society successfully maintained at great cost in an infamous chancery suit against them brought in Oct. 1832 by the Skinners' Company of the City of London.   87 *A report of the deputation of the Irish Society* (London, 1815), p. 70; [H. Schultes], *A concise view of the origin, constitution and proceedings of the Honorable Society of the Governor and Assistants of London of the New Plantation of Ulster, within the Realm of Ireland* ([2nd ed.], London, 1832), 94. The different editions of Schultes' compendia of extracts from the Irish Society's records vary considerably in content and reflect the changes in the Irish Society's policies that occurred during the Thorp's governorship.   88 *A report of the deputation of the Irish Society* (London, [1815]), Appendix A.   89 *NCT*, 21 Nov. 1828.   90 Characterizations of the town commissioners have been pieced together from the following sources – Coleraine TC, PRONI, LA/25/2B/1; *Returns relating to the corporation of the borough of Coleraine, in Ireland*, HC

lack of concern by the Waterford interest for the town commission was demonstrated by the fact that only one of the first town commissioners chosen in December 1828 was a member of the corporation connected with the Waterford interest. During the course of the parliamentary contests that occurred in the borough between 1828 and 1837, however, 6 of the original 21 commissioners were co-opted into the corporation in order to provide much needed support for the Waterford interest. Of the remaining 15 members of that original commission, 5 were among the opponents of the Waterford interest who had applied for admission to the corporation as freemen in order to receive the parliamentary franchise but were rejected. These rejections resulted in both litigation and parliamentary investigation. A further 4 of the original 21 town commissioners were known opponents of the Waterford interest in the town, making the total number of town commissioners opposed to the corporation 9.[91] While it is impossible to classify the remaining six members with certainty, none of them applied for admission to the corporation between 1801 and 1832 or were admitted to its ranks subsequently. They were certainly not numbered among the corporation's foremost supporters. This analysis taken together with the fact that the first chairman of the town commission was an opponent of the corporation strongly suggests that first town commission had a liberal majority.

Analysis of the membership of subsequent town commissions during the period between 1828 and the enactment of municipal reform in 1840 strongly suggests that liberals were in the majority throughout this period. This conclusion is substantiated by the increasingly strident confrontations between the town commission and the corporation. In December 1832 the parliamentary contest in the borough pitted Sir John Beresford for the Waterford interest against William Taylor Copeland, an alderman of the City of London and member of the Irish Society. Copeland, partner and later proprietor of the well-known English porcelain firm of Spode, was a liberal reformer at the time though he later became a follower of Sir Robert Peel.[92] Beresford was elected on the deciding vote of the mayor by a total of 98 votes to 97 but the outcome was challenged in a petition to parliament. In February 1833, while the petition was still before parliament, a riot occurred in Coleraine. Having learned that

1831–2 (409), xxxvi, pp 1–20; *Returns relating to Coleraine corporation*, HC 1834 (91), xliii, pp 2–3; *Third report from the select committee on fictitious votes, Ireland; with the minutes of evidence, appendix and index*, HC 1837 (480), xi, appendix no 13, pp 279–80; and newspaper accounts of elections and public meetings.   91 The classification of these members has been pieced together from a number of sources. For example, the classification of Samuel Lawrence as an opponent of the Beresford interest was derived from the following sources; Irish Society, *Report of a deputation to Ireland in the year 1832* (London, 1832), p. 9; and T.H. Mullin, *Coleraine in modern times*, p. 17.   92 Beaven, *Aldermen of the City of London*, ii, p. 143.

Beresford had decided not to contest the petition against his return to parliament, a crowd of Beresford's supporters expressed their chagrin by attacking the houses of two Copeland supporters with stones.[93]

The victims of the mob had difficulty obtaining justice from the local magistracy. Under the municipal charter the justices of the peace for the town were chosen from among the mayor, recorder and aldermen and had exclusive jurisdiction within the town and liberties. These so-called charter justices were perceived to be 'nominees of an individual and partisans of a party' who exhibited 'a bias and partiality in their magisterial conduct'. Either through incompetence or deliberate omission, the charter justices issued imperfect summonses in this case. The imperfections resulted in the abandonment of the case by one victim and a near dismissal at trial for the other. To add insult to injury some of the charter magistrates expressed a belief that the case 'originated in a conspiracy' on the part of the victims. Fortunately a 'respectable person' had witnessed the riot and corroborated the accusations so that a settlement for compensation was eventually reached.[94] It was the political context of the case that caused the victims' difficulties. The rioters were reportedly led by John Cochrane who was the clerk of the market, a position under the corporation, and a district master of the Orange Order.[95] On the other hand, the victims were opponents of the corporation who had been refused admission to the corporation during the political battles of 1830–2.[96] To complicate matters further, one of the victims, John Caulfield, had been appointed by the town commission to collect the rates.[97] It may have been Caulfield's connection with the town commission that led the 'commissioners for lighting and watching the town' to interfere 'upon a representation of the outrage made to them by the nightly watch under their control'.[98] In this way the conflict pitted the collector of tolls and customs for the corporation against the rate collector for the town commission.

A war of words continued between the town commission and the corporation. In May 1835, shortly after another contested parliamentary election at which Copeland narrowly defeated an alderman of the corporation in Coleraine, Henry Richardson, the town commission censured the mayor for 'certain reflections thrown upon us in our character as commissioners'. The

---

93 *Municipal corporations (Ireland), appendix to the first report of the commissioners, part III, conclusion of the north-western circuit*, HC 1836 (29), xxiv, pp 1028–9. 94 Ibid. 95 Ibid.; *Report from the select committee appointed to inquire into the nature, character, extent and tendency of orange lodges, associations or societies in Ireland: with the minutes of evidence, and appendix*, HC 1835 (377), xv, appendix, p. 43. 96 *Municipal corporations (Ireland), appendix to the first report of the commissioners*, p. 1029; *Returns relating to the corporation of the borough of Coleraine*, p. 9. 97 Coleraine TC, 6 Apr. 1829, PRONI, LA/25/2B/1. 98 *Royal commission to inquire into municipal corporations (Ireland), appendix to the first report of the commissioners*, p. 1029

commissioners also prepared a memorial to the lord lieutenant 'requesting that the chairman of the Commissioners for the time being be invested with Magisterial authority, that the duties incumbent on Commissioners may be more efficiently discharged'. In June 1835 the commissioners also sought a legal opinion concerning their relationship to the corporation.[99]

These legal skirmishes soon gave way to violence during the parliamentary election in 1837. Antagonism between the landed classes and the merchants and manufacturers was a pronounced theme during the election. A champion of the conservative candidate Edward Litton boasted that Litton had the support of the '*resident* and influential gentry' while his opponents were merely 'inhabitants of Coleraine engaged in mercantile speculation'.[1] At the approach of the poll in August 1837 the town commissioners feared violence because of 'serious injury having been done both to persons and houses of a great number of the Inhabitants who voted for the Liberal Candidate at a former Election'. To avoid any further trouble, the town commissioners resolved to increase the number of watchmen and to coordinate their efforts with the Irish constabulary. In spite of these sensible precautions, a series of riots occurred. During these riots watchmen from the town commission were disarmed and detained by order of the mayor of the corporation. The local superintendent of the Irish constabulary convinced the mayor to release the watchmen and attempted to prevent further incidents by ordering all the watchmen to return to the watch house. In spite of these efforts, other watchmen were detained on the orders of the chamberlain, John Boyd. Two of the watchmen were beaten by a mob of conservative supporters in the course of their detention.[2] The identification of the town commission with liberalism was unmistakable to conservatives.

After the election in which Litton defeated a Whig landlord, Leslie Alexander, 129 votes to 77, the town commission sent a memorial to the government outlining the conduct of the corporation.[3] The town commission complained that the officers of the corporation had endangered the lives of the watchmen by 'having operated to direct the fury of the mob against said watchmen'. To add insult to injury, it was the watchmen rather than the leaders of the mob who were bound over by the borough magistrates to face charges of assault. The town commission provided the accused watchmen with legal counsel and asked the Lord Lieutenant to investigate the conduct of the borough magistracy during the election so that 'the authority vested in us as commissioners by said Act of Parliament, may not be either wantonly or ignorantly trampled upon'.[4]

---

99 Coleraine TC, 13 May 1835, 18 May 1835, 1 June 1835, PRONI, LA/25/2B/1.
1 *Ulster Times*, 5 Aug. 1837, 4.   2 Coleraine TC, 16 Oct. 1837, PRONI, LA/25/2B/2.
3 B.M. Walker (ed.), *Parliamentary election results in Ireland, 1801–1922* (Dublin, 1978), p. 263; Coleraine TC, 16 Oct. 1837, PRONI, LA/25/2B/2.   4 Coleraine TC, 16 Oct. 1837,

The politicization of the town commission intensified as municipal reform made its tortuous way through parliament. The municipal reform act received the royal assent in August 1840 and the final meeting of the common council of the corporation occurred in October of that same year. Local conservatives feared municipal reform would fundamentally undermine their position. The ultra-conservative MP for the borough, Edward Litton, depended on the corporation for his seat in parliament and tenaciously defended that power base. Litton led ten Irish Tories in a last-ditch opposition to municipal reform despite the conservative leader Robert Peel's pledge to support reform.[5] Failing in that, Litton attempted to undermine the new municipal order. In July 1842, he presented a bill to parliament to amend the constitution of town commissions.[6] The bill proposed altering the franchise of the town commission by adopting plural voting like that used for the poor law unions. Every inhabitant rated above £5 per annum would have one vote, those rated above £10 two votes. Above that level, an inhabitant would receive an additional vote for every additional £10 in valuation.[7] Intended to help preserve conservative influence in Irish towns and cities Litton's bill ultimately failed, but the anxiety of conservatives concerning the institution of the town commission is revealing. The hitherto underestimated social changes were all too apparent to the supporters of the *ancien régime*.

At the time of the triennial election for the town commission in July 1840 the upcoming dissolution of the corporation in Coleraine left the corporate interest with little choice but to try their fortunes in the town commission. The town commission election for that year was vigorously contested with 47 candidates vying for the 21 positions.[8] It is difficult to gauge the balance between liberals and conservatives precisely as a number of new members were elected. Because the leading figure in the corporation since 1831, John Boyd,[9] was elected chairman of the town commission in August 1840 it appears that the supporters of the corporation gained a small majority.[10] In many ways, the dissolution of the municipal corporations disappointed liberals in places such as Coleraine. They had expected to gain power and patronage. They had not imagined that conservatives would or could challenge them in the more representative town commission.

The dissolution of the corporation undoubtedly altered the nature of the

PRONI, LA/25/2B/2.   5 McDowell, *Public opinion and government policy*, pp 183–4. 6 *Journals of the House of Commons*, v. 97, 29 July 1842, p. 543.   7 *A bill to alter and amend an act of the ninth year of King George the fourth to make provision for the lighting cleansing and watching of cities, towns corporate and market towns in Ireland*, HC 1842 (502), iii, p. 3.   8 Coleraine TC, 7 July 1840, PRONI, LA/25/2B/2.   9 Coleraine corporation minute book, 1 Oct. 1831, PRONI, LA/25/2A/2.   10 Coleraine TC, 1 Sept. 1840, PRONI, LA/25/2B/2.

town commission in Coleraine. Not only had the town commission become the sole focus of municipal politics, but the day to day operations of the town commission became more complicated as result of inheriting many of the powers and all of the property of the defunct corporation. Time and energy had to be devoted to the management of markets, leases, rents, and tenant-right.[11] Opponents of the corporation had relished the prospect of taking over these responsibilities. The reality proved a mixed blessing. Along with the corporation's property the town commission also inherited a large debt. Despite considerable potential revenues, the corporation had borrowed large sums, much of it from its own members who profited handsomely, in order to construct market buildings.[12] As the successor to the corporation, the town commission became responsible for these debts that by 1844 still amounted to £4,000.[13] During the first decade after the corporation's dissolution much of the town commission's resources, political as well as financial, were employed in managing these debts.

The conservatives were obviously not undone by municipal reform. The corporate interest could no longer exclude its opponents from municipal government but they still possessed considerable power and influence. That power and influence was focused on a town commission that was no longer an alternative institution of municipal government with limited resources but the sole municipal authority. In Coleraine, the perilous condition of municipal finances forced liberals to compromise with their opponents. In particular the town commission was indebted to John Boyd.[14] After the final meeting of the corporation the town commission appointed a committee to investigate Boyd's claims to compensation for offices he held under the corporation as well as mortgages he possessed on corporate property. The town commission's investigations were hampered by Boyd's refusal to give up the 'deeds, leases, books, and documents in his possession, as Chamberlain of the late Corporation' on the grounds that these items were securities for the corporation's debts to him.[15]

Boyd eventually allowed an examination of some records and the committee reported in January 1841 that it had 'found several objectionable items', particularly those dating after February 1836 when parliament began serious consideration of municipal reform. If Boyd could not produce satisfactory documentation for each particular debt, the committee recommended that the town commission should 'leave Mr Boyd to establish his claim by law'. Boyd

---

11 Ibid., 10 Nov. 1840, 5 Apr. 1841, 4 Mar. 1844, PRONI, LA/25/2B/2; 2 Mar. 1846, PRONI, LA/25/2B/3. 12 *NW*, 12 Jan. 1841. 13 Coleraine TC, 23 Apr. 1844, PRONI, LA/25/2B/2. 14 As one of its last official acts, the corporation issued a bond to Boyd, then mayor, 'for the balance due him on foot of his account with this Corporation'. Coleraine corporation minute book, 17 Oct. 1840, PRONI, LA/25/2A/2. 15 *NW*, 12 Jan. 1841.

was quick to take up the challenge. In February 1841 the committee was forced to report that 'the several mortgages and bonds' had to be considered legitimate as legal 'judgements have been duly entered on the said bonds'. Boyd increased the pressure upon the town commission by initiating additional proceedings to recover other claims. Because of the threat of further legal costs, the committee recommended conceding responsibility for the debts, arrangement of a payment schedule, and asking Boyd to 'stop all further proceedings, on being paid the [legal] costs already incurred'.[16] Adverse legal judgments had forced the town commission to cut its losses.

The committee's recommendations raised concerns among liberals that the town commission might feel compelled to make a devil's bargain with Boyd. A correspondent from Coleraine sent a copy of the report of concerning Boyd's claims to the *Northern Whig* in the hope of publicizing the travails of Boyd's opponents who had 'honestly done their duty to the town, by resisting every attempt at appropriating the public property'. Liberals were particularly concerned that in exchange for forbearance on his claims, Boyd would be appointed treasurer of the town commission. The duties of treasurer had been expanded to include receiving rents from the former corporate properties and 'the tolls and other income of the town'.[17] These were duties that Boyd had performed to the great advantage of the conservative cause in Coleraine while he was chamberlain of the corporation. Six days after the announcement of the town commission's recognition of his claims, Boyd resigned the chairmanship of the town commissioners.[18] To their credit, however, a majority of both the committee investigating Boyd's claims and the town commission as a whole balked at a proposal that Boyd should be chosen treasurer for the town commission.[19]

The decision to deny Boyd had its costs. Boyd pertinaciously refused to turn over the records of the corporation.[20] His position was strengthened by his election to parliament for the borough in February 1843.[21] Without the corporation's records the town commission could not accurately ascertain its revenue base and was reduced to the pathetic course of writing to the Irish Society for information concerning the property it had provided to the corporation.[22] The Irish Society had been unsuccessfully attempting to uncover information concerning its property in Coleraine since 1814.[23] Large debts and uncertain revenues continued to strain the finances of the town commission until 1845 when it managed to free itself of the corporate debt with an extraordinary loan

---

16 Ibid., 12 Jan. 1841, 16 Feb. 1841. 17 Ibid., 12 Jan. 1841, 16 Feb. 1841. 18 Coleraine TC, 18 Feb. 1841, PRONI, LA/25/2B/2. 19 *NW*, 16 Feb. 1841, 2. 20 Coleraine TC, 11 Feb. 1845, PRONI, LA/25/2B/3. 21 Walker, *Parliamentary election results*, p. 263. 22 Coleraine TC, 7 Mar. 1845, PRONI, LA/25/2B/2. 23 *A report of the deputation of the Irish Society* [1815], p. 70.

approved by the government. It was, however, still unable to gain access to the corporate records held by Boyd.[24] By 1846, the town commission had grown weary of the struggle. Boyd had been compelled by other circumstances (Presbyterian politics, tenant-right and an ambitious conservative landlord) to compromise with liberals in order to retain his parliamentary seat. The political compromises forced upon Boyd, the settlement of his debt, and the continuing need for information concerning the defunct corporation led the town commission to agree to Boyd's appointment as treasurer, a seemingly inconsequential position for a sitting MP, in 1846.[25] The position was, however, one of considerable political utility. In Coleraine the treasurer for the town commission was also land agent for the extensive holdings inherited from the corporation. The potential influence with tenants eligible to vote in a borough with a small constituency could prove invaluable to an ambitious politician. The expedient alliance only lasted until 1852 but Boyd was able to maintain his position as treasurer, despite serious disagreements with the town commission, by his tenacious control of local records until 1860 when Coleraine adopted the 1854 towns improvement act that provided that the treasurer for the town commissioner must be a banking company.[26] Boyd died two years later in 1862.

The tortuous history of the relationship between John Boyd and the town commission has led some to suggest that 'Coleraine politics made a non-sense of party labels'.[27] Upon closer examination through the lens of the town commission it is clear that there was a continuous, if complex, struggle between liberals and conservatives in the 'trim little borough'. Despite the long career of John Boyd, the history of Coleraine was one of considerable change. Between 1828 and 1840 the corporation of the town was challenged by the town commission but the advantages of the corporation with regard to revenues, records and the charter justices precluded a complete transformation. After municipal reform the struggle continued despite circumstances, such as the corporation's debts, that strengthened conservatives. The contests for the town commission continued to be hard-fought. Between 1840 and 1860 all but one of the elections for town commission were contested.

As for parliamentary politics, Coleraine ought not to have survived parliamentary reform in 1832. It was too small a constituency to avoid being bullied or seduced by powerful interests. In a narrow constituency, without the ballot, the influence of political aspirants could be brought to bear with greater force on voters. This does not preclude the existence of identifiable political groups. The history of Coleraine illustrates the importance of local politics in gauging

24 Coleraine TC, 4 Dec. 1843, 23 Apr. 1844, PRONI, LA/25/2B/2; 11 Feb. 1845, PRONI, LA/25/2B/3. 25 *BU*, 20 Sept. 1853. 26 *Coleraine Chronicle*, 25 Feb. 1860. 27 Hoppen, *Elections, politics, and society*, p. 448.

the strength of liberalism. The structure of parliamentary politics lent itself to the influence of landlords or corporate oligarchies but in an institution such as the town commission liberalism could find a niche in even a trim little borough like Coleraine.

During the period between 1814 and 1842 Ulster liberalism did not succeed in overcoming completely the historic accumulation of power by landlords and oligarchies. The hopes raised first by parliamentary reform and then by municipal reform were in many ways disappointed. Divisions among reformers, whether over the virtues necessary for good government or the utility of the Union, at times weakened and exasperated liberals. However, there were considerable achievements. The revolutionary heritage of Ulster liberalism that had proven so divisive was abandoned for a more moderate and practical ideal that was in keeping with political developments not only in Britain but also in France. Ulster liberalism also adapted to the changes in Ulster Presbyterianism that some historians have misinterpreted as its death knell. The efforts of Henry Cooke to harness the undoubted growth of evangelical ideals among Presbyterians to a conservative, pan-Protestant agenda were markedly unsuccessful. Ulster Presbyterians became evangelicals and supporters of the Union, but they did not wed themselves to conservatism. The question would become, could evangelical, Presbyterian liberals cooperate with Catholic reformers, even without the perilous issue of repeal? The pragmatic ideals of Ulster liberals also contributed to a hitherto unrecognized reform of local government in Ulster town and cities in the form of the town commissions. The focus upon parliamentary politics or sectarian issues has caused many historians to overlook the considerable social changes that liberals helped bring about.

CHAPTER THREE

Ulster liberalism and the consolidation
of public opinion, 1842–59

At the close of 1842, the hopes Ulster liberals had placed in parliamentary and municipal reform seemed to have been disappointed. The emergence of repeal as a significant political question had blighted the anticipated harvest. At the parliamentary level, the accommodation between liberals and their conservative foes in Belfast during the parliamentary by-election of August 1842 appeared to confirm that Ulster Presbyterians were becoming aligned with the conservatism and a pan-Protestant ascendancy. At the local level, liberals in Belfast had been routed at the first town council elections after municipal reform. The conservatives captured every seat. Given these events, it is not surprising that some might wonder whether Henry Cooke's premature declaration of unity between liberal Ulster Presbyterians and the Church of Ireland in 1834 had finally come to pass.

Although the explanations have varied, the degeneration of Ulster liberalism has become a widely accepted fact. In the *New history of Ireland*, Oliver MacDonagh concisely summarized the consensus. Ulster liberalism had been in decline since the 1790s until by the 1840s the ascendancy achieved by Henry Cooke among Presbyterians and the popular politics of O'Connell dealt it an all but fatal blow. The historiography that MacDonagh summarized was diverse but of limited use for a detailed consideration of Ulster liberalism. With two exceptions, the commentaries upon Ulster liberalism were small parts of larger works discussing other topics. They lacked the luxury of closely investigating Ulster liberalism over time. The two works that treat Ulster liberalism more directly and in greater detail differ markedly from one another in their approach and conclusions.

In the course of a study that chronicled the degeneration of Ulster liberalism from an idealized conception of the United Irishmen, Flann Campbell described how Ulster liberals were seduced into betraying of the principles of 1798.[1] Henry Cooke and his Tory allies convinced Presbyterians that the economic progress of Belfast was attributable to the Union and the moral superiority of Protestantism. In this way Presbyterians would be distracted from what Campbell considered to be the self-evident need for national independence and a republican form of government. Campbell's approach is

---

1 Campbell, *The dissenting voice*, pp 160–9.

less interested in understanding the efforts of Ulster liberals to adapt to changing circumstances than in condemning perceived betrayals or debasements of the principles of 1798.

In his broader study of Ulster politics before 1886, Frank Wright approached the issue in a markedly different fashion. Wright did not consider the story of Ulster liberalism in terms of the failures of men and women to measure up to an imagined ideal. Rather, Wright described the efforts of liberals to adapt to changing social and economic circumstances along what he conceived of as an ethnic frontier between Britain and Ireland in Ulster. Ironically, Wright believed that 'the relative equalizing of communities' along that frontier drew Catholics and Protestants into 'more reciprocal conflict'.[2] Wright described a 'decay of the colonial structure' as a result of economic developments that resulted in a weakening of the foundations of authority in both the Protestant and Catholic communities. In marked contrast to the persistent oppression outlined by Campbell, Wright argued that Ulster society had changed significantly during this period. In many ways the Protestant ascendancy was seriously weakened. The potency of Wright's intellect was evident in his willingness to consider the possibility that the decay or even the collapse of the colonial structure might not herald liberal success or social peace. The purpose of this chapter is to explain the continued survival and evolution of the liberal tradition in Ulster during the 1840s and 1850s described by Wright. While sharing Wright's belief in significant changes in Ulster society during this period, I have placed greater emphasis on the actions and beliefs of those who contributed to the survival and development of Ulster liberalism than upon the impersonal economic and social forces that affected their efforts.

Presbyterians or Protestants?

One of the most striking signs of the diminished status of Henry Cooke and his conservative allies within Ulster Presbyterianism was the critical analysis of the 1842 meeting of the general assembly that appeared in the newly established Belfast newspaper, the *Banner of Ulster*. Established in June of 1842, the paper was to become a thorn in the flesh for Cooke. The *Banner* differed greatly from the traditional bugbear of conservatism in Ulster, the *Northern Whig*. While the *Whig* tended to be radical in religion as well as politics, its publisher being a Non-subscribing Presbyterian, the *Banner* was unabashedly evangelical in its outlook.

It is interesting to note, as demonstrated in Table 3.1, that three of the four

2 F. Wright, *Two lands on one soil* (New York, 1996), p. 513.

newspapers in Ulster with the largest circulations between 1843 and 1847 were liberal Protestant publications.[3] The three newspapers – the *Banner of Ulster*, *Northern Whig* and *Londonderry Standard* – were all Presbyterian in focus. The substantial circulation of liberal newspapers in Ulster demonstrates again that the failure to elect members to parliament or municipal councils should not be the sole measure of liberal strength. The fact that the oldest of the Presbyterian newspapers, the *Northern Whig*, was associated with Non-subscribing principles while the more recently established *Londonderry Standard* and *Banner of Ulster* were both orthodox and evangelical, also illustrates important changes occurring within Presbyterianism in Ulster that significantly affect liberal fortunes.

The first editor of the *Banner of Ulster* was George Troup, a native of Aberdeen. Prior to his arrival in Belfast, Troup had edited newspapers in Liverpool, Montrose, Aberdeen and Glasgow. Troup was an ardent evangelical who had attended a seceding Presbyterian congregation in Scotland, founded a total abstinence society, and supported the non-Intrusion party led by Thomas Chalmers.[4] It is not surprising, therefore, that the editorial policy of the *Banner* was founded on the belief 'that the advancement of religion in society is the best safeguard of civil liberty, and the surest means of securing the prosperity of any land'. The *Banner* was unreservedly sectarian in the sense that it believed Presbyterianism afforded 'the most reasonable and efficient means' for the spread and development of Christianity and was 'bound to seek its extension'.[5]

Despite being thoroughly evangelical in tone, the *Banner* did not engage in the persistent and pervasive vilification of Catholicism found in the Tory *Ulster Times* or other extreme Protestant publications. Rather, the *Banner* denounced 'fierce expressions' against Catholics as lacking a 'Christian spirit'. This admirable scruple did not, however, prevent the *Banner* from occasionally engaging in strident theological debates and broad characterizations. In 1842, the *Banner* opposed the efforts to increase and consolidate state funding for the Catholic seminary of Maynooth. In 1845, during the controversy surrounding the Charitable Bequests Act for the regulation of legacies made to the Catholic church, the *Banner* remarked that 'intelligent men amongst the Roman Catholics will see the necessary tendency of their faith to nurture and protect despotism, and to injure and retard constitutional interests in all quarters of the globe'.[6]

In politics, the *Banner* at first declared itself independent of existing parties. Those parties had created 'a considerable portion of that political asperity

---

3 This characterization is not limited to the author's evaluation. See J.S. North (ed.), *Waterloo directory of Irish newspapers and periodicals* (Waterloo, ON, 1986).   4 G.E. Troup, *Life of George Troup* (Edinburgh, 1881), pp 18–32; *ODNB*, www.oxforddnb.com accessed 4 Feb 2008.   5 *BU*, 10 June 1842.   6 Ibid., 21 Mar. 1845, 8 July 1842, 17 Jan. 1845.

Table 3.1: Estimated circulation figures for selected newspapers, 1837–47

	1837	1838	1839	1840	1841	1842	1843	1844	1845	1846	1847
Belfast											
Banner of Ulster						692	1,069	855	889	986	832
Belfast Commercial Chronicle	1,135	717	705	737	769	785	776	705	705	705	705
Belfast News-Letter	726	1,144	1,000	962	1,010	808	740	740	692	673	635
Northern Whig	929	955	936	1,119	1,256	1,327	1,378	1,410	1,442	1,500	1,538
Reformer	385	231	154	93							
Ulster Times	853	885	907	769	670	705					
Vindicator			803	832	837	957	769	772	841	846	495
Elsewhere in Ulster											
Coleraine Chronicle									587	750	635
Fermanagh Impartial Reporter	260	250	240	240	337	433	442	384	538	625	577
Londonderry Journal	662	875	721	798	682	769	788	673	673	731	481
Londonderry Sentinel	1,135	981	1,211	1,144	1,125	1,240	1,087	1,163	1,250	1,212	1,385
Londonderry Standard	1,067	894	1,048	1,183	1,221	1,298	1,240	1,394	1,308	1,606	1,740
Newry Examiner	553	494	465	385	324	282	186	272	260	240	208
Newry Telegraph	596	691	676	737	760	788	731	788	763	837	753
National Papers											
Nation							7,856	8,606	6,327	5,760	5,096
Pilot	817	631	824	734	798	649	834	1,094	836	1,094	836

Source: A return of the number of stamps issued to newspapers, and the amount of advertisement duty paid on each of the last two quarters of the year 1843, separately stated; [...] HC 1844 (55), xxxii; Return of the number of newspaper stamps at one penny, issued to newspapers in England, Ireland, Scotland and Wales, from the year 1837 to the year 1850, HC 1852 (42), xxviii; Waterloo Directory of Irish Newspapers and Periodicals.

which, unfortunately distinguishes this country' and exaggerated the problems in Ireland. Tories bewailed seething rebellion in the south and Whigs decried sectarian oligarchy in the north until 'many quiet people believe men walk the streets of our towns with pistols in their pockets'. The result of these dire reports was a reluctance to invest in Ireland. The only statement of political principle that the *Banner* was willing to make in its first edition was that it was 'the duty of the State, and of individuals, to bestow a little more attention towards promoting the physical comfort and intellectual enlightenment of the great body of society'.[7] This statement presaged the significant interest in social reforms that would characterize the *Banner* during its publication.

It is clear from the editorial exchanges between the *Banner* and its rivals, the liberal *Northern Whig* and the Tory *Ulster Times*, that this political neutrality was a polite fiction soon abandoned. The *Banner* was scornful of conservative policies in general and hostile towards any alliance with the Tories. When the *Newry Telegraph* criticized the *Banner* for not supporting a 'combined and harmonising Protestant conservativism', the *Banner* disdainfully replied that it believed that concept a 'cant phrase minted to lull men asleep while their dearest rights and privileges, and the Constitution established by our forefathers in 1688, are undergoing a process of galloping destruction'.[8]

The hostility of the *Banner* resulted in part from simmering discontent with the handling of the issue of lay patronage in Scotland and the marriage question in Ireland. This antagonism over ecclesiastical grievances would be aggravated further by the issue of the disposition of the church properties in the hands of congregations that joined the Non-subscribers in 1844.[9] The animus of the *Banner* towards conservatives was also, as will be seen more clearly with regard to the land question, a result of a fundamental disagreement about how best to reform and improve Ulster society. As emblems of the growing evangelical nature of Ulster Presbyterianism, the *Banner* and the *Londonderry Standard* were also representatives of a renewed emphasis upon a reformulated vision of the godly commonwealth.[10] The very titles of the two papers were allusions to the blue banners of the Covenanters.

The *Banner*'s relationship with what it described as the 'Whig' leadership in Ulster was more complicated. The difficulty was more than a matter of policy. The significant philosophical differences between the *Banner* and the existing liberal leadership represented by the *Northern Whig* would later come to a head over the land question. An additional factor in the disputes between the *Banner* and the existing leaders seems to have been the rivalry between orthodox,

7 Ibid., 10 June 1842. 8 Ibid., 16 Sept. 1842. 9 Ibid., 14 June 1844. 10 The *Londonderry Standard* was established in 1836 by two liberals and remained in publication until 1964; D. Murphy, *Derry, Donegal and modern Ulster*, p. 112; B. Lacy, *Siege city* (Belfast, 1990), pp 179–80.

evangelical Presbyterians who formed the majority of the denomination and the small minority of Non-subscribing Presbyterians who retained considerable social and economic influence. At the time of the election compromise of 1842, the leadership of the Belfast Reform Association that had supported the plan, despite considerable unease among its members, was comprised of Catholics and Protestants in a surprisingly balanced proportion. Catholics comprised 59 of 101 places on the general committee. On the management committee, however, 7 of the 12 members were Protestants.[11]

However, those Protestants in the association's leadership were not representative of the great mass of Presbyterianism. If orthodoxy prevailed among the great majority of Presbyterians, heterodoxy continued to be a hallmark of an influential minority. Many of the long-standing leaders of political radicalism and liberalism in Ulster were perceived as outside the evangelical fold of Ulster Presbyterianism.[12] The president of the Belfast Reform Association, Robert Grimshaw, was a Unitarian.[13] The *Northern Whig,* the oldest and hitherto most influential of the newspapers purporting to represent the Presbyterian community in Ulster, was perceived to be as heterodox as its proprietor, F.D. Finlay, a Unitarian son-in-law of one of the seventeen original Non-subscribing ministers who had separated themselves from the Synod of Ulster in 1830. James Simms, the *Whig*'s editor from 1830 until 1850, was a former divinity student associated with Revd Henry Montgomery who had abandoned his religious calling in the face of accusations of heterodoxy during Cooke's campaign against nonconformity within the Synod of Ulster.[14] In addition to the commercial enterprise of the *Northern Whig*, Finlay and Simms also collaborated in the publication of the weekly organ of the Belfast Reform Association, the *Reformer*, published between 1837 and 1840.[15] In September 1842 the *Banner* accused the *Northern Whig* of being the 'organ of Arianism', under the '*surveillance* of certain Arian preachers', a reference to the Non-subscribing leader Revd Henry Montgomery who was also an active spokesman for the Belfast Reform Association,[16]

By distancing itself from the traditional élite of the liberal party in Belfast, the *Banner* was hoping to appeal to the evangelical majority within Ulster Presbyterianism. This strategy was aided by the disruption of Catholic and Protestant cooperation during the period between 1842 and 1847. Soon after the O'Connellite newspaper the *Vindicator* began publishing in Belfast in 1839, its first editor, Charles Gavan Duffy, had attempted to convince local Catholics to distance themselves from the Protestant-led Reform Association. Despite

11 Slater, 'Belfast politics, 1798–1868', p. 70.   12 P. Brooke, *Ulster Presbyterianism* (1987), pp 156–7.   13 Slater, 'Belfast politics', p. 92; *BU,* 11 Oct. 1844.   14 Presbyterian Historical Society of Ireland, *Extracts from original letters of James McKnight*, pp 5–6.   15 North (ed.), *Waterloo directory*, p. 424.   16 *BU,* 27 Sept. 1842.

Duffy's efforts, the Catholic leadership in Belfast, led by Bishop Cornelius Denvir, continued to support a policy that set aside the issue of repeal as the price for Presbyterian cooperation. O'Connell attempted to aid Duffy in two ways. First, O'Connell's visit to Belfast in January 1841 compromised liberal Protestants in the town and created bad feelings among the embattled advocates of continued ecumenical political cooperation. Second, O'Connell's thorough investigation and public denunciation of the compromise of 1842 that had been supported by both Catholics and Protestants in the Belfast Reform Association further weakened and humiliated the advocates of cooperation. In 1843, proponents of Repeal also gathered support for an Independent Registry Association intended to supplant the Belfast Reform Association.[17] The *Banner of Ulster* was able to accuse the heterodox leadership of the Belfast Reform Association of damaging the liberal cause through its mismanagement of affairs, intimating an over reliance upon Catholic allies. By 1844, the *Banner* concluded that 'the Whigs are useless' and feared that 'Dr Montgomery, with all his liberal pretensions, has succeeded in ruining the Liberal party'. The *Banner* also took special care to draw critical attention to a conference of Irish Unitarians in Belfast presided over by Robert Grimshaw in October 1844.[18] Disaffection with the leadership may have contributed to the apathy of the liberal party in Belfast that allowed a conservative candidate to be returned at a by-election in 1845 without a contest despite the collapse of the Repeal movement and the Independent Registry Association.[19]

When tenant-right became a critical issue during the 1840s, the *Banner* enthusiastically supported efforts at political agitation not only as an opportunity to gain support at the expense of the *Northern Whig* but also in the hope of strengthening Ulster liberalism by drawing support from among the much more numerous evangelical Presbyterians. The question was, could a larger portion of the evangelical majority among Ulster Presbyterians be convinced to support liberalism without threatening the critical but often prickly partnership between Presbyterians and Catholics?

An opportunity to gauge the strength of orthodox liberal Presbyterianism presented itself at a by-election in Coleraine in 1843. As described earlier, the 'trim little borough' of Coleraine had been the scene of significant political struggles at both the parliamentary and local levels. Supported by legal challenges funded by the Irish Society, the liberals who controlled the town commission had achieved some success in their struggles with the corporate interest. However, the corporate interest rallied around John Boyd and preserved itself through a series of machinations that preserved their power

17 Slater, 'Belfast politics', p. 43.   18 *BU*, 21 June 1844, 11 Oct. 1844.   19 Slater, 'Belfast politics', p. 92.

over corporate property by controlling corporate records. This control had proved decisive to their efforts to return conservative candidates for the borough despite significant local opposition. The success of the corporate strategy was demonstrated by the failure of the liberals to field a candidate in the general election of 1841 to oppose the ultra-Tory Edward Litton. Litton had represented the borough since 1837 after a particularly bitter and violent election contest. It was the first occasion since 1830 that no contest had occurred in the borough.

Litton's position in the town was finally undermined by the growing sense of grievance that galvanized the Presbyterian majority in the borough. In the summer of 1842, Litton came under considerable criticism from the Presbyterian community for his conduct with regard to the Church of Scotland and the Presbyterian marriage question. The Coleraine presbytery concluded that Litton had 'failed to exonerate himself from the charge of neglecting the interests of the Presbyterians' and described his conduct in parliament as 'offensive to every consistent Presbyterian'. Under these circumstances, Litton's annual appearance before the electors of Coleraine in September was of greater interest than usual. A confrontation between Litton and his foremost critic, Revd John Brown of Aghadowey, was expected. When Brown was absent, Litton explained that he and his critics had come to an understanding so that 'every accusation of a breach of trust on my part, everything injurious to the character of a man of honour' had been withdrawn. Two weeks later, Brown told a different story. He revealed that Litton had tried to coerce his critics by initiating a libel action against Brown. Along with the libel action, Litton had called upon Brown and the presbytery of Coleraine to meet with him before the public meeting with the constituency. The presbytery had refused but Brown accepted. When the parties met they reached an agreement whereby Brown signed a statement stating that he had never intended to 'impeach the honour' or 'private character' of Litton.[20] For his part, Litton agreed to abandon his legal proceedings unconditionally and pledged that Brown's name would not be mentioned during his address to the constituents. Brown asserted that he had entered into this agreement in order to restore harmony within the community and to prevent violent confrontations between the two sides. Indeed, according to Brown, the local constabulary had already requested reinforcements. Upon learning that he had been attacked by Litton at the meeting in Coleraine, Brown renewed his public criticisms of Litton and the conservatives.

The *Banner of Ulster* ended its silence on the subject with a condemnation of Litton which concluded that 'from the present Parliament, the Presbyterian

20 *BU,* 6 Sept. 1842.

community has no hope of justice in questions affecting their interests, and they will be sacrificed piecemeal, unless a different system is pursued in selecting representatives from any hitherto adopted'. Presbyterians would be better off if a Whig government were in power. Under the previous Whig administration the people of Scotland had to endure lay patronage in theory but in practice they had 'virtually the choice of their ministers'. In contrast, under the Peel administration the appointments were 'obnoxious to the people; men have been thrust into pulpits merely on account of their obsequiousness to the lawyers'. Echoing the arguments made by Brown and others at the general assembly, the *Banner* concluded that 'it is needless for Presbyterian constituencies to quarrel with members of another Church because they do not thoroughly understand their views, and have no desire to promote them when they come in contact with their own opinions and interests'.[21] The moment had arrived for the Presbyterians of Ulster to assert themselves on the political scene.

The opportunity presented itself in October 1842 when Litton was appointed master of chancery by the Peel administration. It was rumoured that the Peel administration had intended to move the then solicitor-general to Coleraine, but that plan was wrecked by the conflict between Litton and Brown. The first candidate to enter the lists was John Boyd. Boyd declared that he had entered the campaign because of 'the necessity of Presbyterians having persons of their own religious sentiments to represent them in Parliament'.[22] Boyd's long history in Coleraine did not inspire confidence among those seeking to reform the borough. He had been associated with the corporation since 1821 and had been chamberlain during the struggle to open the corporation.[23] For these reasons, the *Banner* was sceptical of his candidacy. Because Boyd held 'Conservative opinions, while many of the electors in Coleraine are of Liberal opinions' and were 'sinking their political creed with a view of returning a Presbyterian candidate', the constituents had a right to expect that Boyd would offer them distinct assurances that he would be willing 'to abandon his party and offer them the vigorous opposition which they will deserve from every friend of civil and religious liberty' when Presbyterian interests were at stake. This demand for assurances was given a more concrete form by the influential Brown. As a leading member of the newly-formed Coleraine Church Defence Association, he issued a public letter requesting that Boyd pledge not to step aside for a government nominee or abandon the Presbyterian cause for office. Brown insisted upon the pledges because he believed 'the time is now come when Presbyterians must act vigorously and unitedly, or be overborne', by

21 Ibid. 22 Ibid., 23 Sept. 1842, 18 Oct. 1842. 23 *Return of the number of freemen created in each corporate town in* Ireland *returning members to parliament*, HC 1831–2 (550), xxxvi, p. 3; *Returns relating to Coleraine corporation*, pp 2–3.

the landlords and the established church.[24] The immediate issue may have been religious equality but it was combined with the traditional resentment of the ascendancy which often underlay the reform cause.

Boyd was not the only threat to the borough's independence. Boyd's opponent was Henry Hervey-Bruce, scion of a landed family possessing a considerable estate near Coleraine. Unsuccessful in challenging the Beresfords in the county constituency, Hervey-Bruce hoped to take advantage of the divisions in Coleraine. Over the course of the campaign, it became clear that the doubts about Boyd were overborne by dislike for Hervey-Bruce. A clear sign of this trend was a meeting of the Coleraine Church Defence Association in early November 1842 where Brown and Boyd shared a speaking platform. Boyd's participation was a gesture of reconciliation, but there was still ambivalence. Boyd was allowed to speak on the explicit condition that political matters were excluded.[25] It seems that Brown had not yet fully reconciled himself to support Boyd. It was only a matter of time, however, before the political realities of the situation would prevail.

The Hervey-Bruce interest was able to marshal considerable resources to make extensive purchases of goods in order to curry favour with local merchants possessing the franchise. These goods were then used to 'treat' other prospective supporters. Practices of this sort led some to propose strong countermeasures. It was even suggested that the Coleraine Church Defence Association publicly expose corrupt practices with a view to 'bring the discipline of the Church to bear' upon Presbyterian miscreants at least. The political reality of the situation was that the strength of the Hervey-Bruce interest insured that any division in the Presbyterian community would result in defeat. For this reason, Brown finally declared to his supporters on 14 December 1842, that he believed himself 'under a plain obligation, on public grounds', to declare that he considered it 'expedient for them in the present circumstances to unite in supporting Dr. Boyd at the coming election'.[26]

In addition to Brown's reluctant endorsement, Boyd was able to enlist the services of Samuel McCurdy Greer, a local barrister who had been active in efforts to reform the corporation since 1830.[27] As late as the spring assizes of 1842 Greer had represented the town commission in legal disputes against former corporate officers. The son a Presbyterian minister, Greer was a prominent lay leader and had proposed the establishment of Church Defence Associations at the general assembly during July 1842. With the support of the reformers and the Presbyterian activists Boyd was successful. Boyd polled 106 votes while Hervey-Bruce only managed 84.

---

24 *BU*, 21 Oct. 1842, 25 Oct. 1842. 25 Ibid., 11 Nov. 1842. 26 Ibid., 11 Nov. 1842, 20 Dec. 1842. 27 *Returns relating to the corporation of the borough of Coleraine*, pp 1–20.

In 1842, the by-election at Coleraine, in conjunction with the previously described events of the general assembly, demonstrated three important characteristics of Ulster liberalism during the 1840s. First, the Presbyterian church in Ireland was not dominated by Henry Cooke or political conservatism. Orthodox theology and evangelical devotion were certainly the dominant religious trends, but an impulse for reform that was fuelled, in part at least, by Presbyterian resentment of the privileges of the Church of Ireland Ascendancy continued to exist. That resentment intensified as a result of the crisis in the Church of Scotland and the marriage question in Ireland. Second, the strength of evangelical liberalism was demonstrated by the considerable circulation of the *Banner of Ulster* and the *Londonderry Standard*. Despite the obvious political failures of Ulster liberalism during this period, the fact that three liberals papers, the evangelical *Banner* and *Standard* together with the *Northern Whig*, were three of the four papers with the greatest circulation in the province must be taken into consideration. Thirdly, the by-election at Coleraine demonstrated that despite the great difficulties that remained for liberals attempting to challenge ascendancy power, a significant liberal political presence persisted. Though unable to gain a clear victory at the parliamentary level, Coleraine reformers were able to end the subservience of their borough to powerful landed patrons. Furthermore, while the devil's bargain with Boyd continued undisturbed until the 1850s when another emotional issue, tenant-right, resulted in a challenge to the compromise, the borough had managed to squeeze important concessions from Boyd.

Those who would proclaim the demise of Ulster liberalism by this date must either ignore this evidence or assert that these journals are not truly liberal, that this particular brand of reform differed too greatly from the radicalism of the late eighteenth century to be considered part of the same tradition. It seems unreasonable, however, to expect that Ulster liberalism would not change given the transformations in Ulster society. The realities of an act of Union, an industrial revolution, and government reforms that weakened ascendancy control of municipal institutions were bound to affect political thought. A basic recognition of the need to reform society by removing the privileges of ascendancy persisted. Ulster liberals might not possess the power to achieve the best but they could prevent the worst. Most important of all, many of the Presbyterian ministers who had played such an important role in organizing both local and provincial opposition to Litton became active supporters of tenant-right in part because of their experience in opposing the landed interest in 1842 and 1843.

Tenant-right: conquests, commonwealths and political economy

The starting point for any discussion of the place of the tenant-right movement in the history of Ulster liberalism might naturally seem a simple question – what precisely was tenant-right? This is no easy question. Tenant-right was a customary practice with no clear foundation in common law or statute. The very definition of tenant-right was an integral part of the political debate. Because controlling the definition was at least half the battle, accepting any particular formula espoused by contemporaries, such as the programs of tenant activists, entails accepting assumptions about Irish society that should be critically examined. Tenant-right involved more than a clash over property rights. The political and cultural contexts of tenant-right were at least as important as the economic aspect.

Stipulating the necessity for a critical attitude towards any formula purporting to be the essence of tenant-right, a broad working definition is still required. Tenant-right referred to the practice of out-going tenants in Ulster demanding payments from in-coming tenants who were to replace them. Having originated some time during the plantation of Ulster in the seventeenth century as a means to encourage and sustain English and Scottish colonization, over time tenant-right became a marketable commodity with prospective tenants bidding for the 'good will' or 'interest' of the outgoing tenant. In some circumstances, considerable sums were paid, often equivalent to the rent for a number of years and on occasion even the purchase price of the property. There is a growing consensus among historians that this was the core of tenant-right.[28] Further accretions to this practice, specifically the ideas of fixity of tenure and fair rents that together with the free sale of good-will came to be known as the 'Three F's' of land reform, were the result of efforts to defend and adapt the core of tenant-right to changing circumstances.

During the nineteenth century, establishing the value of tenant-right became a source of considerable conflict. Changes in economic circumstances, particularly those brought about by the general decline in agricultural prices after the end of the Napoleonic wars in 1815, contributed to changes in estate management, especially a growing belief in the need for the consolidation of small holdings. As part of their efforts to consolidate holdings, landlords increasingly sought to regulate tenant-right by either directly limiting the amount paid for tenant-right or insisting that adjoining tenants were given preference over any other bidders.[29]

28 See E.D. Steele, *Irish land and British politics: tenant-right and nationality, 1865–1870* (Cambridge, 1974), p. 28; M.W. Dowling, *Tenant right and agrarian society in Ulster, 1600–1870* (Dublin, 1999); W.E. Vaughan, *Landlords and tenants in mid-Victorian Ireland* (Oxford, 1994), pp 66–71.   29 Wright, *Two lands*, pp 79–103.

Despite its widespread practice throughout Ulster, the extent to which tenant-right lacked any concrete legal recognition can be gauged by the fact that one of the most accomplished legal writers in Ireland during the 1830s, John Finlay, a native of Ulster, did not mention the custom in his detailed treatise on the law of landlord and tenant in Ireland that was intended to explain the differences between English and Irish law 'on a subject in which they differ more than on any other'.[30] Both the nebulous legal standing of the custom and the anxieties that such uncertainty might produce in changing economic circumstances were exemplified in a legal case concerning the construction of a railway between Enniskillen and Dundalk in 1847.

When the railway company and the tenants of the parish of Donaghmoyne in Co. Monaghan could not agree on the amount of compensation due to the tenants, the issue had to be brought before the petty sessions in Carrickmacross. The solicitors representing the tenants sought to defend the amount requested by their clients by citing the market price of tenant-right on the estate in question, but the lawyers from the railway company dismissed their claims by challenging the very legitimacy of tenant-right. Insisting that 'compensation should be estimated in accordance with legal, not imaginary interests', the company's lawyer stated that there was 'no legal principle to sustain such a right' as tenant-right. The practice 'rested altogether upon the will or caprice of the landlord'. As tenant-right was 'not binding on the landlord, the company should not, therefore, be required to pay for an interest of that nature'. The suggestion that tenant-right had no legal standing and might not be used as a criterion for establishing compensation so horrified one of the magistrates that he threatened not to hear the case. In the end, the magistrates chose not to comment upon the validity of the custom but decided upon an amount, £20 per acre, precisely half way between the £7 per acre suggested by the company and the £33 per acre sought by the tenants.[31] If such sums were truly subject to the caprice of landlords or magistrates, tenants had considerable cause for anxiety.

Concerned by what they perceived to be the on-going erosion of an historic right, tenants and their supporters had for some time sought to give the force of statute to tenant-right. In 1835, W.S. Crawford, the Co. Down landlord representing the O'Connellite stronghold of Dundalk, presented a bill to parliament to protect the interests of tenants.[32] After simply obtaining leave to present a bare outline of the bill in 1835, Crawford attempted to gain the support of public opinion in Ulster through public meetings before pressing the measure in parliament in 1836.[33] In his bill Crawford proposed that:

---

30 J. Finlay, *A treatise on the law of landlord and tenant* (Dublin, 1835), p. ix. **31** *BU*, 15 Jan. 1847. **32** R.B. O'Brien, *The parliamentary history of the Irish land question* (4th ed., London, 1880), pp 63–5. **33** *NW*, 5 Nov. 1836.

the tenant (if evicted for any other reason than the non-payment of rent) was justly entitled to compensation, for labour and capital expended, *in such degree as the expenditure of that labour and capital had increased the value of the farm.*[34]

If the bill passed, improvements done with the consent of the landlord were to be recorded in a parochial register so that their value to the property could be easily calculated whenever a change in tenure occurred. There were also provisions for compensation for improvements done without the landlord's permission where necessity and suitability could be proven to a court at quarter sessions. A system for the valuation of improvements was also proposed.[35] Crawford's bill met with considerable opposition from other Irish landlords in parliament and never proceeded beyond a first reading.

As legislation was proposed it became evident that it would be difficult to capture a customary practice such as tenant-right within the bounds of legislation that might be approved by parliament but still satisfy tenants. Both in parliament and in his meetings in Ulster, Crawford admitted that his bill was founded on compromises. Speaking in November 1835 at a dinner in Holywood, Co. Down Crawford acknowledged that while his hosts in Holywood fully supported his bill 'they did not agree with him in every respect; but they gave up minor differences, for the purpose of enabling him to pursue the public good'.[36] The nature of those differences can be better understood by comparing the political language used by Crawford with that of others at the time.

While offering an historical explanation of Irish poverty founded on the hostility between landlord and tenant outside of Ulster, Crawford adopted the language of political economy when he sought support for his legislative program. Crawford did not lay claim to some ancient right established during the plantation but instead spoke of policy. Securing compensation for tenants was a means to ensure investment in agriculture. In Holywood in 1835, Crawford, citing the example of 'most of the great landholders in Great Britain' and Adam Smith, asserted that compensation for improvements would 'create what is so much wanted – capital'. He wanted to make the tenant 'a capitalist, instead of a pauper, and a trusty yeoman, instead of a desperate conspirator'.[37] In many ways, Crawford agreed with the views of orthodox political economy at that time. According to R.D.C. Black, there was a consensus among orthodox economists that the classical model of agriculture espoused by David Ricardo 'applied to a more advanced tenure and agriculture'

---

34 W.S. Crawford, *A defence of the small farmers* ([1839]), p. 112.   35 O'Brien, *The parliamentary history of the Irish land question*, p. 64.   36 *NW*, 5 Nov. 1835.   37 Ibid.

than that practiced in Ireland. In particular, for Ireland to improve its economy the present system of cottier farming had to give way to 'capitalist farming, on the English model'.[38]

Where Crawford differed from most of the economists was his challenge to the axiom that increased agricultural investment could only come when landlords were able to consolidate their holdings into larger, more efficient farms. Crawford feared that such a consolidation would entail great suffering: 'It cannot be concealed, that the reduction of population, and the expulsion of the small holders of land, is a doctrine much favoured by the public.' Furthermore, improvement would still require labour. After consolidation, those improvements would be done by a class of labourers entirely dependent upon wages for their existence, and Crawford feared that this would not provide for a stable society. Instead, Crawford proposed that the tenant rather than the landlord might be the primary agent for improvement and investment. If it were possible, by securing compensation for improvements, to make the desire for land dependent on 'the exertion of industry', that land hunger 'which under other circumstances, would lead into the commission of crime, will operate to his own benefit, and to the good of every interest in the State'.[39]

After his bill had been rejected and quarrels with O'Connell forced him from his seat at Dundalk, Crawford began to speak more harshly of the role of landlords in Irish society. The radicalism that had characterized Crawford's early political career reasserted itself. Crawford described landlords as the beneficiaries of monopolistic privileges conferred on them by the state for the good of society. The quest for land reform was a struggle for 'the just share of all the benefits which the benevolent Creator of the universe has conferred upon all alike, but which the unjust monopolies of human institutions have abstracted from the mass of the community, to confer upon minute favoured portions'. In order to insure that the public good was respected, society had the right to enact 'wholesome limitations and provisions' for the use of that land. Furthermore, Crawford began to employ a labour theory of value to judge the role of landlords in Irish society. Crawford stipulated that '*the most sacred right of property is, to acquire it by industry*'. Irish landlords had not acquired their property by industry, but were given them 'by Henry II, and other successive Monarchs' in order 'to secure the English interest'.[40] Crawford's growing radicalism also manifested itself in a brief flirtation with Chartism. In 1837 Crawford attended Chartist meetings in London and maintained a correspondence and friendly acquaintance with a young Chartist from Donegal, Thomas

---

38 R.D.C. Black, *Economic thought and the Irish question* (Cambridge, 1960), p. 18.   **39** W.S. Crawford, *A defence of the small farmers* (Dublin, [1839]), pp 15, 113.   **40** *NW*, 14 Jan. 1837, Oct. 1837.

Ainge Devyr. In 1836 Devyr published a radical critique of the land system that denounced 'absolute ownership' of land that he dedicated to Crawford.[41] Despite his desire to limit the consequences of orthodox economic theory in Ireland, Crawford was in some ways compelled to use the language of orthodox political economy theory in his efforts to persuade parliament to adopt his proposed legislation.

Crawford was more strident for a time after his disappointments, but he still spoke of reform in terms of the philosophy of natural rights rather than historically constituted rights, social compacts or covenants. Crawford may have appealed to the rational self-interest and intellect of some tenant farmers but he did not excite their emotions. The rhetoric that would excite tenants did not derive from a philosophic radicalism but rather from the rhetoric of a godly commonwealth that was then gaining ground in Ulster.

While Crawford was out of parliament from 1837 until 1841 the land question was somewhat in limbo. The public mind was taken up by other issues, particularly the establishment of an Irish poor law, municipal reform and, most importantly, repeal of the Union. For his part, Crawford was attempting, with little success, to develop the ill-fated Ulster Constitutional Association into a broad reform coalition. After he was offered the seat for the borough of Rochdale in England in 1841, Crawford began to take up the question of land reform again. In July 1843 Crawford proposed a new landlord and tenant bill in parliament but agreed to withdraw the bill later that year when Sir Robert Peel, assured him that a royal commission would investigate conditions in Ireland and recommend specific proposals for land reform. As a result, in 1843 the Devon commission began its Herculean labours.

Despite the appointment of the commission, some reformers in Ulster believed that Crawford's tactics were defective. In October 1843, the *Banner of Ulster* chided Crawford for neglecting to organize public opinion outside parliament.[42] With the hope of arousing more local support for Crawford's proposals, the *Banner* began to publish critical accounts of local estates, particularly the nearby estate of the absentee landlord the marquess of Hertford centred upon the parliamentary borough of Lisburn. Aside from questions of estate management, the luxurious lifestyle of the marquess was a particular target of criticism.[43]

Having voiced complaints about unnecessary delays and the choice of witnesses, the *Banner of Ulster* had been pessimistic about the Devon commission accomplishing anything of importance. The report that appeared

---

41 T.A. Devyr, *The odd book of the nineteenth century* (New York, 1882), pp 136–7, 148–9, 174–5; [T.A. Devyr], *Our natural rights* (Belfast, 1836), p. iii.   42 *BU*, 6 Oct. 1843.
43 Ibid., 14 Nov. 1843.

in February 1845 confirmed this fear and added insult to injury by granting publicity to doubts concerning the economic utility of tenant-right. When in March 1845 the *Times* and the *Dublin Evening Mail* suggested that not only did the tenant-right reduce the amount of capital available to either the landlord or an in-coming tenant to spend on improvements but was feudal in its origin, the *Banner* amusingly remarked that 'though we are not friends of feudalism and its tenures, yet as this is the only decent remnant so far as we remember that has descended to our time, it may be preserved for its curiosity'.[44] The *Banner* became increasingly alienated by the strictly economic examination of the problem as attempts were made to put the commission's proposals into law. The *Banner* was representative of a growing segment of opinion in Ulster that no longer believed that a proposal for compensation for permanent improvements was worth abandoning tenant-right as they conceived it.

Later that same month, the *Banner* made it clear that while it believed that Crawford's proposals for compensation for prospective improvements would be beneficial, particularly outside of Ulster, they should not supplant the custom of tenant-right that 'had been bought and paid for, or inherited, by the present tenantry'. Crawford denied that he intended his legislation to supersede the custom of tenant-right but did not explain how the custom might be preserved from such a fate. He complained that 'I would be anxious, if possible, to establish this custom on a legal and more solid foundation; but I find great difficulty in framing a legal and more solid foundation for that purpose, other than by securing compensation for the labour and capital expended'. This would be the conundrum that would exasperate politicians in both Ireland and Britain for the next twenty years. There was little doubt that tenants in Ulster had invested significant amounts of money in tenant-right, but tenant-right simply could not be justified in simple economic terms and, as a result, did not lend itself to the organization and rationalization of statute. The real question was, if legislation were adopted that only secured prospective improvements, would the market for tenant-right cease to exist? Over the next two years, the exasperation would increase among both politicians and tenants. When the Peel government brought forward legislation intended to provide for compensation for improvements, as recommended by the Devon commission, they were dismayed to find themselves criticized by friend and foe alike. Even Crawford concluded that 'a measure so limited as proposed in the Commissioners' report' would be 'a perfect cancelling of that right which the tenants of Ulster have possessed by immemorial custom'.[45]

In the House of Lords even this bill was opposed with such force, particularly by Irish landlords led by the marquess of Londonderry, that the

44 Ibid., 7 June 1844, 14 Mar. 1845.   45 Ibid., 28 Mar. 1845, 1 Apr. 1845

government was forced to abandon it. After the government surrendered, Crawford attempted to keep the matter before parliament but accomplished nothing else before the session ended.[46] In 1846, the government introduced another bill providing for compensation for prospective improvements. Crawford reluctantly supported the bill and the *Banner* grudgingly admitted that it would probably be beneficial, but criticized it for limiting its provisions to tenants with leases when most tenants had none.[47] Among some tenants, however, the bill aroused an outraged opposition. At a public meeting in Comber, Co. Down in July 1846, resolutions were passed opposing the bill because of its limitations on compensation, especially its restriction to prospective improvements and exclusion of past improvements. Speakers bluntly compared the failure to provide compensation for past improvements to 'robbery'. In order to oppose the measure, it was suggested that a 'Tenant League' be established.[48]

The failure of the bill did little to relieve tenants' anxieties. The economic effects of the Famine, while not as severe as elsewhere in Ireland, were becoming apparent in Ulster. Tenants were concerned that some local landlords, particularly on the Hertford and Londonderry estates, were unwilling to reduce rents during this period of economic hardship.[49] Furthermore, it has been suggested that during the Famine the bottom fell out of the market for tenant-right in Ulster.[50] Tenants believed their very existence on the land was threatened. The early efforts of the new Liberal government under Lord John Russell to cope with the crisis did little to assuage their fears. Not only did the government fail to bring in a landlord and tenant bill of its own, leaving Crawford instead to suffer ignominious defeat yet again, but it outraged tenants with public works proposals that they believed threatened to put the cost for such works on their shoulders rather than those of the landlords. Another proposal by Lord George Bentinck that the poor-rate be levied entirely off the occupying tenant rather than the landlord also caused concern. Tenants began to organize, and in May 1847, while Crawford's bill was still before parliament, public meetings in Derry and Coleraine laid the foundation for the Ulster Tenant-Right Association.[51]

Despite Crawford's efforts the land question had not been a critical issue for Ulster liberals before 1847. Tenants were concerned by changes in estate management practices that threatened to devalue their customary interest in the land and Crawford's legislative efforts were favourably commented upon in the liberal press. As the *Banner* had complained, however, that concern did not

46 O'Brien, *Parliamentary history of the Irish land question*, pp 71–6.   47 Ibid., 77; *BU,* 19 June 1846.   48 O'Brien, *Parliamentary history of the Irish land question*, 77; *BU,* 24 July 1846.   49 *BU,* 6 Nov. 1846, 17 Nov. 1846, 27 Nov. 1846, 1 Dec. 1846.   50 Wright, *Two lands*, p. 128.   51 *BU,* 2 Mar. 1847, 25 May 1847, 1 June 1847.

manifest itself as an organized movement until 1847 for four reasons. First, until the publication of the report of the Devon commission the issue had lacked distinct parameters. Second, the calamitous effects of the Famine made the issue a matter of survival to many tenants and a pressing political and moral problem for the British government. Third, so long as Repeal remained the foremost political issue, Catholic and Protestant cooperation was difficult if not impossible. Fourth, it was not until the evangelicals provided a more effective rhetoric, the pursuit of a godly commonwealth, that Presbyterians began to organize with any effectiveness.

The publication of the report of the Devon commission in 1845 together with the consequent proposed legislation by governments in 1845 and 1846 gave the issue of tenant-right a greater definition and immediacy. When the testimony given before the Devon commission was published, the opinion of many witnesses, including a number of important landlords and agents, that they believed tenant-right was an impediment to agricultural improvement that ought to be curtailed or abolished was remarked upon with concern and outrage at public meetings.[52] Even the commissioners themselves appeared ambivalent about the value of tenant-right, and Crawford, at a public meeting in Crossgar, Co. Down, voiced the concern of many that the commissioners 'were rather disposed to tolerate than approve of it [tenant-right]; – they gave it their sanction, because they thought it would be impractical to abolish it'. This concern increased when the first legislative proposals from government were brought forward in 1845 and 1846. Not only were these proposals unsatisfactory, placing unwelcome limits on the custom that some considered tantamount to its abolition, but owing to their origin with government they seemed to have some chance of passage.[53] Because Crawford's earlier legislative proposals were not supported by the governments of the day and therefore had practically no chance of passage, those bills probably did not arouse the same intensity of opinion as the bills proposed by administrations after 1845.

The second significant factor in making tenant-right a critical issue during the period between 1845 and 1847 was the effect of the Famine upon the agricultural economy. Before the Famine, tenants had complained about encroachments upon tenant-right, but during the Famine tenants briefly experienced what life might be like without the custom. Many hard pressed tenants were willing to sell their interests but almost no one still possessed sufficient capital to purchase those interests. Even landlords who might have wished to take advantage of the situation to consolidate further their holdings were struggling with unpaid rents and the burdens of the poor law.[54] The security

---

52 *NW,* 12 Apr. 1845; *Vin,* 3 May 1845.   **53** *NW,* 12 Apr. 1845, 5 July 1845.   **54** Wright, *Two lands,* pp 121–2.

that the ability to sell one's tenant-right previously had provided was completely undermined by the collapse of the agricultural economy. Tenants were determined to secure their interests and the often-considerable investments that had gone into them against such an impending collapse.

A third impediment to any attempt by Ulster liberals to organize around the issue of tenant-right was that perennial bugbear of Ulster liberalism, the threat of repeal of the Union. When tenant-right became a critical issue, the repeal movement attempted to use the concerns of tenants in order to entice Ulster liberals into making common cause with them. Shortly after the publication of the report of the Devon commission, Daniel O'Connell outlined his plan to attract Ulster tenants to the cause of repeal. Pointing out that there 'seemed to be a formidable conspiracy of the great landlords, backed by the Land Commissioners, to put an end to the tenant-right', O'Connell pledged that the Repeal Association would 'rally for the tenantry in Ulster'. In exchange for the association's support in legalizing the custom and extending it throughout Ireland, 'all we want is their cooperation and assistance'. O'Connell exhorted the tenants of Ulster to put aside past sectarian differences, to avoid betraying 'their own best interests for the purpose of indulging in a frantic fanaticism', and recognize that 'there is but one way to secure the tenant-right in Ulster, and that is by the men of Ulster joining the Repeal Association'.[55] As evidence of the importance attached to the land question, the parliamentary committee of the Repeal Association published three reports commenting upon the Devon commission's report in the first three months after its publication.[56] In June 1845, after the first government tenant compensation bill had been presented to parliament, the Repeal Association issued a further report written by Thomas Davis, the Protestant Young Irelander, that asserted that the government's proposed legislation would 'ABOLISH THE TENANT-RIGHT OF ULSTER', and called upon 'the men of Ulster to take immediate steps to avert the ruin threatened by this bill'.[57]

Despite their own consternation at the Devon commission's report and the legislative proposals of the government, Ulster liberals were not persuaded to forsake the Union by the alarming predictions of the Repeal Association or the hope that an Irish parliament would legalize tenant-right. Recognizing that 'the

55 *BU*, 14 Mar. 1845, 21 Mar. 1845.   56 The three reports were Loyal National Repeal Association, *First report of the parliamentary committee of the Loyal National Repeal Association on the land question* (Dublin, 1845); Loyal National Repeal Association, *Second report of the parliamentary committee of the Loyal National Repeal Association on the land question* (Dublin, 1845); Loyal National Repeal Association, *Third report of the parliamentary committee of the Loyal National Repeal Association on the land question* (Dublin, 1845).   57 Loyal National Repeal Association, *Report of the parliamentary committee of the Loyal National Repeal Association on the tenants' compensation bill* (Dublin, 1845), pp 17–18.

Repealers are endeavouring to gain over the Ulster men, by telling them that "Ulster is in danger"', the *Northern Whig* doubted whether tenant-right was in immediate danger of abolition. Furthermore, in the *Whig*'s estimation the custom was in many ways defective, and it hoped for a more rational scheme of compensation rather than a simple legalization as proposed by O'Connell.[58] The *Banner* applauded many of O'Connell's proposals but expected that reforms would be accomplished without repeal of the Union. The *Banner* furthermore resented any insinuation by O'Connell that sectarian bigotry underlay its objections to repeal or undermined its advocacy of tenant-right. Their support for the Union was practical, founded on its support for agricultural prices, its encouragement of manufactures, and its framework for political and economic stability. At the same time, the *Banner* made it clear that they would not repudiate any alliance for mutual benefit, but seek the repeal movement's support 'to obtain for Ireland a measure equivalent to Mr Sharman Crawford's Bill'.[59] That cooperation would not come, however, at the price of the Union.

Crawford also cast cold water on O'Connell's proposed partnership. Because O'Connell had never seriously supported Crawford's previous efforts at land reform, Crawford complained that 'the people of Ulster had as good a chance in relying on Sir Robert Peel for this measure as on the Repeal Association'.[60] As might be expected, Crawford's comments exasperated advocates of repeal in Ulster. At the Ulster provincial repeal meeting at Dundalk in May 1845, James McConvery, the publisher and proprietor of the Belfast repeal newspaper the *Vindicator*, sarcastically wondered aloud why it was 'by some strange fatuity, that people never can see things in exactly the same light as Sharman does'. McConvery told the crowd that if the Ulster tenant-right were to be preserved 'the rallying cry from North to South, from East to West, must be Ireland for the Irish'.[61] The disagreement over repeal and the personal antagonism between O'Connell and Crawford made an alliance between Catholic and Presbyterian reformers on the land issue doubtful.

In May 1847, the issue of repeal lost much of its impetus with the death of Daniel O'Connell. While internal divisions involving the Young Ireland movement and the catastrophe of the Famine had affected the Repeal movement, contemporaries recognized that the structure of politics had been fundamentally altered by the death of O'Connell. In considering O'Connell's political career, the *Banner* was convinced that 'the demise of Mr O'Connell opens an entirely new book of Irish politics'. In particular, the accusation that public opinion in Ireland was somehow subservient to the will of O'Connell

---

58 *NW*, 27 Mar. 1845.   59 *BU*, 21 Mar. 1845, 25 Mar. 1845, 18 Apr. 1845.   60 *NW*, 12 Apr. 1845.   61 *Vin*, 3 May 1845.

was no longer applicable, and the time was ripe for necessary reforms such as the legalization of tenant-right. Within a fortnight of O'Connell's death, a provincial organization, the Ulster Tenant-Right Association, was being organized by activists in Derry.[62] This association would bring together liberal Protestants and supporters of O'Connell from across Ulster together in a single organization. It was a feat that a powerful, credible repeal movement under O'Connell's direction had prevented.

The fourth element in the development of a popular tenant-right movement in Ulster was the evolution of political rhetoric that would excite the imagination of orthodox Presbyterians. This depended in part on the continued diminution of the influence of the conservative political element among orthodox and evangelical Presbyterians. At the annual meeting of the general assembly in July of 1847 a significant debate occurred over the role of the church in politics. The focus of the controversy was the resolution of the assembly in 1843, during the crises of the marriage question and lay patronage in Scotland, that called upon Presbyterians to defend themselves from the 'powerful influences' trying to wrest from them their 'rights and privileges', through 'a united and faithful discharge of their duty as Christian electors', to secure representation of Presbyterian interests in parliament by electing Presbyterians to parliament.[63] In 1843, Henry Cooke had been sufficiently outraged by this resolution, which he construed to be not only an attack upon the conservative government of Sir Robert Peel but a personal repudiation of himself, that he had pledged not to return to the general assembly until it was rescinded.

Cooke had kept his pledge, but by 1847 he and his followers were concerned that important national political developments together with pressing Presbyterian issues made Cooke's return to the general assembly imperative. Cooke's supporters presented a motion to rescind the 1843 resolution on the grounds that it was an extraordinary response to the marriage crisis and not a permanent principle of the general assembly. After a rancorous debate, the motion was approved and the 1843 motion rescinded by a vote of 43 to 21.[64] Despite the apparent victory of Cooke and his supporters, the size of the vote demonstrated that the general assembly had in no way reached a consensus on this question. While the exact number present on that evening is not certain. The general assembly was well attended, Cooke's intentions having been known for months, and probably comprised more than four hundred ministers. The observation by the *Banner* that a 'considerable number' of the assembly had declined to vote was a profound understatement.

The ambivalence of the assembly can be further discerned by the diversity

62 *BU,* 1 June 1847.   63 Holmes, *Henry Cooke,* pp 156–8; *BU,* 16 July 1847.   64 Ibid.

of opinion among ministers who were usually identified with a particular party within the general assembly. For example, Revd John Edgar, usually a reliable ally of Cooke in conservative causes such as opposition to the national schools, opposed the effort to rescind the 1843 resolution and suggested that it was hypocritical to assert that politics had no place within the general assembly.[65] The assembly had certainly discussed political matters before and would certainly do so again. Edgar further accused the proponents of the motion of attempting to bend the general assembly to the will of one man, his friend Henry Cooke. On the other side, Revd William Dobbin, a self-described opponent of Cooke on most issues, supported the motion to rescind in the hope of preserving peace within the general assembly by bringing Cooke back to the fold.[66] The failure of Cooke to defeat his opponents overwhelmingly was another sign of the surprising effect of the previously discussed union between the Synod of Ulster with the secession synod. The secession tradition produced political opponents to Cooke whose religious orthodoxy could not be impugned. Furthermore, they would provide both the rhetoric and much of the leadership of the tenant-right movement in Ulster.

The effect of the combination of these four factors, the report of the Devon commission, the agricultural crisis, the decline of the repeal movement and the on-going ferment among Presbyterians can be dramatically illustrated by considering a series of meetings that occurred within just a little over a year between February 1847 and March 1848. In February 1847, a meeting of farmers from the counties of Antrim, Down and Armagh was held in Belfast to discuss the so-called Labouchere bill intended to provide compensation to tenants for improvements. At what both the press accounts and the attendees described as a sparsely attended meeting, the principal speaker was Revd Henry Montgomery who lectured the audience not so much on the issue of tenant-right discussed in the resolutions before the meeting but rather on the policy and practice of the poor law.[67] There was no significant Catholic presence at the meeting in the form of either prominent laymen or priests. The meeting was definitely a Presbyterian affair with five ministers in attendance, all of them speaking. Furthermore, of those five ministers, three were Non-subscribers. Montgomery's own description of the meeting as composed of 'the élite of the farmers of this part of Ulster', seems quite apt. The meeting reflected the organizational weakness of the tenant-right movement at that time.

The first signs of the increasing political potential of the issue of tenant-right were evident in the Famine-ravaged countryside of Co. Armagh. On 29 April 1847, a meeting that included both the Presbyterian and Catholic clergy

---

65 Holmes, *Henry Cooke*, pp 99–100; *BU*, 16 July 1847. 66 *BU*, 16 July 1847. 67 *BU*, 2 Mar. 1847.

of the town was held in the courthouse at Newtownhamilton to formulate a petition to parliament on the issue of tenant-right.[68] The importance of the meeting was that it served as an example that was soon picked up both in the press and by prominent leaders in Ulster. Overshadowed by the final scenes of the life of O'Connell, the meeting did not receive attention in the press until some weeks after it occurred. Having taken notice, the *Banner* described the participation of both Protestant and Catholic ministers as a sign that the issue of tenant-right was producing a new movement that was 'a combination of all parties and politics'.[69]

Placing repeal in abeyance for the sake of achieving land reform was also given consideration by the *Vindicator* in the form of a letter from Edward Maginn, the coadjutor to the Catholic bishop of Derry. Maginn had established a reputation as an ardent supporter of O'Connell willing to confront perceived injustices publicly and vociferously. Maginn had not, like the local bishop of Down and Connor, Cornelius Denvir, damaged his credibility among nationalists by becoming involved in the controversial Charitable Bequests board set up by the Peel administration in late 1844. It is a measure of the significant political changes wrought by O'Connell's death and the crisis of the Famine that Maginn, the zealous patriot, was willing, for the moment at least, to forego repeal in order to achieve some measure of land reform. In his letter to the *Vindicator*, Maginn explained that 'even a Repeal of the Union, without the full recognition of your rights, would be of small service to your country'.[70] In this spirit, Maginn was willing to cooperate with efforts of the editor of the *Londonderry Standard*, James McKnight, to establish a provincial tenant-right society.

Although local societies had been established as early as 1846 at Derry and Comber, Co. Down, the establishment of a provincial society, the Ulster Tenant-Right Association, arose out of a committee appointed at a tenant-right meeting at Derry in June 1847. With McKnight as its secretary, the committee concluded that for such an association to succeed it would need the support of both Catholic and Presbyterian clergy. In order to enlist the aid of the Catholic clergy the committee contacted Bishop Maginn who provided a letter endorsing the association that was read at its first public meeting, a dinner for W.S. Crawford at Derry in October 1847. Of the 167 persons attending, at least 29 were clergymen. McKnight understood that much of the power and success of O'Connell had derived from the participation of the clergy and attempted to incorporate that strategy into the new association. The foundation for this cooperation was the deliberate exclusion of any issue other than tenant-right. Maginn wrote that 'in all discussions on this subject, differences on religion and

---

68 *Vin*, 15 May 1847.   69 *BU*, 25 May 1847.   70 *Vin*, 21 Apr. 1847, 19 May 1847.

politics should be placed in abeyance', and the members 'must strongly bar their gates against their introduction'.[71] McKnight confirmed the principle. The Ulster Tenant-Right Association was 'composed of farmers of all views in politics and religion, and inside their association no other subject but that of tenant right was known or would be admitted'.[72]

The first significant fruit of the new association was a large meeting at Ballybay, Co. Monaghan in early January 1848. By now the principle of clerical cooperation was established and the platform was shared by the local Catholic clergy from the town and surrounding countryside as well as two Presbyterian ministers. The speeches at the meeting demonstrated that despite genuine cooperation, significant differences, as expressed in their rhetoric, could not be entirely obscured. In the course of advocating tenant-right the Catholic speakers not only called upon the government to compel landlords to do their duty but made reference to a history of British confiscation and misrule as the fundamental cause for the social and economic crisis. The Revd E. McGowan, Catholic curate from a parish near Carrickmacross, Co. Monaghan, minced few words,

> the genius of British Government, for so many centuries in Ireland, its wars of oppression, its crippling legislation, its taxation monopolies, its anti-Irish prejudices, in reality have reduced Ireland to its present state of poverty.[73]

The animus against British administration that had been nurtured during the Repeal movement was alive and well.

On the other hand, while the Presbyterians also called for the government to compel landlords to accept their responsibilities, they believed that British government in Ireland was the foundation of the tenants' rights. Their goal was to restore those rights. James McKnight believed that 'both justice and wisdom' were to be found in the 'British Parliament' so that the tenants might achieve their aims by demanding 'constitutionally, but firmly, immediate redress'.[74] Likewise, the meeting at Ballybay also provided the first indications that the strategy of reaching out to the orthodox and evangelical majority among Presbyterians advocated by the *Banner* might bear fruit. Both David Bell and his fellow Presbyterian minister David Hanson were orthodox Presbyterians connected with the general assembly. More importantly, both had strong connections to the Seceders. David Bell's congregation of Derryvalley had been established by the Seceders about 1800 and Bell himself, the son a

---

71 *Vin*, 30 Oct. 1847, 3 Nov. 1847. **72** *BU*, 28 Mar. 1848. **73** Ibid., 14 Jan. 1848. **74** Ibid.

seceding minister, was ordained as a Seceder in 1839 just prior the creation of the general assembly in 1840.[75] David Hanson, though he was ordained in 1847 by the general assembly, was an assistant for the aging minister of the former seceding congregation of Drumkeen.[76] Bell and Hanson were not rarities.

By examining newspaper accounts of tenant-right meetings between 1847 and 1852, 95 Presbyterian ministers can be identified as having spoken in some fashion, whether in the form of introduction of a resolution or the delivery of a more lengthy discourse. Of those 95 ministers, 2 belonged to the handful of seceding sects, constituting a score or so of ministers, who had not joined the general assembly in 1840; 3 ministers were Covenanters from the Reformed Presbyterian Synod of Ulster composed of 25 ministers in 1849; 5 were members of the Non-subscribing Presbytery of Antrim that included 13 ministers in 1849; 9 were Non-subscribers from the Remonstrant Synod of Ulster that numbered 32 ministers in 1849; and 76 were members of the general assembly that comprised 514 ministers in 1849.[77]

Of the 76 ministers from the general assembly, 29 came from congregations that had been in the secession synod. Of those 29 ministers 17 had been ordained as Seceders. A further 6 of the 29 ministers representing former secession congregations were ordained after the creation of the general assembly in 1840 but can be counted within the seceding tradition with a degree of certainty because they were not only called by former seceding congregations but were also the sons of secession ministers. The remaining 6 of the 29, while not as clearly connected to the seceding tradition, must have had some affinity with the traditions of the former seceding congregations that called them.

The patterns of participation by Presbyterian ministers at tenant-right meetings require further comment before its significance can be fully understood. To begin with, the seemingly considerable level of participation by ministers from the Presbytery of Antrim and the Remonstrant Synod of Ulster is probably misleading. As shall be seen below, prominent Non-subscribing ministers such as Henry Montgomery and Fletcher Blakely were active spokesmen for the tenant-right movement before the organization of the Ulster Tenant-Right Association and the elaboration of a specific program by James McKnight. By 1849 the Non-subscribers had generally withdrawn from the

---

75 D. Stewart, *The Seceders in Ireland* (Belfast, 1950), pp 310–11. 76 Presbyterian Historical Society of Ireland, *A history of congregations in the Presbyterian Church in Ireland* (Belfast, 1982), p. 419. 77 The accounts of tenant-right meetings were taken from the *Banner of Ulster, Northern Whig* and *Vindicator*. Information regarding ministers and congregations was derived from Stewart, *The Seceders in Ireland;* Presbyterian Historical Society of Ireland, *A history of congregations;* and *Thom's Irish almanac and official directory for the year 1850.*

movement and as shall be seen, prominent Non-subscribers left their former allies to join forces with the opponents of the Ulster Tenant-Right Association.

On the other hand, even the considerable number of Covenanters and Seceders understates their role in the tenant-right movement. Not only did ministers from the seceding and covenanting traditions together constitute 34 of the 95 ministers who spoke at tenant-right meetings between 1847 and 1852, but they were also among the most frequent speakers. It was the practice at tenant-right meetings for local ministers to have some role but for additional speakers, such as James McKnight, to provide the primary address. Ministers from the seceding tradition were among the most frequent speakers on tenant-right platforms: David Bell, John Coulter, John Downes, John Mecredy, William Reid, John Rutherford, J.L. Rentoul and J.B. Rentoul. Of the 53 men who comprised the central committee of the Ulster Tenant-Right Association in 1850 18 were clergymen, all of them Presbyterian ministers. Of those 18 ministers, 9 were from the seceding tradition.[78]

This level of participation by Seceders in political associations was unprecedented. In the most recent consideration of the role of Ulster Presbyterians in politics at the end of the eighteenth century Ian McBride has described how the Seceders, in reaction to the chaos of that time, had abandoned 'the revolutionary programme of the Covenant' and diverted 'their energies towards the preaching of vital religion and the salvation of the individual'. Among the evidence cited by McBride was the fact that of the 60 Presbyterian ministers and probationers suspected of involvement in the rebellion of 1798 only 3 were Seceders while 5 ministers of the much smaller covenanting tradition were involved.[79] Furthermore, McBride correctly observed that the charges of disloyalty against seceding and covenanting ministers ought to be examined very closely as their obstinate refusal to swear any oath that might contradict or undermine their commitment to the principles of the covenant occasionally made them the objects of unwarranted suspicions of involvement in insurrection.

The newly found public spirit among the Seceders was the result of a combination of factors. One significant factor was the crisis in the Church of Scotland. They had been profoundly displeased with the seeming lack of concern about this crisis on the part of Henry Cooke. Cooke seemed willing to put his own conservative political agenda above the needs of fellow ministers in Scotland who had placed their very livings at stake for principle. This displeasure made them willing allies of those who had opposed Cooke's position within the general assembly. The crisis of the Famine was also a factor. The Famine affected the relatively poorer and more rural congregations of the

78 *BU*, 14 June 1850.   79 McBride, *Scripture politics*, pp 83, 232–5.

151

seceding tradition disproportionately more than those of the former General Synod. This made them natural allies of the tenant-right movement. Taken together, their hostility towards Cooke and their support for tenant-right made them potential allies of those Presbyterians who wished to wrest control of the liberal political leadership from the hands of the Non-subscribing élite who were predominant in the Belfast Reform Society.

The significance of tenant-right could not be measured simply by its effect upon agricultural investment or estate management. Tenant-right was intimately connected with conceptions of community. The political rhetoric of the Ulster Tenant-Right Association was replete with religious language and symbolism that premised the reciprocal obligations of landlords and tenants. While modern historians might refer to such obligations as the moral economy, contemporaries more often conceived of it in religious terms akin to the idea of a godly commonwealth. It is not surprising that the ministers who played such a prominent role in the Ulster Tenant-Right Association should have been the source of much of this political language. The forceful, prophetic nature of that language was, however, unprecedented. Before the formation of the Ulster Tenant-Right Association, the discussions of tenant-right by W.S. Crawford and others had been characterized by a more rationalistic approach to the question. Policies were advocated on the grounds of utility. Would they encourage investment or the consolidation of holdings and thereby improve the quality of agriculture? For the ministers of the Ulster Tenant-Right Association, the primary questions were moral. Did the current agricultural system, particularly in light of the catastrophe of the Famine, conform to God's precepts?

The language of reciprocal social obligations that characterized the speeches of the Ulster Tenant-Right Association was systematically outlined in a pamphlet by James McKnight entitled *The Ulster tenants' claim of right* published in 1848. In this lengthy and extraordinarily pedantic work McKnight pressed three fundamental ideas. First, McKnight sought to demonstrate that the relationship between landlord and tenant was founded on the 'essential, inherent trusteeship' of the state for the public welfare. Citing the natural law tradition, McKnight asserted that any ownership of land beyond that which can be occupied and worked by one man alone was dependent upon 'the requirements of public utility alone'. Landed proprietors were responsible stewards. McKnight cited a dictum of Thomas Chalmers' *On political economy in connexion with the moral state and moral prospects of society* first published in 1832 that property ought to be 'in the state of having a *public service* and *obligation* attached to it' rather than 'in the state of *simple* and *unconditional ownership*'. Second, by examining of history of the plantation of Ulster during the seventeenth century, McKnight sought to demonstrate that the custom of tenant-right was established by the crown itself at the same time 'in the self-same public instrument', as the titles of the landed proprietors in Ulster. Tenant-right was essentially 'a direct proprietary interest in the soil', that ought to be considered equal to the claims of landlords. Any attempts to destroy, curtail, or limit tenant-right were regarded as 'daring violations' of the rights of property which the government ought to protect against.[80] The third aspect of McKnight's argument was an attempt to demonstrate how the custom of tenant-right had benefited Ulster and would likely benefit, upon extension, the rest of Ireland. The extreme pedantry of McKnight's work almost certainly limited its direct appeal to the public. Its precepts, however, were effectively recast by the speakers of the Ulster Tenant-Right Association, particularly the Presbyterian ministers.

An early example of this new prophetic tone was a speech at Ballybay in January 1848 of David Bell, the Presbyterian minister of that town. Bell was not only a member of the central committee of the Ulster Tenant-Right Association but also served subsequently on the council of the Tenant League. Bell defended his right to speak publicly for tenant-right on two grounds – the approval of tenant-right voiced by the general assembly in an address to the lord lieutenant and, more importantly, his duty as a minister of Christ. Citing the precepts of the apostle Paul and the example of Christ, Bell proclaimed that it was his duty to God and his fellow man 'to announce to all, that it is His command, "to do justly," and "to love mercy," and to claim from all obedience to His sacred authority'.[81]

With this prophetic authority, Bell and others outlined the duties of landlords to their tenants from biblical and historical precepts. In June 1850, after a public controversy with Lord Castlereagh, Revd J.M. Killen of Comber, Co. Down suggested at the provincial tenant-right demonstration in Belfast that Lord Castlereagh should refer to the Bible for an account 'of that model commonwealth which God had established amongst His own people'. With that account in mind, Killen hoped that Castlereagh would recognize the agricultural crisis was an act of Providence intended 'to expose the hollowness, the thorough unsoundness and extreme danger of the continuance of the present relations betwixt landlord and tenants'.[82]

While such language was extensively used by ministers it was not their exclusive domain. At the June 1850 provincial tenant-right demonstration in Belfast a lay member of the central committee, William Hopkins of Ballymoney, warned landlords that 'it was a dangerous thing to oppress the people, as it was contrary to the God's commands'. The landlords were respon-

---

80 J. McKnight, *The Ulster tenants' claim of right* (Dublin, 1848), pp 6–7, 36.   81 *BU*, 14 Jan. 1848.   82 Ibid., 14 June 1850.

sible for the lives of their tenants and would be judged harshly if those tenants were 'destroyed or exterminated'. Landlords would be 'summoned before the tribunal of the Lord Jesus Christ to give an account of the manner in which they performed the trusts which possession of property conferred'.[83] James McKnight usually focused on the historical practice of the churches in the British Isles rather than citing scriptural principles. At a tenant-right meeting at Newtownards, Co. Down, in October 1851 McKnight defended the participation of ministers in the tenant-right movement from the charge of unwarranted involvement in supposedly secular affairs by quoting passages from the puritan divines Richard Baxter and Thomas Adams together with liturgies from King Edward VI. He hoped to demonstrate that the supposed division between secular and religious issues had little or no relevance in the past. McKnight recited an entire prayer from a primer of Edward VI calling for the Holy Spirit to remind landlords that they were '*Thy* tenants' and ought not '*rack* and *stretch out* the rents' of their tenants. McKnight concluded that no Presbyterian ought to claim allegiance to the puritan tradition 'if he can find nothing but clerical degeneracy in discussions involving the reciprocal obligations of men in society', nor an Episcopalian boast of the martyrdom of Archbishop Cranmer or the piety of Edward VI if 'he reject the economics of Edward's Prayer-book'.[84] McKnight's strategy of including the clergy gave the Ulster Tenant-Right Association a prophetic tone that had a wider appeal than the principles of political economy.

This prophetic tone increasingly isolated and weakened the Non-subscribing élite of Ulster liberalism. This was particularly evident when disagreements about the acceptability of compensation as opposed to the free sale of tenant-right came to the fore during 1850. Disagreements had arisen about the custom's origins and the best means for its preservation during the efforts to secure tenant-right through legislation. Because of his earlier legislative failures, W.S. Crawford had become convinced that whatever the origins and practices of tenant-right had been, successful legislation must accommodate the economic principles and beliefs prevalent in parliament.[85] This meant accepting some form of compensation for improvements rather than the free sale of interest. Crawford was willing to accept compensation for improvements that included some retrospective provision as a necessary compromise, but the Non-subscribing élite went further. They considered compensation preferable to free sale. As early as 1845 the *Northern Whig* believed that compensation would curb extravagant expenditures on tenant-right that were an impediment to agricultural improvement.[86] Many tenants, however, objected to compensation for improvements on the grounds that they

83 Ibid.   84 Ibid., 24 Oct. 1851.   85 *BU*, 28 Mar. 1848.   86 *NW*, 27 Mar. 1845.

or their ancestors had invested considerable sums on tenant-right without regard to the principle of improvement. They feared that if they could not demonstrate that they had made acceptable improvements, their investments would be ignored and completely lost.

By 1850 the divisions over compensation developed into bitter warfare between the *Northern Whig* and the *Banner of Ulster*. The *Northern Whig*, under the editorship of James Simms, continued to advocate compensation for improvements rather than attempting to legalize the customary practice of tenant-right. Indeed, the *Whig* concluded 'that the old right or custom appears to be gone, under the altered circumstances of the times' so that it would be pointless to ask parliament 'to legalize that which has ceased to exist'.[87] As a result of its editorial policy the *Whig* lost whatever influence it might have possessed with the Ulster Tenant-Right Association and was vilified at the provincial meeting of the association in Belfast in June 1850.[88] The alienation of the Non-subscribing élite from the larger tenant-right movement was also evident in July 1850 when the Association of Non-Subscribing Presbyterians, a body comprising the Remonstrant Synod of Ulster, the Presbytery of Antrim and the Synod of Munster, met in Newry. At that meeting, a proposal to petition parliament for tenant-right was rejected by a large majority.[89] This action stood in stark contrast to the proceedings of the general assembly where a petition supporting tenant-right had been passed by 'an immense majority'.

It was a testament to the popularity of the petition in the general assembly that Henry Cooke, who had attempted to undermine the proposal before the gathering, did not speak against it other than to signify his dissatisfaction by attempting to dissuade other opponents of the petition from wasting their breath and the assembly's time. Such passivity on the part of Cooke was singular indeed. Cooke must have suspected that opposition to public sentiment on this issue might further undermine his influence. Not surprisingly, the *Banner* gloated that only the 'Orthodox Presbyterian Church' had advocated 'the maintenance of the poor man's rights, in opposition to the rich man's power, and privilege, and oppression'. The *Banner* furthermore castigated the assertion by the majority among the non-subscribers that tenant-right ought to be held as a strictly political issue. The *Banner* estimated that 'four-fifths of the Bible itself are equally political' and suggested that those 'transcendental gentlemen' too holy to deal with such issues ought to 'join the company of "Enoch and Elias," leaving the materialisms of Bible duty to men of humble Bible attainments'.[90]

In the last few months of 1850 the *Whig* became desperately strident in its

87 Ibid., 22 Jan. 1850. 88 *BU*, 14 June 1850. 89 *BNL*, 23 July 1850. 90 *BU*, 5 July 1850, 26 July 1850.

attacks upon the *Banner* and speciously accused its editor, James McKnight, of advocating illiberal policies while editor of the *Belfast News-Letter*.[91] Perhaps the most striking evidence of the desperation of the Non-subscribing élite occurred in November 1851 when political observers in Ulster witnessed a conjunction of clerical luminaries that few contemporaries would have predicted. At a dinner in honour of the marquess of Downshire at Hillsborough, the organizers brought forward the '*two great Guns* of the North', Henry Cooke and Henry Montgomery, to fulminate against the policies of the Ulster Tenant-Right Association.[92] The spectacle of Montgomery, the champion of theological nonconformity and political liberalism among Presbyterians, making common cause with his nemesis Cooke, the champion of orthodoxy and political conservatism, was certainly incongruous if not wondrous. The *Banner of Ulster* expressed mock delight that ministers who had assailed each other as 'furious bigot' and 'denier of the "Lord that bought him"' were now 'doing everything but hugging one another in token of renewed brotherhood'.[93] Others were repelled by the fraternal levity of men who had 'taught their children to pronounce the shibboleth of party' and 'plunged the province into heartburning and strife for more than twenty years'.[94] The further irony of Montgomery's appearance at the same site where Cooke had announced the alliance of Presbyterianism with Episcopalians under the banner of conservatism in 1834 was not lost on contemporaries.

While the collapse of the repeal movement was an essential precondition for any significant cooperation between Catholics and Presbyterians, McKnight's role should not be underestimated. McKnight had established a reputation for fairness to Catholics without compromising his standing as an orthodox Presbyterian. Frank Wright has correctly observed that McKnight was notable among Protestant journalists for a humane discretion that was perhaps best exemplified by the fact that McKnight 'never let his readers imagine that the Famine in the South was a result of the moral weakness of the people'.[95] As described previously, McKnight began his career on the staff of the *Belfast News-Letter* in 1827 and eventually became editor in 1830. He remained at the paper until 1846 when continued clashes between the proprietor's conservatism and McKnight's moderate liberal views made his position untenable.[96] In 1846 McKnight became editor of the *Londonderry Standard* and remained there until 1849 when he moved to the *Banner of Ulster*.[97] In 1853, he left the *Banner* to return to the *Standard* where he laboured until his death in 1876.

---

91 *NW*, 5 Oct. 1850. **92** John Rogers, *The speech of the Rev. John Rogers, Comber, at the tenant soirée at Anaghlone* (Belfast, [1851]), p. iii. **93** *BU*, 18 Nov. 1851. **94** Rogers, *The speech of the Rev. John Rogers*, p. 9. **95** Wright, *Two lands*, p. 134. **96** Presbyterian Historical Society of Ireland, *Brief biographies of Irish Presbyterians* (Belfast, 1915), p. 13. **97** *BU*, 4 Sept. 1849.

Despite his affiliation with the *News-Letter* McKnight demonstrated a willingness to challenge the shibboleths of his community while at the same time respecting its heritage. McKnight applied his maturing intellect to analyses of that tradition in two pseudonymous pamphlets published in 1836. Both works confronted the widespread assertion that Catholicism was inherently intolerant by comparing it with the historical practice of Presbyterians. In *A letter to those ministers of the Church of Scotland who have lent themselves to the Dens' theology humbug*, McKnight criticized Presbyterians participating in a campaign against the teaching of the works of an eighteenth-century Catholic theologian at Maynooth. That theologian, Pierre Dens, had asserted that magistrates were obliged to punish, even execute, recalcitrant heretics. The teaching of Dens was taken as further evidence of the essential tyranny of Catholicism. Sarcastically dedicated 'without permission' to Henry Cooke, McKnight explained in the preface addressed to his 'Roman Catholic countrymen' that although he fundamentally disagreed with them in matters of religion he would 'never be a party to any scheme for doing you civil or political injustice'. McKnight believed the agitation against the works of Dens was intended 'to get up an artificial alarm amongst the rabble' in order to prevent municipal reform, preserve abuses in the Church of Ireland and 'beguile half-informed Protestants into Orangeism, under the gentle name of "Protestant Associations".'[98]

McKnight defended Catholics in two ways. First, he reiterated the defence Catholics themselves offered. The objectionable portions of Dens' work were limited to a couple of chapters in an eight volume edition that concerned larger issues of theology and canon law. Contemporary Catholics had rejected the sanguinary principles in the work and could not be held accountable for the opinions of one man. Second, McKnight exhorted Presbyterians to examine their own heritage of persecution. In his characteristically pedantic fashion McKnight wound his way through the labyrinthine history of Presbyterianism in Scotland in order to demonstrate that John Knox and the other leaders of the Reformation had espoused doctrines as severe and intolerant as those of Dens. Even more troubling was the fact that, unlike the case of Dens in which the intolerance was advocated by one man, 'the *duty* of the State to root out and destroy heretics' had been 'solemnly sanctioned, both by the Scottish Church and the Scottish Parliament', widely disseminated in popular editions of the reformers' works and enshrined in the Westminster Confession of Faith that remained the doctrinal standard for Presbyterians. Given these facts, McKnight

---

98 Member of the General Synod of Ulster [James McKnight], *A letter to those ministers and members of the Church of Scotland, who have lent themselves to the Dens' theology humbug* (Edinburgh, 1836), pp v–vi.

concluded that it was impossible to imagine 'that intolerance is an exclusive attribute of Roman Catholicism'.[99]

Despite his iconoclasm, McKnight was careful not to alienate his intended audience. He revered Knox and the other reformers; but they had lived in a different time. McKnight also took care not to accuse most Presbyterians of continuing to believe or act upon the intolerant principles contained in their traditional confessions of faith; 'because I know that you live in the nineteenth instead of the seventeenth century'. If, however, Presbyterians could 'tacitly separate what is good and what is bad' in the works of the reformers, 'how comes it that Roman Catholics cannot have the benefit of a similar equitable construction of their opinions'.[1] The combination of iconoclasm and a sense of historical development are very much reminiscent of the nascent liberalism of the eighteenth century in the works of Joseph Pollock, George Douglas, and Henry Joy.

In the second pamphlet, *Persecution sanctioned by the Westminster Confession*, McKnight continued his battle against Cooke over the chosen ground of Presbyterian tradition. In this case, the issue was Cooke's alliance with the covenanting minister Thomas Houston to oppose voluntaryism and support unqualified subscription to the Westminster Confession of Faith. McKnight delivered a withering assault on the early principles of the Covenanters and the Westminster Confession that left little doubt about their unsuitability for the nineteenth century. McKnight pointedly remarked upon the absurdity of Cooke glorifying a covenanting tradition that would have revolted against the 'marriage' of the Church of Ireland and Presbyterians he had proclaimed at Hillsborough in 1834. The covenant required not only the destruction of popery so fervently desired by Cooke and his allies, but also the extirpation of prelacy and the suppression of nonconformity

The principles of the Covenanters also logically entailed a repudiation of William III by Cooke's allies associated with Orangeism. William had formally protested against the persecuting principles of the Scottish coronation oath; and the Covenanters had reciprocated by condemning William's Toleration Acts that, ironically, 'constituted the charter of Presbyterians' in Ireland. As for the Westminster Confession, McKnight caustically observed that because it had been promulgated by statute, 'the doctrinal parts of the Confession, as they stand, are really the work of the English House of Commons, who *altered* them as they would have done the clauses of a bill for the regulation of beer-shops'.[2]

Perhaps the most telling blow against Cooke, however, was McKnight's

---

99 Ibid., pp 15, 18.   **1** Ibid., pp 14, 24.   **2** Member of the Synod of Ulster [James McKnight]. *Persecution sanctioned by the Westminster Confession* (Belfast, 1836), pp iv–vi, 66–7.

observation that even those who had been among the most tenacious adherents of the covenanting tradition had adapted to the changing spirit of the times. The Secession Church of Scotland, who had for some time required subscription to the Westminster Confession at ordination, stipulated that no minister was required to approve any portion 'which teaches or may be supposed to teach, compulsory or persecuting, and intolerant principles in religion'. Even the Covenanters themselves had 'disclaimed the persecuting tenets embodied in the Confession'.[3] After having engaged in iconoclasm on this magnitude it is extraordinary that McKnight was chosen to edit the two most important organs of orthodox Presbyterian opinion in Ulster, the *Banner of Ulster* and the *Londonderry Standard*. McKnight's popularity both as an editor and as a speaker on tenant-right platforms demonstrates that Presbyterianism in Ulster had not been petrified by the challenges of modernity. It also helps to explain the seemingly incongruous alliance between Catholic and evangelical Presbyterian activists during this period.

'Our own capital and industry': local government

In addition to the more widely known drama of the tenant-right movement, Ulster liberals significantly challenged the power of urban patrons in places that had seemed secure Ascendancy citadels. It was not only during the era of Catholic emancipation and parliamentary reform that the establishment of a town commission resulted in local political conflict. When municipal reform was enacted for Ireland in 1840, the legislation provided for the transfer of the powers and property of the abolished corporations to town commissions. The oligarchies that had entrenched themselves in close corporations were now forced to compete in a more representative arena. This sudden change resulted in an increased number of social and political conflicts, some lasting for a decade or more.

Dramas were played out in places rarely disturbed by politics. There seemed little worth fighting over in Bangor, a Co. Down town with a population of just over 3000 in 1841. Although the corporation had been composed entirely of 'members of the Ward family, their friends and allies', the borough had lost its parliamentary representation at the Union. The corporate property consisted of just over fifty-nine acres divided into 'very small' holdings among forty-three tenants and brought in just over £52 in annual rent to the corporation. Even those rents were applied 'generally for public and useful objects'.[4] There were no tolls or customs collected. Yet when the corporation was dissolved as a

---

3 Ibid., pp 70–1.   4 *First report of the commissioners appointed to inquire into the municipal corporations in Ireland*, pp 690–1.

result of municipal reform this paltry portion of corporate property became the ostensible object of a hard-fought struggle.

Despite inclement weather 'persons from the country, as well as from the town' filled the town hall in Bangor on 7 December 1840 to consider establishing a town commission to replace the defunct corporation. Reluctant to relinquish their authority many of the former corporators, including the agent for the Ward family, attended the meeting in order to exert their influence against a town commission. From the outset the corporate interest attempted to have the meeting adjourned on technicalities concerning the requisition. Unfortunately for them, two of the three presiding magistrates with extensive authority over questions of procedure and qualification were the well known liberals W.S. Crawford and his son, J.S. Crawford, who favoured a town commission.[5]

The corporate interest had hoisted themselves on their own petard. This was in fact the second meeting scheduled to consider a town commission. In the hope of avoiding a public discussion of the issue, the corporate interest had ignored a previous notice for a meeting from the lord lieutenant on the grounds that the requisition was incorrectly addressed to the provost of the corporation, an office long vacant. Rather than attempting to establish a corporate history of Bangor, the Lord Lieutenant simply sent a second notice for a meeting to be presided over by three justices of the peace instead of the provost. Had that first notice been accepted, the conduct of the meeting, including any rulings upon electors' qualifications, might have been controlled by the corporate interest. In spite of this initial fumbling, the corporate interest was determined to prevent the establishment of a town commission. The corporation's lawyer warned the meeting that his participation at the meeting was simply intended to provide the legal grounds for the 'quashing of the present proceedings in Queen's Bench'.[6]

The corporate interest understood that the dissolution of the corporation required the transfer of corporate property to some responsible institution; but they reminded the meeting that the law provided for the transfer of corporate property to the board of guardians if no town commission were established.[7] The corporate interest also believed that a board of guardians would be more amenable to their control. One third of the board of guardians consisted of appointed ex-officio guardians drawn from the local justices of the peace. The rest of the board was elected by a system that granted plural votes to wealthier ratepayers. The proposal to transfer corporate property to the board of guardians was clearly intended to preserve traditional, conservative power in Bangor. For the corporate interest another important advantage of the transfer

5 *NW*, 8 Dec. 1840. 6 Ibid. 7 Ibid.

of corporate property to the board of guardians was that it could be accomplished without the trouble of a public meeting.

The proponents of the town commission were eager to publicize the proceedings. When it was suggested that the statute limited admission to the meeting to those eligible for the municipal franchise, W.S. Crawford rejected that interpretation saying he 'could not come to any conclusion opposed to the admission of the public' or 'those who might advocate the legal rights and privileges of the public'. Furthermore, the advocates for the town commission argued that the public interest would be served more effectively by the recovery of 'the property, now in the possession of the Old Corporation, and now applied to purposes not advantageous to the town'. To establish their point they cited published parliamentary evidence describing the revenues from corporate property and 'dilated on the misapplication of these funds'. They urged that the community 'take into their own direction, that which was originally intended for the interests generally, of the inhabitants of Bangor'.[8] The fact that the report of the commissioners investigating municipal corporations had not been particularly critical of affairs in Bangor was less important than the principle of public responsibility and representation.

The issue eventually came to a poll. When at the end of the day the adherents of a town commission held a slight lead, the opponents requested that the poll be adjourned rather than closed because the inclement weather had prevented many people from attending the meeting. An adjournment was reluctantly granted in spite of protests that 'the corporators' intended 'to send out their bailiffs' in order 'to force persons to come forward to vote against their wishes'. As feared, the adjournment benefited the opponents of the town commission, and on the next day a town commission was rejected by a vote of 96 to 76. According to the *Northern Whig* the victory was the result of 'extraordinary exertions made, during the adjournment, on behalf of the Corporation'. Yet, the corporation's supporters were still so closely pressed that 'they were obliged to bring up a number of females to vote', whose qualifications and independence were suspect.[9] Both sides had marshalled considerable resources in a struggle that was less about the paltry property of the corporation than about local authority. It is interesting to note that the government took measures to prevent extended polling where bribery and coercion might be practiced with an amending act in 1843 that provided a two-day limit for polls as well as more explicit rules for terminating proceedings.[10]

Undoubtedly the most bitter of the conflicts concerning the transfer of corporate power and property occurred in Enniskillen. In many ways Enniskillen was typical. It was a close corporation that provided none of the

8 Ibid. 9 Ibid., 12 Dec. 1840. 10 6 & 7 Vict. c. 93, 1843, sect. 23.

ordinary services of watching, cleaning or paving to the town. According to the royal commissioners investigating municipal corporations, the corporation in Enniskillen existed 'for no practical municipal purposes whatever, save those which relate to its property, to the borough court, and to the provost's jurisdiction respecting weights and measures', all of which provided fees and patronage to corporate officials. Like almost everywhere else in Ireland, the corporation in Enniskillen was exclusively Protestant. However, the royal commissioners characterized Enniskillen as unique in the virulence of its sectarianism. They described an atmosphere of palpable fear. Unlike any other town they had visited, the inhabitants had 'a strong sense of apprehension of offending the Patron by coming forward to give evidence in open court' about matters which, 'as it appeared to us, might have been disclosed without giving the slightest case for offence'.[11] This fear was almost certainly related to the Cole family's prominent role in the Orange Order during this period.[12] As a result, the commissioners received 'less assistance from persons not connected with the corporation in Enniskillen, than at any other place which we visited in the progress of our Inquiries'.[13]

Recognizing its atypical aspects, the history of the town commission in Enniskillen is nevertheless a vital source of information about the difficulties that confronted inhabitants trying to manage the transfer of the power and property of corporations to town commissions. Indeed, as will be seen, Enniskillen may have been the primary copybook used for an amending act of 1843 intended to deal with such problems. Furthermore, despite the climate of fear and intimidation, the events were singularly well-documented in the local press. Whereas in other towns there are glimpses of the conflicts with occasional insights into the tactics and strategies of the opposing interests, no comparably detailed and continuous description has yet been recovered. It is unfortunate that the most complete data should be derived from a somewhat atypical town, but having acknowledged this difficulty, the insights gained from this underappreciated transition are compelling.

A town commission actually had been approved in January 1829 at what the *Enniskillen Chronicle* described as 'the most numerous as well as the most clamorous' meeting of its kind in the town. Twenty-one commissioners were selected to be sworn in at the regular monthly meeting in February 1829. At the February meeting, however, the 2nd earl of Enniskillen made an extraordinary personal appearance to explain that the January meeting had been of doubtful

---

11 *Royal commission to inquire into municipal corporations (Ireland), appendix to the first report of the commissioners*, pp 108–67. 12 In Oct. 1828 the 2nd earl of Enniskillen, as Deputy Grand Master of the Orange Order, had announced the revival of the institution in Fermanagh at the court house in Enniskillen, *Clonmel Advertiser*, 11 Oct. 1828. 13 *Royal commission to inquire into municipal corporations (Ireland), appendix to the first report*, p. 1086.

legality because 'there was no proof of notice of the meeting being posted at the church and court-house'. It was further suggested that if the meeting were irregular, the town commissioners might not be able 'to enforce payment of the taxes accordingly'.[14] Given that town commissions at this time depended on the local magistracy to enforce their decisions this statement was as much a threat as an observation. Under these circumstances the provost, who had presided over the first meeting and been responsible for providing public notices, declined to swear in the chosen commissioners

No further efforts were made to establish a town commission until November 1837 when the circumstances had changed considerably. Because the issue of municipal reform was of national interest in 1837, there was considerable public scrutiny of the process. The results could not be blatantly manipulated. A majority of the inhabitants seemed to favour a town commission, and even the conservative local newspaper, the *Enniskillen Chronicle*, supported a town commission as a practical measure.[15] Although previously the creation of a town commission had been frustrated 'by a silly quirk advanced for what was deemed an interested motive', the *Chronicle* hoped that on this occasion 'no such unworthy subterfuge will be suffered to thwart the laudable object now in view'.[16] Uncertain about their ability to defeat the measure in the face of public opinion, the corporate interest attempted to delay the process.

At the meeting the corporate interest conceded the need for improvements but proposed delaying consideration of a town commission until 'the nature of the [corporation] reform expected to be brought forward in parliament' was known. This proposal threatened to disrupt the meeting entirely, but a compromise proposal to adjourn the meeting until March 1838 was accepted on the condition that it was stipulated that if municipal reform failed to pass, a town commission had already been approved.[17] The proponents of a town commission were confident that significant municipal reform of some sort was at hand.[18] Unfortunately the fate of municipal reform was not evident until August 1840.

With the passage of municipal reform in August 1840, the corporate interest could no longer delay public discussion, and a new meeting to consider a town commission was scheduled for 20 October 1840. Alarmed by this prospect, the corporate interest, led by the 3rd earl of Enniskillen, orchestrated a separate meeting of the 'late and present Provosts, with the members of the

14 *EC*, 5 Feb. 1829; a similar effort to undermine the town commission in Newry was defeated at the Armagh assizes with the assistance of Louis Perrin, future member of the royal commission that investigated municipal corporations, *Strabane Morning Post*, 13 Apr. 1830. 15 *LJ*, 28 Nov. 1837; *EC*, 23 Nov. 1837. 16 *EC*, 16 Nov. 1837. 17 Ibid., 23 Nov. 1837. 18 *NW*, 7 Jan. 1837.

Corporation, and a number of respectable inhabitants' at the town hall on 19 October 1840 to consider alternatives to a town commission. The conduct of the meeting illustrated the personal influence wielded by the earl. Casting the event as a gracious effort by the earl to arbitrate on the divisive issue, the chairman of the meeting announced that 'his Lordship was in attendance to answer any questions the inhabitants might wish to be informed on'. A spokesman for the inhabitants favouring the town commission made it clear that they did not have any questions. It was simply a matter of fact that 'a large portion of the town thought the income of the Corporation ought to be applied to the improvement of the town', and 'nothing was looked to but the benefit of a town that was capable, and deserved to be equal to any other town in Ireland'.[19] They were not interested in the continued patronage of the earl of Enniskillen.

The earl tried to protect his authority and influence in the town by accommodating the desire for representative municipal government on his terms. He proposed the creation of a new corporation, elected by £10 householders, using provisions of the municipal reform legislation.[20] Knowing that the £10 franchise was an unpopular amendment to the legislation, the corporate interest attempted to soothe the opposition to the proposed new corporation in two ways.[21] First, they appealed to the inhabitants' financial concerns. They suggested that a new corporation would have more limited powers of taxation than a town commission, and they pledged to use their influence as grand jurors to obtain more county resources for the town in order to minimize municipal rates. Second, they offered more public participation in town affairs by proposing, somewhat dubiously, that the new corporation would 'be composed one half of burgesses and one half of the inhabitants'. The earl graciously assured them that 'he would let it be a fair election of the £10 householders'.[22]

Any hope that the inhabitants might support a new corporation was unrealistic. The immediate difficulty was the same issue that had divided the inhabitants in Bangor – what was to be done with corporate property? In this case an inhabitant asked whether the tolls and customs 'hitherto enjoyed by the corporation', would be applied to the improvement of the town by the proposed new corporation. It was pointed out that these charges had at one time amounted to more than £370 per annum. This was more participation than the earl had envisioned. He answered bluntly that 'the tolls and customs were his property and he could do with them as he pleased'.[23] When further questions were raised about corporate property the earl left the meeting which ended in disarray shortly afterwards.

The following day the provost convened the official meeting to consider a

---

19 *EC*, 22 Oct. 1840.   **20** Ibid.   **21** McIntyre, *The liberator*, pp 258–9.   **22** *EC*, 22 Oct. 1840.   **23** Ibid.

town commission. The number of people seeking to attend the meeting was so great that it had to be moved first from the town hall to the corn market and finally to the court house where the police unsuccessfully attempted to exclude 'non-residents and unqualified persons'.[24] The meeting became a clamorous demonstration of public opinion rather than a private deliberation of the town's élite.

At the court house, the corporate interest threatened to delay any transfer of corporate property to a town commission. The spokesman for the corporate interest predicted that a new corporation would be in place before a town commission 'could obtain a single shilling of the funds' from corporate property. Undeterred, the proponents of the measure proceeded to a poll in a borough where there had not been a contested parliamentary election since before the Union. Lasting three days, the poll was fought with all the tenacity of a contested parliamentary election. The conservatives characterized the contest as nothing less than 'the first struggle of radical intolerance to trample on the Conservative cause of Fermanagh'.[25] The 'radicals' intended to take control of municipal institutions by introducing 'a Five Pound franchise experiment into Enniskillen under the mask of improving the town'.[26] During the contest the corporate interest used its remaining powers to full advantage. Not only did the provost conduct the meeting in a partisan manner that limited debate, but he also permitted the opponents of the town commission to substantially reduce the size of the electorate by means of their near monopoly of municipal records.

This practical disfranchisement was, ironically, founded on an unintended consequence of ecclesiastical reform. It will be recalled that the establishment of a town commission relied upon the rating of the vestry for the initial property qualifications to vote. The corporate interest attempted to use the significant changes in the status of the vestry as an institution of local government to their advantage. At the meeting in 1840 the spokesman for the corporate interest tried to exclude any inhabitant who had not been rated at the last vestry. The counsel for the proponents of the town commission countered this gambit by pointing out that the act permitted anyone not actually rated at the last vestry to make themselves eligible by simply consenting 'to be rated at the next rating'.[27] The corporation's counsel responded that such consent was meaningless because there would be no future vestry rating. The right of the vestry to assess a rate had been abolished by a section of the Irish Church

---

24 Ibid.   25 Ibid., 22 Oct. 1840, 29 Oct. 1840.   26 Ibid., 12 Nov. 1840.   27 Ibid., 22 Oct. 1840; 9 Geo. IV, c. 82, sect. 5, stated 'That when any person shall have become liable to be rated in any such parish at any time after the making of the last preceding rate, and shall consent to be rated in like manner as if he had been actually rated for the same, such person shall, if otherwise qualified, be entitled to vote as if he had been actually rated'.

Temporalities Act of 1833.[28] This interpretation was readily accepted by the provost.[29]

Because the vestry rating used at the meeting dated from 1832, this ruling effectively disfranchised eligible inhabitants whose residences and circumstances had changed since that time.[30] Furthermore, the valuation used for the vestry in 1832 was grossly inadequate. According to an investigation of Irish boroughs prior to parliamentary reform, the houses in Enniskillen in January 1832 were generally valued at 'little more than one-half their real value' and in some cases less than one-third.[31] This was hardly surprising since the last valuation had been conducted in 1800. The 1800 valuation, moreover, remained 'practically unaltered' from the previous valuation in 1731.[32] The tactic of using a grossly inadequate rating and prohibiting declarations of consent to be rated in the future certainly excluded many eligible inhabitants from participation in municipal government.

When the 'consenting' voters, meaning those unrated but willing to be rated, were rejected, the supporters of the town commission asserted that, according to the rector, there had been a more accurate valuation by the vestry since 1832. This was difficult to prove due to the exclusive control of municipal documents exercised by the corporate interest. When the proponents of the town commission called for the rate, the spokesman for the corporate interest produced a list copied from the vestry book with a declaration by a churchwarden verifying that it had been the last rating for the parish.[33] The vestry book itself was never produced, but the provost accepted the copy of the rating and the declaration of the churchwarden in spite of objections. Suspicions may have derived from the fact that the churchwarden in question had been the last recorder for the corporation.[34] The reluctance to produce the vestry book may also have arisen from the fact that rates had been applotted in 1833, 1834 and 1835, and the applotment for 1835 was accompanied by the only significant revaluation of town property since 1731.[35] In each of those years, however, the approval of the applotted rate had been wholly or partially frustrated by popular opposition.[36] In this way the churchwarden's declaration that the 1832 rating was the last rate had a simulacrum of truth. It was the last wholly

28 Ibid.; the counsel for the corporation explicitly referred to 3 & 4 Will. IV, c. 37, sect. 65.
29 Similar strategies to frustrate the transfer of corporate property to town commissions were undertaken successfully in Tuam and Ardee. See *The queen v. Clarges Ruxton, esq., portrieve of the borough of Ardee* in *Irish Law Reports*, 3 (Dublin, 1841). 30 *EC*, 29 Oct. 1840. 31 *Parliamentary representation, Ireland* […], HC 1831–2 (519), xliii, p. 74. 32 W.H. Dundas, *Enniskillen, parish and town* (Dundalk, 1913), pp 64, 52 33 *EC*, 22 Oct. 1840, 29 Oct. 1840. 34 Dundas, *Enniskillen, parish and town*, p. 87; W.C. Trimble, *The history of Enniskillen* (Enniskillen, 1919–21), iii, p. 723. 35 Dundas, *Enniskillen, parish and town*, p. 52. 36 *EC*, 16 May 1833; Dundas, *Enniskillen, parish and town*, p. 55; *EC*, 4 June 1835.

successful rating by the vestry. The corporate interest must have relished the irony of popular opposition to vestry rates providing the means to frustrate popular support for a town commission.

During the first two days of the poll the provost recorded all the votes but excluded any inhabitant not rated by the vestry in 1832 from the official tally. Because the *Enniskillen Chronicle* published a list of all the voters and whether they were accepted or rejected, it can be shown that many of the excluded inhabitants were qualified. They were officially listed as £10 householders in the report of the select committee on fictitious votes in Ireland in 1837. On the third day the provost provided the meeting with a tally of the accepted votes that prompted the supporters of the town commission to abandon the struggle.[37] During the course of the poll, 115 inhabitants voted for the town commission but only 9 were accepted by the provost (29 of the 115 were listed as £10 householders in 1837). 118 inhabitants voted against the town commission but only 23 were accepted by the provost (49 of the 118 were listed as £10 householders in 1837).[38]

An instructive epilogue occurred within a few days of the poll, on 26 October 1840. The board of guardians, now trustees of the property of the corporation that had been dissolved on 24 October 1840, appointed the church-warden who had provided the controversial copy of the rating to the post of collector of tolls and customs for the town market.[39] Some of the manifold sharp practices of the corporate interest in Enniskillen in 1840 were prohibited by an amending act passed in August 1843. The obsolete reference to valuation by the vestry was repealed and replaced by poor law valuation. The clerk for the poor law union was now required to attend any election meeting with the 'Rate or Valuation book of such Union'.[40] The government may very well have used Enniskillen as the copybook for the amending legislation. In February 1843 the *Enniskillen Chronicle* complained that the government had written to a leading proponent of a town commission 'requiring information as to the several meetings of Enniskillen held for the purpose of applying the provisions of the lighting and cleansing act to the town' instead of contacting the responsible corporate official.[41] By March 1843 the amending bill was before parliament.[42]

With the rejection of a town commission in 1840, the struggle to wrest control of the town's institutions from the earl of Enniskillen became focused on the newly created board of poor law guardians. When the board became responsible for the corporate property the earl of Enniskillen used his influence with the guardians to maintain control of that property. Because of the

37 *EC*, 29 Oct. 1840. 38 Ibid., 22 Oct. 1840, 29 Oct. 1840; *Third report from the select committee on fictitious votes*, appendix no 6, pp 201–3. 39 *EC*, 29 Oct. 1840. 40 6 & 7 Vict. c. 93, sect. 10–20. 41 *EC*, 23 Feb. 1843. 42 *Journals of the House of Commons*, v. 98, 21 Mar. 1843, 137.

property qualifications for poor law elections, the earl of Enniskillen was able to control the board. Although his opponents averred 'that his influence was such that he could carry any measure that he took an interest in with the board', he could not control publicity concerning the deliberations of the board of guardians as had been the practice under the corporation.[43]

Until the parliamentary inquiries of 1833, the proceedings of the corporation were 'never made known to the inhabitants at large'.[44] In 1833 the *Enniskillen Chronicle* had confirmed that the inhabitants regarded corporate affairs 'with jealousy and distrust from the nature of the privacy respecting them'. During its first year of existence the board of guardians also deliberated in private, but in this case the poor law commissioners in Dublin issued a rule compelling the guardians to admit newspaper reporters and sent an assistant commissioner to Enniskillen to enforce compliance.[45] This publicity revealed questionable conduct by the board and reinvigorated efforts to establish a town commission.

Once again the occasion for discontent was the management of corporate property. Elected guardians complained that the revenues from corporate property were being spent on the salaries of numerous former corporate officers who were 'not doing anything for that money'. These liabilities amounted to £306 14s. out of an annual income from corporate property of £447 17s. 8d. Although it must have been galling to see such a large percentage of the public revenues supporting the redundant remnants of the corporate patronage system, limited compensation for former corporate officers was provided for by the municipal reform act. Other expenditures were more questionable. In February 1842, the assistant poor law commissioner responsible for Enniskillen reminded the guardians that they were simply the trustees of corporate property. They could only apply revenue from former corporate property to stipulated expenses such as debts acquired before municipal reform, the salaries of former officers and the support of the poor.[46] The guardians could not act as if the corporation's powers had been simply transferred to the board of guardians. In spite of this admonition the board of guardians continued to spend corporate revenues on questionable items.

Only in August 1844 did the resolve of the corporate interest begin to waver. Admitting that inquiries had convinced him that a corporation would be costly, the earl of Enniskillen agreed to submit to public opinion and support a town commission.[47] Unfortunately, the matter was delayed yet again when the board

43 *Lessees of the commissioners of the town of Enniskillen v. The earl of Enniskillen*, in *Irish Law Reports*, 12 (Dublin, 1850), 37.   44 *Royal commission to inquire into municipal corporations (Ireland), appendix to the first report of the commissioners*, p. 1085.   45 *EC*, 26 Sept. 1833, 24 Sept. 1840, 21 Oct. 1841; R.B. McDowell, *The Irish administration* (London, 1964), p. 177.   46 *EC*, 21 Oct. 1841, 10 Feb. 1842.   47 Ibid., 29 Aug. 1844.

of guardians became embroiled in a series of conflicts with the poor law commissioners in Dublin.[48] Once again a significant source of the conflict was the late corporation's property, particularly the application of revenues to the costs of maintaining the poor.[49] By August 1844 the considerable expense of the poor law was becoming evident. There were over £1,000 in cost over-runs for the construction of the work-house after the board of guardians had already borrowed more than £11,000 for that purpose.[50] The guardians were reluctant to strike a rate sufficient to pay these expenses. They hoped to minimize the rate by increasing the revenues from corporate property and then applying that money to poor law expenses.

One untapped source of revenue was the arrears in rents on corporate property. From the outset, the guardians had encountered difficulties collecting the rents. In January 1842 the arrears amounted to £900. By April 1845 the amount had increased to £1,215. However, the board of guardians needed the consent of the poor law commissioners in Dublin to proceed against defaulting tenants. The poor law commissioners refused to approve proceeding against all of the defaulting tenants, but instead recommended that two or three defaulters be prosecuted as examples to the others. The guardians rejected this plan and accused the commissioners of withholding their permission because they preferred the arrears to be used by a town commission rather than applied to poor law expenses. One guardian complained that the commissioners had been 'humbugging' the board of guardians and that there was no point in pursuing defaulters anymore 'as it was certain that commissioners under 9 Geo. 4th would be applied for as soon as the rate is struck, and all the concerns with the corporation, therefore, will be removed from the board'. The guardians obstructed the process by refusing to assist the town clerk in preparing the rate. It was not until December 1845 that the *Enniskillen Chronicle* could announce that 'the poor rate has been struck and now in the process of collection', so that there was no longer any reason for delaying a town commission.[51] Regardless of reason, the process was delayed until August 1846 while the board of guardians continued to seek permission to prosecute all of the defaulting tenants holding corporate property.

Following a struggle that had lasted more than seventeen years, the establishment of the town commission was anticlimactic. When the official meeting was convened in September 1846 a town commission was approved with no opposition and the first twenty-one commissioners selected with practically no disagreement. There was no poll. The *Enniskillen Chronicle* praised 'the

---

48 Ibid., 22 Aug. 1844, 3 Mar. 1845, 6 Mar. 1845.   49 3 & 4 Vict. c. 108, sect. 18.   50 *EC*, 22 Aug. 1844; *An account of the sum total advanced on loan,, on the security of the poor rates in Ireland; for the building of workhouses in Ireland*, HC 1847 (157) lv, p. 9.   51 *EC*, 13 Jan. 1842, 3 Apr. 1845, 11 Dec. 1845.

unanimity that was here manifested' and hoped that 'every party difference will be forgotten; and that the good of the Enniskillen public will be the sole object' of the town commissioners. It proved a forlorn hope. From the first regular meeting there were, according to the *Enniskillen Chronicle,* 'marked signs of distinct political parties' that had been 'the ruin of the public interest' in Enniskillen.[52] As had been the case in Coleraine, establishing a town commission was not a decisive victory for liberals. A struggle to establish the principle of public authority over the property of the defunct corporation continued, with varying degrees of intensity, for the next thirty years. Three days after the first meeting of the town commission, the earl of Enniskillen expressed his disapproval by locking the town commissioners out of the town hall.[53] In response the town commission decided to establish its rights to all of the former corporate property.

As in Coleraine, the town commission needed to gain access to the records of the corporation in order to establish its claims. In this case, those records were in hands of the board of guardians whose chairman, the earl of Enniskillen, refused to release the documents on the grounds that they were necessary for 'the recovery of the arrears owing to them' out of the estate of the corporation.[54] Whether the similarities with the tactics of John Boyd in Coleraine were deliberate or coincidental is unclear. Although the board eventually forwarded some documents to the town commission, neither the minute book, the account book nor the book of record, all of which had been examined by the royal commissioners in 1833, were ever relinquished.[55] The minute books for the years 1801 to 1839 were reported stolen from the town clerk's desk sometime during 1845 or 1846.[56] During a later conflict concerning leases, the plain-speaking editor of the *Impartial Reporter,* William Trimble, advised the town commissioners to secure their leases and other documents in a bank lest they disappear like the corporation's books.[57]

From the few records delivered to them, the town commission discovered numerous irregularities, including leases 'dated years before the paper was manufactured', leases with 'erasures' and leases 'given in reversion'.[58] In effect, the town commission publicly accused the corporation of crudely falsifying documents and illegally transferring property. The fear described in 1833 had

---

52 Ibid., 24 Aug. 1846, 21 Sept. 1846. 53 Enniskillen TC, 1 Oct. 1846, PRONI, LA35/2B/1A. 54 *EC,* 5 Nov. 1846. 55 Trimble, *History of Enniskillen,* iii, p. 1090. 56 In Dec. 1848 a barrister representing the town commission in a legal case against the earl of Enniskillen testified that 'about three years since the desk of the Recorder of Enniskillen was broken into, and the record books, containing the proceedings of the corporation, from the year 1801 to the year 1839 inclusive, stolen from it.' *EC,* 11 Dec. 1848. 57 J.B. Cunningham, *Oscar Wilde's Enniskillen* (2002), p. 29. 58 Trimble, *History of Enniskillen,* iii, p. 1090; Enniskillen TC, 1 Mar. 1847, PRONI, LA35/2B/1A.

given way to open confrontation. By withholding the records, the corporate interest hoped to conceal Byzantine abuses from public scrutiny. Despite legislation forbidding the 'conveyance, alienation, settlement, charge or incumbrance whatsoever of corporate property' while municipal reform was being debated, the corporation had alienated sizeable portions of corporate property.[59]

In one particularly brazen act, the earl of Enniskillen took control of the meat market of the town through an astonishing conflict of interest. The property for the meat market had been leased to the corporation in perpetuity by the Cole family for £21 per year. Although the corporation made a profit of over £400 per year from the market, when the corporation's documents and responsibilities were transferred to the board of guardians, the rent for the meat market due to the earl of Enniskillen went unpaid. As result, the market was ejected for non-payment of rent. In a sublimely absurd moment, the earl of Enniskillen had the ejectment notice served on himself as chairman of the board of guardians.[60] The town commission succeeded in regaining control of the corporate property through a legal case brought by the Irish attorney-general with the town commission as relators. Fearing the earl of Enniskillen's influence might affect the outcome, the case was transferred to Dublin where the town commission prevailed in December 1848.[61] With the revenues from this recovered property, the town commission avoided levying a town rate until 1870.[62]

The actions of the town commission demonstrated the changing order of things in Enniskillen. After years of opposition to the national school system by conservatives and the Orange Order, in September 1847 the commissioners proposed that a National school be built on former corporate property.[63] In order to further emphasize their control of public space, in January 1848 the town commission exercised its statutory authority to rename streets. Previously, political motives occasionally had governed the naming of streets. For example, after the duke of Wellington had voted for Catholic emancipation in 1829, the trendy Wellington Place was renamed Eldon Row after the ultra-Tory peer who had persevered in the opposition to emancipation. In 1848 the town commission was determined to remove some of the symbols of sectarian triumphalism that had characterized the corporation's reign. They changed the name of a primary street through the town from William Street, in honour of

---

59 6 & 7 Will. IV, c. 100; *Lessees of the commissioners of the town of Enniskillen v. the earl of Enniskillen*, in *Irish Law Reports*, 12 (1850), 36–40. **60** *Report of the commissioners appointed to inquire into the state of the fairs and markets in Ireland, part II, minutes of evidence*, HC 1854–5 (1910), xix, p. 480. **61** *Lessees of the commissioners of the town of Enniskillen v. the earl of Enniskillen*, p. 40; Trimble, *History of Enniskillen*, iii, p. 1092. **62** Trimble, *History of Enniskillen*, iii, pp 1093–4. **63** Enniskillen TC, 6 Sept. 1847, PRONI, LA35/2B/1A.

William III of glorious memory, to Castle Lane, signifying the street's proximity to Crom castle.[64] Enniskillen's conservatives were outraged by the changes. The *Enniskillen Chronicle* condemned the town commission as an 'honourable body of good-for-nothings' and a 'noisy band of peace-disturbers' who 'for the purpose of proving their authority, metamorphose the name of the street into another quite the antipodes to that which it was formerly known'.[65]

Another telling symbol of the diminished power of Enniskillen's conservatives was their loss of control of the town hall in 1849. After regaining control of the building, the town commission promptly resolved 'that all Secret Societies be prevented from holding their meetings in this Town Hall'.[66] Aimed at the Orange Order and the earl of Enniskillen, this policy marked a dramatic departure from previous practice. As recently as 1845 the town hall had been the site of meetings by the Orangemen of Fermanagh to protest the dismissal of one of their leaders from the magistracy.[67] In the place of Orange meetings, the town commission presided over a tenant-right meeting in the town hall in July 1850. Among the resolutions was a motion of thanks to the prominent radical politicians W.S. Crawford, John Bright, and Richard Cobden.[68]

The conflicts with the earl of Enniskillen endured. There were occasional truces, such as the brief suspension of hostilities during the passage of the Enniskillen Improvement Act of 1870 that incorporated the town commission, extended the municipal limits and permitted the town to borrow money to build a waterworks.[69] However, as late as 1877 the royal commission considering local government and taxation in Ireland was still investigating events that had occurred forty years previously. The commissioners heard testimony from the current chairman of the town commission, Jeremiah Jordan, a Methodist merchant and tenant farmer who complained that when he was a teenager 'the then provost and burgesses' had 'leased or jobbed away the greater part of the corporate property to relatives or friends'.[70] In 1874, Jordan had briefly presented himself as a Liberal candidate for the borough promising to support fixity of tenure for tenant farmers.[71] Jordan subsequently joined the Land League and was elected MP for Fermanagh South as a Nationalist.[72] He received his political education in the town commission in Enniskillen.

Enniskillen was not the only place where the political quiescence of aristo-

---

64 Trimble, *History of Enniskillen*, iii, p. 1133.   65 *EC*, 10 Jan. 1848.   66 Enniskillen TC, 9 Apr. 1849, PRONI, LA35/2B/1A.   67 *Vin* 21 Aug. 1839, 30 Aug. 1845, 15 Oct. 1845.TC, 9 Apr. 1845.   68 Enniskillen TC, 29 July 1850, PRONI, LA35/2B/1A.   69 *Local government and taxation of towns inquiry commission (Ireland), part I, report and evidence, with appendices*, HC 1877 (1696), xxxix, p. 2.   70 *Local government and taxation of towns inquiry commission (Ireland), part III, report and evidence, with appendices*, HC 1877 (1787), xl, p. 127. 71 *FJ*, 27 Jan. 1874.   72 *Parnellism and crime; the special commission; part xxviii* (London, 1889), pp 5 – 6; *The popular guide to the House of Commons* (London, 1906), p. 78.

cratic domination was disturbed. In Newtownards, Co. Down, the dominant family were the Stewarts, the marquess' of Londonderry, who had controlled local affairs for decades. The Stewarts acquired control of the town in a transaction that illustrated the extent to which parliamentary boroughs and municipal corporations had been deemed chattel even into the nineteenth century. After the Union, James Alexander, the nabob 1st earl of Caledon, had exchanged the borough of Newtownards for that of Newtownlimavady, Co. Londonderry with Robert Stewart, 1st marquess of Londonderry. To complete the transaction, the personnel of the respective corporations were exchanged, 'the friends of each mutually resigning as burgesses in the one, and being elected in the other'.[73] Between that exchange and the investigation of the municipal commissioners in 1833, the corporation met once. A town commission was established in January 1842 in the aftermath of municipal reform. To begin with, as had been the case in Strabane, the habit of relying upon the beneficence and authority of the patron persisted. The town commissioners solicited contributions from the 3rd marquess of Londonderry to help defray extraordinary costs and keep rates down. When in 1842 the town commission outlined its need for £50 for lighting, the marquess expressed a willingness to do everything in his power, 'consistent with what is just', and helpfully, in his mind at least, suggested that along with the £10 he and his sons would contribute and the £20 the commissioners would provide, they might 'set on foot a voluntary subscription' from the 'Gentry and Inhabitants not immediately in the Town, but surrounding and passing constantly through it'.[74]

In 1850 this amicable relationship ended abruptly and very publicly. The occasion for the rupture was a visit by the lord lieutenant, the 4th earl of Clarendon, in September 1850. During the visit, the town commissioners presented an address to the viceroy which, along with the usual salutations, asked Clarendon to use his influence to obtain legislation 'which would secure to the tenant full compensation for all his improvements'. This petition aroused Londonderry's wrath. In a public letter he expressed indignant embarrassment that 'merely the Chairman and Commissioners of my Town, for the watching and lighting of the same' should have made Newtownards 'the only locality where complaint and grievance would be mingled with compliment'. Furthermore, he was offended that 'the inference of injustice broadly hinted against landlordism' should come from an estate where it had been 'the invariable practice from father to son', to adhere to the 'boon' of tenant-right. He believed that the commissioners had joined in the agitation of a few malcontents led by local Presbyterian ministers because their 'commerce, and shops,

---

73 *First report of the commissioners appointed to inquire into the municipal corporations in Ireland*, p. 958. 74 Newtownards TC, 6 Jan. 1842, 6 Apr. 1842, PRONI, LA60/2B/1.

and town' depended on his lordship's tenants' 'favour and custom'. Only the earl of Clarendon's courteous disregard of the affront had prevented the marquess 'from taking those measures of separation from you and your interests which, under other circumstances, I should have felt it my duty to have adopted'.[75]

The town commissioners were not chastened by the marquess' lecture. They responded with a caustic public letter of their own in which they rejected the principal points of Londonderry's letter. The most emotional response, however, was reserved for Londonderry's characterization of them as subservient dependents. They boasted that:

> our own capital and industry, as well as those of our fellow-townsmen, have almost entirely raised the buildings and established the trade of our town; and, consequently, the considerable additions which have thus been made to your rent-roll, and the large sums which the manufacturers have circulated among your tenant *farmers*, place you and them under greater obligations to the inhabitants of the town than they are to either to your lordship, or to that portion of your tenantry to which you refer.

In their ire they went further. Even the marquess' contributions and subscriptions to local institutions, 'taking into consideration the vast sums of money received by you, as lord of the soil' were 'trifling'.[76] This petulant exchange received press coverage in London as well as Dublin, where the *Freeman's Journal* mockingly described the town commissioner's address to the lord lieutenant as 'too great an infringement of feudal rights' to be borne.[77]

The marquess' haughty public denunciations certainly did not demonstrate the polite condescension that an experienced diplomat might have been expected to possess. Even the conservative *Belfast News-Letter* characterized an earlier public letter as 'sharpened by taunts, spiced with sneers, and loaded with sophistries'.[78] Nevertheless, the marquess was not entirely delusional in his apprehension of an organized agitation against him. The affairs of his estate had been widely criticized in the local press, especially in the *Banner of Ulster*. Two Presbyterian ministers, Revds Julius McCullough and Hugh Moore had played prominent roles in meetings on the estate. Furthermore, it would be fair to describe the two ministers as agitators. They both spoke publicly at tenant-right meetings, and McCullough was a member of the central committee of the Ulster Tenant-Right Association for whom Londonderry's letters were indeed a boon.[79]

---

75 Ibid., 11 Sept. 1850, 17 Sept. 1850, PRONI, LA60/2B/1.   **76** Ibid., 27 Sept. 1850, PRONI, LA60/2B/1.   **77** *FJ*, 20 Sept. 1850.   **78** *BNL*, 25 Dec. 1849.   **79** *BU*, 14 June

They were not, however, outside agitators. Not only were they both local ministers, but they were also town commissioners. Moore had been a commissioner since 1844 while McCullough was chosen to replace a deceased commissioner in June 1849. In May 1851, Moore was elected chairman of the town commission.[80] By August 1851 Moore and four other town commissioners who had offended the marquess the year before were served with notices to quit town parks leased to them. True to form, they responded with defiant public letters published both in Belfast and Dublin.[81] A little more than two years later, in February 1854, one of those town commissioners who had been served with a notice to quit, John McKittrick, offered one last affront to the ageing aristocrat who died the following month. When Londonderry ordered an archway into the market-house closed, McKittrick encouraged two weavers to challenge this decision by bringing the masons engaged in the work before the petty sessions on a nuisance charge. This seemingly trivial case was given extensive coverage in press. Interest in the case was sparked by McKittrick's choice of counsel. Whatever remained of the dignity of the marquess was severely assailed by a Belfast solicitor named John Rea, of whom more will be written, in a performance that the *Banner of Ulster* rightly described as astonishing. Rea spent the entire case mocking the marquess, and when the opposing counsel objected that 'parties behind the screen put forward these paupers' only 'to abuse Lord Londonderry in Court' and get 'Mr Rea to make a speech and fling out innuendos', Rea feigned shock that anyone would conceive of such a plan.[82]

In the end Rea lost, and relations improved between the town commission and the 4th marquess of Londonderry, a man of more liberality and discretion who freely provided ground for new markets and let land for industrial use on generous terms. This was in dramatic contrast to his father's explicit contempt for manufacturing and clumsy attempts to manipulate the leases of town parks for political ends. The reconciliation with the new lord of the soil did not yet mark the end of a liberal presence in the town. As late as 1874 Newtownards was considered a liberal stronghold where the town commissioners continued to participate in liberal political causes.[83] The history of the conflict between the town commission and the 3rd marquess illustrates the ability of liberals to find a space for themselves in town commissions, and, more importantly, a willingness to use the town commission to challenge publicly the authority and influence of aristocratic patrons. Similar confrontations occurred in a number of other towns.

At the end of December 1852, a banquet was held in Lisburn to celebrate

---

1850. 80 Newtownards TC, 1 July 1842, 6 Aug. 1849, PRONI, LA60/2B/1. 81 *BNL*, 29 Aug. 1851; *FJ*, 30 Aug. 1851. 82 *BU*, 21 Feb. 1854. 83 Wright, *Two lands*, pp 406–9.

the victory of R.J. Smyth, son of a local landowner, in the first contested election in nearly seventy years in the borough hitherto controlled by the Conway family, the marquess of Hertford. It was an unusual year. Three parliamentary elections had occurred in the small borough located only eight miles from Belfast and noted for its textile industry. The effort to elect Smyth and free the borough from aristocratic control was coordinated by members of the town commission associated with the tenant-right movement. Their involvement began with small steps. After the death of the sitting MP for the borough in November 1851, the first wonder of that year occurred. Previously the opulent 4th marquess of Hertford had forwarded his choice of a candidate for the borough from Paris without any consultation with the town. On this occasion, however, a public meeting of the electors was held in December 1851, and the constituents were presented with a short list of candidates from which to choose.[84]

The evidence indicates that this boon had been coerced from the Hertford interest. Indeed, the *Belfast News-Letter* described the unopposed election as 'the first occasion on which the inhabitants, on their own part, had claimed freely to exercise the elective franchise'.[85] This seems incongruous at first glance. An effort to draft a local candidate not sanctioned by the Hertford interest had failed, and the chosen candidate, J.E. Tennent – the former conservative MP from Belfast, was from the list sanctioned by the marquess. Furthermore, there had been no contest. Nevertheless, reformers considered Tennent's selection a victory. One liberal later recalled that they thought they 'had made a hole in that partition so long stuck up between us and our own rights'.[86] Among Tennent's supporters were liberals on the town commission such as Hugh McCall, a member of the central committee of the Ulster Tenant-Right Association. McCall had proposed Tennent to the December meeting, and at the actual election in January 1852 he was the primary speaker in support of the unopposed candidate.

Despite the taunts of some observers that Tennent was just another Hertford nominee, McCall justified his support for Tennent on two grounds. First, a local committee of six men, 'two Protestants, one Orangeman, two Liberals, and one Conservative', representing the broad spectrum of political opinion in the town had decided upon Tennent 'five days previous to Lord Hertford's *dictum* having been announced'. The decision to redeem the independence of the borough had been made already. McCall contended that times had changed from when 'the manufacture' of an MP for Lisburn had been 'about one of the most ridiculous farces ever attempted under the name of an election'. No longer would a candidate not bother 'to leave his quarters in

84 *BNL*, 5 Dec. 1851.   85 Ibid., 7 Jan. 1852.   86 *BU*, 12 Nov. 1852.

176

Piccadilly' while the electors 'went through all the formalities of a return without ever seeing their representative', much less questioning him about the issues.[87]

Second, Tennent had promised to support tenant-right. At the hustings, after lauding the young Tennent's fight for Greek liberties in the hope of rallying any reluctant liberals, McCall made a show of providing Tennent an opportunity to publicly support tenant-right. More importantly, in his speech Tennent endorsed the particular construction of tenant-right favoured by the Ulster Tenant-Right Association at that time. Tennent stated that a successful bill on the land question must secure for a tenant 'the full equivalent of such improvements as had their origin either in his own capital and labour, or that of others whose interests had descended to, or been acquired by, him'. This was well beyond anything that Tennent's colleagues in parliament were likely to support, but it was part of the price Tennent had paid for the support of the coalition.

By the time of the general election in July 1852, liberals were complaining that Tennent had not held to the bargain. After the conservatives came to power in February 1852, Tennent became known as 'the bully of the ministry' unleashed upon supporters of more radical interpretations of tenant-right. Despite these grumblings, Tennent was able to retain his seat without a contest by deftly playing upon sectarian fears in order to disrupt the coalition built around the freedom of the borough and tenant-right at the end of 1851. Wise to the divisions among Protestants in Ulster, Tennent did not cry that the established church was in danger, but in a bravura cultural analysis which extended to architecture and painting he proclaimed that the very Reformation was in peril. He also wisely did not abandon tenant-right completely, but now spoke of compensating a tenant 'for the permanent value conferred on his farm' rather than a purchased or inherited interest. At the hustings, Hugh McCall conceded that this election 'might be called a walk-over', but warned that 'the case might be different on another occasion'.[88]

In December 1852, the third election in twelve months occurred when Tennent resigned in order to become secretary to the Board of Trade. On this occasion the Hertford interest supported the lord advocate for Scotland, John Inglis, who needed a seat in parliament after having lost at a Scottish constituency at the general election. This attempted reassertion of the 'system of nomineeism' reinvigorated the coalition from December 1851. They organized support for R.J. Smyth, the son of a local landlord who was chairman of the town commission. The liberals supported Smyth, the self-described moderate conservative, as part of the effort to end Hertford control of the

87 *BNL*, 5 Dec. 1851, 7 Jan. 1852.   88 Ibid., 17 April. 1852, 12 July 1852.

borough, but they were also mollified by Smyth's endorsement of free trade and tenant-right, including compensation for past improvements. Smyth was elected during a particularly violent campaign which pitted divided local Orangemen against one another.

In the aftermath of the election, the Hertford interest undertook an extensive campaign of retaliation against Smyth's supporters. According to the journalist James Godkin, notices to quit were served on every Smyth supporter who did not possess a lease.[89] The town commission was included among the defaulters, and the marquess of Hertford withdrew his contributions for watching and cleansing so that the commissioners were forced to raise rates to the maximum permissible levels.[90] The liberals were not passive in the face of these attacks. In May 1853, John Rea was unleashed upon the grand jury at the presentment sessions for the barony when claims for compensation by conservatives whose property had been damaged during the election were considered. Rea claimed to represent 'Mr McCall, Mr Belshaw, and the constitutional party of Lisburn generally', and called upon two town commissioners as witnesses.[91] In 1855, at the first triennial election for the town commission after Smyth's victory, the agent for the Hertford estate appeared unexpectedly and explained that he believed the commissioners needed an infusion 'of some new blood' and 'trusted the list he would now present would exhibit the requisite infusion'.[92] Caught unaware, the liberals protested impotently as they were purged from the town commission. However, the setback was only temporary. In 1858 the liberals regained positions on the town commission and by 1859 the chairman of the commission was one of the liberals who had been purged in 1855.[93]

There were documented struggles of varying intensity and duration concerning the use of public buildings, rents from former corporate lands, and tolls collected at markets or fairs in the following Ulster towns: Bangor, Ballymoney, Coleraine, Enniskillen, Lisburn, Monaghan, Newtownards and Strabane. These struggles were schools for politics that allowed Ulster liberals to organize. In 1857 the success of liberals in town commissions in Ulster resulted in an optimistic editorial entitled 'The Progress of Liberal Feeling in Ulster' in the *Ulsterman*, the Catholic newspaper published in Belfast. It recounted liberal successes in places formerly known for their conservatism. A salutary change had made the province 'more wise, more tolerant, more free from sectarian discord, more regardless, in political and social intercourse, of differences of creed'. For the *Ulsterman*, the newly found health in the body politic was most evident in the government of towns that were formerly 'the strongholds of Orangeism and bigotry'. Cookstown, for example, had been

89 J. Godkin, *The land-war in Ireland* (London, 1870), pp 335–7. 90 *BU*, 4 Feb. 1853. 91 *BU*, 4 Feb. 1853. 92 *BNL*, 3 July 1855. 93 *BNL*, 4 Aug. 1859.

'rank with Orangeism', but by January 1857 it was 'quite pure and healthy' in its 'political atmosphere'. Likewise, Enniskillen, formerly 'the very centre of fanatic violence', was now 'a decent, well-conducted town boasting of its liberal constituents, its liberal Town Commissioners, and only the other day of its Catholic Municipal Governor'.[94] In a short time the town commission in Ulster had indeed wrought a transformation in political fortunes in many towns. The authority of the urban patrons had been significantly weakened. Institutions representing public opinion had been consolidated. The question would be whether the practical collapse of aristocratic authority would result in a better society.

94 *Ulsterman*, 19 Jan. 1857.

CHAPTER FOUR

The seeds of division and the land of hope, 1860–76

On the eve of a parliamentary general election in the summer of 1865, many Ulster liberals believed that they had reached a critical juncture. The three newspapers representing the broad spectrum of liberal opinion in Ulster, the *Banner of Ulster, Ulster Observer* and *Northern Whig*, considered what they all admitted to be the weak, indeed humiliating, condition of liberalism at the parliamentary level. The *Banner* confessed that,

> since the first election under the Reform Act, the representation of Ulster has become more and more Tory, until now one would suppose that the great electoral body of Liberals had forsaken the political faith of their forefathers, and adopted the principles of their hereditary enemies.[1]

For its part, the Catholic *Observer* believed it 'humiliating', and 'monstrous', that two conservatives should represent Belfast when, 'unless professions be a lie and hypocrisy a recognised rule of conduct among us', the majority of Belfast's eligible voters were liberals.[2] Representing non-subscribing Presbyterianism since 1824, the *Northern Whig* directed its outrage at the degraded condition of the Presbyterian community. Citing statistics from the 1861 census, the first to publish data on religious affiliations, the *Whig* complained that in their 'own ancient settlements', where their 'social and political influence ought to be predominant', Presbyterians were instead 'held and disposed of, politically, like chattels, by a few Episcopalian peers and their sons'.[3]

Forced to recognize the full extent of their difficulties, all three sections of the liberal coalition, evangelical Presbyterians, non-subscribing Presbyterians and Catholics, agreed that the root of the problem was the division that had arisen between Catholic and Presbyterian liberals. Although they differed considerably in assigning responsibility for the divisions, their explanations provide clues to the social and political developments during the period between 1859 and 1876 that threatened to make the always-difficult alliance between Catholics and Presbyterians practically impossible. From this re-

---

1 *BU*, 15 June 1865. 2 *UO*, 4 July 1865. 3 Orthodox, *Letters to the Presbyterians of Ulster on the general election of 1865* (Belfast, 1865), p. 6.

evaluation in 1865, a brief period of ambivalent political experimentation occurred during which a fragile foundation for future cooperation was established. With the re-emergence of the land question as a unifying concern, that cooperation resulted in considerable successes during the general election of 1874. However, those successes masked significant underlying threats to the foundations of Ulster liberalism. The consolidation of liberal public opinion was threatened by social and cultural developments that encouraged confessional solidarity at the expense of common public spheres. In Ulster's towns and cities where the populations had rapidly increased, the simple solidarity of creed was easier to recreate and maintain than more complex relationships.

Preachers and missionaries: liberal Protestant public opinion

In 1865 the *Banner of Ulster* believed that the current division among liberals was the result of distrust implanted among many Presbyterians by O'Connell's agitation for repeal of the Union together with significant changes in the nature of Catholic leadership. The *Banner* lamented the passing of Catholic bishops they considered liberal and cooperative, such as Daniel Murray and William Crolly, and their replacement by the perceived leader of Ultramontane policies in Ireland, Paul Cullen. The *Banner* hinted that it was the hostility towards Cullen among liberals that contributed to a defection of some 'luke-warm Liberals' during the so-called Papal Aggression of 1850. The most significant factor, however, in the division between Protestants and Catholics was 'a growing tendency', engendered by the increasing ultramontane spirit, 'among a certain portion of Roman Catholic electors to separate from Liberal Protestants'. The *Banner* complained that this alienation even led some Catholics 'to select Tories rather than Protestant Liberals as their representatives'.[4] For the *Banner*, the failure of Belfast Catholics to support the candidacy of Thomas McClure in 1857 was a particularly galling demonstration of the damaging effects of the ultramontane tendency.

Concerns about changes in the nature of Catholicism during the 1850s and 1860s were not unfounded. By the late 1840s, some Ulster liberals commented upon aspects of the changes documented by Emmet Larkin as comprising a devotional revolution throughout Ireland in the decades after the Famine. It was not only the perceived changes in the policies and attitudes of the hierarchy that disturbed liberal Protestants. They believed that the attitudes and behaviour of the Catholic laity towards them had been fundamentally affected as well. Taken together, these changes were deemed ominous threats to the development of liberalism in the province.

4 *BU*, 15 June 1865.

In 1848 the former Congregationalist minister James Godkin published an anonymous article in the *North British Review* describing the advent of changes in popular devotional practices among Catholics. Godkin observed that inexpensive devotional literature inculcating Marian devotions was becoming readily available. Godkin reviewed a number of tracts, such as a Dublin edition of selections from the writings of Alphonsus Liguouri (1696–1787), founder of the Redemptorist order of missionary priests, intended for use by sodalities and confraternities. Godkin was concerned that the inculcation of popular Marian devotion demonstrated that 'the Church of Rome is about to assume a new attitude in this country'. Godkin's anxiety was not the product of a fervent anti-Catholicism eager to denounce popish idolatry. While critical of Marian devotion, Godkin eschewed what he complained of as 'offensive and opprobrious epithets, printed in vehement capitals'.[5] Godkin described the Marian devotion as more akin to 'hero-worship' than idolatry and acknowledged that it had some pastoral advantages.

Godkin had acquired considerable liberal credentials by 1848. In what was almost a paradigm during the nineteenth century, Godkin came to liberalism from a seemingly incongruous evangelical background. Born in 1806 at Gorey, Co. Wexford, Godkin was a convert from Catholicism who described his experience 'as a devoted member of the Church of Rome, as a Sceptic in that communion, as a Convert to Protestantism, but still unrenewed in heart and, finally, as a Believer in JESUS', in a book that went through at least three editions between 1836 and 1845.[6] Because of his conversion, Godkin's subsequent ordination as pastor of a Congregational church at Armagh in 1834 was of 'peculiar interest' to the community and the press. Godkin's early career seemed to reflect the proverbial zeal of the convert. He spoke frequently at temperance society meetings, published an account of his conversion, participated in public religious controversies,[7] and became involved in missions under the auspices of the Irish Evangelical Society, an organization of agents from various Protestant denominations but practically controlled by Congregationalists.[8]

From such beginnings, it might be thought that Godkin had been struck blind on the road between Armagh and Belfast before becoming a liberal.

5 [J. Godkin], 'Mariolatry', *North British Review*, 8 (1848), 341–2. The anonymous article is attributed to Godkin in Walter Houghton (ed.), *The Wellesley index to Victorian periodicals, 1824–1900* (London, 1966–89).   6 J. Godkin, *A guide from the church of Rome to the church of Christ* (2nd ed., Dublin, 1836), p. vi. A third edition was published in Belfast by the *Banner of Ulster* in 1845.   7 *BNL*, 9 Sept. 1834, 18 Sept. 1835, 22 June 1838, 20 Nov. 1838.   8 An excerpt from Godkin's journal during his missions appeared in 'Irish Evangelical Society', *Congregational Magazine*, n.s. 9 (1845), 6971; J. Godkin, *The religious history of Ireland* (London, 1873), p. 231.

However, for all his evangelical ardour, Godkin was of a liberal cast of mind at least as early as 1837. That year, while still a minister in Armagh, he was involved along with a number of leading Ulster radicals, including William Sharman Crawford and Robert Grimshaw, in the Friends of Religious Liberty.[9] Godkin's liberalism became more pronounced when he moved to Belfast in 1838 and founded a weekly newspaper, the *Christian Patriot.* In the pages of the *Patriot* Godkin espoused a curious blend of philosophic radicalism and evangelical enthusiasm. Godkin believed that the 'Baconian philosophy' that characterized 'science and political economy' was affecting religion as well and 'working a revolution in the churches'. The spirit of the age was 'practical' and even churches were being 'tried by this test of utility'. Far from a dangerous development, Godkin believed this spirit was 'in strict harmony with the genius of the Gospel' and would finally allow Christianity to realize its potential. Echoing the recurrent theme of liberal iconoclasm, Godkin also believed that societies passed through stages so that 'no society, civil or sacred, can be as wise in its infancy as in its maturity'.[10]

For Godkin, attempts by some evangelicals to enforce confessional uniformity in the name of tradition were a mask for intolerance. Such evangelicals typically recalled past leaders because in seeking 'shelter under some plausible pretence' they understood that nothing could be 'more plausible to a Protestant people than the example of the Reformers'. Like McKnight, however, Godkin was not afraid to criticize aspects of a Reformation that at times 'was more a revolt against intolerable tyranny, than a battle for great *principles*'. Godkin was also a proponent of 'united education' in the belief that it would teach the Protestant that his Catholic countryman was not 'a persecuting traitor, whom oath cannot bind nor kindness conciliate'. Conversely, Catholics would no longer imagine their Protestant brother an 'irreligious tyrant' or 'scowling bigot'.[11] Despite quarrels with Godkin's ardent evangelical opinions, the *Vindicator*, Belfast's Catholic paper at that time, described the *Christian Patriot* as 'an anti-Tory journal'.[12]

After a fire in March 1840, the *Christian Patriot* closed, but Godkin continued to be both missionary and liberal, publishing evangelical tracts and iconoclastic attacks on the established churches while journeying between mission stations.[13] Godkin's iconoclasm reached a new level in 1845 with the publication of an essay advocating Repeal that was awarded a prize by Daniel O'Connell's Loyal National Repeal Association. Godkin emphasized in the

9 *NW*, 12 Jan. 1837. 10 J. Godkin, *The touchstone of orthodoxy* (Belfast, 1838), pp iii, 40. 11 Ibid., pp 41, 43, 201. 12 *Vin*, 3 July 1839. 13 *BNL*, 17 Mar. 1840; during the period between 1840 and 1845 Godkin wrote the following: *Apostolic Christianity* (Dublin, 1842); *Lent lectures on Romanism and Puseyism* (Belfast, 1843); *The church principles of the New Testament* (London, 1845).

advertisement to the essay that his support for Repeal was founded on three preconditions – adherence to peaceful and constitutional methods; that 'Irish Protestants, generally, shall concur in demanding it'; and that 'inviolable security be given that neither the Church of Rome nor any other church shall ever be established or endowed in this country'.[14] Godkin's logic failed to convince most of his fellow liberals about the possible merits of Repeal and so alienated his fellow missionaries that his connection with the Irish Evangelical Society ended.

Godkin's advocacy of a qualified Repeal did not end his connection with Ulster liberalism. After a brief sojourn in England as a journalist that began in 1847, Godkin returned to the province in late 1849 in order to edit the *Londonderry Standard* after James McKnight left that paper for the *Banner of Ulster*. As editor of the *Standard* Godkin was an important figure in the tenant-right movement in Ulster and spoke frequently at meetings and demonstrations throughout the province. When McKnight returned to the *Standard* in November 1854, Godkin began a nearly decade long career as editor of the Dublin newspaper the *Daily Express* and Irish correspondent to the *Times* of London.[15] Beginning in 1865, Godkin published a series of articles on Irish affairs in the *Fortnightly Review* that formed the basis of a handful of books. Godkin's writings purportedly influenced English public opinion to accept disestablishment of the Church of Ireland as well as land reforms. In 1873 Queen Victorian bestowed a pension on Godkin at the behest of William Gladstone.

Of particular interest are Godkin's later accounts of the changes in Irish Catholicism that he first perceived in 1848. In 1867, Godkin published *Ireland and her Churches* with the intention of demonstrating the necessity for disestab-lishment of the Church of Ireland. In his description of Catholicism, Godkin claimed that the Catholic 'revival' of the 'last quarter of a century' has 'taken a direction in regard to doctrine and worship which may be regarded as an innovation of very grave import'.[16] Godkin described in detail the intense devotional practices that had been fostered by a zealous Catholic clergy. Citing Enniscorthy, Co. Wexford, as the most thorough example of this devotional transformation, Godkin observed that the Catholic churches of that town were open to large numbers of worshippers receiving the sacraments of confession and communion at all hours. In 1873 Godkin published *A religious history of Ireland* in which he commented further upon the effects of religious revival within the Catholic community. One important result was 'the greatly increased

---

14 J Godkin, 'The rights of Ireland', in Loyal National Repeal Association, *Repeal essays* (1845), p. [288].   15 *BU*, 7 Nov. 1854.   16 J. Godkin, *Ireland and her churches* (London, 1867), p. 303.

sway of the Roman Catholic priesthood over their flocks'. Godkin feared that this development correlated with an increase in ultramontane power that sometimes rendered Catholics, who were 'naturally lovers of freedom and fair play', into reluctant enemies of liberalism. The conservatism of the increasingly powerful ultramontanism within Catholicism discouraged cooperation between liberal Catholics and Protestants. Perhaps reminiscing about his cooperation with local Catholic curates in Armagh city in the Friends of Religious Liberty or his participation in the tenant-right movement during the 1850s, Godkin complained that by 1873 the toasts of the O'Connellite era advocating civil and religious liberty were no longer heard among Catholics. Instead, there was increasingly 'no alternative left to Liberal Catholics but the revolt of outraged reason against legitimate authority'.[17]

Godkin was a prime example of how a perspicacious liberal was concerned by changes in Catholicism. He was not the only articulate witness to these trends. The newspapers of the 1850s and 1860s contained numerous accounts of parish missions conducted by various religious orders throughout Ireland. Recent scholarship by Emmet Larkin has described the extraordinary number of parish missions undertaken in Ireland in the period between the first parish mission given by Irish Vincentians in the diocese of Dublin in 1842 until 1880. According to Larkin's investigations, the various religious orders active in Ireland visited each of the thousand Catholic parishes in Ireland at least twice between 1842 and 1880.[18]

While differing in particulars according to the order responsible, missions were typically conducted by five or six priests and lasted several weeks according to the numbers in attendance. Penitence and the need for sacramental reconciliation were the central themes of a series of daily sermons intended to awaken the faithful to the many ways in which they might transgress and imperil their salvation. Before the Famine, people responded in such large numbers that they practically overwhelmed the resources of the clergy. After the Famine, the dolorous mortality and emigration caused by that calamity combined with an increase in the number Catholic clergy contributed to an increasing ratio of priests to people that helped to maintain the sacramental devotion inspired by these missions. In this way, Larkin concludes that 'in literally a generation, the Irish people *as a people*, were transformed into those pious and practicing Catholics they have essentially remained right down to the present day'.[19]

Such a fundamental social change was bound to affect other relationships in

17 Godkin, *Religious history of Ireland*, pp 269, 280–1.   18 E. Larkin and H. Freudenberger (eds), *A Redemptorist missionary in Ireland, 1851–1854* (Cork, 1998), p. 11.   19 E. Larkin, 'The parish mission movement in Ireland, 1850–1875', typescript of a paper presented.

a region where Catholicism could not easily insulate itself from a small Church of Ireland Ascendancy but was confronted with sizeable Protestant communities. Recent scholarship has confirmed Godkin's aforementioned perception of the potential for social divisions created by the Catholic revival wrought by these parish missions. An important element of the Redemptorist missionary program, for example, was an attempt to inculcate 'an ideology which defined Catholics over against their Protestant neighbours', by discouraging interdenominational marriages and mixed education while at the same time sponsoring 'a whole gamut of social, recreational and educational societies', in order to encourage Catholic solidarity.[20] It is reasonable to wonder at what point the desires of Catholics to preserve and strengthen their community conflicted with the desires of many middle-class Catholics and Protestants to create and maintain a sense of commonweal. How did the emphasis on group solidarity limit the opportunities for interdenominational cooperation in the creation of a non-sectarian public sphere? Protestant liberals would soon begin to imagine that a principle of sectarian separatism was being inculcated by Catholic leaders that would threaten the civil society they were striving to construct and maintain.

In part, renewed efforts to create and reinforce Catholic solidarity were intended to combat a perceived threat of proselytism. In 1852, the most influential proponent of parish missions in Ireland, the archbishop of Dublin and papal apostolic delegate, Paul Cullen, hoped to create a corps of missionaries 'to wipe out the proselytizers everywhere'.[21] Apprehensions of a campaign of proselytism in Ulster were not unfounded. The Home Mission of the Synod of Ulster had been established in 1826 in order 'to supply with religious instruction and ordinance of the Gospel' to isolated Presbyterians in the south and west of Ireland.[22] At that time, the Home Mission explicitly denied any intention to proselytize Catholics.[23] Subsequently, the question of proselytism became more ambivalent. By 1835, the Home Mission hoped to assist not only isolated Presbyterians in the west and south but also Ulster Presbyterians lacking sufficient religious instruction and, most notably, 'the ignorant of our countrymen of all sects, especially the Irish-speaking population'.[24] Despite the denials of proselytism and the simple reality that the resources of all varieties of clergy were increasingly overstretched in many parts of Ireland, the Catholic hierarchy believed that Presbyterians were taking advantage of difficult situations in order to proselytize poor Catholics. Archbishop Cullen hoped that the missionary priests would counteract this threat.

20 J. Sharp, *The reapers of the harvest* (Dublin, 1989), p. 31.   21 Larkin, 'The parish mission movement in Ireland'.   22 R. Blaney, *Presbyterians and the Irish language* (Belfast, 1996), p. 74.   23 Holmes, *Our Presbyterian heritage*, p. 111.   24 Blaney, *Presbyterians and the Irish language*, p. 78.

During the 1850s, new concerns were aroused by an organized campaign of open-air preaching conducted by a group of evangelical Presbyterian ministers. In July 1852, the evangelical Presbyterian minister of Tullylish, Co. Down, John Johnston, formally requested the imprimatur of the general assembly for a system of open-air preaching, modelled in part on the activities of the Free Church of Scotland in the cities of Edinburgh and Glasgow, that had been tried for seven years previously by a handful of ministers in Ulster. Formally approved the following year, Johnston justified open-air preaching on the grounds of necessity. Johnston claimed that 'one fourth of the population in the country and one-half in the towns, never enter a place of worship' so that they were 'practical heathens, without God, without Christ, and without hope in the world in general'. To remedy this calamity deemed worse than famine or cholera, ministers were recruited for an arduous circuit of open-air preaching. According to the first annual report on open-air preaching to the general assembly, a minister would leave on Monday 'to preach every evening for five days at a different town' before returning to his congregation at the weekend.[25]

As the system developed over time, groups of towns were organized into a route. In each synod, a convener organized the resources of the Presbyterian churches along the routes to support the peripatetic ministers. Each minister along a route was required to keep a diary describing specific aspects of his experiences. That diary was to be forwarded expeditiously to the convener who collated the data and made abstracts to be included in the annual report. These abstracts seem to confirm the denials of proselytism. The primary categories for describing the audiences were 'church going people', often from the local Presbyterian congregation, and the 'poor' who were the intended audience. Certainly, some ministers occasionally noted with pleasure the presence of Catholics, but the presence of Catholics was not considered a measure of the effectiveness of the scheme. During the year from July 1852 to July 1853, 18 ministers were reported to have preached to about 30,000 people. By 1858, during a particularly wet summer, 56 ministers, nearly a tenth of the ministers in the general assembly, reported conducting 357 services outdoors for more than 57,000 listeners.[26]

Whatever the intentions and priorities of the ministers, open-air preaching was bitterly resented by Catholic public opinion. In July 1854, the *Ulsterman* complained of the 'perpetration of open-air abuse of the Catholic faith' in Strabane by a trio of Presbyterian ministers preaching from the steps of the market-house. The *Ulsterman* reported that its local correspondent feared 'that a repetition of this miserable exhibition will lead to riots' by Catholics outraged

---

25 *BU*, 17 July 1852, 26 July 1853.   26 *Eighth annual report of open-air preaching by ministers of the General Assembly … 1858* (Belfast, 1859), pp 4, 14–15.

at 'filthy attacks uttered against all they hold sacred and venerable'.[27] A convener for the synod of Derry and Omagh in 1858 acknowledged that 'at one station a very formidable opposition was organized' and that sometimes such opposition included remonstrances from 'magistrates and others in high quarters, who evidently did not understand the object in view'.[28] It is interesting to note that the convener for the open-air mission of the synod of Derry and Omagh in 1858 was Revd Richard Smyth, a future Liberal MP.

There were certainly justifications for misunderstanding open-air preaching. Some of the ministers involved, such as Henry Cooke, were justly notorious in the Catholic community. Furthermore, the general assembly did not have a monopoly on street preachers. Exponents of a more controversial style of open-air preaching, emphasizing attacks upon Catholic doctrines rather than the broader precepts of the gospel, were also present in Ulster's towns and cities. In December 1856, the Belfast Parochial Mission was established by the Episcopal minister Thomas Drew of Christ Church. Drew was a well-known conservative who had aroused the particular ire of James McKnight during 1854. In the pages of the *Banner of Ulster* McKnight excoriated the Christ Church Protestant Association that, according to its charter as quoted by McKnight, endorsed 'the recovery of all ground lost in the struggle for PROTESTANT ASCENDANCY', repeal of Catholic emancipation and the abolition of 'nunneries'.[29] In its campaign against 'spiritual despotism' the Belfast Parochial Mission organized anti-Catholic sermons by well-known controversialists.[30] During the summer of 1857, Drew's mission encountered resistance from the Catholic community, organized in part by the *Ulsterman*, as well as local authorities fearing disturbances. After encountering violent opposition to its sermons in August 1857, the Belfast Parochial Mission cancelled its series of sermons.

Others were not dissuaded. The Presbyterian minister Hugh Hanna was determined to defend the principle of open-air preaching. The general assembly was ill-served by the circumstances that allowed Hanna, one of only a handful of ministers involved with Orangeism at this time, to become a symbol of the open-air missions. An angry crowd of Catholics, encouraged by a broadside secretly published by the *Ulsterman*, gathered to prevent a speaker from the Belfast Parochial Mission from preaching at the customs house. Upon learning that the mission had abandoned its public services, the crowd made its way to Hanna's sermon and attacked the listeners gathered there. A serious riot lasting for several days ensued. As a result, 'roaring Hugh Hanna' became a lasting image of open-air preaching in Ulster that resonates to this day.[31] While

27 *Ulsterman*, 22 July 1854.   28 *Eighth annual report of open-air preaching*, p. 15.   29 *BU*, 22 July 1854.   30 S. Farrell, *Rituals and riots* (Lexington, VA, 2000), p. 145.   31 A statue of

Hanna was not representative of the open-air preachers within the general assembly, his career demonstrated the potential for communal violence resulting from open-air preaching.

Although parish missions conducted by the Catholic missionary orders were intended for Catholics, not the conversion of Protestants, these missions sometimes also became occasions for sectarian violence. In Belfast in 1852 and again in 1853, a mission cross erected by the Rosminians in Friar's Bush cemetery aroused the ire of Orange mobs who attempted to destroy it. During late June and early July 1853, a Rosminian mission in Lisburn drew a sizeable number of Catholics from other parishes, particularly Belfast just seven miles distant. According to reports in the *Ulsterman*, large numbers of penitents were leaving the mission at 9.30 p.m. and returning at 4.30 a.m. the next day.[32] The inevitable increase of pedestrian traffic created by the mission unfortunately coincided with the season for traditional, though at the time theoretically proscribed, Orange celebrations. Loyalist truculence was exacerbated by a singular defeat suffered by the conservatives in December 1852 at the first contested election for the borough since before the Union. When a group of local Protestants described in press accounts as Orangemen harassed Catholics travelling to and from the chapel, serious rioting was only avoided by a strong constabulary presence. The *Ulsterman* reported that during the mission 'considerable apprehension was entertained in Belfast and Lisburn'.[33]

In September 1854, a Redemptorist mission at Newtownlimavady, Co. Londonderry, caused serious rioting when the small force of six constables was overwhelmed by circumstances similar to those in Lisburn. According to the constabulary the mission drew at least five thousand Catholics to the town that had a population of 3,205 in 1851 but only 2,732 in 1861. Roughly two-thirds of the population belonged to Protestant sects, and Presbyterians accounted for nearly sixty per cent of those Protestants. The Catholic chapel simply could not accommodate the numbers, and services were held in a nearby field. Like Lisburn there were complaints of Catholics being harassed as they journeyed back and forth through the area. Furthermore, the *Ulsterman* accused a local Church of Ireland rector and a Presbyterian minister of having conducted controversial sermons and lectures to coincide with the mission. Despite these

Hanna erected in north Belfast was damaged by an IRA bomb in 1970. Local loyalists destroyed a temporary peace monument erected on the empty plinth in 1995. Subsequently, loyalists, outraged by the perceived usurpation, convinced the Belfast city council to re-erect the restored statue in its original location against the advice of both nationalist councillors and some Presbyterian elders who feared the symbol might ignite further violence in a particularly volatile section of the city. Jane Leonard, 'Memorials to the casualties of conflict: Northern Ireland, 1969–1997' electronic text available at ds.dial.pipex.com/town/estate/y013/reports/memorials/memorials.pdf (1997), pp 27–8. **32** *Ulsterman*, 13 July 1853, 29 June 1853. **33** Ibid., 7 July 1853.

alleged provocations, the mission had proceeded peacefully without extraordinary security arrangements. At the last of the unusual out-door services, however, the ordinary admonition to the penitents to depart in quiet reflection was deviated from with disastrous results. All of the witnesses agreed that three cheers for the Pope, Archbishop Cullen and the owner of the field was the immediate occasion for the violence. Whether from fear or anger, a crowd of Protestants, described by the correspondent of the *Ulsterman* as Orangemen, attending services at the nearby Church of Ireland parish church of Balteagh rushed into the street upon hearing the cheers. After some confusion, an affray began which overwhelmed the constabulary and resulted in injuries and considerable damage to Catholic property.

Both the parish missions and open-air preaching became involved unwittingly in the pattern of ritual displays by sectarian fraternal societies such as Orangemen or, less frequently, Hibernians. These groups staked out contending sectarian claims for control of public places and occasions such as fairs, markets, town squares and town halls.[34] Parish missions did not include elaborate Corpus Christi processions or public religious ceremonies in Ulster but the enthusiasm generated by the missions filled towns with Catholics from the nearby countryside. Often these crowds accompanied the priests as they proceeded to and from the chapel. Contemporary Catholic accounts of riots arising from parish missions generally described their antagonists as being Orangemen who were roused to violence by the diatribes of anti-Catholic preachers. The organization and mobilization of the Catholic community certainly was an affront to the Orangemen's self-described principle that 'where you could walk, you were dominant'.[35] For their part, Catholics seem to have made little distinction between the varieties of open-air preaching. They perceived all open-air preaching as insults or efforts at proselytism. The ministers involved were little better than Orange auxiliaries to be repelled with force if necessary. The possibility for cooperation between Catholics and Protestants upon liberal political issues was practically undermined by violent confrontations.

By the early 1860s, some Presbyterians began to recognize that their efforts to create and consolidate liberal political institutions in Ulster were fundamentally threatened by an upsurge in sectarian associations and violence. An important example of this increased Presbyterian anxiety was the work of John Brown, Presbyterian minister of Aghadowey, Co. Londonderry. During a

---

34 I am deeply indebted to my colleague Sean Farrell for bringing this issue to my attention as well as for providing a typescript of an unpublished paper on this topic, 'Setting the stage: ritual and sectarian violence in nineteenth-century Ulster', presented to a seminar at the Institute of Irish Studies at Queen's University Belfast.   35 M.W. Dewar et al., *Orangeism* (1967), p. 118; as quoted by Farrell, 'Setting the stage'.

lengthy ministry lasting for nearly sixty years until his death in 1873, Brown published more than thirty pamphlets and has been described as the most prolific, though it must be said not always the most profound or elegant, Irish Presbyterian writer of the nineteenth century.[36] In many ways, his writings are emblematic of the development of Ulster liberalism among Presbyterians during his lifetime.

Brown's first publication in 1820 was an encomium on education intended to raise money for the newly founded Belfast Academical Institution. The pamphlet reflects many of the characteristics of Ulster liberalism at that time. For Brown, education contributed to civil liberty by social reform as opposed to revolution. 'By teaching men the danger of innovation', education does not 'hastily overturn old institutions but gradually smoothes down their asperities'. Having been educated in Glasgow, Brown also believed in the progress of humanity through stages of civilization. One of the more surprising aspects of Brown's early writing was a strong sense of Irish identity and historical grievance. Brown complained that in Ireland 'the energies of her peasantry are paralyzed by the iron grasp of ruthless minions, her wealth squandered in the giddy circles of a haughty rival, and her population' compelled 'to crouch to superiors in foreign lands, being literally hewers of wood and drawers of water'.[37]

Although Brown's early writings commented upon political questions, spiritual and pastoral issues were the focus for a time. Brown's political sentiments were governed by an evangelical sensibility that occasionally led him into unseemly temporary alliances with political conservatives.[38] As discussed previously, those temporary alliances ended during the 1840s when Brown's battles with Henry Cooke helped to weaken conservativism among Presbyterians. By 1857, Brown was a committed opponent to that 'phantom called Conservatism'.[39] During the 1850s, a seemingly incongruent combination of an evangelical sensibility with political liberalism characterized Brown's writings. In 1855, Brown published a sermon describing the spiritual struggle of a nonconformist Catholic farmer against the efforts of the Catholic clergy to bring him back within the fold that in some ways suggested the kinds of changes in Catholicism described by Godkin, but Brown's hostility towards Catholicism was more manifest.[40] At the same time, Brown remained committed to a political liberalism that included Catholics as political allies.[41] By 1864, Brown was increasingly concerned that sectarianism might

36 T.H. Mullin, *Aghadowey* (Belfast, 1972), p. 170.   37 John Brown, *The importance of learning to society* (Belfast, 1820), pp 11–13, 27.   38 D.H. Akenson, *The Irish education experiment* (London, 1970), p. 170.   39 J. Brown, *The elective franchise, a sacred trust* (Coleraine, 1857), p. 12.   40 J. Brown, *Barney McLees* (Belfast, 1855).   41 Brown, *The elective franchise*, p. 15.

undermine the liberal institutions that had developed in Ulster during the nineteenth century.

In 1864, Brown published probably his most famous work, *Social peace promoted by the Gospel*.[42] The pamphlet consisted of the text of an open-air sermon Brown delivered at Ringsend, Co. Londonderry to an audience of Catholics and Protestants. The sermon was intended to quell an outbreak of sectarian affrays that had begun at local fairs and escalated to party processions and assassinations in the villages and countryside between Coleraine and Newtownlimavady. Delivered early in Brown's ministry, in 1826, the timing of the publication of the sermon and the accompanying introduction make it clear that the increasing communal discord of the 1860s was the real subject of the pamphlet.[43] Brown was anxious that the disturbances that had occurred in the 1820s were becoming commonplace again. 'I mention these facts', Brown wrote in 1864, 'in the hope that Presbyterians will understand that it is quite possible to live, as I have lived, in the exchange of kindness with Roman Catholic neighbours'.[44]

Brown's primary complaint against party processions and sectarian associations was their subversion of morality. The very real differences between Catholics and Protestants could not excuse violence or separation. At the individual level, sectarian hatred imperilled the soul because 'no act of devotion can be accepted by God so long as we cherish unkind feelings to our fellowmen'. Communal discord also endangered the physical welfare of individuals: it was 'destructive of personal comfort' and an obstruction 'to the improvement of our beloved fatherland'. The time and expense resulting from involvement in sectarian associations such as the Orange Order were 'utterly ruinous to poor men'. Party conflict also threatened the community as whole. They made human justice all but impossible. An impartial observer of the criminal trials resulting from sectarian violence would 'see poor hapless creatures in a state of high excitement, so blinded by passion that the most intelligent judges and juries can only guess what is true'. Because deliberation and rationality did not govern such circumstances, Brown advised that all controversial speeches and sermons should be abandoned in times of excitement. Whatever the intentions of a speaker, 'the rude rabble rush to conflict, ready, in the name of party to indulge in brutal acts of violence' after even a formal debate. Brown also warned that 'party factions' distorted the virtues of leadership so that 'generally the worst and most unscrupulous of men gain an ascendancy in the cabals of such parties'.[45]

In the same year, Brown published a lecture specifically concerned with the

---

42 J. Brown *Social peace promoted by the gospel* (Derry, 1864).   43 Mullin, *Aghadowey*, pp 184–5.   44 Brown, *Social peace*, p. iv.   45 Ibid., pp 8, 11, 15–16.

traditional marches and commemorations at Derry. In his discourse Brown reiterated his denunciation of sectarian associations as damaging to the individual. Party processions 'often lead to intemperance, and thus prepare for brawls and discord' so that participants were 'injured physically and morally, and their social peace and harmony are eventually destroyed'. In this pamphlet, however, Brown added political and philosophical reasons to his pastoral criticisms. Politically, Brown believed conservatives were attempting to usurp the legacy of the siege. Brown observed that the first commemoration of the siege had been celebrated by local Catholics, including the bishop, but by 1864 the commemorations tended 'to confirm and extend the power of a political party who would not grant to others the advantages that they claim for themselves'. Catholics were estranged from the revived commemorations by 'the processions of noisy youths and all the kindred noises of "Roaring Meg"' as well as 'military displays' and 'insulting demonstrations'. Together these provocations caused Catholics to forget that the siege 'secured lasting benefits to all parts of the British community'. Somewhat tactlessly, Brown reminded Catholics that 'they now share the privileges of British subjects' and were indebted to Protestants 'for the legislation that removed their fetters'.[46] Brown's failure to mention the efforts of Daniel O'Connell and the Catholic Association probably did little to foster good feeling among Catholics, but Brown's intention was to maintain a political alliance of liberal Presbyterians and Catholics.

Brown believed Catholics ought to join the celebrations of the heritage of the Glorious Revolution. As William of Orange had joined with the Pope against Louis XIV, Catholics and Presbyterians should maintain their alliance against their common foes, the Tories. The continuation of that liberal alliance was more important than annual commemorations of the events of the siege. Because Tory manipulations of the commemorations had alienated Catholics, 'such celebrations should be confined to decades or jubilees' in a gradual effort to restore the comity that had existed between the communities. Philosophically, the commemorative tradition did not comport with the current stage of society. Reflecting the continuing influence of the Scottish enlightenment upon a generation of ministers educated at Glasgow, Brown suggested that the martial values appropriate at the time of the siege were inappropriate for an increasingly commercial city. Citizens ought to turn away from celebration of the martial prowess of the past and apply themselves to practical matters. 'In former times it was well that brave men preserved religious and civil freedom', but now the inheritors of their sacrifices 'should labour to extend the blessings of civilization'. Brown's particular hope was that the city would become the site of a new college 'whose mission will be not to train men

46 J. Brown, *Two lectures* (Derry, 1864), pp 11–14.

as much for war and violence as to diffuse the blessings of science and concord' with the hope of giving 'to our earth by their wisdom and industry some resemblance of Eden before man rebelled against God'.[47]

Aside from the galvanizing effects of sectarian violence, Ulster liberalism was also threatened by Protestant fears that the changing political principles of Catholics were beginning to affect daily life. In October 1859, the *Banner of Ulster* complained that during the previous two years the policies of the archbishop of Dublin and papal legate, Paul Cullen, had achieved almost total ascendancy within the Catholic community. The willingness of the 'Liberal and Independent press of the Roman Catholic community of Ireland' as represented by the *Freeman's Journal,* 'the noblest and ablest of Liberal journals', to accede to a pastoral from the Irish bishops in the summer of 1859 condemning the principle of mixed education was evidence of the victory of the ultramontane principles of the hierarchy. From this perceived abandonment of the *Freeman's Journal's* 'high and independent antecedents', the *Banner* concluded that 'there no longer exists in Ireland a Roman Catholic Liberal press'.[48] In January 1860, the *Banner* further suggested that 'a Liberal political creed and an abject submission to a domineering hierarchy are essentially incompatible'.[49]

Perhaps more disconcerting than the policy of denominational separatism espoused by the Catholic clergy, was the fear that such a policy might be gaining acceptance among British politicians. During the period between Lord Palmerston's formation of a minority government in 1855 and the election of 1865 there was no secure majority in parliament. This was, in the words of E.D. Steele, 'the setting for Palmerston's unenthusiastic play for the votes of Irish members, and of Disraeli's pursuit of an alliance between the Tories and the Irish Catholics'.[50] Ulster liberals worried that British politicians were willing to barter the reforms of the previous three decades. For the *Banner of Ulster,* this devil's bargain was exemplified by the abandonment of the principle of non-sectarianism for the denominational principle in the reformatory schools established by parliament in 1858.[51] When the system was practically operating in early 1860, the *Banner* described it as 'a dangerous and embarrassing precedent for future legislation' because 'of its distinct departure from the non-sectarian basis of the National Board and the Queen's Colleges'.[52]

Concerns about the principles underlying Irish reformatories also were voiced by a Presbyterian minister from Derry who was becoming a leader within Ulster liberalism. In 1861, Richard Smyth, acknowledging the aid and influence of James McKnight, published a lengthy critique of the reformatories

---

47 Ibid., pp 14, 234. 48 *BU,* 25 Oct. 1859. 49 *BU,* 7 Jan. 1860. 50 E.D. Steele, *Palmerston and Liberalism, 1855–1865* (Cambridge, 1991), p. 324. 51 21 & 22 Vict. c. 103. 52 *BU,* 7 Jan. 1860.

entitled, *Philanthropy, proselytism and crime*.[53] Early in his career Smyth was identified with the evangelical wing of Presbyterianism. In 1855, he was called to a congregation in Westport, Co. Mayo, and his reports to the general assembly on missionary efforts in Connacht together with his prominent advocacy of open-air preaching occasionally aroused the ire of the Catholic press.[54]

Smyth's earliest publications were more remarkable for their evangelical zeal than their political acumen.[55] Smyth became, however, a leading figure in a flowering of liberalism in Derry centred on Magee college, the Presbyterian seminary, where he was appointed professor in 1865. By the time of his premature death in 1878, Smyth was an established leader among Ulster liberals and had been elected to parliament with the combined votes of Catholics and Presbyterians in Co. Londonderry. Smyth and his allies sustained a tradition of evangelical liberalism that had first emerged during the tenant-right campaign led by James McKnight and attempted, with some success, to cooperate with Catholics. Before such cooperation was established, however, significant disagreements would have to be addressed.

Smyth's assessment of the new reformatories was blunt. They were 'a reversal of all enlightened legislation for the management of public institutions of this country'. The establishment of the denominational system would aggravate already dangerous divisions in Irish society with the 'sectarian Reformatories carrying on a guerrilla warfare against the non-sectarian institutions of the country'. Smyth believed that the reformatories would be the model for establishing the denominational model in education. He averred, seemingly histrionically, that it was only a matter of time before the Catholic hierarchy would demand 'separate Union Workhouses, separate gaols' and, ultimately, 'the end will be a separate army to establish a separate government'.[56]

Smyth believed that the denominational principle contributed to a false perception that Ulster was divided between a monolithic Protestantism and a unified Catholicism. The reformatories act broadly divided reformatories into two categories, Protestant and Catholic. While Smyth did not believe that the legislature intended any disrespect to Presbyterians, the act grouped 'into one promiscuous mass, the Episcopalians, Presbyterians, Quakers, Jews, Unitarians, Latter-Day saints, Methodists, and Baptists, under the one denomination of *Protestant*'. Smyth opposed this parliamentary Protestant union with as much

53 R. Smyth, *Philanthropy, proselytism and crime* (Derry, 1861).   54 Latimer, *A history of the Irish Presbyterians*, p. 499. For an example see the lengthy denunciation of 'Smith' in an editorial of the *Ulsterman*, 20 July 1857.   55 R. Smyth, *Life for the nations: a plea for India* (Derry, 1857); R. Smyth, *Ireland & Italy* (Derry, 1860).   56 Smyth, *Philanthropy*, pp 8, 35, 87.

feeling as an earlier generation had rejected Henry Cooke's Hillsborough banns.[57]

The false dichotomy encouraged by the denominational system obscured the fact that Catholics were not united in support for the denominational principle. According to Smyth, the policy was the product of an 'Ultramontane faction, who had a narrow majority in the Synod of Thurles, but who have a mere fraction of adherents among the intelligent Catholic *laity* of Ireland'.[58] Unlike Ulster conservatives who often seemed to consider all Catholics as political and theological reprobates, Smyth believed that liberalism might flourish among Catholics if the ultramontane spirit were contained. His further conviction that adherence to liberal principles would inevitably lead Catholics to Protestantism of their own accord must be considered in this context.

Smyth also believed that the reformatories undermined Presbyterian and Catholic liberals alike by encouraging the surrender of an individual's liberty of conscience to the perceived needs of sectarian solidarity. Smyth complained that perhaps the worst aspect of the system was that *'no provision is made for a change in the religious opinions of the inmates'*. Society, even in the laudable interest of preserving communal harmony, had no right to cooperate in the restraint of individual conscience. Not even parents had a right to interfere in the religious conviction of young men and women who had reached the age of discretion.[59]

Taken together, the views of Godkin, Brown and Smyth demonstrate that the fears of Presbyterians were significant and had at least some foundation in reality. The changing attitudes of the Catholic hierarchy and laity certainly had to be considered by liberal Protestants. With the apparent willingness of conservative British governments to trade upon sectarian issues, the concerns of liberals became magnified. Even with these concerns, the continued political failures eventually brought liberal Presbyterians to consider two difficult questions. Could liberalism survive without cooperation between Catholics and Protestants? Were Catholics interested in cooperation?

Lawyers and laymen: Catholic public opinion

For their part, Catholics were quick to remind the public that the Presbyterians had not always been reliable allies. In July 1865, the Belfast Catholic newspaper, the *Ulster Observer*, reacted strongly to a series of pseudonymous letters in the *Northern Whig* (letters attributed to James Godkin in the catalogue of political and religious pamphlets collected at Magee college). The letters in the *Whig* bemoaned the political failures of Ulster Presbyterians and ascribed them to the

---

57 Ibid., pp 35, 54–6. **58** Ibid., p. 87. **59** Ibid., pp 54–5.

swaggering dominion of Ascendancy aristocrats in Ulster.[60] The Catholic *Ulster Observer* used the occasion of this Presbyterian rallying cry to outline its perception of the role of Presbyterians in contributing to the divisions within liberalism. The *Observer* believed that the role of Presbyterians within conservatism was at least as significant as their contributions to liberalism. The *Observer* asserted that 'throughout Ulster the vast majority of the Presbyterian body is either actively or passively associated with the most illiberal and most intolerant section of the community'.[61] This was a painful reminder to liberal Presbyterians that prominent members of their own community, notably Revd Henry Cooke, were indeed among the staunchest allies of the conservatives.

In addition, the *Observer* criticized Presbyterians for placing more importance on their own particular sectarian grievances than in the general welfare of liberalism. 'Pure Presbyterianism', the *Observer* predicted, 'would be no improvement upon pure Toryism'. Instead, Catholics were 'the pillar of the Liberal party in the province' and 'the Liberal Protestants of Ulster can effect nothing without the assistance of the Catholic body'.[62] Despite their bold assertion, the difficulty for liberal Catholics was that they simply lacked the political strength in and of themselves to form a sufficient foundation for Ulster liberalism. This weakness had two primary causes – relative socio-economic deprivation and considerable internal divisions. The relative socio-economic deprivation was dramatically demonstrated in the case of Belfast. In the course of Belfast's dramatic growth as a commercial and industrial centre during the nineteenth century, its Catholic community eventually surpassed that of Newry in importance in the province. Frank Wright has demonstrated that the relatively small size of middle-class Catholic communities outside of Belfast further magnified the importance of Belfast's Catholic commercial and professional community that was in many ways rather modest in size, wealth and influence. By 1864, Catholics comprised about a third of the city's population but were disproportionately poorer than their Protestant neighbours. In 1864 Catholics paid only nine per cent of the local taxes and occupied only thirteen per cent of the houses rated at £8 or more per annum.[63]

In an era of property qualifications this economic weakness correlated directly with political weakness. Catholics comprised only 13 per cent of the municipal electorate and 16 per cent of the parliamentary voters.[64] If they were united and well-led Catholics might have played a decisive role in a liberal victory in Belfast, but they could not have been the foundation of a liberal party with any hope of success. Protestants would inevitably provide the greater number of supporters in any successful liberal coalition. Assuming that Frank

60 Orthodox, *Letters to the Presbyterians of Ulster*, p. 6.   61 *UO*, 1 July 1865.   62 Ibid.
63 Wright, *Two lands*, p. 295.   64 Ibid.

Wright's analysis of the relative wealth and influence of Belfast Catholics as compared with their co-religionists in other Ulster towns and cities is correct, then the social and political weakness of Catholics in comparison with their numbers assumes a broad importance throughout Ulster. Even in Newry, where practically two-thirds of the population were Catholic, Catholics could not elect a member to parliament without the help of a small liberal Presbyterian community. In return for their cooperation, Presbyterians had been permitted to choose a member of their own communion as the town's liberal candidate for parliament.

Aside from their economic weakness, the quality of leadership in the Catholic community was also sometimes dubious. In Belfast in particular, clerical leadership was handicapped by divisions. During the period between 1835 and 1865 the bishop of the Catholic diocese of Down and Connor responsible for Belfast was Cornelius Denvir, a former professor of natural philosophy at Maynooth. Denvir created powerful enemies among his fellow bishops and clergymen by his cooperation with the Charitable Bequests commission and his support for the principle of united education in both the national schools and the Queen's Colleges. According to Ambrose Macaulay, relations between Denvir and his flock consequently deteriorated until Denvir 'withdrew more and more from public meetings and public affairs'.[65] Unlike some of his more outspoken colleagues among the bishops, Denvir believed that Catholics had made and might continue to make gains by cooperation with liberal politicians and policies.

With the ascendancy of Paul Cullen in the Irish hierarchy Denvir's position became even more precarious. Denvir's support for united education made him unpopular with the proponents of denominational education led by Cullen. Cullen and his allies portrayed Denvir's cautious pastoral approach and circumspect cooperation with liberal policies to papal authorities as deriving from a timorous nature when they might equally have been interpreted as sensible efforts to avoid compromising his liberal allies.[66] In 1860 a coadjutor bishop, Patrick Dorrian, was appointed to the diocese. Whatever effect this appointment may have had upon pastoral affairs it did little to restore clerical influence in politics. Dorrian's appointment created a situation possibly worse than a community with no leadership, a community with divided leadership.

While clerical leadership was lacking, the lay leadership of the Catholic community was worse. Perhaps because of their community's apparent economic weakness, the Catholic leadership short-sightedly placed considerable hope in the strategy of the pugnacious and erratic solicitor John Rea to

---

65 A. Macaulay, *Patrick Dorrian* (Dublin, 1987), p. 56. 66 J.J. Silke, 'Cornelius Denvir and the "spirit of fear"', *Irish Theological Quarterly*, 53 (1987), 136–9.

undermine the conservative political machine in Belfast by legal rather than political means. Born about 1822, Rea was the son of a Presbyterian grocer who served for a time as clerk of the market, an office under the municipal corporation, until his son's legal career brought about his dismissal. In 1837, Rea was apprenticed to Edward O'Rorke, a Catholic solicitor involved in liberal politics during the 1840s.[67] Rea later served a short term as assistant clerk of the peace for Belfast from 1841 until 1843. Rea's experiences gave him a birds-eye view of the establishment of a Byzantine Tory political machine in Belfast by the solicitor John Bates. Rea was in many ways the person best suited to defeat that machine, but he proved a disaster for liberalism in Belfast.

When the passage of municipal reform for Ireland ended the reign of the Donegall interest over the close corporation, John Bates ingeniously manipulated the provisions of the new legislation in order to establish a Tory monopoly in the corporation. At the first elections for the town council after municipal reform, Bates capitalized upon technical errors by liberals at the registry to pad the burgess rolls with doubtful conservative electors while at the same time removing qualified liberal electors.[68] As a result, Bates' Tories captured all forty seats for the town council in 1842. In the aftermath of the victory, Bates became both the town clerk and the solicitor for the conservative party.

Bates used his position as town clerk to consolidate the Tory monopoly by continuing to disfranchise liberal electors through a clever manipulation of the complexities and defects in municipal law. Among the qualifications for the municipal franchise was the requirement that all local taxes be paid. In Belfast there were six such taxes. Led by Bates, the conservatives managed to gain control of 5 of the 6 bodies responsible for these taxes. As a result, they could control the appointment of both the valuators and collectors for the various rates. With control of theses bodies, the conservatives not only manipulated the valuations to their advantage but they also frustrated the efforts of qualified liberal electors to pay all of the requisite taxes. In particular, the collectors for the parish and borough rates were unavailable when liberal ratepayers sought to pay their taxes. According to parliamentary investigations, between 1843 and 1854 an average of 2,747 people qualified for the municipal franchise according to the burgess rolls. However, during this period an average of 1,345 potential electors could expect to be disqualified for failure to pay local rates, often the most trivial of those rates.[69] Both the government and Belfast liberals understood the nature of Bates' manipulations but efforts to counter them were ineffective.[70] Bates successfully outmanoeuvred his opponents through a

67 *BNL*, 19 May 1881; *Vin*, 2 May 1840, 13 Nov. 1844; *NW*, 29 Aug. 1840, 13 Aug. 1842, 20 Jan. 1844. 68 Slater, 'Belfast Politics', p. 248. 69 Ibid., pp 250–1. 70 An example of government efforts to remedy the situation was an amending act of 1843, 6 & 7 Vict. c. 93, which sought consolidate and regulate the collection of local rates.

combination of sharp practice and a dexterous application of the finer points of municipal legislation and the private bill system for local improvements.

The genius of Bates was illustrated immediately after the conservative victories in the town council elections in 1842. One municipal institution remained in liberal hands, the police commission. The police commission seemed a secure bulwark from which to resist conservative monopoly. It will be recalled that the police commission was part of a bicameral improvement commission established in 1800 and significantly amended in 1816. The police commission comprised 25 people – 12 commissioners who served for life along with the 12 burgesses and mayor of the corporation serving as *ex-officio* members. After the dissolution of the corporation removed the *ex-officio* members, the police commission was controlled by liberals who had been a majority among the 12 commissioners since 1837. That control was brief. In 1843 Bates contended that the burgesses of the unreformed corporation ought, as a matter of course, to be succeeded by the burgesses of the reformed corporation. This meant everyone who met the property qualifications for the municipal franchise, according to Bates' valuators, and paid their rates, due to Bates' collectors, was now a burgess and therefore an *ex-officio* police commissioner. After an unsuccessful legal challenge by Belfast liberals and the rump of the old Donegall interest, in January 1844 the Tory burgesses swamped the old commissioners and passed a resolution transferring the powers of both the police committee and police commissioners to the town council.[71]

Bates established a municipal monopoly with greater patronage and power than any surviving corporation in Ireland. Bates had acquired not only the powers of the reformed corporations but also the powers of the older improvement commission. Bates subsequently fortified the already considerable powers of the combined institutions through a controversial series of private improvement acts that enabled conservatives to subvert further the safeguards against oligarchy built into the reformed corporations. Bates was able to deflect much of the opposition that such a policy might have aroused in Belfast and in London by pleading necessity. Belfast needed extraordinary municipal powers in order to deal with extraordinary growth and development.

Bates' machine was finally destroyed when John Rea undertook a successful legal challenge of the town council's exercise of the extraordinary fiscal powers garnered through Bates' improvement acts. As a young solicitor, Rea became involved in the Young Ireland movement and spent nine months in jail in 1848 as a result of this affiliation.[72] Rea established his reputation for pugnacious rhetoric through his involvement in legal cases, beginning with his defence of a number of Young Irelanders, with political overtones.[73] His forensic endurance

---

71 Slater, 'Belfast Politics', p. 254. 72 *BNL*, 19 May 1881. 73 See for example his

was legendary and frequently maddened opponents and allies alike. Rea is reported to have spoken for more than four hours at a meeting of the parish vestry in Belfast.[74] During the early 1850s, Rea was generally considered an asset by liberals and was employed in a variety of cases ranging from elections and riots to disputes over vestry rates or the control of public property. Rea seized upon every opportunity to harass or ridicule his conservative opponents, including judges. For example, in May 1853 Rea appeared before a grand jury presentment session in Lisburn for the barony of Upper Belfast and systematically opposed claims by conservatives for compensation for damages to property incurred during a riotous by-election for the borough. The amounts in question were trifling, almost all less than £5, but Rea goaded his conservative opponents by challenging every detail.[75]

Rea's tactics, however, soon began to alienate some of his liberal allies. Not only did his constant vituperation make tactical compromises impossible, but some became convinced that Rea was attempting to use the popularity and influence resulting from his legal performances to further his own, more radical, agenda rather than the greater liberal cause. In May 1854 the *Banner of Ulster* dramatically broke with Rea who had recently been hired to defend the paper in a libel case. According to the *Banner*, Rea publicly expressed 'his magnanimous expectations' that in return for his legal services the *Banner* 'must lay its editorial independence under his feet, and must sacrifice its public duties to Mr John Rea's eccentricities'. The *Banner* supported Rea in challenging vestry assessments and municipal finances or proposing sanitary reforms; but Rea's outlandish manner was estranging an 'influential party in the community' and 'instrumentally, at least, doing the work of Toryism'.[76]

While Rea had been repudiated by McKnight in the *Banner*, he was strongly supported by Denis Holland in the pages of the *Ulsterman*, Belfast's Catholic newspaper. With that support, Rea announced in August 1854 that he would challenge the Tory monopoly of municipal offices by standing for town councillor for the most Catholic ward in Belfast, Smithfield. The Bates' machine responded by summarily dismissing Rea's father, a conservative, from his position as clerk of the market. Rea retaliated by becoming involved in a suit against Bates and a number of town councillors alleging abuse of their various financial powers. The suit accused the town councillors of exceeding limits upon borrowing money and misapplication of borrowed funds. The *Ulsterman* conceived of the suit as a means to topple the Bates machine and accordingly

participation presentment session for the barony of Upper Belfast at Lisburn in the aftermath of a fiercely contested parliamentary election in that town, *Ulsterman*, 11 May 1853; or his challenging of the Londonderry interest at a petty sessions in Newtownards, *Ulsterman*, 8 Feb. 1854.   **74** *BU*, 25 April 1854, 13 May 1854.   **75** *Ulsterman*, 11 May 1853. **76** *BU*, 13 May 1854.

lent their support to Rea's efforts to publicize the allegations against Bates during the municipal election campaign that expanded from Smithfield to all five wards in the city.[77] With the Bates' machine intact and lacking any significant Presbyterian support, Rea was crushed in every ward.

Publicity concerning Rea's allegations, however, began to have some affect upon municipal affairs. Writers more temperate than Rea published detailed descriptions of the chicanery of Bates' machine.[78] In June 1855 Rea succeeded in chancery when the court found the defendants guilty of the main allegations and ordered them personally responsible for the £273,000 illegally borrowed and misappropriated during the previous ten years.[79] It seems clear that the town councillors had not been guilty of gross corruption in the sense that they or their supporters defalcated with corporation funds. Aside from some inflated contracts, the borrowed funds were spent upon real improvements of various kinds. The Bates' machine was more concerned with retaining political power than personal profit. The corporation, however, had exceeded its legal powers. Bates was undone. Having lost the confidence of the town council and facing financial ruin, Bates resigned in July 1855 and died in September of the same year.[80] Without Bates, the Tory machine collapsed and the burgess roll practically tripled.[81] In August 1855 Rea himself together with five other liberals, including the first Catholic to sit on that body, Bernard Hughes, were elected to the town council.

Rea's success was a pyrrhic victory for liberalism in Belfast. Some of those who had cooperated with the chancery suit in the hopes of destroying the Bates' machine were horrified by the scope of the court's decision. They accused Rea of usurping control of the suit from more sober agents and purposes. William Girdwood, an attorney originally from Lurgan and a former member of the Ulster Tenant-Right Association central committee, claimed, with the corroboration of the *Banner,* that he rather than Rea had initiated the suit in chancery 'to put an end to the late Town Clerk's system', but not 'to embarrass the creditors' of the corporation or 'ruin or harass with litigation' individual town councillors.[82] A number of liberals were anxious about Rea's motives and the likely effects of the chancery decision upon future municipal development. The future credit and development of the city was more important than punishment of the remnants of Bates' machine. For this reason, the chamber of commerce, a 'haven for disillusioned Liberals' with 'little sympathy for the Corporation in its disarray' sent a delegation to the attorney-

77 Slater, 'Belfast Politics', p. 255. 78 Slater cites a work by a liberal solicitor Samuel Bruce who subsequently became a town clerk, Slater, 'Belfast Politics', p. 256; another important work was, James Kennedy, *The evils of the act for the regulation of municipal corporations* (Belfast, 1855). 79 Chambers, *Faces of change,* p. 169. 80 Ibid., p. 256. 81 Slater, 'Belfast Politics', pp 256, 285. 82 *BU,* 14 July 1855.

general seeking forbearance until a bill to protect member of the Corporation from personal financial responsibility could be submitted to him.[83] The case was once again ensnarled in chancery.

This was the beginning of a ten-year struggle to mitigate the effects of the original chancery decree that bitterly divided liberals. Not surprisingly, conservatives were even more desperate to reach some accommodation and made overtures to moderate liberals. The conservatives proposed a compromise whereby they would abandon their exclusionary practices, even resigning seats in the town council in favour of liberals, in exchange for liberal support for a private improvement bill that would indemnify the culpable town councillors and secure the credit of the town. Liberals became divided into what were referred to as pro-compromise and anti-compromise factions. Rea led the anti-compromise party composed of the Catholic community and the radical Non-subscribing elite. Many of Rea's supporters were willing to accept a compromise whereby the town councillors in question would be responsible for the legal costs of the chancery suit and the failed private improvement bills, but indemnified for the money illegally borrowed but spent on public facilities.[84] Rea, however, as the relator in the suit, was irreconcilable and frustrated all efforts at compromise. Rea rejected a proposal worked out by a committee of the chamber of commerce that included the local leader of the more advanced liberals, Robert Grimshaw.[85]

Over time, the divisions hardened, and Rea's rhetoric did little to conciliate moderates. A prime example of his forensic extravagance was a speech during the parliamentary election for Belfast in 1857 when liberal divisions contributed to a conservative victory. While claiming he 'would not again wish to see the country involved in civil war', Rea nonetheless praised the rebels of 1798 and 1848 and hoped to see 'a monument erected to their memories and deeds'. Rea desired Ireland to 'possess what Dr Drennan and men such as he wrote and suffered for, and what Theobald Wolfe Tone and men such as he fought and died for'.[86] In this and other speeches Rea attempted to bind together what would later become known as the constitutional and physical force traditions of Irish republicanism.[87] Some Ulster radicals were willing to cooperate with Rea in the hope of furthering their cause but for most liberals the militant rhetoric with its republican allusions was anathema.

The extent to which Rea and the chancery suit became the focal point of liberal divisions can hardly be exaggerated. During the period between 1852 and 1859 Rea was strongly supported in pages of the *Ulsterman*, the self-

---

83 Chambers, *Faces of change*, p. 171.   84 Wright, *Two lands*, p. 217.   85 Slater, 'Belfast politics', p. 279.   86 *Ulsterman*, 9 Mar. 1857.   87 For another example, see Rea's speech before the Catholic Institute in Belfast, St Patrick's Day 1863, *UO*, 19 Mar. 1863.

described organ of the Catholic community edited for almost all of this period by Denis Holland, a fellow Young Irelander. Holland left the *Ulsterman* in 1858, just prior to the paper's failure, and founded the *Irishman*. That newspaper, published first in Belfast and then in Dublin, was for a time the semi-official organ of early Fenianism.[88] Together Rea and Holland consistently advised Ulster's Catholics to adopt an independent, uncompromising stance not only with regard to conservatives but also towards liberal Protestants. When a new Catholic newspaper, the *Ulster Observer*, began publication in Belfast during 1862 the prime question soon became would it support Rea and his strategies? The *Northern Whig* asserted that it would be foolish for the Catholic community to continue supporting Rea as even 'the compact body of Liberals' who initially had supported Rea now rejected him. Rea had 'assailed, defamed, and vilified' potential allies until his fervid oratory had 'served but to swell streams of abuse into torrents of vituperation'. Rea's public life had become 'a succession of indecent brawls and outrages on every form of order'. Despite the admonition, the *Observer* continued to support Rea and liberals continued to be divided. At the municipal elections in November 1863, liberal candidates were unexpectedly defeated in the Catholic stronghold of Smithfield ward. Supporters of the unsuccessful candidates acknowledged that some liberals had refused to vote for candidates associated with Rea.[89]

In February 1864, the stalemate in the Dickensian chancery suit gave way to arbitration by the chief secretary Edward Cardwell. That arbitration allowed indemnification for the special respondents through a private improvement bill in exchange for certain reforms. Rea did not, probably could not, accept defeat quietly. In July 1864, Rea was forcibly removed from a House of Lords committee considering the private improvement bill. The immediate aftermath of the failure of Rea's mulish obstructionism was a period of flux while all the parties were compelled to reconsider their positions. In 1864, however, the possibility for reconciliation between the 'anti-compromise' liberals, comprised primarily of Catholics, and the 'pro-compromise' liberals was hindered by serious sectarian violence in the city during August.

Ironically, the riot may have been the occasion that convinced some in the Catholic community of the necessity of cooperation with liberal Protestants in order to defeat conservative policies. There was not, however, consensus about a strategy to supersede the blunderings of John Rea. During the course of the riots a crisis occurred when some Catholics considered taking up arms to defend themselves from Orange mobs and the reputedly partisan corporation police, the justly notorious Belfast Bulkies. For the first time in Belfast's history

88 R.V. Comerford, *The fenians in context* (Atlantic Highlands, NJ, 1985), pp 95–7.   89 *NW*, 5 Jan. 1863, *UO*, 26 Nov. 1863.

a group of Catholics, led by the growing number of labourers and artisans loosely referred to as 'navvies', retaliated in a significant way by attacking Protestant churches and national schools, including one particularly horrific instance when an attempt was made to wreck a school with children in it.[90] At first these reprisals seem to have been a spontaneous, frustrated response to partisan policing and provocations by Protestant mobs.[91] Whatever the provocation, the violence brought the wrath of both the Protestant mobs and the authorities down upon the 'navvies', and they were forced back into the predominantly Catholic enclave in the western portion of the town known as the Pound.[92] The Catholic rioters found themselves besieged and in the unenviable position of having to rely upon men with whom they had traded blows, both the Bulkies and the Irish constabulary, to defend them from angry Protestant mobs. It was at this critical moment that a community meeting was held to consider the formation of a self-defence organization.

The venue for this deliberation was the Belfast Catholic Institute. Founded in 1859 the Catholic Institute was a voluntary organization that embodied both the increasing spirit of denominationalism that concerned many Protestant liberals as well as a potential weakening of the role of the clergy in Catholic society that alarmed the Catholic hierarchy.[93] With the support of several wealthy Catholic merchants and shareholders, the institute acquired a house where Catholics might gather for social and educational purposes. A reading room containing books and periodicals was maintained and lectures on practical arts such as mechanics and chemistry were presented to Catholic working men.[94] According to the *Banner of Ulster,* at the first meeting of the institute its founders were disappointed that they 'had not met with the encouragement which they had anticipated from the Roman Catholics of the middle classes of society in Belfast' and had been refused the aid of Bishop Denvir.[95] Denis Holland voiced similar complaints in the pages of the *Irishman,* his newly formed proto-Fenian newspaper.[96]

During the riots of 1864, Catholics gathered at the institute to decide upon a course of action. Despite a circular by Bishop Dorrian warning against retaliation and 'meetings called without the proper authority' by 'self-appointed' leaders, William McCoy, subsequently a leader in the amnesty movement for Fenians imprisoned or transported for their participation in an abortive insurrection in 1867, proposed a self-defence organization that was approved by acclamation. In the emotion of the moment Catholic working men had rejected

90 Budge and O'Leary, *Belfast,* p. 82; Wright, *Two lands,* pp 261–9. 91 Wright, *Two lands,* p. 261. 92 Ibid. 93 Wright described two threats to Catholic solidarity, increased social interaction with secular or 'Protestant' institutions and the repudiation of clerical influence as demonstrated in Ribbonism or Fenianism, *Two lands,* p. 296. 94 Macaulay, *Patrick Dorrian,* p. 140. 95 *BU,* 14 July 1859. 96 Macaulay, *Patrick Dorrian,* p. 140.

the authority of their clergy and seemed determined to pursue a course of action that would lead them into dangerous conflict with the secular authorities.

At this critical juncture, the editor of the *Ulster Observer*, A.J. McKenna, preserved a measure of Catholic unity and probably prevented a disastrous collision between the Catholic community and the secular authorities. Rather than appealing to authority or morality, McKenna provided a realistic assessment of the likely outcomes of a policy of self-defence – almost certain defeat and the alienation of a sympathetic liberal administration in London. McKenna counselled the crowd to send a delegation to Dublin to petition the central government to relieve them from corrupt and partisan local authorities by appointing government commissioners to supersede the local magistrates. McKenna understood, however, that the crowd would only accede to this sober approach if they believed that more immediate measures were being undertaken to protect their lives and property. Something had to be done. Therefore, McKenna proposed that while Catholics should not appear in the streets in armed ranks, as elements of the Protestant community supposedly had, they need not be passive victims of aggression. If necessary, Catholics could and should defend their homes. Furthermore, McKenna proposed the appointment of a committee to collect money and deliberate upon any future steps.[97] McKenna attempted to direct the angry and anxious energy of the community away from retaliation.

In the aftermath of the riots, McKenna and Dorrian came to very different conclusions about the lessons to be drawn. Dorrian was determined to restore and increase the influence of the clergy in the community. To this end, Dorrian set about undermining the independence of the Catholic Institute. With cunning bordering on deceit and the robust exercise of his full episcopal authority, including the threat of excommunication, Dorrian forced a complete reorganization of the Catholic Institute. With the encouragement of recent papal pronouncements fulminating against perceived secular threats to religious authority, Dorrian did not limit himself to the Catholic Institute but set stringent conditions, supported by the threat of excommunication, for any future associations.[98]

By late 1866, Dorrian had arranged the complete dissolution of the Catholic Institute. In so doing, Dorrian believed that he was preserving the Catholic community from the effects of its close, daily intercourse with Protestants in Belfast. The questioning of clerical authority, such as that which occurred during the riot of 1864, was a result of 'the Presbyterian leaven' having made some in the Catholic Institute 'wish to have themselves entirely free from all Ecclesiastical control'.[99] The same concerns about Catholic solidarity that had

97 *UO*, 18 August 1864.   98 Macaulay, *Patrick Dorrian*, pp 140–7.   99 Ibid., p. 150.

formed part of the impetus for parochial missions and denominational education led clerics such as Dorrian to attempt the preservation of clerical authority and denominationalism as the foundations of Catholic solidarity.

Politically, Dorrian was convinced that Catholic separatism was the foundation for a necessary policy of independent opposition in parliament similar to that envisioned by the failed Independent Irish Party. He had expressed his hostility towards too close a cooperation with those outside the Catholic, nationalist community previously. In August 1864, Dorrian wrote to a fellow cleric, 'I look upon Whiggery as the Evil Genius of Ireland, a few offices for traitors and starvation & oppression for the rest of the Catholic people'.[1] The increasing evidence of frustration among Catholics as demonstrated by support for Fenianism and the behaviour of the working classes of Belfast during the riots of 1864 convinced Dorrian that some outlet for the peaceful expression of Catholic grievances was necessary. When Cardinal Paul Cullen launched the National Association in order to achieve disestablishment of the Church of Ireland, land reform and secure denominational education in December of 1864, Dorrian was one of its strongest supporters.[2]

A.J. McKenna, on the other hand, seems to have concluded that Catholic solidarity, however desirable and beneficial, could not of itself adequately protect and promote Catholic interests in Ulster. It was only as a part of a larger liberal alliance that Ulster Catholics could expect to advance. McKenna's convictions concerning the necessity of close alliance with British liberals brought him into conflict with Dorrian. The outcome of that conflict fundamentally affected the future relationship between the Catholic community and Protestant liberals. Ironically, McKenna had been chosen for the *Ulster Observer* in the belief that he would be amenable to clerical oversight.[3] Born in Co. Cavan and a former student for the priesthood at Maynooth, McKenna certainly lived up to these expectations at the beginning of his editorship by supporting denominational education and denouncing secret societies. In the *Observer* in March 1863 McKenna also advocated a policy of independent opposition, advising his readers to 'be independent of both parties, using each in so far as they can make each useful to the promotion of their own ends'.[4]

By June 1864, however, McKenna's editorials had aroused private condemnation by Dorrian.[5] On a personal level, Dorrian almost certainly resented the growing prestige of the young editor. As McKenna spoke to meetings throughout the province, he was increasingly regarded as the spokesman and champion of Ulster Catholics. With regard to public policy, McKenna began to

---

1 From a letter by Dorrian quoted in Emmet Larkin, *The consolidation of the Roman Catholic Church in Ireland, 1860–1870* (Chapel Hill NC, 1987), p. 289. 2 Ibid., pp 312–13. 3 Macaulay, *Patrick Dorrian*, p. 194. 4 *UO*, 26 Mar. 1863. 5 Macaulay, *Patrick Dorrian*, pp 196–7.

speak against the policy of independent opposition that Dorrian cherished. In February 1864 McKenna cast cold water on efforts to revive the Independent Irish Party. McKenna suggested instead that only an alliance of Irish, English and Scottish farmers that would elicit the cooperation of British politicians such as Richard Cobden and John Bright could succeed. In April 1864, McKenna further criticized the policy of independent opposition by concluding that, even if English liberals 'travesty a glorious cause', the 'amalgamation of the Catholic and Tory parties' that a policy of independent opposition might require was an 'impossibility'. 'Liberals as we are, and always have been', Catholics ought not to 'turn our backs on the cause to which our conscience and intelligence lead us to give an honest and consistent support'.[6]

McKenna probably further antagonized Dorrian by his advocacy of some of the ideals of continental Catholic liberalism. McKenna explicitly lauded Comte de Montalembert as a symbol of the essential liberalism of Catholicism.[7] Montalembert advocated increased political liberty and participation in government by a broader segment of society as the best means to secure Catholicism. The church was protected from unwarranted interference by the state by enlisting the faithful to control that state.[8] In a similar vein, McKenna exhorted Catholics to be less dependent upon clerical and secular leaders, even those as great as O'Connell. Reliance upon authoritarian leadership had left Catholics 'helpless' and 'incompetent' when that leadership failed. Perhaps with Young Ireland and the continental revolutions of 1848 in mind, McKenna acknowledged that mistakes would be made, that people would 'fall into many errors and commit many follies, and be guilty of many indiscretions'. However, from the experience of governing themselves 'order will come, and, when it does come, it will be abiding'.[9] For Dorrian, McKenna's advocacy of Catholic liberalism might very well seem akin to the malign influence of Presbyterian culture and values.

In 1865, after the riots and during Dorrian's campaign against the Catholic Institute, McKenna openly criticized the National Association of Cardinal Cullen that Dorrian warmly supported.[10] Furthermore, in opposition to the policy of the National Association, McKenna supported the candidature of Tristram Kennedy in Co. Louth in April 1865. McKenna understood, however, that his position was vulnerable. In June 1865 McKenna wrote to the chief whip of the Liberal party, Henry Brand, asking for some action be taken to support the alliance of Catholics and liberal Protestants in Belfast lest he be forced to surrender to clerical pressure and support the National Association.[11]

---

6 *UO*, 27 Feb. 1864, 5 Apr. 1864. 7 Ibid., 5 Apr. 1864, 12 Apr. 1864. 8 R.H. Soltau, *French political thought in the 19th century* (New York, 1959), pp 172–3. 9 *UO*, 5 Apr. 1864. 10 Ibid., 4 Feb. 1865. 11 Slater, 'Belfast Politics', pp 163–4.

In response to McKenna's pleas for aid, the national liberal leadership arranged for an outsider, Lord John Hay, to contest the borough. It was hoped that an outsider who had no role in the bitter quarrels of the previous years might reunify the various strands of liberalism. In this at least, Hay was partly successful. Although Hay was thoroughly defeated by his conservative opponents, he managed for the first time in more than fifteen years to organize and maintain a semblance of unity among liberals. Catholics, liberal Presbyterians, and radicals all supported Hay publicly in the days before the election. After the election, liberals did not engage in mutual recriminations despite some very real grounds for suspicion and complaint.

Before the election, prior to Hay's announcement as a candidate, an overly optimistic account of liberal strength in the town intended to persuade liberals to contest the election suggested that 1,749 of the 3,566 electors in the town were liberals. Of those 1,749 liberal electors, 729 were supposed to be Catholics, 700 Presbyterians, 170 Unitarians and 150 others divided amongst Methodist, Episcopalians and Quakers. Liberals had hoped that 1,550 supporters might actually vote, including 700 Catholics. After the election, the conservative *News-Letter* attempted to sow seeds of disunity by asserting that Catholics had been abandoned by their Presbyterian allies. According to the *News-Letter*, all but two of the hoped-for Catholic votes had been cast for Hay, but liberal Protestants had only provided 293 of a hoped for 850 votes.[12] To the *News-Letter*'s disappointment, however, the failure of more than 550 supposed-liberal Protestants to vote was ascribed by all of Hay's supporters, with considerable cause, to hasty preparations, Tory chicanery and intimidation. As a result, all sections of liberalism agreed to the formation of the Ulster Liberal Society in the hope of undoing the accumulated abuses of the registration system that had accrued during the long Tory monopoly of municipal government.

The lack of recrimination about a very real disparity in performance was in part the result of the fact that the two leaders of the Catholic community had much to gain from continued cooperation with liberals. Catholic unity might have been seriously damaged during the election in July. Bishop Dorrian had sole control of the diocese since May 1865 and was an inveterate opponent of liberals such as Hay. Dorrian hoped, however, that a liberal government might grant concessions on Catholic higher education, a primary concern of the National Association.[13] It may have been this hope and the deference paid by Hay to Dorrian that prevented unseemly divisions during the 1865 parliamentary election. For his part, McKenna not only believed that the liberal alliance was the best hope for reforms in Ireland but he also understood that

---

12 Ibid., pp 165, 173.   13 Larkin, *The consolidation of the Roman Catholic church in Ireland*, p. 447.

liberal Protestants might prove useful allies against Dorrian. McKenna's role in the revival of liberal hopes was vital. Besides his support for cooperation with liberals, the spectacle of McKenna and the Catholic Institute resisting Dorrian convinced some liberal Protestants that Catholicism had not fallen completely to the 'Ultramontane' threat, that Catholics were not a monolith.[14]

While the general election of 1865 laid a new foundation for liberal cooperation, there were still considerable difficulties. To begin with, the conflict between Dorrian and the Catholic Institute became a public scandal in October 1865. Dorrian was severely criticized not only in the conservative press but in the *Banner of Ulster* as well. Describing Dorrian's circular concerning Catholic associations as possessing 'a spirit of the most bigotted Ultramontanism', the *Banner* accused him of having 'driven into retirement' Bishop Denvir, 'whose views in many respects were in unison with those of such moderate and tolerant prelates as Drs. Crolly, Murray and Doyle'.[15] The fears of Ultramontanism were revived.

This fear was also evident in February 1866 when Presbyterians debated the question of higher education. At that time, the liberal government seemed willing, as Dorrian had hoped, to grant charters to both the Catholic university and Magee college for affiliation with the Queen's colleges.[16] Despite the temptation of official recognition for Magee, the general assembly rejected this plan. Although the assembly was overwhelmingly against the plan, there was a bitter debate as to what the grounds of opposition ought to be. For liberals, led by Revd John MacNaughtan, the opposition ought to be based on concerns very similar to those that Richard Smyth had described in 1863 with regard to denominational reformatories. Such a plan would establish the denominational system in higher education. Such a system would prove disastrous to private conscience and civil liberty. A dissenting individual or group within any particular denomination might find themselves isolated and persecuted. At its crudest, the argument was made that the dominant 'Ultramontane' faction in Catholicism would crush dissent as Bishop Dorrian had coerced the Catholic Institute. Obviously such a line of argument had the disadvantage of being perceived, sometimes with good reason, as little more than anti-popery.

The conflicts in the Catholic community between Dorrian and McKenna as well as the divisions between Presbyterians and Catholics concerning education contributed to the failure of the liberals in Belfast to contest two by-elections for the borough in 1866. However, within two years, new circumstances led to a period of political experimentation from 1868 until 1874 that demonstrated both dangerous developments threatening the annihilation of Ulster liberalism as well as greater opportunities for coalition between Catholics and

14 *BU,* 29 July 1865.   15 Ibid., 28 Oct. 1865.   16 Wright, *Two lands,* pp 301–8.

Presbyterians. By the general election of 1874 a strange spectacle presented itself to many of Ulster's electors – a genuine contest between liberals and conservatives in a large number of parliamentary constituencies.

Parades and politics: general election of 1868

At the general election of 1868 Ulster liberals, particularly those in Belfast, were forced to adapt to substantial changes in the structure of politics. The Representation of the People (Ireland) Act of 1868 did not affect Ireland as dramatically as the parallel English parliamentary reform of 1867, but the changes were significant. Although the franchise for the county constituencies that formed the bulk of parliamentary representation in Ireland remained virtually unchanged from that established in 1850, in the boroughs a decrease in the property qualifications for occupiers resulted in sizeable increases in the number of electors. Throughout Ulster the borough electorate increased by 131 per cent during the period from 1866 until 1868.[17] See Table 4.1.

Furthermore, the aggregate number obscures the remarkable increase in the number of electors in prosperous manufacturing and commercial towns such as Belfast where the number of electors had increased from around 3600 to just more than 12,000.[18] More than a quantitative change, the electoral reform resulted in a qualitative change in the electorate. For the first time, a considerable number of the new electors were working men, both skilled artisans as well as industrial workers.[19]

While Ulster liberals had earnestly advocated the extension of parliamentary reform to Ireland, their emphasis had been a redistribution of seats rather than an extension of the franchise. The *Banner of Ulster* complained bitterly of the under representation of Belfast and questioned the complete lack of representation of growing towns such as Newtownards, Portadown, Lurgan or Ballymena, particularly if compared with decaying towns in the south and west of Ireland that still returned members to parliament while their populations markedly decreased.[20] The *Banner* reserved its harshest criticism, however, for the reduction of the qualification for the occupier franchise to £4. According to the *Banner* this change was likely to enfranchise men in the 'wretchedness and demoralisation that lies between North Street and Smithfield' who, 'in point of intelligence and morality', ought 'not to be invested with such a trust'.[21]

It was somewhat surprising that the *Banner* should have objected so strenuously to a £4 occupier franchise for parliament when the £5 qualification for

---

17 B.M. Walker, *Ulster politics* (Belfast, 1989), p. 40. 18 Wright, *Two lands*, p. 315. 19 Walker, *Ulster politics*, p. 40. 20 *BU*, 24 Mar. 1868. 21 Ibid.

Table 4.1: Changes in borough electorates in Ulster due to Franchise Act of 1868

Boroughs	Electors 1866	Electors 1868	% Increase electors	Population 1861	Population 1871	% Increase population
Belfast	3,615	12,168	237	119,393	174,412	46
Lisburn	272	469	72	8,585	9,326	9
Derry	863	1,483	72	20,875	25,242	21
Armagh	421	603	43	9,320	8,976	-4
Newry	557	796	43	13,108	14,158	8
Enniskillen	245	341	39	5,820	5,836	0
Dungannon	177	245	38	3,994	3,886	-3
Coleraine	252	346	37	6,236	6,588	6
Downpatrick	181	241	33	4,317	4,155	-4
Carrickfergus	1,201	1,290	7	9,417	9,397	0
Total	7,784	17,982	131	201,065	261,976	30

Source: Brian Walker, 'The Irish Electorate, 1868–1915', *IHS*, 18 (1973).

the town commission clearly had been to the advantage of liberals in towns throughout Ulster for nearly forty years. It was concern about the growth of Orangeism that caused Ulster liberals to fear the new franchise. As early as June of 1867, John Rea, who for all his manic demagogy understood the potential of franchise reform to disrupt the existing structure of politics in Belfast and other towns in Ulster as well as anyone, gleefully predicted a significant increase in the political influence of Orangeism. The *Banner of Ulster* anxiously concurred, noting that 'in Belfast and all over Ulster, the Orangemen are a powerful body and their influence will be greatly increased when the Reform Bill takes effect'.[22] Orangeism was not a new phenomenon in Ulster but the changing circumstances in many Ulster towns magnified its potential to unleash the kinds of sectarian conflict and violence that galvanized Catholics and Protestants into mutually hostile groups. In Belfast as well as a number of other growing commercial or industrial towns in Ulster, a mixture of demographic and environmental change created explosive social conditions.

Explanations of the increasing importance of Orangeism have been largely connected with discussions of the increase in sectarian clashes in Ulster towns and cities. Early scholarship on this subject suggested that the deterioration in communal harmony in places such as Belfast was directly related to the increasing rural migration into urban areas. This migration increased the proportion of Catholics in places such as Belfast and threatened Protestant social and political dominance.[23] It was further suggested that the rural folk,

22 Ibid., 18 June 1867, 11 Apr. 1868. 23 For a discussion of this historiography see

Catholic and Protestant, brought with them a tradition of sectarian animus and violence. These explanations have been challenged by scholars and must be substantially qualified. The absolute numbers of Catholics certainly increased in many Ulster towns as their populations increased during the nineteenth century. Whether the proportion of Catholics in these towns increased is a more daunting question. One of the great gaps in our knowledge of nineteenth-century Ireland is the religious composition of towns and cities before 1861.

Beginning in 1861, data on religious professions was included in the published reports of the census. The data on religious professions collected before that time have been lost with one important exception. In 1835, parliamentary commissioners investigating education in Ireland published the data on religious professions from the 1831 census together with their own data collected in 1834.[24] Unfortunately, the unit of measurement was the civil parish rather than the townlands and municipalities used in later accounts so that the religious composition of towns cannot easily be reconstructed to any useful extent. With the possible exceptions of Armagh town, where the population of the town comprised more than ninety per cent of the civil parish's population, and Belfast, where the population of the somewhat amorphous conurbation described as the 'town and suburbs' comprised eighty-seven per cent of the population of the civil parish, it is practically impossible to use the parochial data from 1834 as a kind of statistical sample from which to extrapolate the data for towns. Even with other sources of information to guide and limit the extrapolation, the margins of error are simply too great to be useful in any discussion of the changing religious composition of towns before 1861.[25] With the added complication of shifting municipal boundaries, the question of the changing religious composition of most towns becomes practically impossible to unravel before 1861.

If it is assumed that the flourishing economy of Belfast made it the primary magnet for Catholic migration in Ulster, then a qualified discussion of the changing proportion of Catholics in Ulster towns can be undertaken. Because of its importance, more information concerning the changing demography of Belfast can be gleaned than for other towns. Furthermore, because the population of Belfast comprised practically ninety per cent of the population of the civil parish where it was located, the data concerning religious profession from the investigation of public instruction in 1834 may be used with care.

Farrell, *Rituals and riots*, pp 127–32. **24** *First report of the commissioners of public instruction, Ireland*, HC 1835 (45, 46, 47), xxxiii–xxxiv. For a more detailed discussion of the usefulness of this data see David Miller, 'Irish Catholicism and the Great Famine', *Journal of Social History*, 9 (1975), 81–3. **25** The difficulties of determining municipal boundaries have been described by W.E. Vaughan and A.J. Fitzpatrick in *Irish historical statistics: population, 1821–1871* (Dublin, 1978).

Table 4.2: Populations of towns in Ulster, 1831–61

Town	1831			1841			1851			1861			1831–61
	Area in acres	Pop.	Pop. density	Area in acres	Pop.	Pop. density	Area in acres	Pop.	Pop. density	Area in acres	Pop.	Pop. density	Population increase
Portadown	NA	1591	NA	54	2505	46	54	3091	57	54	5528	102	247%
Lurgan	NA	2842	NA	121	4677	39	121	4205	35	121	7772	64	173%
Belfast*	457	44,770	98	1872	75,308	40	1872	97,784	52	5637	119,393	21	167%
Newtownards	NA	4442	NA	365	7621	21	365	9566	26	365	9542	26	115%
Ballymena	NA	4067	NA	90	5549	62	90	6136	68	90	6769	75	66%
Banbridge	NA	2469	NA	117	3324	28	117	3301	28	117	4033	34	63%
Omagh	NA	2211	NA	73	2947	40	73	3054	42	73	3533	48	60%
Derry*	241	14,030	58	497	15,196	31	497	19,727	40	497	20,519	41	46%
Dromore	NA	1942	NA	67	2110	31	67	1862	28	67	2531	38	30%
Comber	NA	1377	NA	95	1964	21	95	1790	19	95	1713	18	24%
Lisburn*	818	6201	8	231	6284	27	231	6533	28	231	7462	32	20%
Ballymoney	NA	2222	NA	86	2490	29	86	2578	30	86	2600	30	17%
Cookstown	NA	2883	NA	154	3006	20	154	2993	19	154	3257	21	13%
Limavady	NA	2428	NA	515	3101	6	515	3205	6	515	2732	5	13%
Cavan	NA	2931	NA	170	3749	22	170	3034	18	170	3118	18	6%
Dungannon	138	3758	27	230	3801	17	230	3835	17	230	3984	17	6%
Larne	NA	2616	NA	96	3345	35	96	3076	32	96	2766	29	6%

Source: W.E. Vaughan and A.J. Fitzpatrick (eds), Irish historical statistics: population, 1821–1971 (Dublin, 1978).

*Refers to towns for which the data have been taken from, Parliamentary representation, Ireland [...], HC 1831–2 (519), xliii. Collected in the summer of 1831 these data have the significant advantage of delineating the area considered.

Table 4.3: Catholic population of Belfast, 1784–1881

Year	Population of Belfast	Catholic population	Catholics as % of population
1784	13,650	1,092	8
1808	25,000	4,000	16
1834	61,600	19,712	32
1861	119,393	41,406	35
1871	174,412	55,575	32
1881	208,122	59,975	29

Belfast was certainly not a typical Ulster town in many ways but rather might be assumed to be at the extreme margin with regard to Catholic migration. During the period between 1831 and 1861 only the much smaller towns of Portadown and Lurgan exceeded the astonishing rate of growth of Belfast: see Table 4.2.

There was also a significant increase in the proportion of Catholics in the town during the period. Given the dominance of its economy, the increase was probably larger than any other town, with again the possible exceptions of Portadown and Lurgan. See Table 4.3.

However, a number of scholars have observed that the marked growth in the proportion of Catholics seems to have occurred during the period between 1808 and 1834, more than two decades before Belfast was regularly ravaged by sectarian riots.[26] While an increase in the proportion of Catholics in some Ulster towns such as Belfast, Lurgan and Portadown was almost certainly a significant factor in the increase in sectarian tension evident from the 1860s, it does not seem to have been a sufficient cause. Indeed, the Catholic proportion of many Ulster towns declined during the period between 1861 and 1881 when sectarian tensions worsened in many places: see Table 4.4. The Apprentice Boys existed, with important lapses related to the history of government policy towards party processions, before the so-called age of riots. In the most recent study of the phenomena of sectarian violence in Ulster during the nineteenth century, Sean Farrell has remarked that an under appreciated factor in the increase in sectarian tension was the urban environment. With Protestant and Catholic workers 'neatly packed' in increasing numbers into their respective ghettos, 'activists could easily manufacture the kind of provocative incidents that led to widespread and prolonged bouts of communal rioting'.[27] Farrell might have added that the development of better transportation networks, including railways, permitted activists to mobilize their followers in an unprecedented fashion. As early as the 1850s Orange leaders in Enniskillen were organizing trips to Derry where the iconography of loyalism might be seen in stone.

26 Farrell, *Rituals and riots*, p. 129. 27 Ibid., pp 130–1.

Table 4.4: Populations of towns in Ulster, 1861–81

Town	1861				1871				1881				1861–81
	Area in acres	Pop.	Pop. density	% Catholic	Area in acres	Pop.	Pop. density	% Catholic	Area in acres	Pop.	Pop. density	% Catholic	Pop. increase
Belfast	5,637	119,393	21	34	5,991	174,412	29	32	5,991	208,122	35	29	74%
Larne	96	2,766	29	28	216	3,288	15	26	216	4,716	22	23	70%
Lisburn	231	7,462	32	27	239	7,876	33	26	639	10,755	17	21	44%
Londonderry	497	20,519	41	58	1,933	25,242	13	55	2,164	29,162	13	55	42%
Portadown	54	5,528	102	34	654	6,735	10	29	654	7,850	12	26	42%
Banbridge	117	4,033	34	25	769	5,600	7	22	769	5,609	7	22	39%
Ballymena	90	6,769	75	24	472	7,931	17	22	469	8,883	19	21	31%
Lurgan	121	7,772	64	35	851	10,632	12	37	851	10,135	12	34	30%
Comber	95	1,713	18	5	95	2,006	21	5	95	2,165	23	4	26%
Newry	629	12,179	19	65	701	13,364	19	65	701	14,808	21	66	22%
Carrickfergus	129	4,028	31	15	120	4,212	35	13	120	4,792	40	12	19%
Cookstown	154	3,257	21	45	187	3,501	19	44	187	3,870	21	41	19%
Bangor	274	2,531	9	6	824	2,560	3	7	824	3,006	4	8	19%
Ballymoney	86	2,600	30	31	516	2,930	6	28	516	3,049	6	29	17%
Omagh	73	3,533	48	62	73	3,724	51	58	73	4,126	57	59	17%
Armagh	269	8,801	33	55	1,092	8,946	8	52	1,092	10,070	9	50	14%
Limavady	515	2,732	5	32	572	2,762	5	35	572	2,954	5	37	8%
Coleraine	547	5,631	10	26	207	6,082	29	22	207	5,899	28	21	5%

Dungannon	230	3,984	17	55	230	3,886	17	55	230	4,084	18	54	3%
Letterkenny	66	2,165	33	68	395	2,116	5	71	395	2,188	6	70	1%
Belturbet	225	1,789	8	63	1,141	1,759	2	66	1,141	1,807	2	66	1%
Strabane	253	4,184	17	60	253	4,309	17	62	253	4,196	17	67	0%
Castleblayney	82	1,822	22	66	185	1,809	10	69	185	1,810	10	69	-1%
Enniskillen	210	5,774	27	56	230	5,836	25	56	230	5,712	25	60	-1%
Dromore	67	2,531	38	31	258	2,408	9	23	258	2,491	10	21	-2%
Cavan	170	3,118	18	75	493	3,389	7	75	497	3,050	6	75	-2%
Clones	52	2,390	46	55	181	2,170	12	50	181	2,216	12	55	-7%
Downpatrick	278	3,692	13	45	278	3,621	13	45	278	3,419	12	47	-7%
Newtownards	365	9,542	26	12	483	9,562	20	11	483	8,676	18	10	-9%
Cootehill	107	1,994	19	70	449	1,851	4	72	451	1,789	4	74	-10%
Ballyshannon	352	3,197	9	81	760	2,958	4	80	759	2,840	4	78	-11%
Monaghan	170	3,799	22	70	177	3,632	21	67	177	3,369	19	73	-11%
Antrim	136	2,137	16	23	197	2,020	10	27	197	1,647	8	22	-23%

Source: W.E. Vaughan and A.J. Fitzpatrick (eds), *Irish historical statistics: population, 1821–1971* (Dublin, 1978).

The rapid, unplanned expansion of sectarian ghettos also overwhelmed existing social institutions. There was not enough housing much less a sufficient number of schools and churches. The squalid conditions certainly concerned contemporaries. Graphic descriptions of the poverty of urban Belfast, such as those provided by the Congregationalist minister Revd W.M. O'Hanlon, encouraged both Protestant and Catholic ecclesiastics to undertake missions to redeem the denizens of the Pound and the Sandy Row.[28] Unfortunately, these missions themselves became a further catalyst for sectarian distrust as accusations of proselytism or neglect, many warranted, were exchanged between Catholic and Protestant groups. As has been observed previously, many of the leaders of liberal Presbyterianism in Ulster were evangelicals involved in missions or open-air preaching. Missions of mercy sometimes inadvertently contributed to the construction of bulwarks of confessional solidarity. Belfast liberals feared that the 1868 franchise reform would bring those who manned these bulwarks into the polity.

In the short term, however, Ulster liberals were fortunate that the qualitative change in the electorate occurred at a moment of discontent within the conservative ranks. Rank-and-file Tories dissented from several policies of their leadership in an unprecedented fashion. In Belfast, conservative activists and ultra-Protestants criticized the compromise with liberals over the chancery bill that allowed liberals, even Catholic liberals, on to the town council and disbanded the corporation police. They were further displeased by the establishment of a new financial system that essentially destroyed the longstanding differential rating system for the police rate, the tax assessed by the improvement commission that provided the bulk of municipal revenue. In a seemingly practical proposal to consolidate the numerous local taxes that had been the source of much of the past political chicanery, the conservatives undermined the graduated scale of taxation and effectively transferred the burden of taxation from the highest valued property in the town to the more modest owners of property.[29] The *Banner of Ulster* estimated that the consolidated borough rate would double the taxes on property rated at £20 or less.[30]

Throughout Ulster, discontent with local policies was compounded by unease at the efforts of the minority government of the conservative leader Disraeli to secure the continued endowment of the Church of Ireland by offering concessions on education and endowment to the Catholic hierarchy.[31] Ulster conservatives became divided between those who wished to preserve government support by 'levelling up', that is providing supposedly equal state support to both Catholicism and Protestantism, and 'levelling down', meaning

28 W.M. O'Hanlon, *Walks among the poor of Belfast* (Belfast, 1853). 29 Wright, *Two lands*, pp 223, 284–7. 30 *BU*, 31 Jan. 1867. 31 T. MacKnight, *Ulster as it is*, 2 vols (1896), i, pp 152–3.

the abolition of all ecclesiastical endowments. In general, the aristocratic leadership of Ulster conservatives seems to have favoured the policy of 'levelling up' while many rank and file Tories, especially those ultra-Protestants or evangelicals appalled at the prospect of supporting 'Romish errors' tended to support 'levelling down'. In 1868 conservative discontent with local issues and national policies became focused around one minor landlord from Co. Down, William Johnston.

Johnston became a celebrated figure in 1867 because of his opposition to the Party Processions Act of 1850 forbidding party demonstrations and parades such as those of Orangemen or Apprentice Boys.[32] Johnston came into conflict with the government as well as the leaderships of the Orange Order and the conservative party, both of whom urged obedience to the law.[33] After two months imprisonment for leading an Orange procession from Newtownards to Bangor, a thoroughly Protestant area in Co. Down, Johnston sought to use his status as an Orange martyr as the basis for a parliamentary campaign in Belfast in 1868. Despite clear evidence of Johnston's popular support, including an impressive demonstration in Belfast, the conservative leadership selected two other candidates. Considering this snub a betrayal of the conservative cause, Johnston decided to oppose the official Tory candidates. During the campaign, Johnston emphasized the social divisions between the aristocratic leadership of the conservative party and the Tory rank and file whose influence seemed to be increasing.

Even with popular support, Johnston understood that in order to defeat the established Tory leadership he would need allies. As early as May 1868 Johnston met with liberals in Belfast to consider collaboration against the estab-lished conservative leadership in Belfast.[34] Liberals found the opportunity to foster division among their enemies too great a temptation to resist. The early overtures between liberals and Johnston were not acted upon until August. After the Belfast Liberal Association selected Thomas McClure as their candidate on August 19, the strategy of pairing votes with Johnston was first publicly endorsed by two influential liberals, James McKnight of the *Londonderry Standard* and Revd John MacNaughtan.[35] McClure, a tobacco manufacturer and member of the Presbyterian Representation Society, had been an unsuccessful candidate for Belfast in 1857 when liberals had been divided and Catholics, led by the *Ulsterman*, had refused to support him.[36] In September 1868 Johnston, not having significant personal wealth, was offered

32 Farrell, *Rituals and riots*, p. 156.   33 A. McClelland, 'The later Orange Order' (1973), pp 126–7.   34 Wright, *Two lands*, p. 326.   35 McKnight's editorial from the *Londonderry Standard* endorsing such a strategy was published in the *BU*, 25 Aug. 1868; Wright, *Two lands*, p. 326.   36 J. Magee, *Barney: Bernard Hughes of Belfast, 1808–1878* (Belfast, 2001), pp 79–80.

financial support for his campaign by two leading liberals.[37] The strategy of cooperation succeeded and both McClure and Johnston were elected.[38]

It might seem as if nothing more than a common foe held together this seemingly incongruous coalition. The seeming revolution within loyalism led by Johnston depended upon a rare arrangement of circumstances, what might be called a Gladstonian moment, that permitted widely divergent political motivations and philosophies to coalesce around a common policy. Liberal Protestants remained opposed to party demonstrations even though they complained about a lack of impartiality by the government, accusing it of leniency towards demonstrations supporting Fenian prisoners.[39] Liberal Catholics certainly could not sympathize with Johnston's Orange agenda. At that particular moment, however, there were a number of issues that facilitated cooperation. Despite significantly different motives, both Johnston and liberal Presbyterians agreed on the principle of levelling down in ecclesiastical matters and supported disestablishment of the Church of Ireland. Johnston's rationale for levelling down was thoroughly anti-Catholic, a determined opposition to any state support for Catholicism. Presbyterian sentiment on the issue was developing during the course of 1868 but by the time of the election in November the *Banner of Ulster* had accepted the growing consensus among liberal Presbyterians in favour of disestablishment.[40] Ulster liberals supported levelling down for a variety of reasons – objections to the 'indiscriminate endowment' of truth and error, the incompetence of the state to discriminate in matters of private conscience, the injustice of any unequal dispersal of state funds, and fears of the extension of the denominational system in society.[41]

Frank Wright observed that under the leadership of Revd John MacNaughtan, the differences between a '"rationalist" egalitarianism and "No Popery"' among Presbyterians were obscured so that 'those who believed in religious equality on principle, and those who saw it as a "barrier to Romanism" might coexist'.[42] This broad framework for cooperation had the advantage of achieving the widest possible support among Presbyterians, especially with the numerous and powerful evangelical element. The disadvantage of the 'levelling down' approach was its sometimes negative effect upon cooperation between Presbyterians and Catholics. Along with the important issue of disestablishment, liberal Presbyterians also found common ground with Johnston on the issues of tenant-right and the ballot as a means to undermine the aristocratic domination of the rural constituencies. Indeed, in the pages of the *Londonderry Standard*, James McKnight, commented that 'in these circum-

37 Wright, *Two lands*, p. 326. 38 Walker, *Ulster politics*, pp 61–2. 39 *BU*, 3 Mar. 1868; 28 Mar. 1868. 40 Ibid., 26 Sept. 1868. 41 All of these views, including some incongruous combinations, were expressed at one meeting in Belfast discussing disestablishment, *BU*, 8 Feb. 1868. 42 Wright, *Two lands*, p. 314.

stances, were Mr Johnston not an Orangeman, he would be popularly set down as an "advanced Liberal" if not complimented with the name of a "radical".[43]

Catholic support for the both McClure and Johnston was more problematic. The leadership of the Catholic community remained divided. Bishop Dorrian had arranged the removal of A.J. McKenna from the editorship of the *Ulster Observer* at the end of 1867. Dorrian had not, however, gained complete control of the field. In February 1868 McKenna launched a new paper with a title allusive of a spirit of cooperation between Catholic and Presbyterian reformers, the *Northern Star*. Dorrian attempted to counter McKenna's new journal by establishing a rival Catholic paper, the *Ulster Examiner,* under his practical control in March 1868. Despite this effort, Dorrian's influence was clearly attenuated. His hopes for the National Association had been disappointed. The association had failed to gain widespread support among Catholics and faced determined opposition from liberal Presbyterians.[44] Dorrian was also at odds with the city's wealthiest Catholic, Bernard Hughes. During the election of 1868, both McKenna and Hughes strongly supported the candidacy of Thomas McClure as well as a tactical alliance with Johnston.[45]

Elsewhere in 1868 coalitions of Catholic and Presbyterian voters achieved success without relying upon conservative divisions, but the results presaged an ambivalent future for liberals in Ulster towns. In Newry, William Kirk, a Presbyterian merchant who had been elected in 1852 and 1857 as a tenant-right candidate, defeated Viscount Newry and Mourne, grandson of the proprietor of much of the borough's property, with 386 votes to 379. The victory was the result of a lop-sided coalition consisting of just over 350 Catholic voters and around 30 liberal Presbyterians. Although nearly two-thirds of the population of Newry was Catholic, property qualifications for the franchise ensured that Catholics could not carry the constituency by themselves. In 1868 Catholic voters only comprised 362 (45%) voters out of a total electorate of 797: see Table 4.5. Presbyterians accounted for 210 (26%) voters, members of the Church of Ireland comprised another 190 (24%), and assorted smaller Protestant denominations made up the remaining 35 (4%) of the electors. With such an imbalance, it is not surprising that Catholics began to wonder why one of their own was not selected as the liberal candidate.[46]

They had been previously. Newry liberals had chosen Catholic candidates in

43 Quoted in *BU,* 25 Aug. 1868.   44 For the limited appeal of the National Association see Emmet Larkin, *The consolidation of the Roman Catholic Church in Ireland,* pp 391–3. For an example of the antagonism of Ulster liberals to the National Association see the editorial of the *Banner of Ulster,* 13 Apr. 1867.   45 *BU,* 17 Oct. 1868.   46 P. Bew and F. Wright, 'The agrarian opposition in Ulster politics, 1848–87', in S. Clark and J.S. Donnelly, Jr (eds), *Irish peasants: violence and political unrest, 1780–1914* (Madison, WI, 1983), p. 203

Table 4.5: Parliamentary poll, Newry, 1868

Candidates	Church of Ireland votes	Church of Ireland votes valued between £4 and £8	Presbyterian votes	Presbyterian votes valued between £4 and £8
William Kirk	9	1	30	1
Viscount Newry	174	45	171	25
Unpolled	7	0	9	0
Total	190	46	210	26

Source: Brian Walker, *Ulster politics: the formative years, 1868–86* (Belfast, 1989).

1831, 1832, 1835 and 1837. In 1835, D.C. Brady became the only Catholic elected for an Ulster constituency before 1874.[47] Because Catholics provided a large portion of the vote in the borough, liberal Presbyterians seem to have been willing to support this arrangement. That successful sectarian compromise was subsequently challenged on two fronts. First, after their defeat in 1835, the Needham interest began to exert tighter control over their property in the borough in order to make certain that all of their tenants were politically reliable. This meant no Catholics and, it must be assumed, only trustworthy Presbyterians.[48] Second, the issue of repeal divided liberals during the 1840s. These divisions were painfully evident in 1841 when Brady declined to contest the seat. Instead an outsider, Sir J.M. Doyle, came forward with the support of local repealers. However, when pressed at the selection meeting to confirm his support for repeal, Doyle refused.[49] Undoubtedly Doyle and the local repealers understood that although supporting repeal might be necessary to win support for his candidacy among many Catholics, it would be fatal in any constituency where liberal Presbyterian votes were needed for victory. Doyle was defeated by the largest margin of victory in that constituency during ten contested elections between 1832 and 1880.[50]

47 Walker, *Ulster politics*, p. 64.   48 *Report from her majesty's commissioners of inquiry into the state of the law and practice in respect to the occupation of land in Ireland*, HC 1845 (605, 606), xix, p. 424.   49 *NW*, 5 June 1841.   50 Walker, *Parliamentary results*, p. 307.

Other Protestant votes	Other Protestant votes valued between £4 and £8	Catholic votes	Catholic votes valued between £4 and £8	Total votes	Total votes valued between £4 and £8
6	1	341	102	386	105
23	6	11	7	379	83
6	0	10	3	32	3
35	7	362	112	797	191

Sectarian cooperation was restored during the 1850s, when repeal was no longer an issue, and William Kirk, a liberal Presbyterian linen merchant, won contests in 1852 and 1857. Throughout this period, the predominance of the Catholic community in Newry was given recognition in the town commission where the chairmen were leading Catholic liberals.[51] The franchise reform of 1868 placed the delicate sectarian balance within liberalism under further stress by increasing the disparity between Catholic and Presbyterian support. As might be expected, the franchise reform of 1868 had a greater affect upon the Catholic community. A third of the Catholic electors who voted in 1868 were valued between £4 and £8 and would not have been eligible for the franchise at previous elections: see Table 4.5. The Church of Ireland vote benefited slightly less, with twenty-five per cent of the total comprised of these new voters. Only twelve per cent of the Presbyterian vote was comprised of these new voters.

The fears that lower class Protestant voters would be a source of strength for conservatives seem realized in a close examination of the poll in Newry in 1868. Table 4.5 demonstrates that not only did lower-class Church of Ireland voters support the conservative candidate but their lower-class Presbyterian counterparts did so as well. It might be expected that only one of the forty-six new Church of Ireland voters supported Kirk, but the fact that only one of the

---

51 Newry TC, PRONI, LA58/2B/3, 29 Nov. 1853; Canavan, *Frontier town*, pp 154–5.

twenty-six new Presbyterian voters valued between £4 and £8 voted for Kirk is remarkable. The democratization of the franchise in Newry contributed to growing Catholic political power but threatened the future of liberalism in the town. This 'perverse development of democratization', as Wright described it, threatened to destroy the foundations for a society governed by a public opinion that had been created between 1814 and 1828 and consolidated during the 1840s and 1850s.

The victory of liberals in the city of Derry was also accomplished without any conservative division. During the period between 1832 and 1860 the parliamentary seat for the city of Derry had been held by a wealthy Whig, Sir Robert Ferguson. Ferguson had succeeded in building a broad coalition of support in the city after the corporate interest had collapsed because of financial irregularities brought to light during a dispute with the Irish Society.[52] Despite a significant growth in population over the course of the century (see Table 4.2 and Table 4.4), caused in part by the migration of Catholics from the immediate hinterland and the development of sectarian ghettos, the Protestant Fountain and Catholic Bogside, the city was relatively free of sectarian violence. Local prohibitions on party processions about the city's famed walls had helped to limit occasions for violence.[53] After the death of Ferguson in 1860, however, the city's tranquillity was increasingly in peril. At the by-election in 1860 a three-way contest occurred. The nominal conservative candidate was William McCormick who, like Ferguson before him, emphasized local economic development rather than party issues so as not to alienate the sizeable number of Presbyterian and Catholic voters. The constituency at the time seems to have comprised about 800 voters, of whom 200 were Catholic. The two liberal candidates were Samuel McCurdy Greer and George Skipton. Greer was a barrister who had been involved in liberal politics since the 1830s when he was a participant in the struggles against the Beresford interest in Coleraine. He was subsequently elected MP for Co. Londonderry at the general election of 1857 as a supporter of tenant-right after losing a by-election for the same constituency earlier in the same year as a candidate of the Presbyterian Representation Society. Greer was associated with an influential evangelical Presbyterian element in the city that was supported by a number of wealthy Presbyterian industrialists. The evangelicals had established the *Londonderry Standard*, Magee college, and the Derry Presbyterian City Mission. McCormick won the 1860 by-election with 327 votes to Greer's 309 and Skipton's 84. Greer's narrow defeat by McCormick in 1860 was a result of the divided liberal vote, including a splintering of the Catholic vote.[54]

---

52 Wright, *Two lands*, pp 60–1.   53 Farrell, *Rituals and riots*, p. 150.   54 D. Murphy, *Derry, Donegal and modern Ulster*, pp 113–14.

At the general election of 1865, McCormick retired and the conservative candidate was Lord Claud Hamilton, son of the marquess of Abercorn. Unlike the moderate McCormick, Hamilton's candidacy galvanized Catholic and Presbyterian opinion behind the perennial liberal candidate, Samuel McCurdy Greer. Despite the coalition of Catholics and Presbyterians, Greer was narrowly defeated, 379 votes to 331, purportedly because of Hamilton's exploitation of his territorial influence to intimidate Presbyterian shopkeepers. Rather than surrendering to mutual recriminations in the aftermath of defeat, the alliance of Catholics and Presbyterians was secured and reinforced by their shared opposition to Hamilton's efforts to 'transform the hitherto apolitical Apprentice Boys from their neutral role in Protestant politics by capturing the leadership of the organization'. The local Catholic community had long been hostile to commemorations of the siege but Presbyterian opinion, led by McKnight's *Standard,* became increasingly hostile to the commemorations as Hamilton and the new leadership of the Apprentice Boys began to organize special trains to the city from other areas of Ulster.[55]

At the general election of 1868, Hamilton was opposed by Richard Dowse. Despite attempts at intimidation by Hamilton's supporters, Dowse won with 704 votes to Hamilton's 599. Three significant factors contributed to liberal success. First, the franchise reform of 1868 resulted in a dramatic increase in the number of Catholic voters from about 200, or roughly 24% of the total electorate in 1860, to 563, 38% of the total electorate in 1868: see Table 4.6.

Second, the particular vibrancy of the liberal Presbyterian community in Derry should not be overlooked. The liberal party in Derry was able to attract a larger portion of eligible Presbyterian voters, 33%, than in Newry, 14%. Furthermore, of those Presbyterians who did not actively support the liberal cause, a sizeable number did not support the conservative candidate either. Of the Presbyterian electors in Derry 15% declined to vote, while only 4% of Newry's Presbyterian voters did not vote. In addition, not only did Presbyterians make up 22% of Derry's population as opposed to 12% in Newry, but Derry was also located in a region with a sizeable Presbyterian population rather than a heavily Catholic district. In Derry the Presbyterians also possessed institutions, such as a seminary and newspaper, that were absent in Newry. The third element contributing to liberal success in the city was the leadership of the Catholic community. The Catholic bishop of Derry, Francis Kelly, was moderate in his political views and marked out for special thanks by Dowse after his victory.[56] This contrasted markedly with Belfast where the

---

55 Ibid., p. 116.   56 Walker, *Ulster politics,* p. 63. For a description of the more moderate political outlook of Kelly see Emmet Larkin's works, *The consolidation of the Roman Catholic Church in Ireland,* and *The Roman Catholic Church and the home rule movement in Ireland, 1870–1874* (Chapel Hill, NC, 1990).

Table 4.6: Parliamentary poll, Derry city, 1868

Candidates	Church of Ireland votes	Presbyterian votes	Other Protestant votes	Catholic votes	Total
Richard Dowse, Q.C.	13	163	27	501	704
Lord Claud J. Hamilton	275	259	43	22	599
Unpolled	20	75	31	40	166
Total	308	497	101	563	1,469

Source: Brian Walker, *Ulster politics: the formative years, 1868–86* (Belfast, 1989).

animus of Bishop Dorrian towards liberals made him a reluctant ally at best. This contrast between the approaches of Dorrian and Kelly would have dramatic consequences for liberal fortunes in the future.

The fragility of the liberal gains in the boroughs in 1868 became evident even before the general election of 1874. The first test was a by-election in the city of Derry in early 1870. Dowse was opposed by Robert Baxter, an English solicitor and member of the Plymouth Brethren. During the period since the general election, the explosive issue of party processions in the city had arisen anew. A working-class Catholic organization, the so-called Liberal Working Men's Defence Association, began to hold amnesty demonstrations around the city. Despite the entreaties of local authorities and liberal leaders, the attorney-general doubted whether the amnesty demonstrations could be banned.[57] Liberal leaders understood the potential threat to their coalition and called for a ban on all processions. The *Londonderry Standard* ridiculed the conservative position that:

> rejoices in the 'civil and religious liberty' of party and rebel processions all Ireland over, Fenianism disporting itself without let or hindrance provided only that Apprentice Boyism may have the privilege of destroying the trade, endangering the peace, and deranging all social relationships of Derry two or three times a year.[58]

The amnesty demonstrations provoked a backlash among local Apprentice Boys who began to chafe at the discipline of local conservative leaders and invited the champion of loyalist democracy, William Johnston, to the city. Soon Catholic reinforcements were arriving from Inishowen while Protestant reserves poured in from the Coleraine area. By the time of the by-election in

---

57 Murphy, *Derry, Donegal and modern Ulster*, pp 120–3; Wright, *Two lands*, p. 421.   58 *Londonderry Standard*, 1 Jan. 1870.

Table 4.7: Parliamentary poll, Derry city, 1870

Candidates	Church of Ireland votes	Presbyterian votes	Other Protestant votes	Catholic votes	Total
Richard Dowse, Q.C.	15	143	14	508	680
Lord Claud J. Hamilton	301	245	31	15	592
Unpolled	40	125	44	40	249
Total	356	513	89	563	1,521

Source: Brian Walker, *Ulster politics: the formative years, 1868–86* (Belfast, 1989).

February 1870, the situation in the city was explosive. It is a credit to the strength of the liberal coalition in Derry that despite these circumstances, Dowse was able to defeat Baxter, 680 to 592, in much the same fashion as had been accomplished at the general election in 1868: see Table 4.7.

The liberal coalition in Newry was not so fortunate when William Kirk died in December 1870. During the summer and fall of 1869 Newry had been the scene of sectarian affrays and a Fenian amnesty demonstration. In July 1870 there were also numerous clashes in towns in the hinterland of Newry.[59] Given these circumstances, the liberal coalition faltered and no candidate was chosen to oppose Viscount Newry. The weakened state of the coalition between Catholics and Presbyterians in the town could not overcome the effects of the sectarian violence of the time.

Even in Derry the liberals succumbed to circumstances in 1872. The efforts of liberals, the central government, and even the local conservative leadership to ban processions in the city during 1871 and 1872 were defeated by a legal decision against the military enforcement of the ban won by John Rea in early 1872.[60] Rea's victory helped bring about a repeal of the Party Processions Act that had disastrous consequences for Derry and liberal prospects in parliamentary boroughs throughout Ulster. As the critical month of August arrived, when the relief of the siege was commemorated by the Apprentice Boys and Lady's Day was celebrated by Catholics, there were no legal means to prevent provocative processions by either party. Under these circumstances a by-election was held in the city during November 1872.

The liberal candidate was Christopher Palles, the new Catholic attorney-general for Ireland. At first, Palles seemed likely to succeed as the conservative vote in the city appeared in peril of splitting over the issue of processions. There were two candidates vying for the conservative vote, Bartholomew McCorkell and Charles Lewis. Lewis was an English solicitor and Presbyterian

59 Wright, *Two lands*, pp 416–17. 60 Ibid., p. 421.

chosen by the Conservative central office in London and approved by a meeting of local conservatives nearly three months before the election. McCorkell, a wealthy shipowner who described himself as a 'progressive constitutionalist', was supported by working class loyalists estranged from the traditional conservative leadership for having chosen an outsider and for attempting to ban party processions.[61] Fortunately for the conservatives, their liberal opponents became even more divided. Palles was, in reality, as unsuited to the circumstances as a candidate could be. His support among the Catholics was ambivalent at best. Palles had been responsible for the notorious prosecutions of Catholic bishops in Galway for unduly influencing an election earlier that year during which it was perceived that the judge had insulted Catholicism. Despite support from Bishop Kelly, at the particular urging of Cardinal Cullen, Palles was excoriated in the Catholic press, especially in the *Ulster Examiner* controlled by Bishop Dorrian. To make matters worse, for the first time there was a home rule candidate from Belfast, J.G. Biggar, in the race who threatened to divide the Catholic vote. Biggar's supporters used violence and intimidation to disrupt meetings on behalf of Palles.

Among Presbyterians, Palles also faced considerable difficulties. Before his selection for Derry, Palles had been an unsuccessful candidate for Co. Meath where during the campaign he had supported the policies of Cardinal Cullen with regard to denominational education.[62] The potential damage of this issue among liberal Presbyterians was compounded by the fact that Lewis explicitly opposed denominational education. The conservatives had wisely chosen a Presbyterian whose views on education might drive a wedge between liberal Presbyterians and Catholics. In addition, at the last possible moment, the split among conservatives was healed and McCorkell withdrew. In the first election in Ireland under the Secret Ballot Act passed in 1872, Lewis won with 696 votes to Palles' 522 votes. Biggar and McCorkell brought up the rear with 89 votes and 2 votes respectively. The liberal coalition had lost 158 votes since 1870.

It is clear that both liberal Presbyterians and Catholics abandoned Palles. Because of the secret ballot it is not possible to determine the denominational breakdown of the 1872 vote with the same precision as in 1868 and 1870. However, contemporary press accounts supplied the statistics in Table 4.8.

Assuming these numbers are correct, the Catholic portion of the liberal vote had declined by around 100 votes, the greatest part of them almost certainly defections to Biggar. Since 1870, the liberal Presbyterians had lost just about 40 voters. While the conservatives may have gained some voters through improved registration, it is clear that a considerable portion of the 104 votes they had

61 Walker, *Ulster politics*, p. 81; Murphy, *Derry, Donegal and modern Ulster*, p. 126.   62 Larkin, *The Roman Catholic Church and the home rule movement in Ireland*, p. 153.

*Table 4.8: Denominational composition of the
liberal vote in Derry City, 1872*

Church of Ireland	9
Presbyterian	101
Other Protestants	3
Catholic	409
Total	522

Source: Desmond Murphy, *Derry, Donegal and modern
Ulster, 1790–1921* (Londonderry, 1981).

gained since 1870 were disaffected liberal Presbyterians. Despite losing the
election, the liberal coalition in Derry once again provided evidence of its
vitality. Given the rancour of the campaign and the increasing sectarian
divisions within the city, the result was far from catastrophic. Unfortunately,
both groups within the coalition blamed one another for the defeat and the
mutual recriminations certainly contributed to the defeat of liberal candidates
during the next two elections.

The complete collapse of the liberal hopes that had been aroused by the
victory of McClure and Johnston in Belfast was the most dramatic evidence of
the perilous state that Ulster liberalism found itself in because of efforts to
maintain confessional solidarity in a rapidly changing society. In many ways
William Johnston and Bishop Dorrian were pursuing a similar ideal for society
in Ulster. Wright observed that Johnston, in order to preserve and expand the
Orange Order, hoped to transform its relationship with Catholics. Unlike his
predecessors, Johnston rejected the idea that the purpose of Orangeism was to
deter Catholics from disloyalty. Instead, Johnston advocated a kind of 'levelling
up' of marching rights. Far from attacking Amnesty demonstrations, Orangemen ought to recognize an 'equality of rights' for Catholic processions.
Johnston accepted, indeed encouraged, the ideal of equal marching rights for
Catholics. Johnston hoped that the prohibition of Orange processions as a
threat to public order would cease if all processions were accepted as commemorations intended 'to maintain a solidarity entirely internal to their participants'
rather than as an expression of control of an area or location.[63] Orangeism and
Catholicism would remain diametrically opposed, but if allowed to control
themselves they could reach a peaceful equilibrium. Dorrian's strident support
for a denominational system for all social institutions, from the school to the
political party and the graveyard, was in many ways similar to Johnston's vision
of society. Peace between the sects might be achieved if the equal right to
construct and enforce confessional solidarity were respected. Liberals were

63 Wright, *Two lands*, p. 342.

anathema because their ideals of individual liberty weakened the construction of confessional solidarity. Indeed, liberals were suspected of being sympathetic to the greatest threat to social peace – proselytism.

Johnston's vision of a transformed Orangeism collapsed in the summer of 1872 when the practical establishment of equal marching rights in Belfast brought about by the repeal of the Party Processions Act resulted in massive rioting. Neither Catholics nor Protestants accepted the commemorative ideal but rather sought to exert control of territory. Johnston's ideals were abandoned and the conservative leadership in Belfast came to a critical agreement with Dorrian tantamount to dividing the city along denominational lines. According to Wright, 'the Conservative leadership and the Belfast Catholic leadership came to an effective understanding whereby each operated to curb any kind of procession or display within the city boundary'.[64] The agreement afforded conservatives a chance to re-establish their control of the town by enlisting the support of frightened liberal Presbyterians who supported them in their efforts to rein in the remnants of Johnston's independent Orange movement. Similarly, Dorrian was 'intent upon breaking the Presbyterian liberalism which supported national education' and restraining the troublesome independent element as represented by A.J. McKenna. McKenna had died in April 1872 at the age of thirty-eight and his newspaper's interests were absorbed by the *Ulster Examiner* before the year was out. In these circumstances, Belfast liberals had no practical chance of success at the general election of 1874. The breach within conservatism had been healed and in 1873 a reorganization of the local conservative party resulted in the reintegration of Orangeism into party. In order to assuage Orange feeling, Johnston was now an official conservative candidate. Presbyterian sensibilities were also recognized by the selection of a Presbyterian merchant, J.P. Corry, as the other conservative candidate. Thomas McClure tried to defend his seat but was handily defeated as a result of liberal Presbyterian and Catholic dissension.[65]

The failure of liberalism in Belfast was perceived by Ulster liberals, both Catholic and Protestant, as a warning about the possible fracturing of public opinion in Ulster arising from the pursuit of confessional solidarity in the public sphere whether it be in the form of denominational education or party processions. With varied success, they continued to battle against these trends in society. In Belfast, Revd John MacNaughtan, although he had supported the tactical alliance with Johnston in 1868, continued to denounce both party processions and denominational education as threats to civil society. In Derry, the liberal Presbyterian community, organized around James McKnight's

64 Ibid., p. 337.   65 Walker, p. 112.

Londonderry Standard, continued to resist the denominational system. As part of that effort, in 1873 Revd Thomas Witherow, a professor of church history at Magee college, published a popular, iconoclastic account of the events of the Siege of Derry in the hopes of teaching his countrymen 'to look at the past in a calm and kindly spirit, to rise superior to the passions of an evil age, and henceforth to rival each other, not in fields of blood and war, but in the arts of industry and peace'.[66] Witherow's appeal to faith and reason could not overcome other social and demographic trends in crowded Ulster towns when the violence that he so deplored galvanized popular opinion and threatened deliberative public opinion.

'Scattered to the winds': local government

The developing threat to deliberative public opinion was becoming increasingly apparent in the sphere where Ulster liberalism had been most successful – local government. Sectarian division and discrimination have a long and sordid history in local government in Ulster. The straightforward exclusion of Catholics from the unreformed municipal corporations and the subsequent chicanery and gerrymanders of local government in the state of Northern Ireland during the twentieth century have become notorious. It might therefore be assumed the history of the town commission in Ulster would demonstrate a similar pathology. In 1876 a select committee of parliament investigating local government and taxation in Ireland considered the sectarian aspect of town commissions. William Neilson Hancock, a distinguished professor of political economy and experienced civil servant whose brother had served as the chairman of the town commission in Lurgan, informed the committee that by 1876 sectarian divisions had become a significant feature in a number of Ulster town commissions.[67] Hancock cited Armagh, Ballymena, Lisburn, Lurgan, Newtownards and Portadown as particularly egregious examples of sectarian exclusivity in local government. In 1876, there were no Catholic town commissioners in any of those towns.[68] Hancock admitted, however, that this exclusion was a relatively recent phenomenon.

Far from being a continuous story of discrimination and exclusion, Catholics themselves had considered town commissions to be a cause for optimism. It will be recalled that the establishment of the town commission was in large part a result of the efforts of Catholics in Newry. The drafting of the legislation as well as its passage through parliament were primarily the work of

66 T. Witherow, *Derry and Enniskillen in the year 1689* (3rd ed., Belfast, 1885), p. vi. 67 T.A. Boylan and T.P. Foley, *Political economy and colonial Ireland* (New York, 1992), pp 163–4. 68 *Report from the select committee on local government and taxation of towns (Ireland)*, HC 1876 (352), x, p. 16.

the first Catholic barrister in Ulster, Patrick O'Hanlon, and his son, Hugh M. O'Hanlon. The younger O'Hanlon was himself an important and unrecognized influence upon Irish affairs as a result of his position as parliamentary counsel to the Irish Office in London beginning in 1831. At the Irish Office, O'Hanlon drew upon the experiences and knowledge gained while working on the novel permissive legislation for Newry in order to draft some of the most complicated and important legislation affecting Ireland during the nineteenth century.[69]

In August 1828, Hugh M. O'Hanlon returned to Newry from London to explain the legislation for town commissions to a meeting of inhabitants and to advocate adoption of the act. Held during a particularly tense period of O'Connell's ongoing agitation for Catholic emancipation, the reporter from the *Newry Commercial Telegraph* remarked upon the absence of 'a number of gentlemen who usually take a prominent part in our meetings'. Knowing that any untoward partisan display might endanger the adoption of the act by an already divided town, the chairman of the meeting admonished the speakers not to refer to any 'extraneous matter' unconnected with the act. In the course of his oration, however, O'Hanlon clearly intended that the legislation should be considered in the context of the on-going struggle for Catholic emancipation. Having described the process by which the legislation had been passed as evidence of the republican spirit that 'animated and invigorated' the British constitution, O'Hanlon added, though 'in breach of your chairman's injunction', that of this constitution –

> not one word of praise shall pass my lips, except coupled with an expression of the deepest sorrow, that the blessings and franchise of this great, glorious, free and happy Constitution are not even yet enjoyed in full equality and participation by all descriptions and classes of people.

In his peroration O'Hanlon also alluded to his father's service on the Catholic Board as a reminder to him to 'hold fast to the cause of the portion of the country, who are my own tribe and kin [...] the oppressed and degraded Roman Catholics of Ireland'.[70] O'Hanlon was representative of a generation of Ulster Catholics who still considered themselves as joint heirs of the British constitutional tradition in Ireland.[71]

---

69 O'Hanlon's considerable role in the legislative process is described in a letter from O'Hanlon to Sir Robert Peel, 24 Feb. 1844, BL, Add. MSS 40540, ff. 336–338.   70 *Newry Commercial Telegraph*, 19 Aug. 1828.   71 The history of the relationship of the O'Hanlon family with Catholicism became complex over time. Patrick O'Hanlon was criticized for sending Hugh M. O'Hanlon to Trinity College, Dublin and accused, correctly, of officially conforming to the Church or Ireland sometime around 1814 by the irascible Watty Cox; *Irish Magazine*, 7 (1814), 238; 8 (1815), 74, 77, 190. Cox's accusation was corroborated by

Although almost all of the disabilities against Catholics had been officially removed at the end of the eighteenth century, Catholics still rarely held public offices. The religious composition of that first town commission in Newry was remarkable for the time. Eleven of the 21 town commissioners in 1828 were Catholic.[72] Furthermore, not only were Catholics frequently chairmen, but in Newry, the town commission even afforded Catholics the opportunity to challenge the policies of less representative institutions such as the board of guardians.[73] It might fairly be asked, however, whether Newry was not the exception rather than the rule. With its numerous and relatively prosperous Catholic community, Newry might be expected to have a greater participation of Catholics in local government than elsewhere in Ulster. Even in towns with Catholic majorities, the property qualification for the municipal franchise combined with the generally greater relative prosperity of Protestants placed Catholics at a distinct disadvantage. Indeed, if a town did not adopt the Towns Improvement Act of 1854 that reduced the qualifications for the municipal franchise and mandated the division of towns into wards, any vote upon strictly confessional lines would almost certainly have resulted in Catholics being excluded from every town commission in Ulster, with the possible exception of Newry. Were town commissions elected on strictly confessional lines?

Catholics were not excluded from town commissions during the first three decades of their existence. While it is difficult to establish the religious background of every town commissioner with any certainty, an examination of local histories together with accounts of public meetings concerning explicitly religious issues, such as parochial meetings against the Charitable Bequests Act of 1844, have yielded interesting results. In 1844 in Portadown, one of the offending towns cited by Hancock in 1876, 4 of the 21 town commissioners, or just less than 20 per cent, were Catholic.[74] At the time Catholics probably composed a little less than a third of the total population and almost certainly an even smaller proportion of those eligible to vote for town commissions. With this in mind, four Catholic town commissioners was probably more than proportionate with the Catholic population and influence in the town. Given the reputation of the town as a sectarian cockpit, the number is astonishing. It is

O'Hanlon himself in 1825; *The speech of Daniel O'Connell, esq., at the Catholic aggregate meeting at the freemason's hall* (1825), p. 23. Whether that conversion arose from conviction or expediency is unclear, but O'Hanlon's continued connection with the Catholic cause and the significant difficulties encountered by Catholics in the legal profession at that time suggest the latter. One of Hugh M. O'Hanlon's brothers, W.M. O'Hanlon, became a Congregationalist minister in 1835 while his father was in India; 'Memoir of the late Rev. W.M. O'Hanlon', *Evangelical Magazine and Missionary Chronicle*, n.s. 34 (1856), 2404. 72 'Dr. Blake of Dromore, and Father O'Neill of Rosstrevor', *The Irish Monthly*, 18 (1890), 250–1. 73 Newry TC, PRONI, LA58/2B/3, 29 Nov. 1852; Canavan, *Frontier town*, pp 154–5. 74 *Vin*, 1 Jan. 1845.

not possible at this time to measure the Catholic representation on all of the town commissions with any precision, but during the 1830s and 1840s Catholics were represented in many towns, such as the notorious Armagh, Coleraine, Dungannon, Enniskillen, Lurgan, Portadown and Strabane mentioned by Hancock in 1876, where any contested election for town commissioners along sectarian lines would have resulted in the complete exclusion of Catholics. Instead, in places where contested elections were infrequent, such as Portadown, Catholics were included in the arrangements that divided the representation among the various interests in the town. In places, where elections were frequently contested, such as Coleraine, Catholics were typically included in the liberal lists. Sectarian divisions were not yet the societal fault lines that they would become.

It will be recalled that in 1857, the *Ulsterman* had commented upon liberal successes in Ulster, particularly with regard to what it described as 'sectarian discord'. Despite the optimism of the *Ulsterman*, there was evidence of growing sectarian tension in some towns. During the 1840s, the town commission in Strabane, another one of the offending towns cited by Hancock in 1876, had challenged the marquess of Abercorn's claims to control the property of the defunct corporation, particularly the income derived from tolls and customs. Formerly a prosperous market town, during the nineteenth century Strabane was in economic and demographic decline. Already an isolated conclave in a heavily Catholic area, the percentage of the town identified as Protestants declined steadily during the nineteenth century. Using the admittedly imperfect data from the 1834 committee on public instruction, Protestants had made up about half of the town in 1831. By 1861 they were only 40 per cent of the population; and by 1881 that percentage had further decreased to 33 per cent. In 1845, the conflict between the town commission and the Abercorn interest was settled by the government granting a warrant to the town commission for the former corporate property and income, including the tolls. With the common cause of opposition to the aristocratic magnate gone, a new politicization resulted in more frequent contested municipal elections. In July 1850, the first contested election for the Strabane town commission occurred and was connected with local tenant-right politics.[75] Unfortunately, this new politicization did not bring about communal harmony.

At the municipal election in 1853, 35 candidates vied for the 21 positions, including a number of Catholics proposed and seconded by Presbyterians as a sign of the cooperative spirit fostered by the tenant-right movement.[76] After the election, an anonymous correspondent to the *Londonderry Sentinel*, a conser-

---

75 Strabane TC, 14 Dec. 1840, 20 Nov. 1845; 1 July 1850, PRONI, MIC 159/reel 2.
76 Ibid., 4 July 1853, PRONI, MIC 159/reel 2.

vative paper, asserted that a group of commissioners and electors had cooperated on 'high Protestant principle' to defeat John Devlin, one of the more outspoken Catholic candidates.[77] Another correspondent, writing under the pseudonym of 'Peeping Tom' for the *Ulsterman*, reported that the sectarian opposition to Devlin included many who had claimed 'the credit of being at least *quasi-liberals*', including the chairman of the town commission, William Ramsay. For their part, the accused plotters attributed the accusations to Devlin's supporters who wished 'to disturb the peace and harmony of the town'. There were certainly unruly spirits in Strabane who tested the bounds of liberal cooperation. Devlin was associated with a young barrister in the town, Thomas Neilson Underwood, whose intemperate language at a Tenant League meeting at Omagh in 1850 had been criticized by James Godkin.[78] A descendant of the United Irish leader Samuel Neilson, in 1860 Underwood would establish a secret society, the Sons of St Patrick, closely associated with Fenianism.

While Presbyterian ministers and Catholic priests continued to share tenant-right platforms in the town during 1854 and 1855, the proceedings of the town commission became increasingly acrimonious.[79] Disputes arose over compromises undertaken by the town commission with the Abercorn interest during the struggle over corporate property and the conduct of Ramsay as chairman. The conflicts compelled the town commission to consult with solicitors to draft legal opinions on the issues in contention.[80] A restoration of municipal comity was probably not helped by a Redemptorist mission in the town during October and November 1853 or a series of Protestant open-air sermons on the steps of the market-house in July 1854.[81]

Among the ministers participating in the preaching described by the *Ulsterman* as 'filthy attacks' upon all that Strabane's Catholics held 'sacred and venerable', was Revd Alexander Porter Goudy, a grandson of the famous Revd James Porter of Greyabbey executed in 1798.[82] Like James Godkin, John Brown and Richard Smyth, Goudy was an evangelical liberal who had made his reputation among Presbyterians during confrontations with Henry Cooke. Goudy created a controversy by his early reticence to join with Catholic priests in organizations supporting tenant-right. Although he subsequently overcame these scruples, the damage to his reputation among many Catholics was probably irreversible.[83]

By July 1856 the *Ulsterman* concluded that 'the harmony and good feeling' that had previously existed in Strabane was 'scattered to the winds' in order 'to

---

77 *Ulsterman*, 30 July 1853.   78 *NW*, 29 Oct. 1850.   79 *BU*, 16 May 1854; 19 May 1855.
80 Strabane TC, 27 July 1853, PRONI, MIC 159/reel 2.   81 *Ulsterman*, 22 July 1854.
82 W.T. Latimer, *Ulster Biographies* (2nd ed., Belfast, 1897), p. 74.   83 A.P. Goudy, *Right versus might* (Derry, 1852), p. 5.

gratify the over-heated Protestantism of a few fanatics'. The occasion for their pessimism was the municipal election in July 1856. As the election approached, there was an attempt to avoid what looked to be an acrimonious poll by adopting a list of twenty-one candidates. At the nomination meeting, however, two lists were proposed. The first list was brought forward by Underwood and included seven Catholics, with the outspoken Devlin. An alternative list proposed by Ramsay, the *'quasi-liberal'* who had been anonymously accused of sectarianism in 1853, included only two Catholics. Unable to resolve the disagreements over the lists, the dreaded poll went ahead; and after a hard-fought contest lasting two days, no Catholics were elected town commissioner.[84]

In the mutual recriminations following the election, Devlin and the *Ulsterman* ascribed the outcome to sectarianism and a desire to conceal corruption concerning former corporate property. Devlin boasted that his opponents rightly feared that if elected, he 'would prove as troublesome in Strabane as John Rea had done in Belfast'. He condemned the 'bigoted clique' who had 'thrown off the mask' of liberality and inaugurated 'the reign of intolerance' in Strabane. He also disdainfully rejected a plan 'to heal the wounds which this election has caused', in which three or four of the elected commissioners would step aside and allow Catholics to be elected in their stead. In their defence, Devlin's opponents asserted that the other Catholic candidates had suffered from identification with Devlin whose intemperate attacks on his fellow townsmen made him unacceptable to the majority of electors.[85] In Strabane, a number of the conditions that threatened the liberal public sphere elsewhere in Ulster were drawn together in a toxic combination. After having achieved some success at limiting the power of the local patron, increasing confessional solidarities combined with the emulation of Rea's obstructionist tactics undermined the comity and cooperation that had existed in Strabane's town commission.

Perhaps the most striking example of the discontinuity of sectarian division and discrimination occurred in Armagh. With a population almost evenly divided between Catholics and Protestants, Armagh had been a reliable liberal seat at the parliamentary level since 1832. The patronage of the Protestant archbishop of Armagh had been supplanted in a series of contested elections; and by 1840 Col. J.D. Rawdon had transformed the borough into a safe seat. Liberals also controlled the town commission. The records for the town commission from Armagh are at present missing, possibly destroyed, but from the lists of commissioners taken from the local press it is clear that liberals were the majority in the town commission at its establishment in 1833 and from 1848 until 1860.[86] Liberal control of the town commission did not begin to falter until the collapse of the liberal interest at the parliamentary level.

84 *Ulsterman*, 16 July 1856. 85 Ibid. 86 *AG*, 2 July 1848, 12 July 1851, 7 July 1854, 10

The first signs of weakness on the part of the liberal interest occurred during the general election of July 1852. At that election, Rawdon was forced to withdraw at the last moment, supposedly due to irregularities arising from the new system of registry under the 1850 Franchise Act.[87] Rawdon and his supporters did not mention the fact that the Catholic archbishop of Armagh, Paul Cullen, refused to support the liberals because Rawdon had voted with the government of Lord John Russell for the Ecclesiastical Titles Bill.[88] The lack of recrimination was perhaps the result of hopes that the liberal interest might reverse this setback. The town's sole newspaper, the *Armagh Guardian*, had supported Rawdon and was confident that despite his defeat the policy of 'Social Progress and Conservative Reform must go on until the dross of the past is clear removed, and all our institutions conducted for the benefit of the whole community'.[89] Cullen lamented the fact that his policy had meant victory for a 'black orangeman', but he was only beginning to understand that Ulster liberals, whatever their considerable faults, were preferable to the conservatives. Had he foreseen the consequences of the weakening of the liberal interest in the town, Cullen might have reconsidered his decision.

At the triennial election of town commissioners in July 1854, the confidence of the *Guardian* seemed well-placed as the liberal interest survived the parliamentary setback. There was no contest, but liberals made up a majority of the commissioners selected. In late 1855, the difficulties confronting liberals became all too apparent during a by-election in which liberals had high hopes of recovering the seat. Two conservative candidates had entered the field and liberals hoped that they might rebuild their coalition supporting Rawdon. They believed that a coalition of liberal Protestants and Catholics could muster 141 votes out of an expected 374 to be cast. With the conservative vote split, this would be more than enough for victory. The liberal committee appointed to canvass the constituents was, however, appalled to discover that they could not rely upon a unified Catholic vote. A veteran liberal reported that forty-five Catholic voters were going to defect. Furthermore, the committee believed that some of those faithless Catholics had been registered at liberal expense by John Rea but were now 'making the best market of the power we contributed to place in their hands'. There was also speculation that the defectors might be holding out for a different candidate. Catholic members of the coalition confirmed the committee's analysis but counselled perseverance in the hope that 'even yet public opinion may shame the 45 deserters out of their inconsistency'.[90] They

July 1857, 6 July 1860. 87 Ibid., 10 July 1852. Rawdon's supporters blamed their own neglect and hinted that conservatives had tampered with the valuations on which the new franchise system was founded. 88 E. Larkin, *The making of the Roman Catholic Church*, p. 174. 89 *AG*, 17 July 1852. 90 Ibid., 30 Nov. 1855.

were not, and the liberal effort was abandoned. No liberal would be elected for the constituency for another thirty years.

The confusion created by the collapse of the liberal interest at the parliamentary level was evident at the triennial elections for town commissioners in 1857 and 1860. In 1857, seventy people were nominated for the twenty-one positions, but, in order 'to prevent the turmoil and bad feeling inseparable from a contest', a compromise was reached whereby the first twenty-one people nominated were selected. While liberals still appear to have composed the majority, they were increasingly divided along sectarian lines. By the time of the municipal election in 1860 the sectarian divisions were hardening and a contested election could not be averted. Thirty-nine candidates were nominated and in the end thirteen Catholics were elected in a contest where only 257 out of approximately 700 qualified voters participated.[91]

The Catholics of Armagh had achieved a pyrrhic victory. The already divided liberal interest within the town was now confronted by outraged conservatives. In 1860, the Armagh Protestant Association was organized in the city to counteract 'an organization of the Romanists, called the "Catholic Committee". In 1863, the hubris of the Catholic committee was decisively punished. The Armagh Protestant Association organized a slate of twenty-one candidates and provided the constituents with a printed list of those candidates together with an account of the association's grievances and objectives. They complained that a Catholic majority on the town commission misrepresented the sectarian balance of power in the city. Although the population was evenly divided among Catholics and Protestants, the 'number of rated Protestants is nearly double the number of Roman Catholics, and the valuation of Protestants is five times that of Roman Catholics'. Furthermore, the Catholic committee somehow had abused its majority on the town commission 'to object to educated, intelligent and respectable Protestants on the jurors' list, and to claim for Romanists a few degrees removed from the monkey the important position of jurors'. These facts compelled the association 'to re-establish the Protestant character of the city'.[92]

Despite the serious threat of the association, liberals in Armagh did not re-establish the coalition between Catholics and Protestants that had controlled the city for three decades. Instead there were three lists – a pink list for the Armagh Protestant Association candidates, a white list for the Catholic committee candidates and a yellow list 'representing the old Whig party'.[93] The association won decisively, returning all twenty-one candidates. This was the genesis of the sectarian exclusion that William Neilson Hancock had described in 1876.

91 Ibid., 10 July 1857; 6 July 1860.   92 Ibid., 10 July 1863, 24 July 1863.   93 Ibid., 10 July 1863.

Hancock's explanation of that exclusion was that 'a panic seems to have got in' that Catholics were soon to have a majority in the constituency.[94] The truth of Hancock's analysis was in some ways undeniable. Protestant fears that any change in the constitution of the town commission would upset the delicate balance of sectarian power was almost certainly a principle reason Armagh was one of the few places not to adopt the superior powers provided by the 1854 towns improvement act until 1898. Under that act the qualification for the municipal franchise would have been reduced from £5 to £4, and that for town commissioner from £20 to £12. Yet, it must be asked whether Hancock's explanation contains within it another assumption that was more widespread in 1876 than in 1828. Namely, by 1876 Hancock believed that Catholics and Protestants in Ulster would not cooperate within the public sphere.

Hancock told the royal commissioners that sectarian divisions in Ulster were such that he had little doubt that if Catholics were the majority of the municipal constituency in Armagh, no Protestants would be town commissioners in Armagh. At that moment, a simple majority of a party in a constituency meant exclusion from office for the other. There was little possibility of 'a fair proportion of Catholics getting in by having a certain number of Protestants voting for them'. According to Hancock, 'compromises of that sort are hard to carry out in Ulster'.[95] For this reason, Hancock proposed that a cumulative voting system similar to proportional representation should be adopted so Catholics and Protestants might be represented according to their relative strengths. He was in effect suggesting a model for a different society. When the town commission was created, there was an underlying assumption that an ideal public good could be realized when private interests were restrained by public institutions. Adequate services could be provided to towns when the interests of a local landlord or oligarchy were restrained. A limited public sphere was created. For nearly fifty years after its creation the system functioned more or less upon these lines. The system broke down because society had developed in such a way that a common public sphere was increasingly impossible to achieve. Catholics and Protestant were no longer coming together to deliberate on the common good. Instead, the deliberations were exclusive to each community. If there were sufficient common interests a tactical alliance might develop, but the communities were, as Ulster liberals had feared, increasingly divided along confessional lines. The fate of the town commission, an institution created by a liberal ethos, was a foretaste of the difficulties that would confront liberals on a larger stage as society in Ulster became increasingly divided between the supposedly irreconcilable interests of Protestants and Catholics, and unionists and nationalists.

94 *Report from the select committee on local government and taxation of towns (Ireland)*, p. 16.
95 Ibid.

Land of hope? The general election of 1874

Fortunately for Ulster liberals, the province was not made up entirely of towns with crowded sectarian ghettos. In 1874, the issue of tenant-right provided a basis for Catholic and Presbyterian cooperation. For only the second occasion since the Union, Ulster liberals would contest more than half of the nineteen constituencies in the province. Furthermore, they won seven seats and mounted significant challenges to conservative candidates in all but a few constituencies. The surprising resurgence of liberalism was dependent upon three related issues – the maintenance of Catholics in the liberal alliance, the ambitions of Presbyterians and the importance of the land question in Ulster politics.

During the 1870s a new force emerged in Irish politics that threatened to undermine Catholic support for liberalism – the home rule movement. In 1874, under the leadership of Isaac Butt, fifty-nine home rule candidates were elected in Ireland. In Ulster, however, home rule was less significant. Only two constituencies, Cavan and Monaghan, were contested. Although two seats in Monaghan were won by home rulers, the full potential of the Catholic vote in Ulster was not mobilized on behalf of the home rule cause. Unlike Catholic voters elsewhere in Ireland, the electors and leaders of the Catholic community generally supported the Liberal party.

In reality there was no real alternative for Catholics in Ulster. Even Patrick Dorrian came to understand this fact. In October 1873, in reply to a query from Isaac Butt about possible support for his home rule League in Ulster, Dorrian explained his doubts about the prudence of giving public support to the home rule movement in Ulster. 'My adhesion in any way would', he believed, 'irritate rather than sooth the opponents of home rule in this part'.[96] Dorrian's support would create divisions. In those areas where only a Presbyterian-Catholic alliance could succeed, support of a home rule candidate was impractical. Such support would in all probability result in the defection of a sizeable portion of the Presbyterian party. Therefore, a less desirable, but more pragmatic course was suggested by Dorrian. 'I think Catholics would sometimes do well', he advised, 'to forbear even when in the right, and that they ought to taught to do so'. In practical terms, this policy meant that Catholics should support liberal Presbyterians. An active home rule agitation would divide Catholics, frighten liberal Presbyterians, and only strengthen the conservative cause.

The situation among Presbyterians was more complicated. As seen earlier, Presbyterians were divided in their affections. A number of Presbyterians were convinced that there was little room for them in a conservative party dominated

96 Larkin, *The Roman Catholic Church and the home rule Movement in Ireland*, p. 256.

by landlords belonging to the established church. The effect on alienated Presbyterians was clearly demonstrated in Belfast in the general elections of 1868 and 1874. In 1868, it will be recalled, the conservative party in Belfast selected, despite the warnings of some, two Episcopalians, Sir Charles Lanyon and John Mulholland, to represent their cause. The failure to recognize the claims of the city's sizeable Presbyterian community enabled liberals to take advantage of discontent. Thomas McClure, who had unsuccessfully contested the seat previously, was able to draw a number of Presbyterians away from the conservatives.

In 1874 the conservatives were more solicitous toward the Presbyterian community and selected a prominent Presbyterian businessman, James P. Corry, as a candidate. In 1868, Corry had supported McClure. The wisdom of this tactic was not, however, appreciated by conservatives elsewhere in the province. With the exception of Derry city, no conservatives in the other boroughs and counties in Ulster were willing to concede a measure of representation to the Presbyterian community. In contrast, liberals utilized this Presbyterian discontent to its fullest advantage in 1874. Six of the sixteen liberal candidates were Presbyterians. Of the six successful candidates, four were Presbyterian. Most significantly, Presbyterians began to challenge the conservative strongholds in the county constituencies.

In many ways, the land question was the ideal issue for liberals. Until the land question was directly tied to home rule it seemed a safe common ground for cooperation. As long as Presbyterians believed that Catholics were interested in participating in a voluntary association for a common public good, the fears of isolation and separatism, whether in education or in politics, were somewhat obviated. Once again it was the issue of tenant-right that animated Presbyterians and Catholics alike. In January 1874, a national tenant-right conference was held in Belfast. Ironically, although the tenant-right movement strongly supported the liberal government of William Gladstone, the focus of the conference was the inadequacy of his land act of 1870. Like William Sharman Crawford before him, Gladstone had discovered that any measure that might pass through parliament would not satisfy the demands of the tenants in Ulster. Again, like Crawford before him, Gladstone built his bill upon the foundation of compensation for improvements and disturbance rather than the enforcement of any plantation covenant or moral economy.[97] Furthermore, in defining what was described as a custom, Gladstone accepted many usages which tenant-right advocates such as James McKnight considered unwarranted accretions that fundamentally undermined the original intentions

97 For an explanation of the passage of the bill and its provisions, see E.D. Steele, *Irish land and British politics* (1974).

of tenant-right.[98] This dissatisfaction manifested itself in a call for legislation to remedy the shortcomings of the act. The enthusiasm for the land question together with the new protections provided to tenants by the ballot resulted in unprecedented parliamentary successes for Ulster liberals in the hitherto impregnable county constituencies. Among the three liberals returned were James Sharman Crawford, son of William Sharman Crawford, and Richard Smyth the Presbyterian minister and professor at Magee college in Derry. In the boroughs, liberals were elected for Coleraine, Newry and Dungannon. In all of the liberal victories, the alliance of Presbyterian and Catholic voters were significant factors.[99] Furthermore, liberals mounted considerable unsuccessful challenges in several other constituencies. The land question seemed to provide Ulster liberals with a means to reinvigorate the cooperation between Catholics and Presbyterians that was essential to their success.

However, like the Volunteer consensus of a century before, the appearance of cooperation and conciliation regarding the land question concealed a broad divergence in the motivations and ultimate aims of Catholics and Presbyterians with regard to the land. Evidence of this diversity was evident at the tenant-right conference in Belfast in 1874. The general harmony of the proceedings was broken by an exchange between the Presbyterian minister Archibald Robinson of Broughsnane, Co. Antrim and Joseph G. Biggar, a merchant and home rule advocate from Belfast, over a lecture on the land question by Thomas Robertson, a tenant-right advocate from Athy, Co. Kildare. In a paper on 'Yeoman and Peasant Proprietorships' that concluded that, 'the feudal system must be abolished' by constitutional means, 'if possible', or it would be in a few years 'overthrown by force', Robertson asserted that even the inadequate land act of 1870 had been wrested from the Gladstone by the violence of the Fenians.[1] Robinson, an evangelical liberal, could not accept this rejection of the fundamental cornerstone of the British constitutional tradition in Ireland and a dispute between himself and Biggar over the validity of Robertson's assertion threatened to disrupt the conference but for the timely intervention of Samuel McElroy, editor of the *Ballymoney Free Press*.[2] Frank Wright has perspicaciously observed that despite their tactical alliance on policy, 'the assumptions underlying political practice were beginning to be delineated "nationally"'.[3] Liberal Protestants such as Robinson supported Gladstone because they believed that Ireland's needs could be met by the British constitutional tradition. Unfortunately, in Ulster that tradition was, even among liberals committed to civic equality, intimately bound up with an evangelical

98 Wright, *Two lands*, 434; for an interesting theory on the evolution of tenant-right as a tool for land management rather than tenant protection see M.W. Dowling, *Tenant-right*, pp 252–3. 99 Walker, *Ulster politics*, pp 106–8. 1 *NW*, 21 Jan. 1874, 8. 2 Ibid. 3 Wright, *Two lands*, p. 443.

temperament that fired much of their desire for reform. During the general election, Thomas McClure, the MP for Belfast, described the source of his liberalism to a meeting of the Belfast Presbyterian Association. McClure declared that he 'stood before the meeting and the community as a Liberal' who had 'imbibed these views from the lips and lectures of Dr. Chalmers'.[4] Unfortunately, Catholics in Ulster and elsewhere in Ireland increasingly could not imagine room for themselves in the godly commonwealth envisioned by McClure. For them, the heritage of conquest of a 'landlord Parliament and an Episcopal Parliament' conceived by the delegate from Kildare would become their reality.

During the period between 1859 and 1876, the faith of Ulster liberals in the British constitutional tradition was tested. The successes that they had achieved with regard to local government were threatened by the attempts of both Catholics and Protestants alike to preserve their respective cultural identities in the face of considerable social changes. The common public sphere was threatened by the missionaries who in the course of serving their communities also erected bulwarks of confessional solidarity. In many towns across Ulster, liberal gains were dramatically reversed. The apparent successes associated with the land question masked the growing weakness of Ulster liberalism. Without a common public sphere the middle path became increasingly precarious.

4 *NW*, 4 Feb. 1874.

Conclusion

> Notre vraie doctrine, notre vrai drapeau est le spiritualisme, cette philosophie aussi solide que généreuse. [...] elle repousse également la démagogie et la tyrannie; elle apprend à tous les hommes à se respecter et à s'aimer, et elle conduit peu à peu les sociétés humaine à la vraie république, ce rêve de toutes les âmes généreuses, que de nos jours en Europe peut seule réaliser la monarchie constitutionelle.[1]
>
> Victor Cousin, *Du vrai, du beau et du bien* (2nd ed., 1854), pp iv–v.

Ulster liberalism had its origins in an era of armed men determined to recover and secure a constitution. By 1880, however, Ulster liberals were ambivalent about the men who had stood arrayed before congregations in the 'blue swallow–tail-coat' of Revd William Bruce's Lisburn True Blues or the regimentals of Revd Robert Black's Dromore Volunteers. Describing the lives and writings of Presbyterian Volunteers a century before, Revd Thomas Witherow, professor of church history at Magee college and editor of the *Londonderry Standard*, characterized the movement as a 'mania, which infected so strongly every class of the population of Ulster'.[2] It was not so much the Volunteers' political ideals, which Witherow barely commented upon, but their manners that seemed outlandish.

It was, Witherow lamented, an 'intensely political but feebly religious age'. Speaking of one minister's Volunteer sermons, Witherow remarked that 'they were slightly sprinkled' with the precepts from the Gospels but profuse 'with exhortations to virtue and valour'. In his portrayal of another preacher who 'did not escape' the 'Volunteer mania', Witherow recounted a description of a venerable pastor whose 'intimacy with the Latin classics', particularly his favourite orator Cicero, 'gave a complexion, I conceive, to his way of thinking and speaking'.[3] For liberal Presbyterians of Witherow's generation, the prince of orators was more likely to be Thomas Chalmers and references to classical writers and classical virtues were noticeably absent.[4]

---

1 Translation: Our true doctrine, our true banner is spiritualism, that philosophy as solid as it is generous. [...] it repels equally demagogy and tyranny, it teaches all men to respect and love themselves, and little by little it guides human societies to the true republic, that dream of all generous souls, which in our time can be realized in Europe only by constitutional monarchy. 2 Witherow, *Historical and literary memorials*, pp 204, 221–2, 277. 3 Ibid., pp 222–3. 4 T. Witherow, *The autobiography of Thomas Witherow* (1990), pp 54–5.

These changes in manners and political rhetoric were neither suddenly introduced nor simply explained, but there had been signs of things to come. In September 1803, William Bruce once again preached to armed men – the Belfast Merchants' Infantry organized to defend against the abortive insurrection of Robert Emmet. In contrast to the sartorial finery of the Lisburn True Blues, the Belfast merchants wore only a simple black cockade.[5] They maintained this new-found simplicity even at a review of the Belfast yeomanry before the lord lieutenant in 1804. In a painting of that procession that hangs in the Harbour Office in Belfast, Bruce can be seen in full profile, soberly dressed against a background of martial frippery. Furthermore, in 1803 Bruce no longer expounded the social advantages of the knowledge and use of arms. He explained instead that although war was 'so repugnant to the precepts of the Gospel, that many have doubted whether the profession of Arms be consistent with the profession of Christianity', there were occasions when duty required a man to bear the sufferings of war and 'defend those whom Providence has committed to his care'.[6] Likewise, in 1803 Bruce's citations and examples were mostly biblical rather than classical or historical.

It would be overly simplistic to explain the change in Bruce and others as merely a frightened reaction to the violence and disorder of the previous decade, though those experiences certainly affected them. While the influence of the Scottish sociologists apparent in Joseph Pollock's *Letters of Owen Roe O'Nial* was only slowly taken up in explicit terms by other writers, Pollock's devaluation of a mechanistic conception of a mixed constitution in favour of an increased consideration of the role of social changes upon political systems became more widespread. By 1808, William Bruce, the epitome of a civic republican during the 1780s, had himself had taken up the study of society. He wondered whether the Polybian cycle was still applicable to the circumstances of Britain and Ireland:

> May we, in these islands, venture to congratulate ourselves, that we have at length attained to a state of society, in which opulence and refinement are compatible with liberty and religion, commerce with learning, and the virtues of peace with military glory; or have we cause, 'like the Roman patriots', to reflect with regret on the rusticity and ignorance of our more virtuous ancestors?[7]

Furthermore, a re-evaluation of political principles in light of the bloody panorama of Europe during the period of the French Revolution and

---

5 *Belfast Literary Society*, p. 31. 6 W. Bruce, *The Christian soldier* (n.d. [1803]), pp 1, 13.
7 W. Bruce, 'The influence of political revolutions on the progress of religion and learning' in *Select papers of the Belfast Literary Society* (1808), p. [156].

Napoleonic Empire was not limited to supposedly frightened reformers in Ulster.

Throughout Europe, men and women were critically reconsidering and reinterpreting the history of those decades. The reading public in Ulster was aware of these debates, and selections or references from Madame de Staël and Benjamin Constant appeared in Belfast publications.[8] In 1834, readers of the *Belfast News-Letter* were treated to extensive front-page coverage of a debate that touched upon the philosophical origins of the French Revolution. James McKnight, using the pseudonym 'A Presbyterian', accused John Ferrie, a professor at the Belfast Academical Institution, of undermining the morality of future Presbyterian ministers by teaching ideas akin to those of the repudiated 'infidel philosophers of the last century', such as Voltaire, Diderot and Helvétius, who were considered responsible for the apostasy of revolutionary France. The corruption of youth is rarely noteworthy; more interesting was the imputation that Ferrie was out of step with philosophical trends. Specifically, the professor had neglected 'the unceasing labour of the anti-sceptical party in France' led, according to McKnight, by Pierre-Paul Royer-Collard and Victor Cousin, to banish 'the trashy scepticism of other days'. The fact that Cousin also acknowledged that his ideas were influenced by the Scottish philosophers Dugald Stewart, Thomas Reid and, according to McKnight, Thomas Chalmers, was further cause to take notice of these labours.[9]

McKnight usefully placed a debate about curriculum in Belfast in the larger context of a European discussion about the role of religious faith in society. Immensely influential in French society and government during the period between 1815 and 1848, Cousin and his fellow 'spiritualists' were liberals trying to undo the work of those republicans who had sought to separate faith from science, philosophy and politics.[10] In the larger Atlantic world, the role of religious faith in social reform in the United States during the period between 1815 and 1848 has become widely recognized.[11] In this context, the increasing correlation between Ulster liberalism and evangelical religion was not anomalous much less proof of political apostasy. In 1850, McKnight, after a mission to London to lobby for tenant-right legislation, confided to the Young Ireland MP Charles Gavan Duffy, that he was 'persuaded that Divine Providence is making a special opening for the Emancipation of the Irish Masses'.[12]

---

8 *BMM*, 11 (Oct. 1813), 314–17; *BNL*, 10 Oct. 1817; *BNL*, 18 Aug. 1829. **9** *BNL*, 12 Sept. 1834; McKnight was identified as the author on the title page of his *The Ulster tenants' claim of right* (1848). **10** J. Goldstein, *Console and classify* (1989), p. 257; F. Furet, *Revolutionary France, 1770–1880* (1992), p. 316. **11** D. Howe, *What God hath wrought: the transformation of America, 1815–1848* (2007), pp 194–5. **12** Gavan Duffy correspondence, PRONI, T1143/2.

At least one French observer was also hopeful about the prospects for liberalism in Ulster and seemed to endorse the opinion of George Benn, Belfast's first significant historian, in 1823 'that the spirit of political opposition' had by 'no means evaporated' although it was 'less regarded than in the exalted times when all were armed and patriotic volunteers'.[13] Far from bemoaning any diminution of the radical republicanism of the 1790s, in 1839 Gustave de Beaumont believed that by abandoning the idea of an Irish republic Presbyterians had become 'les meilleurs athlètes qui puisse avoir l'Irlande moderne dans la lutte toute légale qu'elle a engagée'. This improvement was due, in part at least, to the commercial spirit which is 'adverse aux révolutions violentes' and fosters social mobility without succumbing to the indolence or privilege of the aristocrat. Furthermore, Beaumont believed that the number of Presbyterians willing to make common cause with Catholics was increasing while the anti-Catholic party was diminishing.[14] Beaumont, like many others, mistakenly imagined that the Non-subscribers rather than evangelical Presbyterians were the engine of this change.

By 1890, the signs of Presbyterian and Catholic cooperation that Beaumont had perceived in 1839 were an almost forgotten relic. In 1890, the Jesuit periodical *The Irish monthly*, published a short account of the life of Revd Michael Blake, Catholic bishop of Dromore. In describing Blake's cathedral town of Newry, the author was particularly struck by the composition of the town commission in 1828. Despite being a 'frontier-town of the Black North, here we have, the year before Emancipation, the Commissioners chosen alternately from Catholics and Protestant' in a way similar to that suggested for associations in 1811 by the former Newry resident William Drennan.[15] In 1890 this cooperation seemed singularly remarkable. Drennan, it will be recalled, had predicted that liberal success was predicated upon sectarian cooperation. In 1839, Beaumont had feared that such cooperation might not persist. If the circumstances were to change, if Catholics and Presbyterians were no longer united by a common enemy, Beaumont doubted that harmony could be maintained between such dissimilar elements. In many ways the history of town commissions in places like Armagh, Lisburn, Newtownards and Portadown seemed to confirm Beaumont's fears for the future of sectarian cooperation. Beaumont did not, however, believe this outcome was inevitable. Over time, through shared battles and victories liberalism might endure – 'chaque culte pourrait bien à la longue se modifier assez pour que l'accord durable des deux cessât d'être impossible'.[16]

---

13 G. Benn, *The history of the town of Belfast* (1823), p. 65.   **14** G. de Beaumont, *Irlande sociale, politique et religieuse*, 2 vols (1839), ii, pp 66–7, 81. Translation: 'the best athletes that modern Ireland could have for legal warfare in which she is engaged'. The commercial spirit which is 'adverse to violent revolutions'.   **15** 'Dr Blake of Dromore', *The Irish Monthly*, 18 (1890), 250.   **16** Beaumont, *Irlande,* ii, pp 68–9. Translation: 'each creed, in the long run,

Beaumont could not predict the kinds of changes in religious practice that concerned James Godkin. As Catholic and Protestant missionaries sought to renew or preserve their communities during a period of significant social change, the reinforcement of communal solidarity in some ways undermined the common public sphere that Beaumont had encountered. Another difficulty was the fact that this public sphere was predicated on a tacit acceptance of a British constitutional tradition. Some Ulster liberals believed that this tradition was widely accepted among a certain class of society. In 1869, James McKnight, during the course of evidence before a royal commission investigating a fatal riot in Derry in April 1868, expressed the opinion that among educated men of all creeds 'there might be no dispute in relation to the extent of civil, political, and religious liberty that we at present enjoy'.[17] This sentiment in some ways echoed George Douglas' criticism, while editor of the New York newspaper the *Western Star and Harp of Erin* in 1813, of Catholics who had walked out of a liberal political meeting in Derry during which a toast to the 'Glorious memory' of William III had been offered. According to Douglas, there was unanimity among the 'the historians of Europe' that the 'English revolution of 1688' had 'not only preserved what liberty remains in Britain' but also 'all that liberty which is now enjoyed in America'.[18]

It was this conviction that had led Douglas to help organize the centenary commemorations of the Siege of Derry. By 1869, however, Ulster liberals such as McKnight no longer supported celebrations of the siege and believed that the government ought to proscribe them. Far from celebrating an epoch in the history of liberty, McKnight believed that in 1869 the commemorations had become party displays intended to glorify the victory of one group over another. They also tended to result in violence because 'there are parties who fancy themselves, or may happen to be, representatives of the original party to the quarrel'.[19] In order to counteract these fancies, in 1873 Thomas Witherow published a history of the siege that attempted to place that event firmly and finally in the past. By means of a tender iconoclasm that demonstrated that no party held a monopoly on gallantry or disgrace during the siege, Witherow hoped to persuade his readers that Ireland had changed significantly since 1689. In 1873 Ireland possessed a constitution under which government was 'simply the reflection of popular opinion' so that 'moral force can really accomplish what rebellion only aims at'. Because the circumstances were different from the period of the siege, Witherow believed what Joseph Pollock had only hoped in

might be modified enough so that a durable agreement would cease to be impossible!' **17** *Report of the commissioners of inquiry, 1869, into the riots and disturbances in the city of Londonderry, with minutes of evidence and appendix,* HC 1870 (5), xxxii, p. 169. **18** *Western Star and Harp of Erin,* 13 March 1813. **19** *Report of the commissioners of inquiry, 1869, into the riots and disturbances in the city of Londonderry,* p. 169.

1793, that 'valour is at a discount, and pugnacity anything but a virtue'. Yet, despite improvements in society and culture, Witherow conceded that significant differences between Catholics and Protestants persisted, and careless or malignant men might easily arouse passions that still smouldered. For this reason, Witherow mocked those men whose highest ambition was to 'flaunt a party-coloured flag [...] full in the face of some sober and industrious neighbour'.[20]

In 1897, Revd W.T. Latimer, a Presbyterian minister from a small village near Dungannon, published a history intended to place another conflict fully and finally in the past. In his *Ulster biographies, relating chiefly to the rebellion of 1798*, Latimer set out to explain what he described as 'the great civil and religious oppression' that had caused the rebellion and led a small number of Presbyterians to take up arms. Like his fellow liberals, Godkin, McKnight and Witherow, Latimer placed his remarkably critical account of the rising in the context of a British constitutional tradition that had granted reforms 'more radical than [Revd James] Porter was hanged for demanding'.[21] In their efforts to adapt a British constitutional tradition to their own times, Ulster liberals from Joseph Pollock to James McKnight were attempting to persuade Catholics and Protestants, nationalists and unionists, that the events of the past need not control the beliefs and actions of the present. To paraphrase François Furet, they wanted to declare both the Glorious Revolution and the Rising over.

---

20 T. Witherow, *Derry and Enniskillen in the year 1689* (1873), pp 322–3, 330. **21** W.T. Latimer, *Ulster biographies, relating chiefly to the rebellion of 1798* (1897), p. [iii].

Sources and bibliography

PRIMARY SOURCES

ARCHIVAL SOURCES

Public Record Office of Northern Ireland, Belfast (PRONI)
Ballymoney town commission minute book, LA17/2B.
Coleraine corporation minute book, LA/25/2A.
Coleraine town commission minute book, LA/25/2B.
Downpatrick town commission minute book, LA/31/2B.
Dungannon town commission minute book, LA/34/2B.
Enniskillen town commission minute book, LA35/2B/1A.
Lurgan town commission minute book, LA51/2B.
Newry town commission minute book, LA58/2B.
Newtownards town commission minute book, LA60/2B/1.
Portadown town commission minute book, LA/64/2B.
Strabane town commission minute book, MIC159.
Downshire papers, D607.
Dungannon election papers, T2181.
Gavan Duffy correspondence, T1143.
Sharman Crawford papers, D856.
Tennent papers, D1748.

Armagh Public Library (Primate Robinson's Library), Armagh
Armagh Corporation Grand Jury minute book.

Centre for Research Libraries, Chicago
Gladstone papers, Papers of the prime ministers of Great Britain 8 (Woodbridge, CT, 1993).
Liverpool papers, Papers of the prime ministers of Great Britain 3 (Brighton, 1983).
Peel papers, Papers of the prime ministers of Great Britain 2 (Brighton, 1980).
Pitt the Younger papers, Papers of the prime ministers of Great Britain 1 (Brighton, 1981).

PARLIAMENTARY RECORDS

An act for erecting and continuing lights in the city of Dublin, and the several Liberties
    adjoining; and also in the cities of Cork and Limerick, and liberties thereof, 6 Geo. I, c. 18.
An act for further explaining and amending the several acts of parliament now in force for
    erecting lamps in the city of Dublin and liberties thereof, 11 Geo. II, c. 19.
An act to revive and amend an Act made in the sixth year of his late majesty King George the
    First, 15 Geo. II, c. 11.
An act for the more effectual enlightening of the city of Dublin and the liberties thereof; and
    for the erecting of public lights in the other cities; towns-corporate, and market-towns in
    the kingdom, 33 Geo. II, c. 18.
An act for continuing, reviving, and amending several temporary statutes, 5 Geo. III, c. 15.

An act for amending the laws relative to the lighting and cleansing of several cities, and for establishing market juries therein; and for other purposes, 13 & 14 Geo. III, c. 20.

An Act for paving, cleansing, lighting, and improving the several Streets, Squares, Lanes, and Passages within the Town of Belfast, 40 Geo. III, c. 37.

An Act to make Provision for the lighting, cleansing, and watching of Cities, Towns Corporate and Market Towns in Ireland, in certain cases, 9 Geo. IV, c. 82.

An Act to restrain the Alienation of Corporate Property in certain Towns in *Ireland*, 6 & 7 Will. IV, c. 100.

An Act to Amend an Act of the Third and Fourth Years of Her Present Majesty for the Regulation of Municipal Corporations in Ireland, 6 & 7 Victoria, Cap. 92.

An Act to Promote and Regulate Reformatory Schools for Juvenile Offenders in Ireland, 21 & 22 Vict. Cap. 103

Journals of the House of Commons
Hansard Parliamentary Debates, 3rd series (1830–91).

Report from select committee on the constitution of committees on private bills, HC 1825 (457), v.

Return of the names of all cities and towns in Ireland, which have made application to the lord lieutenant for permission to adopt the provisions of the 9th Geo. IV c. 82 [...], HC 1829 (140), xxii.

Returns relating to the corporation of the borough of Coleraine, in Ireland, HC 1831–2 (409), xxxvi.

Parliamentary representation, Ireland [...], HC 1831–2 (519), xliii.

Return of the number of freemen created in each corporate town in Ireland *returning members to parliament*, HC 1831–2 (550), xxxvi.

Returns relating to Coleraine corporation, HC 1834 (91), xliii.

First report of the commissioners appointed to inquire into the municipal corporations in Ireland, HC 1835 (23,24,25,27,28), xxvii–xxviii.

First report of the commissioners of public instruction, Ireland, HC 1835 (45, 46, 47), xxxiiixxxiv.

Report from the select committee appointed to inquire into the nature, character, extent and tendency of orange lodges, associations or societies in Ireland: with the minutes of evidence, and appendix, HC 1835 (377), xv.

Cities and towns improvement, Ireland, HC 1836 (306), xlvii.

Municipal corporations (Ireland), appendix to the first report of the commissioners, part III, conclusion of the north–western circuit, HC 1836 (29), xxiv.

First report from the select committee on fictitious votes, Ireland; with the minutes of evidence and appendix, HC 1837 (308), xi.

Third report from the select committee on fictitious votes, Ireland; with the minutes of evidence, appendix and index, HC 1837 (480), xi.

A bill to alter and amend an act of the ninth year of King George the fourth to make provision for the lighting cleansing and watching of cities, towns corporate and market towns in Ireland, HC 1842 (502), iii.

Return of the names of those towns in Ireland in which the act of 9 Geo. 4 c. 82 has been brought into operation wholly or in part, HC 1843 (632), l.

A return of the number of stamps issued to newspapers, and the amount of advertisement duty paid on each of the last two quarters of the year 1843, separately stated; [...], HC 1844 (55), xxxii.

Report from her majesty's commissioners of inquiry into the state of the law and practice in respect to the occupation of land in Ireland, HC 1845 (605, 606) xix.

An account of the sum total advanced on loan,, on the security of the poor rates in Ireland; for the building of workhouses in Ireland, HC 1847 (157), lv.

Return of the number of newspaper stamps at one penny, issued to newspapers in England, Ireland, Scotland and Wales, from the year 1837 to the year 1850, HC 1852 (42), xxviii.

Return of the names of the several towns in Ireland for which town commissioners are now appointed under the act 9 Geo. 4, c. 82, HC 1852–3 (678, 971), xciv.

Report of the commissioners to inquire into the state of the fairs and markets in Ireland, HC 1852–3 (1674), xli

Report of the commissioners appointed to inquire into the state of the fairs and markets in Ireland, part II, minutes of evidence, HC 1854–5 (1910), xix.

Report of the commissioners of inquiry, 1869, into the riots and disturbances in the city of Londonderry, with minutes of evidence and appendix, HC 1870 (5), xxxii.

Report from the select committee on local government and taxation of towns (Ireland), HC 1876 (352), x.

Report from the select committee on local government and taxation of towns (Ireland); with the proceedings of the committee, HC 1878 (262), xvi.

NEWSPAPERS AND MAGAZINES

Armagh Guardian

Banner of Ulster

Belfast Mercury

Belfast Monthly Magazine

Belfast News-Letter

Coleraine Chronicle

Enniskillen Chronicle and Erne Packet

Exile

Freeman's Journal

Londonderry Journal

Londonderry Sentinel

Londonderry Standard

Newry Commercial Telegraph

North British Review

Northern Star

Northern Whig

Strabane Morning Post

Ulster Observer

Ulster Times

Ulster Times

Ulsterman

United Irishman

Vindicator

Western Star and Harp of Erin

CONTEMPORARY BOOKS AND PAMPHLETS

A letter to Henry Flood, esq., on the present state of representation in Ireland (Belfast, 1783).

A report of the committee of the Irish Society respecting their charter (London, 1815).

Beaumont, Gustave de, *Irlande sociale, politique et religieuse*, 2 vols (Paris, 1839).

Benn, George, *The history of the town of Belfast* (Belfast, 1823).

Black, Robert, *Substance of two speeches, delivered of the General Synod of Ulster at its annual meeting in 1812* (Dublin, n.d. [1812]).

Bradshaw, Thomas (ed.), *The general directory of Newry, Armagh and the towns; Dungannon, Portadown, Tandragee, Lurgan, Waringstown, Banbridge, Warrenpoint, Rostrevor, Kilkeel, Rathfriland, &c for 1820 containing an alphabetical list of the merchants, manufacturers, and inhabitants in general; and historical accounts of the respective towns* (Newry, 1819).

Brown, John, *The importance of learning to society and the Christian ministry, illustrated, in an appeal to the congregation of Ballymena, in September last in aid of the funds for supporting a divinity professorship under the care of the Synod of Ulster in the Belfast Academical Institution* (Belfast, 1820).

—— *Barney McLees: a sermon on Christ's priesthood, preached in Aghadowey Presbyterian church on the 7th of January, 1855* (Belfast, 1855).

—— *The elective franchise, a sacred trust: a tract for the times* (Coleraine, 1857).

—— *Social peace promoted by the gospel* (Derry, 1864).

—— *Two lectures* (Derry, 1864).

Cantwell, John, *A treatise on tolls and customs* (2nd ed., Dublin, 1829).

Crawford, William, *A history of Ireland* (Strabane, 1783).

Crawford, William Sharman, *A defence of the small farmers* (Dublin, n.d. [1839]).

Crombie, James, *A sermon on the love of country; preached before the First Company of Belfast Volunteers on Sunday, the 19th of July, 1778* (n.p. [Belfast], 1778).

—— *The propriety of setting apart a portion of the Sabbath for the purpose of acquiring the knowledge and use of arms; a sermon preached before the Belfast Volunteer Company, on the 4th of March, 1781, in the old dissenting meeting house, and published at their request* (Belfast, 1781).

Davitt, Michael, *The fall of feudalism in Ireland* (London, 1904).

Devyr, Thomas Ainge, *Our natural rights* (Belfast, 1835).

—— *The odd book of the nineteenth century* (New York, 1882).

Dickson, William Steel, *Sermons on the following subjects* (Belfast, n.d. [1778]).

—— *A narrative of the confinement and exile of William Steel Dickson* (Dublin, 1812).

Dillon, William, *Life of John Mitchel*, 2 vols (London, 1888).

Documents relative to Lord Killmorey's intended police bill for the town of Newry (Newry, 1824).

Douglas, George, *Derriana* (Derry, 1794).

—— (ed.), *Paine versus religion; or, Christianity triumphant* (Baltimore, 1803).

—— *Forensic eloquence: sketches of trials in Ireland for high treason, etc, including the speeches of Mr Curran* (Baltimore, 1804).

'Dr Blake of Dromore, and Father O'Neill of Rosstrevor', *The Irish Monthly* 18 (1890), 248–61.

[Drennan, William], *Letters of Orellana, an Irish helot to the seven northern counties* (Dublin, 1785).

—— *A second letter to the Right Honorable William Pitt* (Dublin, 1799).

Eighth annual report of open–air preaching by ministers of the General Assembly of the Presbyterian Church in Ireland, 1858 (Belfast, 1859).

Emerson, James, *Letters from the Aegean* (New York, 1829),

Extracts from original letters of James McKnight, LL.D. (Belfast, 1916).

Falkiner, Caesar Litton, *Studies in Irish history and biography, mostly in the eighteenth century* (London, 1902).

Finlay, John, *Letters addressed to the Irish government, on local taxes, the Irish collieries, &c.* (Dublin, 1822).

—— *A treatise on the law of landlord and tenant* (Dublin, 1835).

Fisher, Joseph R., *The end of the Irish parliament* (London, 1911).

Gale, Peter, *An inquiry into the ancient corporate system of Ireland, and suggestions for its immediate restoration and general extension* (London, 1834).

Godkin, James, *A guide from the church of Rome to the church of Christ* (2nd ed. Dublin, 1836).

—— *The touchstone of orthodoxy, or essays on the present state of the churches* (Belfast, n.d. [1839]).

—— *Apostolic Christianity: or, The people's antidote against Romanism and Puseyism* (Dublin, 1842).

—— *Lent lectures on Romanism and Puseyism, with replies to several Roman Catholic priests* (Belfast, 1843).

—— 'Irish Evangelical Society', *Congregational Magazine*, n.s. 9 (1845), 69–71.

—— 'The rights of Ireland', in Loyal National Repeal Association, *Repeal essays* (Dublin, 1845) pp [286–466].

——*The church principles of the New Testament* (London, 1845).

—— 'Mariolatry', *North British Review*, 8 (1848).

—— *Ireland and her churches* (London 1867).

—— *The land-war in Ireland* (London, 1870).

—— *The religious history of Ireland* (London, 1873).

Goudy, Alexander P, *Right versus might; or, Irish Presbyterian politics discussed* (Derry, 1852).

Gracchus [William Bruce], *A vindication of government addressed to the people of Ireland, and dedicated by permission to the majority in both houses of parliament* (Dublin, 1784).

Hempton, John (ed.), *The siege and history of Londonderry* (Derry, 1861).

Historical Manuscripts Commission, *Manuscripts and correspondence of the James, first earl of Charlemont* (London, 1891).

Hume, John, *A sermon preached in the cathedral church of St Columb's Derry, on the commemoration of the 7th of December 1688* (Derry, 1788).

Irish Society, *A report of the deputation of the Irish Society* (London, 1815).

—— *Report of a deputation to Ireland in the year 1832* (London, 1832).

Joy, Henry & William Bruce, *Belfast politics; or, a collection of the debates, resolutions and other proceedings of the town, in the years, MDCCXCII and MDCCXCIII* (Belfast, 1794).

[Joy, Henry], *Historical collections relative to the town of Belfast from the earliest period to the Union with Great Britain* (Belfast, 1817).

Kennedy, James, *The evils of the act for the regulation of municipal corporations in Ireland illustrated in the case of the Belfast town council* (Belfast, 1855).

Killen, W. D, *Reminiscences of a Long Life* (London, 1901).

Latimer, W. T, *Ulster biographies, relating chiefly to the rebellion of 1798* (2nd ed., Belfast, 1897).

—— *A history of the Irish Presbyterians* (Belfast, 1902).

Lenihan, Maurice, *Limerick; its history and antiquities* (Dublin, 1884).

Lessees of the commissioners of the town of Enniskillen v. The earl of Enniskillen, in *Irish Law Reports*, 12 (1850).

MacKnight, Thomas, *Ulster as it is: twenty-eight years' experience as an Irish editor*, 2 vols (London, 1896).

[James McKnight], Member of the General Synod of Ulster, *A letter to those ministers and members of the Church of Scotland, who have lent themselves to the Dens' theology humbug, showing from the Westminster Confession of faith, the larger catechism, and other authorized documents that John Knox and our Protestant reformers, together with assemblies of the kirk, and even the national Kirk of Scotland itself, have all sanctioned the intolerant principles ascribed to Peter Dens* (Edinburgh, 1836).

—— Member of the Synod of Ulster, *Persecution sanctioned by the Westminster Confession; a letter addressed to the clergy, eldership and laity of the Synod of Ulster; showing, from the history and proceedings of the Westminster divines, and the public records of the Church of Scotland, the doctrines of intolerance to which the late vote of unqualified subscription has committed the Synod of Ulster* (Belfast, 1836).

—— *The Ulster tenants' claim of right ; or, land ownership a state trust; the Ulster tenant–right an original grant from the British crown, and the necessity of extending its general principle to the other provinces of Ireland, demonstrated; in a letter to the Honourable Lord John Russell* (Derry, 1848).

McNeill, Mary, *The life and times of Mary Ann McCracken, 1770–1866* (Dublin, 1960).

McSkimin, Samuel, *The history and antiquities of the county of the town of Carrickfergus* (Belfast, 1832).

Madden, Daniel O. (ed.), *The speeches of the Right Hon. Henry Grattan* (Dublin, 1871).

'Memoir of the late Rev. W.M. O'Hanlon', *Evangelical magazine and missionary chronicle* n.s. 34 (1856), 240–4.

Montgomery, Henry, *A funeral sermon of the death of John McCance, esq, MP, delivered in the meeting-house of Dunmurry* (Belfast, 1835).

O'Brien, Richard Barry, *Parliamentary history of the Irish land question, from 1829 to 1869* (4th ed., London, 1880).

O'Hanlon, William M., *Walks among the poor of Belfast and suggestions for their improvement* (Belfast, 1853).

Orthodox [James Godkin?], *Letters to the Presbyterians of Ulster on the general election of 1865* (Belfast, 1865).

Paine, Thomas, *Letter from Thomas Paine to George Washington* (Baltimore, 1802).

[Pollock. Joseph], *Letters of Owen Roe O'Nial* (Dublin, 1779).

Pollock, Joseph, *Letters to the inhabitants of the town and lordship of Newry* (Dublin, 1793).

Porter, J.L., *Life and times of Henry Cooke* (Belfast, 1875).

Presbyterian Layman, *Historical view of the Catholic question; in a series of strictures on Dr Miller's letter to Mr Plunkett* (Belfast, 1827).

The proceedings of the association of the Friends of the Constitution, Liberty and Peace, held at the King's Arms tavern, in Fownes-street, Dublin, December 21, 1792 (London, 1793).

The queen v. Clarges Ruxton, esq., portrieve of the borough of Ardee in *Irish Law Reports*, 3 (1841).

Reid, James Seaton, *History of the Presbyterian church in Ireland*, 3 vols (Belfast, 1867).

Review of the lion of old England: or, The democracy confounded (Belfast, 1794).

Rogers, John, *A sermon preached at Lisnavein, otherwise Ballybay new erection, on Saturday June 10, 1780 to the Lisnavein Independent Volunteers, Trough Volunteers, Lisluney Volunteers, and Monaghan Rangers* (Edinburgh, 1780)

Rowan, Archibald Hamilton, *Autobiography of Archibald Hamilton Rowan, esq.* (Dublin, 1840).

Schultes, Henry, *A concise view of the origin, constitution and proceedings of the Honorable Society of the Governor and Assistants of London of the New Plantation of Ulster, within the Realm of Ireland* (London, 1822).

Smyth, Richard, *Ireland & Italy: a sermon, preached in the First Presbyterian Church, Londonderry, on the twelfth of August, 1860, being the anniversary of the relief of Derry* (Derry, 1860).

—— *Life for the nations: a plea for India* (Derry, 1857).

—— *Philanthropy, proselytism and crime: a review of the Irish reformatory system, with a Glance at the Reformatories of Great Britain, and at Mr, Maguire's industrial schools bill* (Derry, 1861).

—— 'The life and times of Dr Henry Cooke' *British and Foreign Evangelical Review*, 21 (1872), 209–41.

The speech of Daniel O'Connell, esq., at the Catholic aggregate meeting at the freemason's hall (London, 1825).

The standard orange song book: a collection of loyal & constitutional songs, original and select (Armagh 1848).

Teeling, Charles Hamilton, *Sequel to personal narrative of the 'Irish rebellion' of 1798* (Belfast 1832).

Troup, George Elmslie, *Life of George Troup, journalist* (Edinburgh, 1881).

Witherow, Thomas, *Derry and Enniskillen in the year 1689* (Belfast 1873).

—— *Historical and literary memorials of Presbyterianism in Ireland, 1731–1800* (Belfast, 1880).

SECONDARY SOURCES

Adonis, Andrew, *Making aristocracy work: the peerage and the parliamentary system in Britain, 1884–1914* (Oxford, 1993).

Akenson, Donald H., *The Irish education experiment: the national system of education in the nineteenth century* (London, 1970).

Aspinall, Arthur, *Politics and the press, c.1780–1850* (London, 1949).

Barnard, Toby Christopher, 'Historiographical review: farewell to old Ireland', *Historical Journal*, 36 (1993), 909–28.

—— *A new anatomy of Ireland: the Irish Protestants, 1649–1770* (New Haven, CT, 2003).

—— 'The eighteenth-century parish', in E. FitzPatrick and R. Gillespie (eds), *The parish in medieval and early modern Ireland* (Dublin, 2006), pp 297–324.

Bartlett, Thomas, *The fall and rise of the Irish nation: the Catholic question, 1690–1830* (Savage, MD, 1992).

Beaven, Alfred B., *The aldermen of the city of London,* 2 vols (London, 1913).

Beckett, James Camlin, *The making of modern Ireland, 1603–1923* (2nd ed., London, 1981).

Beer, Samuel H., *British politics in the collectivist age* (New York, 1969).

Belfast Literary Society, 1801–1901: historical sketch with memoirs (Belfast, 1902).

Bew, Paul and Frank Wright, 'The agrarian opposition in Ulster politics', in S. Clark and J.S. Donnelly (eds), *Irish peasants: violence and political unrest, 1780–1914* (Manchester, 1983), pp 192–229.

Black, R.D. Collison, *Economic thought and the Irish Question, 1817–1890* (Cambridge, 1960).

Blackstock, Allan 'The social and political implications of the raising of the yeomanry in Ulster: 1796–1798', in D. Dickson, D. Keogh and K. Whelan (eds), *The United Irishmen: republicanism, radicalism and rebellion* (Dublin, 1993), pp 234–43.

Blaney, Roger, *Presbyterians and the Irish language* (Belfast, 1996).

Bond, Maurice F., *Guide to the records of parliament* (London, 1971).

Borsay, Peter and Lindsay J. Proudfoot, 'The English and Irish urban experience, 1500–1800: change, convergence and divergence', in P. Borsay and L.J. Proudfoot (eds), *Provincial towns in early modern England and Ireland: change, convergence and divergence* (Oxford, 2002), pp 1–27.

Boylan, Thomas A. and Timothy P. Foley, *Political economy and colonial Ireland: the propagation and ideological function of economic discourse in the nineteenth century* (New York, 1992).

Briggs, Asa, *The making of modern England, 1783–1867: the age of improvement* (New York, 1965).

Brooke, Peter, *Ulster Presbyterianism: the historical perspective, 1610–1970* (New York, 1987).

Budge, Ian and Cornelius O'Leary, *Belfast: approach to crisis: a study of Belfast politics, 1613–1970* (New York, 1973).

Burrow, J.W., *Whigs and liberals: continuity and change in English political thought* (Oxford, 1988).

Campbell, Flann, *The dissenting voice: Protestant democracy in Ulster from plantation to partition* (Belfast, 1991).

Canavan, Tony, *Frontier town: an illustrated history of Newry* (Belfast, 1989).

Cannon, John, *Parliamentary reform, 1640–1832* (Cambridge, 1973).

Chambers, George, *Faces of change: the Belfast and Northern Ireland chambers of commerce and industry, 1783–1983* (Belfast, 1984).

Chart, D.A. (ed.), *The Drennan letters* (Belfast, 1931).

Christie, Ian R., *British 'non–elite' MPs, 1715–1820* (Oxford, 1995).

Clark, J.C.D. *English society, 1688–1832: ideology, social structure and political practice during the ancien régime* (Cambridge, 1985).

Clarkson, L.A., 'Population change and urbanisation, 1821–1911', in L. Kennedy and P. Ollerenshaw (eds), *An economic history of Ulster, 1820–1940* (Manchester, 1985), pp 137–57.

Clifford, Frederick, *A history of private bill legislation*, 2 vols (London, 1885–7).

Colby, Thomas, *Ordnance survey of Ireland: county Londonderry* (Limavady, 1990).

Comerford, R.V., *The Fenians in context: Irish politics and society, 1848–1882* (Atlantic Highland, NJ, 1985).

Connolly, Sean J., 'Mass politics and sectarian conflict, 1823–30', in W.E. Vaughan (ed.), *A new history of Ireland*, v: *Ireland under the Union, i: 1801–1870* (Oxford, 1989), pp 74–107.

—— 'Eighteenth-century Ireland: colony or *ancien régime?*', in D.G. Boyce and A. O'Day (eds), *The making of modern Irish history: revisionism and the revisionist controversy* (London, 1996).

Cookson, J.E., *The friends of peace: anti-war liberalism in England, 1793–1815* (Cambridge, 1982).

—— *The British armed nation, 1793–1815* (Oxford, 1997).

Crossman, Virginia, *Local government in nineteenth-century Ireland* (Belfast, 1994).

Cullen, L.M., *An economic history of Ireland since 1660* (London, 1981).

Curtin, Nancy J., *The United Irishmen: popular politics in Ulster and Dublin, 1791–1798* (Oxford, 1994).

—— '"Varieties of Irishness": historical revisionism, Irish style', *Journal of British Studies*, 35 (1996), 195–219.

d'Alton, Ian, *Protestant society and politics in Cork, 1812–1844* (Cork, 1980).

Daly, Mary E., 'Irish urban history: a survey', in *Urban History Yearbook, 1986* (Leicester, 1986), pp 61–72.

Dewar, M.W., John Brown and S.E. Long, *Orangeism: a new historical appreciation* (Belfast, 1967).

Dickinson, Harry Thomas, 'Irish radicalism in the late eighteenth century', *History*, 82 (1997), 266–84.

Dowling, Martin W., *Tenant-right and agrarian society in Ulster, 1600–1870* (Dublin, 1999).

Dundas, William Harloe, *Enniskillen, parish and town* (Dundalk, 1913).

Dunne, Tom, 'Popular ballads, revolutionary rhetoric and politicisation', in H. Gough and D. Dickson (eds), *Ireland and the French Revolution* (Dublin, 1989), pp 139–55.

Durey, Michael, *Transatlantic radicals and the early American republic* (Lawrence, KS, 1997).

Eastwood, David, 'Local Government and Local Society', in H.T. Dickinson (ed.), *A companion to eighteenth-century Britain* (Oxford, 2002), pp 40–54.

Elliott, Marianne, *Partners in revolution: the United Irishmen and France* (New Haven, CT, 1982).

—— *Wolfe Tone: prophet of Irish independence* (New Haven, CT, 1989).

Farrell, Sean, *Rituals and riots: sectarian violence and political culture in Ulster, 1784–1886* (Lexington, 2000).

Fontana, Biancamaria, *Benjamin Constant and the post-revolutionary mind* (New Haven, 1991).

Foster, R.F., *Modern Ireland, 1600–1972* (New York, 1988).

Gillespie, Raymond et al., *Belfast: part I to 1840,* Irish Historic Towns Atlas 12 (Dublin, 2003).

Gough, Hugh and Gilles Le Biez, 'Un répubicanisme ambigu: l'Irlande et la Révolution Française', *Annales Historiques de la Révolution Française*, 294 (1994), 321–30.

Gough, Hugh, 'France and the 1798 rebellion', in *The great Irish rebellion of 1798*, ed. Cathal Póirtéir (Boulder, CO, 1998).

Gray, John, 'A tale of two newspapers: the contest between the *Belfast News-Letter* and the *Northern Star* in the 1790s', in J. Gray and W. McCann (eds), *An uncommon bookman: essays in memory of J.R.R. Adams* (Belfast, 1996), pp 175–98.

Gribbon, Sybil, 'The social origins of Ulster unionism', *Irish Economic and Social History*, 4 (1977), 66–72.

Habermas, Jürgen, *The structural transformation of the public sphere: an inquiry into a category of bourgeois society* (Cambridge, MA, 1989).

Halévy, Elie, *A history of the English people in the nineteenth century.* 6 vols (New York, 1961).

Hempton, David and Myrtle Hill, *Evangelical Protestantism in Ulster society, 1740–1890* (New York, 1992).

Hill, Jacqueline, *From patriots to unionists: Dublin civic politics and Irish Protestant patriotism, 1660–1840* (Oxford 1997).

Holmes, Andrew R., *The shaping of Ulster Presbyterian belief and practice, 1770–1840* (Oxford, 2006).

Holmes, R.F.G., *Henry Cooke* (Belfast, 1981).

—— *Our Irish Presbyterian heritage* (Belfast, 1985).

—— 'United Irishmen and Unionists : Irish Presbyterians, 1791 and 1886', in W.J. Sheils and D. Wood (eds), *The churches, Ireland and the Irish: papers read at the 1987 Summer meeting and the 1988 winter meeting of the Ecclesiastical History Society* (Oxford, 1989), pp 171–89.

Hone, J. Ann, *For the cause of truth: radicalism in London* (Oxford, 1982).

Hope, Valerie, *My Lord Mayor: eight hundred years of London's mayoralty* (London, 1989).

Hoppen, K.T., *Elections, politics and society in Ireland, 1832–1885* (Oxford, 1984).

Jamieson, John, *The history of the Royal Belfast Academical Institution* (Belfast, 1959).

Jenkins, Brian, *Era of emancipation: British government of Ireland, 1812–1830* (Kingston, 1988).

Johnston, Edith M., *Great Britain and Ireland, 1760–1800: a study in political administration* (Edinburgh, 1963).

Jupp, Peter, 'Urban politics in Ireland, 1801–1831', in David Harkness and Mary O'Dowd (eds), *The town in Ireland: Historical Studies 13* (Belfast, 1981), pp 103–24.

—— *British politics on the eve of reform: the Duke of Wellington's administration, 1828–1830* (New York, 1998).

Kelly, James, 'The glorious and immortal memory: commemoration and Protestant indentity in Ireland, 1660–1800', *Transactions of the Royal Irish Academy*, Sect. C. 94 (1994), 25–52.

Kiberd, Declan, *Inventing Ireland* (Cambridge, MA, 1996).

Kirkland, Richard, 'Questioning the frame: hybridity, Ireland and the institution', in C. Graham and R. Kirkland (eds), *Ireland and cultural theory: the mechanics of authenticity* (New York, 1999), pp 210–28.

Lacy, Brian, *Siege city: the story of Derry and Londonderry* (Belfast, 1990).

Lambert, Sheila, *Bills and acts; legislative procedure in eighteenth century England* (Cambridge, 1971).

Larkin, Emmet, *The making of the Roman Catholic Church in Ireland, 1850–1860* (Chapel Hill, NC, 1980).

—— *The consolidation of the Roman Catholic Church in Ireland, 1860–1870* (Chapel Hill, 1987).

—— *The Roman Catholic Church and the home rule movement in Ireland, 1870–1874* (Chapel Hill, NC, 1990).

—— and Herman Freudenberger (eds), *A Redemptorist missionary in Ireland, 1851–1854: memoirs by Joseph Prost, C.S.R.* (Cork, 1998).

—— 'The parish mission movement in Ireland, 1850–1875', typescript of a paper presented.

Leonard, Jane, 'Memorials to the casualties of conflict: Northern Ireland, 1969–1997', Electronic text available at http://ds).dial).pipex).com/town/estate/yo13/reports/memorials/memorials).pdf (Belfast, 1997).

Macaulay, Ambrose, *Patrick Dorrian, bishop of Down and Connor, 1865–68* (Dublin, 1987).

McBride, Ian, 'Ulster and the British Problem', in R. English and G. Walker (eds), *Unionism in modern Ireland: new perspectives on politics and culture* (New York, 1996), pp 1–18.

—— '"When Ulster joined Ireland": anti–popery, Presbyterian radicalism and Irish republicanism in the 1790s', *Past and Present*, 157 (November 1997), 63–93).

—— *The siege of Derry in Ulster Protestant mythology* (Dublin, 1997).

—— *Scripture politics: Ulster Presbyterianism, and Irish radicalism in the late eighteenth century* (Oxford, 1998).

—— 'Reclaiming the rebellion: 1798 in 1998', *IHS*, 31 (1999), 395–410.

McClelland, Aiken, 'The later Orange Order', in T.D. Williams (ed.), *Secret societies in Ireland* (New York, 1973).

McCord, Norman, *British history, 1815–1914* (2nd ed., New York, 2007).

MacDonagh, Oliver, 'The economy and society, 1830–1845', in W.E. Vaughan (ed.), *A new history of Ireland*, v: *Ireland under the Union, i : 1801–1870* (Oxford, 1989), pp 218–41.

—— *The emancipist: Daniel O'Connell, 1830–1847* (London, 1989).

McDowell, R.B., *Ireland in the age of imperialism and revolution, 1760–1801* (Oxford, 1979).

—— *The Irish administration, 1801–1914* (London, 1964).

—— *Irish public opinion, 1750–1800* (London, 1944).

—— *Public opinion and government policy in Ireland, 1801–1846* (London, 1952).

McFarland, Elaine W., *Ireland and Scotland in the age of revolution* (Edinburgh, 1994).

Macintyre, Angus, *The liberator: Daniel O'Connell and the Irish party, 1830–1847* (New York, 1965).

Magee, Jack, *Barney: Bernard Hughes of Belfast, 1808–1878* (Belfast, 2001).

Maguire, William Alexander, *Living like a lord: the second marquis of Donegall, 1769–1844* (Belfast, 1984).

—— *The Downshire estates in Ireland, 1801–1845: the management of Irish landed estates in the early nineteenth century* (Oxford, 1972).

—— (ed.), *Letters of a great Irish landlord : a selection from the estate correspondence of the third marquess of Downshire, 1809–1845* (Belfast, 1974).

Mandler, Peter, *Aristocratic government in the age of reform: Whigs and Liberals* (Oxford, 1990).

Miller, David, 'Irish Catholicism and the Great Famine', *Journal of Social History*, 9 (1975), 81–98.

—— *Queen's rebels: Ulster loyalism in historical perspective* (New York, 1978).

Moody, Theodore William, F.X. Martin, F.J. Byrne, W.E. Vaughan, Art Cosgrove, and J.R. Hill (eds), *A new history of Ireland*, 9 vols (Oxford, 1982–2005).

Morris, Robert John and Richard Rodger, 'An introduction to British urban history, 1820–1914', in R.J. Morris and R. Rodger (eds), *The Victorian city: a reader in British urban history, 1820–1914* (New York, 1993), pp 1–39.

Mullin, Julia E., *New Row: the history of the New Row Presbyterian Church, Coleraine, 1727–1977* (Antrim, 1976).

—— *The presbytery of Coleraine* (Belfast, 1979).

Mullin, T.H., *Aghadowey: a parish and its linen industry* (Belfast, 1972).

—— *Coleraine in Georgian times* (Belfast, 1977).

—— *Coleraine in modern times* (Belfast, 1979).

Murphy, Desmond, *Derry, Donegal and modern Ulster, 1790–1921* (Derry, 1981).

O'Brien, Gerard, 'The unimportance of public opinion in eighteenth-century Britain and Ireland', *Eighteenth-Century Ireland: Iris an dá chultúr*, 8 (1993), 115–27.

O'Connell, Maurice R., *Irish politics and social conflict in the age of the American Revolution* (Philadephia, 1965).

—— (ed.), *The correspondence of Daniel O'Connell*, 7 vols (New York, 1972–1999).

O'Ferrall, Fergus, *Catholic emancipation: Daniel O'Connell and the birth of Irish democracy, 1820–30* (Atlantic Highlands, NJ, 1985).

O'Flaherty, Éamon, 'Urban politics and municipal reform in Limerick, 1723–62', *Eighteenth-Century Ireland: Iris an dá chultúr*, 6 (1991), 105–20.

Ó Snodaigh, Pádraig, 'Some police and military aspects of the Irish Volunteers', *Irish Sword*, 13 (1978), 217–29.

—— 'The "Volunteers of '82": a citizen army or armed citizens? a bicentennial retrospect', *Irish Sword*, 15 (1983), 177–88.

Owen, David John, *A short history of the port of Belfast* (Belfast, 1917).

Parry, Jonathan Philip, *The rise and fall of Liberal government in Victorian Britain* (New Haven, CT, 1993).

Pocock, John Greville Agard, *The Machiavellian moment: Florentine political thought and the Atlantic republican tradition* (Princeton, 1975).

——*The ancient constitution and the feudal law: a study of English historical thought during the seventeenth century: a reissue with a retrospect* (New York, 1987).

—— *Virtue, commerce, and history: essays on political thought and history, chiefly in the eighteenth century* (Cambridge, 1985).

Polasky, Janet L., *Revolution in Brussels, 1787–1793* (Brussels, 1985).

Potter, Matthew, *The government and people of Limerick, 1197–2006* (Limerick, 2006).

Robbins, Caroline, *The eighteenth century commonwealthman* (New York, 1968).

Royle, Stephen Arthur, 'Industrialization, urbanization and urban society in post-Famine Ireland *c.*1850–1921', in B.J. Graham and L.J. Proudfoot (eds), *An historical geography of Ireland* (San Diego, 1993), pp 258–92.

Prest, John, *Liberty and locality: parliament, permissive legislation, and ratepayers' democracies in the nineteenth century* (Oxford, 1990).

Sharp, John, *The reapers of the harvest: the Redemptorists in Great Britain and Ireland, 1843–1898* (Dublin, 1989).

Silke, John J, 'Cornelius Denvir and the "spirit of fear"', *Irish Theological Quarterly*, 53 (1987).

Smyth, Jim, *Men of no property: Irish radicals and popular politics in the late eighteenth century* (New York, 1992).

Slater, Gerard James, 'Belfast politics, 1798–1868' (PhD, New University of Ulster, 1982).

Small, Stephen, *Political thought in Ireland, 1776–1798: republicanism, patriotism, and radicalism* (Oxford, 2002).

Soltau, Roger Henry, *French political thought in the 19th century* (New York, 1959).

Steele, E.D., *Irish land and British politics: tenant-right and nationality, 1865–1870* (Cambridge, 1974).

—— *Palmerston and liberalism, 1855–1865* (Cambridge, 1991).

Stewart, A.T.Q., *The narrow ground: the roots of conflict in Ulster* (London, 1977).

—— *A deeper silence: the hidden origins of the United Irishmen* (London, 1993).

Stewart, David, *The Seceders in Ireland with annals of their congregations* (Belfast, 1950).

Strain, Robert William Magill, *Belfast and its Charitable Society: a story of urban social development* (London, 1961).

Sweet, Rosemary, *The English town, 1680–1840: government, society & culture* (New York, 1999).

Thorne, R.G. (ed.), *The history of parliament: the House of Commons, 1790–1820*, vol. 1 (London, 1986).

Tilly, Charles, *Popular contention in Great Britain, 1758–1834* (Cambridge, MA, 1995).

Trimble, William Copeland, *The history of Enniskillen with reference to some manors in co. Fermanagh and other local subjects*, 3 vols (Enniskillen, 1919–21).

Tone, Theobald Wolfe, *Life of Theobald Wolfe Tone*, ed. Thomas Bartlett (Dublin, 1998).

Vaughan, William Edward, *Landlords and tenants in mid-Victorian Ireland* (Oxford, 1994).

Wahnich, Sophie, 'Les républiques – soeurs, débat théorique et réalité historique, conquêtes et reconquêtes d'identité républicaine', *Annales Historiques de la Révolution Française*, 294 (1994), 165–78.

Wahrman, Dror, *Imagining the middle class: the political representation of class in Britain, c.1780–1840* (New York, 1995).

Walker, Brian Mercer, *Ulster politics: the formative years, 1868–1886* (Belfast, 1989).

Whelan, Kevin, 'Reinterpreting the 1798 rebellion in County Wexford', in Dáire Keogh and Nicholas Furlong (eds), *The mighty wave: the 1798 rebellion in Wexford* (Dublin, 1996).

—— *The tree of liberty: radicalism. Catholicism and the construction of Irish identity, 1760–1830* (Cork, 1996).

Wright, Frank, *Two lands on one soil: Ulster politics before home rule* (New York, 1996).

York, Neil Longley, *Neither kingdom nor nation: the Irish quest for constitutional rights 1698–1800* (Washington, DC, 1994).

REFERENCE WORKS

British Biographical Archive, Database in *World Biographical Index*, K.G. Saur.

Dictionary of National biography.

Dictionary of Irish biography.

English short title catalog, 1473–1800, Database, British Library and ESTC/NA.

Houghton, Walter (ed.), *The Wellesley index to Victorian periodicals, 1824–1900* (Toronto, 1966–89).

Keane, Edward, Beryl Phair and Thomas U. Sadleir (eds), *King's Inns admission papers, 1607–1867* (Dublin, 1982).

Newman, Kate (comp.), *Dictionary of Ulster biography* (Belfast, 1993).

North, John S. (ed.), *The Waterloo directory of Irish newspapers and periodicals, 1800–1900: Phase II* (Waterloo, 1986).

Walker, Brian M. (ed.), *Parliamentary election results in Ireland, 1801–1922* (Dublin, 1978).

Vaughan, W.E. and A.J. Fitzpatrick, *Irish historical statistics: population, 1821–1871* (Dublin, 1978).

Index